The Origin of Evil Spirits

The Origin of Evil Spirits

The Reception of Genesis 6:1–4 in Early Jewish Literature

Revised Edition

Archie T. Wright

Fortress Press
Minneapolis

THE ORIGIN OF EVIL SPIRITS
The Reception of Genesis 6:1–4 in Early Jewish Literature, Revised Edition

Fortress Press Edition © 2015

Cover design: Joe Reinke
Cover image: Illustration for John Milton's "Paradise Lost" by Gustave Doré, 1866. Public domain.

Library of Congress Cataloging-in-Publication Data
Print ISBN: 978-1-4514-9032-9
eBook ISBN: 978-1-4514-9654-3

The paper used in this publication meets the minimum requirements of American National Standard for Information Sciences — Permanence of Paper for Printed Library Materials, ANSI Z329.48-1984.

Manufactured in the U.S.

Table of Contents

Preface to the Second Edition

This monograph is a second revised edition to the revision of my doctoral thesis, "Breaching the Cosmic Order: The Biblical Tradition of Genesis 6:1–4 and its Reception in Early Enochic and Philonic Judaism." The thesis was submitted to the Faculty of Theology at the University of Durham in February 2004. I am very grateful to Dr. Jörg Frey and Dr. Henning Ziebritzki for their initial interest in my topic and the subsequent approval for the WUNT 2 series. What follows in the volume is a minor revision of the initial publication by Mohr Siebeck.

While undertaking the revision of the manuscript I took seriously the reviews/critiques prepared in various journals by the following individuals (in alphabetical order): Paul J. Brown, Philip R. Davies, David Instone-Brewer, T. Klutz, Grant Macaskill, Mark D. Owens, Finny Philip, Paolo Sacchi, and Sean Winter. Each of these scholars offered very helpful comments that I am certain would improve the content and argument presented in the volume. However, due to time limitations, I was unable to address all of the issues in the revision, but I do plan to address those deemed significant in future essays or a complete rewrite of the present volume. Nevertheless, one or two comments should be made concerning the interpretation of the Watcher Tradition that seemed to be a concern of nearly all the reviewers. First, it was not my intention to suggest that the so-called "origin of evil spirits" was the only interpretation one could come up with when reading the Book of Watchers. There are certainly others including George Nickelsburg's connection to the Wars of the Diadochi or to the corruption of the Temple priesthood. Second, I must also affirm the comments of Paulo Sacchi and Philip Davies that I may have overemphasized the role of Genesis 6:1–4 in the development of the Book of Watchers (i.e. underemphasized the role of other possible sources); however, if Genesis 6:1–4 is not the source for the author of the Book of Watchers, then both authors must have had access to the same tradition if one considers the parallels between Genesis chapter 6 and *1 Enoch* chapter 6.

I would like to thank each of the reviewers for their very helpful comments and I look forward to further interaction with them.

Archie T. Wright
Norfolk, Virginia, 2013

Preface

This monograph is a revision of my doctoral thesis, "Breaching the Cosmic Order: The Biblical Tradition of Genesis 6:1-4 and its Reception in Early Enochic and Philonic Judaism." The thesis was submitted to the Faculty of Theology at the University of Durham in February 2004. I am very grateful to Dr. Jörg Frey and Dr. Henning Ziebritzki for their initial interest in my topic and the subsequent approval for the WUNT 2 series. I appreciate their editorial suggestions, which have no doubt improved the quality of the work. I would especially like to thank Tanja Mix for her patience and tremendous assistance in bringing the manuscript to completion.

Most who have attempted to complete a Ph.D. will say that it is one of the loneliest tasks that a person can experience. In part, this is true. However, a Ph.D. is never the work of a single individual, but it involves the efforts a special group of people in the student's life. Thus, a grateful acknowledgement for the academic, spiritual, financial, and emotional support must be given, although one cannot express enough gratitude in these few lines. For me, this list of people could produce many pages, so I must limit my heartfelt thanks to a special group of individuals.

I offer a great many thanks to Ken and Lenore Mullican who have been a source of inspiration and encouragement during the process and in the years prior to moving to Durham. They have shown their loving friendship through prayer and financial support. Many thanks go to Kenny and Stephanie Mullican whose friendship, prayer, and financial support have been invaluable. The same must be said of Chad and Debbie Cox, Felipe Ornelas, and Dr. John Swails. I must also give special thanks to long-time friends Scott and Kathy Rex and Janet Koons for their support and prayers. I also must single out my brother Tom for his encouragement and financial support. All my family deserves especial merit for their encouragement and support throughout the process.

Of course, there are many in Durham who have been especially helpful. Thanks to all at St. John's College, college officers, staff, and students who have made Durham a home away from home. Special thanks must be given to Brad and Kori Embry. They have been true friends. The same must be said for Ron and Kathy Herms and their four beautiful children (Annaliese, Jaeden, Adrienne, and Avrielle). Finally, I must thank Mark Bonnington for being a good friend and always an encourager.

Prior to taking up a place at Durham, I had heard many nightmarish stories about Ph.D. supervisors and all the difficulties that come with that relationship. However, I can give only praise to my two supervisors, Professor Loren T. Stuckenbruck and Professor C.T. Robert Hayward. Both have shown why they are experts in their field. The knowledge they have given, the direction they have offered, and the patience they have shown, made working with them a memorable experience. Most of all they have offered a hand of friendship that I hope will continue in the years ahead. Special thanks must also be given to the faculty of the Abbey House for their valuable insight and to the staff for their administrative support.

I am grateful to all who have assisted in reading and offering suggestions to the drafts of the thesis and eventually the book. However, I take full responsibility for the content of this work.

Finally, I must thank the Lord for the calling and ministry that he has placed on my life. Without His wisdom and spiritual guidance, none of this would have been possible. I pray this work will bring light and knowledge to the Kingdom.

Archie T. Wright
Durham, England 2005

Abbreviations

AB	*Anchor Bible*
ABD	*Anchor Bible Dictionary*
ANET	*Ancient Near Eastern Texts Relating to the Old Testament*
ANRW	*Aufstieg und Niedergang der römischen Welt*
Ant.	Josephus, *Jewish Antiquities*
b.	Babylonian Talmud
1 Bar	*1 Baruch*
B.C.E.	Before Common Era
BDB	Francis Brown, S. R. Driver, and C. A. Briggs, *The New Brown – Driver – Briggs – Gesenius Hebrew and English Lexicon with an Appendix Containing the Biblical Aramaic.* Peabody, MA.: Hendrickson, 1979
Ber.	*Berakot*
Bere.	*Bereshith*
BibOr	Biblica et Orientalia
BJS	Brown Judaica Studies
BN	*Biblische Notizen*
BSOAS	*Bulletin of the School of Oriental and African Studies*
BW	*Book of Watchers*
c.	century
ca.	circa, about
CBQ	*Catholic Bible Quarterly*
CBQMS	Catholic Bible Quarterly Monograph Series
CD	Cairo Genizah Damascus Document
C.E.	Common Era
cf.	compare
ch(s).	chapter(s)
1, 2 Chr	1. 2 Chronicles
col(s).	column(s)
ConBNT	Coniectanea Biblica: New Testament
1, 2 Cor	1, 2 Corinthians
CRINT	Compendia rerum iudaicarum ad Novum Testamentum
CSCO	Corpus scriptorium Christianorum orientalium
Dan	Daniel
Deut	Deuteronomy
Did.	*Didache*
diss.	dissertation
DJD	Discoveries in the Judean Desert
DNTB	*Dictionary of New Testament Background: A Compendium of Contemporary Biblical Scholarship*
DSD	*Dead Sea Discoveries*
DSS	*Dead Sea Scrolls*
Eccl	Ecclesiastes

ed(s).	editor(s), edition
1 En	*1 Enoch*
Eth.	Ethiopic
Exod	Exodus
Exp Tim	*Expository Times*
Ezek	Ezekiel
f.	following
fasc.	fascicle
frag(s)	fragment(s)
Gal	Galatians
Gen	Genesis
Hab	Habakkuk
Hag	Haggai
HB	Hebrew Bible
Il.	Homer, *Iliad*
Od.	Homer, *Odyssey*
Hos	Hosea
HSCP	*Harvard Studies in Classical Philology*
HTR	*Harvard Theological Review*
HUCA	*Hebrew Union College Annual*
ibid.	in the same place as the previous citation(s)
idem	the same author
IEJ	*Israel Exploration Journal*
Isa	Isaiah
JBL	*Journal of Biblical Literature*
Jdt	Judith
Jer	Jeremiah
JJS	*Journal of Jewish Studies*
JNES	*Journal of Near Eastern Studies*
Jos. As.	*Joseph and Aseneth*
Josh	Joshua
JSJ	*Journal for the Study of Judaism in the Persian, Hellenistic, and Roman Periods*
JSJSup	Journal for the Study of Judaism Supplements
JSNT	*Journal for the Study of the New Testament*
JSNTSup	Journal for the Study of the New Testament Supplements
JSOT	*Journal for the Study of the Old Testament*
JSOTSup	Journal for the Study of the Old Testament Supplements
JSP	*Journal of the Study of the Pseudepigrapha*
JSPSup	Journal of the Study of the Pseudepigrapha Supplemental Series
JSS	*Journal of Semitic Studies*
JTS	*Journal of Theological Studies*
Jub	*Jubilees*
Judg	Judges
J.W.	Josephus, *Jewish War*
1, 2 Kgs	1, 2 Kings
LAB	*Liber antiquitatum biblicarum* (Pseudo-Philo)
LAE	*Life of Adam and Eve*
Lam	Lamentations
LCL	Loeb Classical Library

Lev	Leviticus
Lk	Luke
LXX	Septuagint (Greek O.T.)
m.	Mishnah
1, 2, 3 Macc	1, 2, 3 Maccabees
Mal	Malachi
Matt	Matthew
Mk	Mark
MSS	Manuscripts
MT	Masoretic Text of the O.T.
n.	note
Nah	Nahum
Nid.	*Niddah*
NovT	*Novum Testamentum*
N.T.	New Testament
NTT	*Norsk Teologisk Tidsskrift*
Num	Numbers
O.T.	Old Testament
OTP	*Old Testament Pseudepigrapha*, Charlesworth Edition
OTS	*Oudtestamentische Studiën*
Pesaḥ	*Pesaḥim*
PG	Patrologia Graeca
Philo of Alexandria	
Abr.	*De Abrahamo*
Agr.	*De Agricultura*
Cher.	*De Cherubim*
Conf.	*De Confusione Linguarum*
Congr.	*De Congressu*
Contempl.	*De vita contemplativa*
Decal.	*De Decalogo*
Det.	*Quod Deterius*
Deus.	*Quod Deus immutabilis sit*
Ebr.	*De Ebrietate*
Fug.	*De Fuga et Inventione*
Gig.	*De Gigantibus*
Her.	*Quis Rerum Divinarum Heres*
Hypoth.	*Hypothetica*
Ios.	*De Iosepho*
*Leg.*1, 2, 3	*Legum allegoriae* I, II, III
Legat.	*De Legatione ad Gaium*
Migr.	*De Migratione Abrahami*
Mos. 1, 2	*De vita Mosis* I, II
Mut.	*De Mutatione Nominum*
Opif.	*De Opificio Mundi*
Plant.	*De Plantatione*
Post.	*De Posteritate Caini*
Praem.	*De Praemiis et Poenis*
QE	*Quaestiones et Solutiones in Exodum*
QG	*Quaestiones et Solutiones in Genesin*
Sacr.	*De Sacrificiis Abelis et Caini*

Sobr.	*De Sobrietate*
Somn.	*De Somniis*
Spec.	*De Specialibus Legibus*
Virt.	*De Virtutibus*
PRE	Pirke Rabbi Eliezer
Prov	Proverbs
Ps(s)	Psalm(s)
Ps. Sol.	*Psalms of Solomon*
PVTG	Pseudepigrapha Veteris Testamenti Graece
Rab.	*Rabbah*
RB	*Revue biblique*
repr.	reprinted
RevQ	*Revue de Qumran*
1, 2 Sam	1, 2 Samuel
Sanh.	*Sanhedrin*
2TP	Second Temple Period
SBLDS	Society of Biblical Literature Dissertation Series
SBLSP	*Society of Biblical Literature Seminar Papers*
Sib. Or.	*Sibylline Oracles*
Sir	Sirach
SJLA	Studies in Judaism in Late Antiquity
STDJ	Studies on the Texts of the Desert of Judah
Sus	Susanna
T. Sol	*Testament of Solomon*
T12P	*Testaments of the Twelve Patriarchs*
T. Asher	*Testament of Asher*
T. Benjamin	*Testament of Benjamin*
T. Dan	*Testament of Dan*
T. Gad	*Testament of Gad*
T. Issachar	*Testament of Issachar*
T. Joseph	*Testament of Joseph*
T. Judah	*Testament of Judah*
T. Levi	*Testament of Levi*
T. Naphtali	*Testament of Naphtali*
T. Reuben	*Testament of Rueben*
T. Simeon	*Testament of Simeon*
T. Zebulun	*Testament of Zebulun*
TDNT	*Theological Dictionary of the New Testament*
Tg(s).	Targum(s)
1, 2 Thess	1, 2 Thessalonians
Tob	Tobit
TS	*Theological Studies*
vol(s).	volume(s)
VTSup	Supplements to Vetus Testamentum
Wis	Wisdom of Solomon
WMANT	Wissenschaftliche Monographien zum Alten und Neuen Testament
WUNT	Wissenschaftliche Untersuchungen zum Neuen Testament
ZAW	*Zeitschrift für die alttestamentliche Wissenschaft*
Zech	Zechariah
Zeph	Zephaniah

Chapter 1

Introduction

1.1 The Problem

The research presented here is concerned with the reception history of Genesis 6.1–4 in early Enochic and Philonic Judaism during the Second Temple Period (hereafter, 2TP). I suggest that the non-specificity inherent in the biblical text of Genesis 6.1–4 opened the basis for the later emergence of an aetiology of evil spirits as Jewish authors engaged with the text. As a result, Genesis 6.1–4, particularly its interpretation in *1 Enoch* 6–16, played an important part in the development of demonology during the 2TP.

Accordingly, by the turn of the Common Era there was in place a worldview within Judaism in which the activity of autonomous or semi-autonomous evil spirits was regarded as a reality. This view is exemplified in the ministry of Jesus as described in the Synoptic Gospels of the New Testament. By contrast, there is little evidence in Jewish literature during the earlier biblical period for such evil spirits. The understanding of demonic affliction found in the Jewish Scriptures (both Hebrew and Greek traditions) does not contain any references to autonomous or semi-autonomous evil spirits that are able to afflict humanity at will. When they are mentioned in the Hebrew Bible (hereafter HB), evil spirits are seen as beings sent by God to accomplish God's plan in the lives of individuals and the nation of Israel (see e.g. Num 5.14–15, 30 – spirit of jealousy; 1 Kgs 19.7, Isa 37.7 – lying spirits; Hos 5.4 – spirit of whoredom; Judg 9.23, Job 4.12–16 – spirits in the service of God; 1 Sam 16.14–23; 18.10–12; 19.9–10 – evil spirit upon Saul). The LXX translates various Hebrew terms[1] related to some type of wild beast that lurks about in the night or in the wilderness as a demonic creature.[2]

---

[1] There are just twenty-one occurrences in the LXX of the term δαιμόνιον (δαίμων), with all but one outside the Pentateuch (Deut. 32:17). The Hebrew term translated demon in the LXX varies: צִי (δαιμόνια, Isa 34.14; 13.21 – desert creature); שָׂעִיר (δαιμόνια [Isa 13.21 – hairy goat], also ὀνοκένταυριος [Isa 34.14, 13.21], ματαίοις [Lev 17.7 – goat demon], and εἰδώλοις [2 Chr 11.15 – satyrs]); שֵׁד (δαιμονίοις, Deut 32.17, Ps 106 (105).37, 38 – demon). All English translations are from NASV.

[2] See Edwin Yamauchi, "Magic or Miracle? Diseases, Demons and Exorcism," in *Gospel Review: The Miracles of Jesus* (ed. David Wenham and Craig Blomberg;

This raises the question of how the presence of categorically evil spirits could have emerged in the writings of the first century C.E. Since no material comparable to an episode such as, for example, Mark 5.1–20 exists in the HB, we must look elsewhere.[3] It is in this search that we encounter the *Book of Watchers* (*1 En* 1–36 = *BW*). This third-century B.C.E. pseudepigraphic composite work offers the oldest extant record of the origin of evil spirits in Judaism (see ch. 2 for question of the date of the document). As suggested above, the non-specificity inherent in Genesis 6.1–4 provided the authors of *BW* the opportunity and the biblical authority, to further develop a demonology in the 2TP. Such a view is substantiated through an examination of the continued development of the tradition around the turn of the era. In what follows, this study will attempt to reveal how the reception of Genesis 6.1–4 encouraged the development of the demonology and anthropology in the 2TP. I will endeavour to ascertain what Jews of the 2TP understood with regard to the origin and activity of evil spirits by examining the development of the concept of evil spirits alongside a developing understanding of human nature (anthropology) in early Jewish literature. Along with *BW*, I will address the interpretation of Genesis 6.1–4 in the *Book of Jubilees*, the treatises of Philo of Alexandria, and other Pseudepigrapha for any insights they might offer. In addition, I will discuss the taking up of the concept of evil spirits from the Watcher tradition by the authors of the Dead Sea Scrolls. Each of these texts sheds a particular light on the investigation and reflects significant developments of demonology and anthropology in this period.

The enigmatic nature of these sources requires an introductory caveat. One must resist approaching these sources in an attempt to find clear paths through the traditions. Clarity of this type is obfuscated by inherent complexities. Rather, it is fitting to offer plausible stages of development in the various documents. The historical disparity between the various sources only serves to validate this approach, which may offer a better view of the developing Jewish understanding of the origin of evil. These stages of growth may have merged to make possible the diversity of the

---

Sheffield: JSOT, 1986), 89–183. Yamauchi argues that the demonology in Israel is restrained in comparison to Mesopotamia. See Edward Langton, *Essentials of Demonology: A Study of Jewish and Christian Doctrine, Its Origin and Development* (London: Epworth, 1949). Langton contends that restraint in respect of the Babylonian and Assyrian influences was due to the desire "to affirm the belief in Yahweh as the one true God." This restraint, he argues, is the reason for the lack of references to demonology among the early Hebrews.

[3] For the most recent examination of demonic activity in the New Testament, see Eric Sorensen, *Possession and Exorcism in the New Testament and Early Christianity* (WUNT 157; Leiden: Mohr Siebeck, 2002).

tradition of demonic affliction encountered in the New Testament. Andy Reimer maintains:

In this task of reconstructing demonologies, one must seek to hold a tension between an integrated and consistent reading of a text or body of texts and an awareness of the sociology of knowledge 'gaps' in any religious sect's worldview. The history of demonology has certainly shown that attempts by texts such as 1 Enoch to rationalize entities that are by definition chaotic, irrational and typically open to all out speculation are bound to fail. Scholarly attempts to reconstruct any sort of ancient demonology will always have to work in the midst of chaos.[4]

Reimer is correct in his assertion that the demonology of *1 Enoch* is indeed chaotic. However, it may be possible that we can ease the sense of chaos by examining the matter of demons and evil spirits alongside a rather less chaotic anthropology, which was emerging in the 2TP at the same time as an interest in demons, was becoming apparent.

1.2 The Approach

I will attempt to unpack what can only be described as a very complicated collection of traditions that serve as the background of the "Watcher tradition" in *BW*. In an effort to trace the development of this tradition, I will subject two specific texts to close analysis. The first is Genesis 6.1–4 which, given its many peculiarities, has presented considerable difficulty for modern interpreters. The great variety of interpretations of this passage in early Jewish literature reveals that it presented similar difficulty for scripture exegetes and commentators in the post-biblical and later rabbinic periods.[5] As this thesis will attempt to demonstrate, Genesis 6.1–4 served as the source for the story of the origin of evil spirits in our second key text, *1 Enoch* 1–36.

1.2.1 Structure of the Thesis

The present study is divided into five main sections. The first section consists of the introduction and a chapter that reviews recent research of *BW* which followed the publication of J. T. Milik's *The Books of Enoch: Aramaic Fragments of Qumrân Cave 4* in 1976. It is necessary to present a detailed history of the research of *BW* in light of the questions raised (and

---

[4] Andy M. Reimer, "Rescuing the Fallen Angels: The Case of the Disappearing Angels at Qumran," *DSD* 7 (2000): 353.
[5] I shall draw on exegetical traditions in the Targumim and Midrashim which, though late, may provide some insight into ways Jewish readers were attempting to understand Gen 6 during the 2TP.

not raised) in the past concerning the structure, date, interpretation, and function of the Watcher tradition.

The second section offers a detailed discussion of Genesis 6.1–4, which includes the various biblical traditions (e.g., "divine council of God") that may lie behind the passage in its present form, and interpretations of the passage by later Jewish writers in the rabbinic period (see ch. 3). This is not an exhaustive examination of every relevant biblical text or non-Jewish works, but rather a presentation of the themes that the author of Genesis 6.1–4 may have been familiar with when he wrote the passage. I shall attempt to identify what aspects of the biblical tradition allowed the author(s) of *BW*[6] to interpret the Genesis passage with the negative elements that are present in *1 Enoch*'s version of the story.

In the third section, we shall examine the primary text that will serve as the starting point of the tradition of the affliction of humanity by evil spirits in the 2TP, *BW*. This will include three chapters that deal specifically with relevant portions of *BW* (*1 En* 6–16), i.e., the author's use of the biblical tradition of the *bene elohim*. The author's interpretation of the *bene elohim* is subdivided into the Asa'el tradition (Instruction motif) and the Shemihazah tradition (see *1 En* 4). A chapter will follow that focuses on the crux of *BW*, the rebellion motif (see ch. 5). This chapter will consider the effects of the actions of the angels on themselves, their offspring, and humanity. Following this discussion, I shall examine the reception of the Watcher tradition, and its "giantology"[7] and anthropology in other Early Jewish literature, in particular, the *DSS* (see ch. 6).

The fourth section will examine the treatises of Philo of Alexandria of which *De Gigantibus* is the primary focus (see ch. 7). Within *BW* and the writings of Philo, I shall highlight anthropological themes that weigh heavily in the discussion of affliction by evil spirits in the 2TP. In the final section, I shall conclude with a summary of the points of the thesis and its contribution to future research of the demonology and anthropology of Early Judaism.

---

[6] It is the consensus of Enochic scholars that there were likely multiple authors involved in the writing of the various sections of *BW*, however for the sake of reading ease I will use only the singular "author."

[7] This is a term coined in discussion with Loren Stuckenbruck about categorizing this section of the Watcher tradition. It is difficult to call it "demonology" if we consider that nowhere in chs. 6–16 are the angels, giants, or their spirits explicitly identified as demons.

1.2 Argument and Scope of the Present Study

Much of recent research on *1 Enoch*, in particular on *BW*, has focused on source and text-critical aspects of the third century B.C.E. material.[8] Previous research has centred on the traditions that are alluded to in *BW*, i.e. Greek, Near Eastern, and Israelite. This approach has added tremendous insight into the method by which the Jewish community in the

---

[8] This material will be discussed in detail in ch. 2: "*1 Enoch* 1–36 *The Book of Watchers*: History of the Documents and a Review of Recent Research." See e.g. William Adler, "Berossus, Manetho, and 1 Enoch in the World Chronicle of Panodorus," *HTR* 76 (1983): 419–42; John J. Collins, "The Apocalyptic Technique: Setting and Function in the Book of Watchers," *CBQ* 44 (1982): 91–111, idem, "Methodological Issues in the Study of 1 Enoch: Reflections on the Articles of P.D. Hanson and G.W. Nickelsburg," in *SBL Seminar Papers, 1978* (Missoula: Scholars Press, 1978), 315–22; Maxwell J. Davidson, *Angels At Qumran: A Comparative Study of 1 Enoch 1–36,72–108, and Sectarian Writings From Qumran* (JSPSup 11 Sheffield: JSOT Press, 1992); Devorah Dimant, "The Fallen Angels in the Dead Sea Scrolls and in the Apocryphal and Pseudepigraphic Books Related to Them" (Ph.D. diss., Hebrew University 1974 [Hebrew]); idem, "The 'Pesher of the Periods' 4Q180 and 4Q181," *Israel Oriental Studies* 9 (1979): 71–102; idem, "1 Enoch 6–11: A Methodological Perspective," in *SBL Seminar Papers, 1978* (Missoula: Scholars Press, 1978), 323–39; Jonas C. Greenfield and Michael E. Stone, "The Enochic Pentateuch and the Date of the Similitudes," *HTR* 70 (1977): 51–65; Paul Hanson, "Rebellion in Heaven, Azazel and Euhemeristic Heroes in 1 Enoch 6–11," *JBL* 96 (1977): 195–223; Ronald S. Hendel, "Of Demigods and the Deluge: Toward an Interpretation of Genesis 6.1–4," *JBL* 106 (1987): 13–26; J.T. Milik, *Books of Enoch: Aramaic Fragments of Qumran Cave 4* (Oxford: Clarendon Press, 1976); idem, "Problemes De La Litterature Henochique a La Lumiere Des Fragments Arameens De Qumran," *HTR* 64 (1971): 333–78; Carol Newsom, "The Development of 1 Enoch 6-19: Cosmology and Judgment," *CBQ* 42 (1980): 310–329; George W. E. Nickelsburg, *1 Enoch 1: A Commentary on the Book of 1 Enoch, Chapters 1–36; 81–108*, (Hermeneia; Minneapolis: Augsburg Fortress, 2001); idem, "Apocalyptic and Myth in 1 Enoch 6–11," *JBL* 96 (1977): 383–405; idem, "Enoch, Levi, and Peter: Recipients of Revelation in Upper Galilee," *SBL* 100 (1981): 575–600; idem, "The Books of Enoch in Recent Research," *RelSRev* 7 (1981): 210–17; Brook W.R. Pearson, "Resurrection and the Judgment of the Titans: in LXX Isaiah 26:19," *JSNTSup* 186 (1999): 33–51; Andy M. Reimer, "Rescuing the Fallen Angels"; James H. Scott, *Adoption as Sons of God* (Tübingen: J. C. B. Mohr, 1992); Michael E. Stone, "The Book of Enoch and Judaism in the Third Century B.C.E.," *CBQ* 40 (1978): 479–492; Loren T. Stuckenbruck, "The 'Angels' and 'Giants' of Genesis 6:1–4 in Second and Third Century B.C.E. Jewish Interpretation: Reflections on the Posture of Early Apocalyptic Traditions," *DSD* 7 (2000): 354–77; idem, *The Book of Giants From Qumran, Texts, Translation, and Commentary* (TSAJ 63; Tübingen: J. C. B. Mohr), 1997; David W. Suter, "Fallen Angel, Fallen Priest"; James C. VanderKam, "Enoch Traditions in Jubilees and Other Second-Century Sources," *SBL Seminar Papers, 1978* (Missoula: Scholars Press, 1978), 229–51; idem, *1 Enoch, Enochic Motifs, and Enoch in Early Christian Literature* (CRINT 4; Assen, The Netherlands: Van Gorcum, 1996); and M.L. West, *The East Face of Helicon* (Oxford: Clarendon Press, 1997).

Second Temple Period formulated its theology and traditions, the sources
for its theology and traditions (both oral and written), and the manner in
which these sources were collected. This has established a firm foundation
for future research of the theological message of these documents, which
until now has been inadequately addressed.

A further portion of previous research was undertaken in an effort to
determine the function of *BW* (see section 2.8.0). Arguments concerning
the function of *BW* have centred on why was there such a need for an
explanation of the origin of evil during this period of Israelite history? I
will present three main theories of interpretation that include 1) the
oppression of Israel by the Hellenistic rulers, 2) the origin of evil through
the rebellion of angels, and 3) the story as a polemic against the priesthood
in Jerusalem.

In summary, these scholarly works have shown that the *1 Enoch* 1-36 is
made up of complex layers of traditions that, in general, find their origins
in Genesis 6. It is no surprise that *BW* is such a complex literary
construction, considering its origins lie in this enigmatic passage that
invited so much speculation!

Genesis 6.1-4 tells the story of the *bene elohim* and their encounter with
the daughters of humanity which resulted in the birth of the *gibborim*. The
passage is positioned in the biblical narrative as a prelude to the judgment
of the Flood. However, on the surface nothing in the biblical text of
Genesis 6.1–4 demands that the reader understand those verses in a
negative light, that is, as depicting some action or event that is considered
inappropriate or dubious. It is necessary to evaluate the traditions (e.g., the
negative aspects of the "angels of the nations") that underlie Genesis 6.1–4
in order to assess properly why the text is commendable as the starting
point of the Watcher tradition.[9] This is to say, the Watcher tradition
represents a type of biblical synthesis and exposition; it is the
"superimposition" of negative traditions on to the relatively neutral
position of Genesis 6.1–4 (i.e., it is rewritten Bible). In doing so, I shall
attempt to identify possible sources that the author of Genesis 6.1–4 may
have had in mind while writing the narrative, sources which may have left
the text open to a negative interpretation by the author of *BW*.

The vocabulary of Genesis 6.1–4 in both the Hebrew and Greek
traditions, i.e. בני האלהים (*bene haElomim*) נפלים (*Nephilim*), גברים
(*Gibborim*) and γίγαντες, (*gigantes*) invited various interpretations in the
early post-biblical and the later rabbinic periods. These interpretations
include those which contain detrimental nuances about the characters in
the story that could lead to a negative understanding of the text, or portray
the characters in a positive or neutral light.

---

[9] These traditions will be discussed in detail in ch. 3 below.

The Hebrew expression *bene elohim* evokes images of the heavenly court of God where the "sons of God" ruled over the nations or acted as intermediaries between the God of Israel and his people (see ch. 3, section 3.2.2). Within this tradition, we find possibilities for Genesis 6.2 to take on negative imagery sanctioning the introduction of rebellious angels in *BW*. The term *gibborim* evokes images of the great heroes of Israel in the biblical period, and at the same time is used as a description of the most imposing גבור in the HB, Nimrod (see ch. 3, section 3.2.4.2). Nimrod is identified in the LXX tradition as a γίγας; and it is implied that he played an active role in the rebellion of the people at the Tower of Babel. This datum alone leaves sufficient room for a negative interpretation of the Genesis 6 text. The LXX translates גבורים with the Greek term γίγαντες, which calls to mind the characters of the Greek myths of Hesiod (*Theogony* and *Works and Days*) and Homer (*Iliad*). As will be shown below, it is also possible that this translation also contributed to *BW*'s negative portrayal of the offspring of Genesis 6.4. I shall argue that the biblical tradition of Genesis 6.1–4, perhaps not immediately apparent, served as a starting point for the author of *BW* as he presented his story of the origin of evil spirits.

The negative interpretation of the biblical tradition of Genesis 6.1–4 in *BW* is centred on the *bene elohim*. It is difficult to imagine that the author of *BW* arbitrarily chose this story to present the origin of evil spirits; therefore, it is likely that this tradition had been developing long before it was unveiled as the Watcher tradition (although no direct proof, other than the biblical data listed above and in the following discussion, can be mustered). It is in this tradition that the author discloses the rebellious nature of the angels, which results in the devastation of the earth and humanity (see ch. 4, section 4.2.0).

Within this story of rebellion, scholars of *BW* have argued for at least two streams of tradition identifying a leadership group amongst the angels on which the blame of the rebellion is placed, the Asa'el (Instruction) motif and the Shemihazah motif. Each of these streams adds a particular dimension to the rebellious action of the angels, resulting in the blame for devastation of the earth being placed on the angels in one account, (Shemihazah) and being partially shifted to humanity for its part in the other (Asa'el/Instruction).

I shall discuss the author's introduction of the Instruction/Asa'el motif and possible motivation for this expansion of the Genesis story (see ch. 4, sections 4.3.0–4.3.4). Much debate has been devoted to the identity of Asa'el and his role in *BW*. He is originally one of the leaders of the angels in the opening verses of *1 Enoch* 6, but is later identified as the angel responsible for teaching humanity the art of war and beautification of women (i.e. the use of cosmetics), which brings about the corruption of the earth. Several scholars have proposed that he is connected to the character Azazel in Leviticus 16, but as will be seen, this theory has no proper foundation at the time *BW* was written. It seems likely that the author's purpose in using the Instruction motif (although this is difficult to determine with any certainty) was to connect the action of the *bene elohim* in Genesis 6 with the judgment of the Flood, placing blame for the disaster on both the angels and humanity.

The primary strand of the story is undoubtedly the Shemihazah tradition (see ch. 4, sections 4.4.0–4.4.3). The author blames the angels for the corruption of creation. Shemihazah and the angels have rebelled against God by crossing into the realm of physical contact with humanity: they have breached the cosmos. The rebellion of the angels and in particular the consequences of their actions, are the focus of the narrative (see ch. 5, section 5.2.0–5.4.0). It is within this tradition that we find motifs of impurity and corruption of the earth and humanity. Each of these is dealt with by the cleansing of the Flood. Alongside these motifs, we are told of the birth of the offspring, who, although characterized as relatively neutral in Genesis 6.4, are portrayed as categorically evil in *BW*. It is here that the synthetic nature of *BW* comes to full view—the punishment of the Flood is a result of the *negative* activity recorded in Genesis 6.1–4. The activity of these figures becomes the central point of the author's story as the rebellious angels are removed from the scene and the interaction of the evil spirits with humanity becomes the focus (*1 En* 15–16). At this point, we can identify the author's giantology, which describes the spiritual nature of the giants as evil, their actions as merciless, and their future as irredeemable (see ch. 5, section 5.4.1–5.6.0). Within the author's introduction of evil spirits, he reveals a glimpse of an anthropology that portrays humanity as defenceless against the attack of these creatures.

It will be shown that other Jewish writers will take up this giantology and anthropology in the 2TP (see ch. 6). These authors pressed the motifs of the Watcher tradition into a more dualistic framework in which good and evil spirits attempt to influence human souls. At the same time, an ethical dualism is developed, which posits an internal struggle in the human spirit to live righteously (follow God) or do evil (abandon the Law and service of God). This is an overriding theme in several of the Qumran documents, as is demonstrated in several of the "incantation" prayers (see ch. 6, 6.6.2).

It seems, however, that this explanation of the problem of human suffering was not easily accepted in every Jewish community. The writings of Philo of Alexandria reveal an interpretation of Genesis 6.1–4 that differs markedly from that found in *BW* (see ch. 7). In *De Gigantibus*, Philo rejects the notion that the giants are evil spirits; rather, they function as personifying metaphors for pleasures and vices of the human flesh (see ch. 7, section 7.4.0–7.4.2). In this manner, Philo is formulating an anthropology that assigns the responsibility of evil to human choice. Philo's anthropology corresponds with the internal struggle of the human soul that is found in some of the *DSS*.[10] His demonology begins with a person's decision whether or not to pursue the desires of the flesh. This internal struggle can be affected by external forces, which are not spirits *per se*, but vices. These vices combine with the fleshly desire of the person, which leads him or her to corruption. Despite Philo's apparent rejection of the demonic interpretation of Genesis 6 found in *BW*, his anthropology has clear affinities with some of the thinking preserved in the Dead Sea documents. Philo's interpretation of the giants reflects diversity within Judaism with respect to the problem of human suffering, a diversity that is also reflected in the New Testament.

1.4 Summary

This thesis discusses the reception of Genesis 6.1–4 (Greek and Hebrew traditions) in Early Jewish literature, in particular, *1 Enoch* 6–16 and the writings of Philo of Alexandria. It will be shown that a primary interpretation of the Genesis passage by these authors involved the understanding of human suffering, that is by demonic affliction in the Watcher tradition and human choice in Philo. While other scholars argue that the story presented in *BW* is simply the author's explanation of an oppressive political situation that Israel is facing, I contend that *BW* can be identified as the author's account of the origin of evil spirits based on his interpretation of Genesis 6.1–4. It should be recognized that this understanding is primarily expressed in *1 Enoch* 15–16. It is clear that the giantology and anthropology, which are presented in BW, serve as a backdrop for what would follow in the developing anthropology and demonology in the *DSS*, the Pseudepigrapha, and the Gospels.

The developing anthropology and demonology in these documents reveal a diverse theological community within Judaism in the centuries around the turn of the era. They suggest the likelihood that the author of *BW* indeed intended the message of the book to offer some explanation for the existence and function of evil spirits in the world of third-century B.C.E. Jews. In arguing along these lines, I part company from the views of Suter, Dimant, and others. This thesis advocates that the message of *BW* may be read aetiologically rather that strictly paradigmatically. Although a

---

[10] See ch. 6, section 6.3.0.

reading which suggests the story is a metaphor for the political situation in Israel at the time is not ruled out, the evidence presented here suggests that *BW* represented the worldview of at least a significant group of Jews in the 2TP, which believed that evil spirits were a reality that they faced on a daily basis.

Before examining the primary source materials themselves, I shall present a thorough evaluative overview of the history of research of *BW* in chapter 2. I include the history of the texts, an outline of the structure of the book, a brief summary of the book, a short excursus on notable terms in *BW*, the foci of the research, i.e., the date, place, and author; theories of source criticism; and the theories of interpretation and function of the book. This evaluation reveals that although this research is invaluable to understanding *BW*, more investigation needs to be done relating to theological issues of the document. This attention to recent research is of particular importance since the major developments in this area of study have transpired during the last three decades. It is in relation to these developments that the focus of this thesis is best delineated.

Chapter 2

1 Enoch 1–36: The Book of Watchers:
A Review of Recent Research

2.1 Introduction

Since the discovery of the Dead Sea Scrolls, there has been an increasing interest by scholars in *1 Enoch* 1–36, the *Book of Watchers*. This is due primarily to the publication of the 4QEn fragments by J.T. Milik in 1976. Milik presents a major edition that contains the Aramaic fragments of *1 Enoch* from Qumran Cave 4.[1] He has included the text of the fragments, his translation and notes, and his reconstruction of the text. Milik provides an evaluation of the extant literature by comparing what he calls "specimens of the original text" to his reconstruction and translation, while also offering an introduction to the history of the early Enochic literature.

The major problem with Milik's book, as many have pointed out,[2] is that in many places the Aramaic text he presents is in fact a reconstruction based on his comparison of the 4QEn fragments with the extant Greek and Ethiopic texts. To this end, he has been properly criticized; his work all too easily may lead to the illusion that a great deal more of the Aramaic documents is extant from Qumran than is actually the case. However, the contribution of Milik's work far outweighs its shortcomings.

As a result of the publication of the Qumran material, several theories have been set forth that consider the major areas of concern about *BW* (i.e. date, place and authorship, source criticism of the myths behind *BW*; and interpretation of the function of *BW*). This chapter will endeavour to present a history of the recent research on *BW*. In order to prepare a backdrop of the review of the previous research, I will first present a brief

---

[1] Milik, *Books of Enoch*.

[2] See reviews by James Barr, review of J.T. Milik, Books of Enoch: Aramaic Fragments of Qumran Cave 4, JTS 29 (1978): 517–30; Sebastian Brock, JJS 29 (1978): 98–99; J. Greenfield and Michael Stone, Numen 26 (1979): 89–103; James A. Sanders, JBL 97 (1978): 446–47; Loren T. Stuckenbruck, "Revision of Aramaic—Greek and Greek—Aramaic Glossaries in The Books of Enoch: Aramaic Fragments of Qumran Cave 4 by J. T. Milik," JJS 41 (1990): 13–48; James C. VanderKam, "Some Major Issues in the Contemporary Study of 1 Enoch: Reflections on J.T. Milik's Books of Enoch: Aramaic Fragments of Qumran Cave 4," Maarav 3, (1982): 85–97.

record of the extant texts of *1 Enoch* 1–36, a short discussion of the structure of *BW*, and finally a summary of the contents.

2.2 History of the Texts

Modern research on *1 Enoch* had its beginning in 1773 with the discovery of the whole of *1 Enoch* by James Bruce who brought three Ethiopic manuscripts back to Europe. This discovery led eventually to no less than 12 translations (English, French, and German) in the nineteenth century, highlighted by August Dillmann's translation and commentary edition in 1853.[3] The discovery of the Akhmim Greek manuscript of *1 Enoch* 1–32 in 1886/87 (and subsequent publication in 1892/93)[4] greatly advanced the research of *BW* in the Greek tradition. R. H. Charles' translation and commentary, published in 1912, contained the most extensive text-critical apparatus and commentary on *1 Enoch* to date. Following Charles' publication, the majority of research concerning *1 Enoch* through 1950 focused on the eschatological aspects and the "Son of Man" of the Similitudes.[5]

A significant advance for the research of *BW* took place with the initial publications (1951, 1955, and 1958) of the Aramaic fragments discovered at Qumran.[6] Milik's monograph containing the fragments of *1 Enoch* and the *Book of Giants*[7] has been a decisive catalyst to further study of *BW*. Michael Knibb published a new translation of the Ethiopic with text-critical apparatus that included the Qumran fragments and the extant Greek texts in 1978.[8] This two-volume work provides a copy of the Ethiopic *1 Enoch* 1–108 (vol. 1) along with a translation and commentary (vol. 2) that compares the various Ethiopic and Greek texts with the Aramaic fragments. A second English translation by Ephraim Isaac followed in 1983.[9] In 1984, Siegbert Uhlig published a German translation based on

---

[3] For a thorough review of the textual tradition, see Nickelsburg, *Commentary*, 9–20, 109–112.

[4] Published by Bouriant (1892) and Lods (1892/93).

[5] The majority of the research was done by Christian scholars; see comments ibid., 114.

[6] See review of material in Milik, *Books of Enoch*. See also Nickelsburg, "Enoch in Recent Research," for a review of the research during this period.

[7] See Stuckenbruck, *Book of Giants* and Émile Puech in *DJD*, vol. XXXI (Oxford: Clarendon, 2001) for a thorough study of the Book of Giants fragments.

[8] Knibb, *Ethiopic Enoch*.

[9] Ephraim Isaac, "1 Enoch," in *The Old Testament Pseudepigrapha* (2 vols.; ed. James H. Charlesworth; New York: Doubleday, 1983–85), 1:5–89. Isaac has not incorporated the Aramaic fragments in his translation.

multiple Ethiopic MSS not incorporated in previous translations by Charles, Knibb, and Isaac.[10] In 1985, Matthew Black published what would be an attempt to expand Charles' 1912 edition with text-critical notes and commentary.[11] Black's two works have analysed the extant Greek manuscripts. The first of Black's volumes presents the extant Greek manuscripts and their textual variants, while the second provides a short introduction, translation, commentary, and textual notes on the variants of the extant Greek manuscripts.

In 1993, Patrick Tiller published a comprehensive introduction and commentary to the *Animal Apocalypse* (chs. 85–90) that is based on multiple Ethiopic MSS, Greek fragments, and the Qumran fragments.[12] In 2001, George Nickelsburg published a long awaited comprehensive introduction and commentary on *1 Enoch* chapters 1–36 and 81–108. The first volume of what is a two-volume commentary on *1 Enoch*[13] includes his own English translation with the apparatus of the variant readings in the Ethiopic, Greek, and the Aramaic fragments from Qumran. He has also included a verse-by-verse commentary that explores what he describes as the "major philological, literary, theological, and historical questions" concerning its place in Hellenism, 2TPJudaism, and early Christianity. In doing so, Nickelsburg has produced a tool that will be appreciated by anyone doing research in what is one of the most important books of 2TP Judaism.

2.3 Structure of the *Book of Watchers*

The *Book of Watchers* is one of the five major sections of *1 Enoch*, although the final section (chapters 91–108) may be subdivided into four smaller sections.

Chapters 1–36 – Book of Watchers
Chapters 37–71 – Book of Parables
Chapters 72–82 – Astronomical Book (Book of the Luminaries)

---

[10] See Siegbert Uhlig, Das äthiopische Henochbuch (JSHRZ 5/6; Gütersloh: Mohn, 1984). For details of these additional manuscripts, see Nickelsburg, *Commentary*, 17.

[11] Matthew Black, *Apocalypsis Henochi Graece* (PVTG 3; Leiden: Brill, 1970) and idem, *The Book of Enoch or 1 Enoch* (SVTP 7; Leiden: Brill, 1985).

[12] See Patrick A Tiller, *A Commentary on the Animal Apocalypse* (Atlanta: Scholars Press, 1993). This section of *1 Enoch* plays an important role alongside *BW* in the interpretation of Gen 6.1–4.

[13] The second volume was released in 2011; see George W. E. Nickelsburg and James C. VanderKam, *1 Enoch 2: A Commentary on the Book of 1 Enoch, Chapters 37-82.* (Hermeneia; Minneapolis: Fortress, 2011).

Chapters 83–90 – Animal Apocalypse (or Book of Dreams)
Chapters 91–108 – Epistle of Enoch[14]

Following the publication of the fragments from Qumran Cave 4,[15] it is now thought that *1 Enoch* was written in Aramaic, and then translated into Greek and later Ethiopic.[16] The five sections of *1 Enoch* as a whole are fully extant only in Ethiopic because the Ethiopic Church preserved it as an authoritative writing.[17] *BW* is itself thought to be a composite document that is normally divided into these subdivisions:

Chapters 1–5 – introduction
Chapters 6–11 – traditions of Asa'el and Shemihazah groups of angels[18]
Chapters 12–16 – reintroduction of Enoch and his interaction with the angels
Chapters 17–19 – Enoch's first heavenly journey
Chapter 20 – list of archangel names

---

[14] Nickelsburg argues (see ibid., 8) that chapter 91 is an editorial section that leads into the Epistle of Enoch (92–105). Chapters 106–107 are identified as a birth narrative from the Book of Noah and chapter 108 is considered an appendix that provides words of assurance to the righteous.

[15] See Milik, *Books of Enoch*. Milik recognizes 11 manuscripts that correspond to four of the five divisions of *1 Enoch*. The Book of Parables has yet to be identified among the fragments of Qumran (p. 7).

[16] Edward Ullendorf and Michael Knibb have argued that the translators of the Ethiopic edition had in front of them both the Aramaic and Greek versions; see Edward Ullendorf, "An Aramaic 'Vorlage' of the Ethiopic Text of Enoch?" (Problemi attuali di scienza e di cultura, quaderni 48; Rome: Accademia Nazionale dei Lincei, 1960): 259–67; and Knibb, *Ethiopic Enoch* (Oxford: Clarendon, 1978), 2:27–46. James VanderKam has argued that the translators depended on the Greek text exclusively; see James C. VanderKam, "The Textual Base for the Ethiopic Translation of 1 Enoch," in *Working with No Data: Studies in Semitic and Egyptian Presented to Thomas O. Lambdin*, (ed. D. M. Golomb; Winona Lake, Ind.: Eisenbrauns, 1987), 247–62. For other arguments related to the Vorlage of the Ethiopic translations, see Klaus Beyer, *Die aramäischen Texte vom Toten Meer* (Göttingen: Vandenhoeck & Ruprecht, 1984), 225–58; H. F. Fuhs, "Die Aethipsche Uebersetzung des Henoch: Ein Beitrag zur Apokalyptikforschung der Gegenwart," BN 8 (1979): 36–56; Joseph A. Fitzmyer, "Implications of the New Enoch Literature from Qumran," TS 38 (1977): 332–45; Erik W. Larson, "The Translation of Enoch: From Aramaic Into Greek" (Ph.D. diss., New York University, 1995); Michael Sokoloff, "Notes on the Aramaic Fragment of Enoch From Qumran Cave 4," Maarav 1 (1978–1979); and James Barr, "Aramaic-Greek Notes on the Book of Enoch I, II," JJS 23 (1978): 187–98.

[17] See R.H. Charles, *The Book of Enoch*, (London: SPCK, 1912. Repr., ed. Paul Tice; Escondido, CA: The Book Tree, 2000), xiv–xxix for a survey of the extant texts. Cf. Nickelsburg, *Commentary*, 9–20, 109–112.

[18] Several have argued that chapters 6–11 are original to the now lost "Book of Noah." See e.g. Alexander, "Sons of God," 60 and Paolo Sacchi, *Jewish Apocalyptic and its History*, (JSPSup 20; trans. William J. Short; Sheffield: Sheffield Academic, 1990), 213.

Chapters 21–36 – Enoch's second heavenly journey

In all likelihood, each of these sections was written by a different author and brought together by an editor or editors at a later date. However, the possibility that it is a single author should be given consideration. As will be argued below, different strands of the tradition may be found in the various sections (e.g. chs. 6–11 likely contain two strands of the tradition – Asa'el and Shemihazah).

BW (especially 6–11) is arguably the earliest Jewish apocalyptic writing that takes up the story found in Genesis 6.1–4. Palaeographical evidence makes it plausible to date *BW* as a whole (i.e. 4Q201, 4QEn[a]) to the early second century B.C.E. or possibly the late third century.[19] At this early stage, *BW* likely consisted of the narrative that is recognized as chapters 6–11 and 12–16.[20] Fragments found at Qumran support the suggestion that chapters 1–5 were incorporated as an introduction to chapters 6–16 during the early stages of the composition.[21] A *terminus ad quem* of the last third of the first century B.C. is suggested for the later chapters of *BW* (i.e. 17–36) that describe the heavenly journeys of Enoch. This is based on the fragments of 4QEn[c +d] that contain the only extant Aramaic text of these chapters.[22]

R. H. Charles proposed in his edition that chapters 1–5 were written as an introduction to the whole collection of *1 Enoch* as a final section to the work. Chapters 1–5, which describe the offence of those who have turned from the covenant of God, the coming judgment and the restoration of the earth, are thought to be eschatological in nature.[23] The Aramaic fragments of 4QEn have since proven Charles' findings incorrect. Due to the dating assigned to the fragments of chapters 1–5 and 6–11 identified as 4QEn[a],[24]

---

[19] It should be noted that 4QEn[a] contains only a small portion of *BW*, i.e., frag i – 1.1–6; ii – 2.1–5.6; iii – 6.4–8.1; iv – 8.3–9.3,6–8; v – 10.3–4; vi – 10.21–11.1; 12.4–6. Loren Stuckenbruck suggests 4Q201 frag 6 corresponds to *1 Enoch* 13.8 (see discussion below)

[20] Milik, *Books of Enoch*, 140–41. Milik and others conclude that the Vorlage of 4Q201 originated as early as the third century. See also Nickelsburg, *Commentary*, 7; Stone, "Book of Enoch and Judaism," 484; and Hanson, "Rebellion in Heaven," 219–20.

[21] It is generally acknowledged that *BW* consisted of several different components which were likely separate traditions interwoven to form the early stage of *BW*. See e.g. Milik, *Books of Enoch*; Nickelsburg, "Apocalyptic and Myth"; Newsom, "Development of 1 Enoch"; Hanson, "Rebellion in Heaven"; Collins, "Apocalyptic Technique"; and Dimant, "Methodological Perspective."

[22] See Milik, *Books of Enoch*, 178–222.

[23] For a detailed study of chapters 1–5, see Lars Hartman, *Asking for a Meaning: A Study of 1 Enoch 1–5*, (ConBNT 12; Lund, Sweden: CWK Gleerup, 1979). Hartman argues that these chapters offer the reader clues on how to understand the chapters that follow.

[24] Milik, *Books of Enoch*, 140, 144. Milik argues that 4QEn[a] dates from early second century B.C.E. while *1 Enoch* 83–90 cannot be dated earlier than 164 B.C.E.

it has been determined that *1 Enoch* 1–5 is an introduction to *BW* (chs. 1–36) only.[25]

2.4 Summary of the Content of the *Book of Watchers*

The content of *1 Enoch* reveals that the author was particularly captivated by the traditions found in Genesis 5–9. James VanderKam and others have argued that a "special form of Judaism," Enochic Judaism, reflects the author's fascination in particular, with the story of the "sons of God" and the "daughters of men" in Genesis 6.1–4.[26] The narrative of *1 Enoch* 6–16 focuses on the Watcher angels (= *bene haelohim*) and their intrusion into the physical world. The story describes how the Watchers (i.e. the rebellious angels) chose to rebel against God by swearing an oath to go to the earth and engage with the daughters of humanity to produce offspring of their own. A comparison of the two passages, Genesis 6.1–2 and *1 Enoch* 6.1–2, reveals a close similarity between the two stories:

Genesis 6.1 And it came about that humanity began to multiply upon the face of the earth and daughters were born to them. 2. And the angels saw that the daughters of humanity were good to behold, and they took for themselves women from whomever they chose.

1 Enoch 6.1 And it came to pass, when the sons of men had increased, that in those days there were born to them fair and beautiful daughters. 2. And the angels, the sons of heaven, saw them and desired them. And they said to one another: "Come, let us choose for ourselves wives from the children of men, and let us beget for ourselves children."[27]

---

[25] Nickelsburg suggests that chapters 1–5 are an introduction to a "full–blown Enochic Testament" that included chapters 1–5+6–11+12–33 or 36+81.1–82.4+91 and parts of 92–105, but admits the evidence is indecisive. See Nickelsburg, *Commentary*, 25. See also Sacchi, Jewish Apocalyptic, 48.

[26] This a far too simple explanation for Enochic Judaism. Enochic Judaism appears to encompass a widespread sectarian movement of which Qumran was likely a part. The sect(s) thought itself to have received authoritative literature by revelation and that the possession of such literature validated it as the elect community of God. It is plausible to suggest that the writings from the Qumran library which are identified as Qumran sectarian were part of the large community of Enochic Judaism. See James C. VanderKam, *Enoch: A Man for All Generations* (Columbia, SC: University of South Carolina, 1995), vii; Gabriele Boccaccini, *Beyond the Essene Hypothesis: The Parting of the Ways between Qumran and Enochic Judaism* (Grand Rapids/Cambridge: Eerdmans, 1998); David R. Jackson, *Enochic Judaism Three Defining Paradigm Exemplars*, (London: T&T Clark, 2004); and Sacchi, *Jewish Apocalyptic*.

[27] Translation from Knibb, *Ethiopic Enoch*, 2:67. There is the question of who is relying on whom in this tradition. Milik has argued that the *1 Enoch* traditions preceded

From this point forward, however, the author of *BW* embarks on an elaborate narrative that departs from the Genesis story detailing the effect of these relationships upon the angels, humanity, and creation.

It has been argued that at least two distinct strands of the angel story can be delineated within chapters 6–16 (Shemihazah and Asa'el). Each of the strands assigns at least part of the blame for the coming judgment of the earth to the angels.[28] The first strand contains the story of Shemihazah and his two hundred followers who take women to sire offspring of their own.[29] The giant offspring that are born from the relations are the primary cause of the violence and destruction on the earth, which, in turn, results in the Flood (cf. *gibborim* in Gen 6.4).

This same group of angels has a role in the second strand of chapters 6–16, which begins in chapter 8. This is the story of the angel Asa'el, whose original mission on the earth was to teach the arts of civilization for the good of humanity. However, the apparently improper use of the knowledge by humans resulted in their own corruption and the punishment of the Watcher angels. The author of *BW* has made it clear that the Watchers have rebelled by having sexual relations with women (Shemihazah tradition) and teaching humanity the rejected forms of knowledge (Asa'el/Instruction tradition).[30] Following the introduction of the Watchers and the Instruction motif, the story continues with the outcry of humanity because of the destruction caused by the giant offspring, which in turn solicits a response from heaven. The author of *BW* incorporates an

---

the Genesis material and that the author of Genesis compressed the *BW* version because of the audience's familiarity with the story. See Milik, *Books of Enoch*, 31.

[28] Dimant has written a detailed interpretation of chapters 6–11 in which she argues for three basic strands within the story. The first is an account of the angels from Gen 6.1–4 who have sexual relations with women and produce giant offspring. The second story, which Dimant argues combined with the first, is a description of how angels led humans into sin by secret instruction and resulted in the appearance of demons and judgment by the Flood. Dimant contends that the third strand, which identifies Asa'el as the leader of the angels, is related to Gen 6.11–12. This story describes the teaching of the arts of civilization to humans, which cause them to sin, corrupt the angels, and bring about the Flood. See Dimant, "Fallen Angels," 23–72.

[29] One question that has perhaps been overlooked concerning this part of the tradition is: 'Why did the angels want to sire offspring in the first place?' Was it a simply matter of lusting after the beauty of the daughters of men? Or was there a tradition in Early Judaism that perhaps revealed the driving force behind the Watchers' desire to have children?

[30] The angels are accused of teaching a "worthless mystery," see e.g. *1 Enoch* 7.1; 8.1–3; 9.6–8a; 13.2b. It is possible that the author or redactor included the Instruction motif into the story in order to place part of the blame for the judgment of the earth on humanity to draw a parallel to the Genesis narrative.

eschatological element into the story beginning in 10.13,[31] which describes the coming of a heavenly epoch following the cleansing of the earth from the evil caused by the interaction of the angels and humanity.

Chapters 12–16 begin within the context of Genesis 5.21–24 and the time that Enoch spent with the angels.[32] Beginning in chapter 12, Enoch is told to go and tell the Watchers of heaven of their approaching destruction as punishment for their sin. He goes first to Asa'el, tells him of his punishment, and then proceeds to tell the rest of the Watchers about their punishment.[33] They in turn, plead with him to intercede with God on their behalf. Chapter 13 describes the Watchers' request for absolution and Enoch's petitioning of heaven. Chapter 14, the longest in this section, depicts Enoch's vision and message to the Watchers; they will be judged and will not have peace. In chapters 15 and 16, God tells Enoch about the sins of the Watchers and their offspring, and that, because of their sin, they shall have no peace.[34] The central theme of these chapters is the story of the angels who sinned by having sexual relations with women and the evil spirits that emerge from the bodies of the giants upon their death.

The final section of *BW*, chapters 17–36, describes the heavenly journey of Enoch. While on the journey, he is shown various elements of the cosmos that play a part in the eschatological message of the author, i.e. Sheol, the ends of the earth, places of punishment, Paradise, God's throne, the tree of life, and Jerusalem. Also, during the journey, he is given heavenly knowledge by an archangel that would be used to counter the teachings of the Watchers.[35]

It is important now to discuss the focus of recent research of *BW* that has studied the work from a redactional or source critical approach. Scholars have made great progress in this area attempting to reach an "original" *1 Enoch* text. Many theories have been presented regarding the

---

[31] Eschatology is first introduced in chapters 1–5.

[32] The LXX has translated אֶת־הָאֱלֹהִים in Gen 5.22 as τῷ θεῷ "with God". It is clear that the author of *1 Enoch* 12.2 has interpreted this as the angels: "And all his [Enoch] doings were with the Holy Ones and with the Watchers in his days."

[33] Cf. 4Q203 8. 6–10.

[34] Compare also 4Q203 frag 13.3 – [. . . שלום לכה איתי [לא די] – "that there will be no peace to you." Text from Florentino García Martínez and Eibert J.C. Tigchelaar, eds., *Dead Sea Scrolls Study Edition* (2 vols.; Leiden and Grand Rapids: Brill and Eerdmans, 1997–98), 1:410.

[35] There is a similar theme found in *Jubilees* in which the scribe and prophet Moses is given heavenly knowledge (i.e. message from God concerning the covenant) by the angels and directly from the mouth of God. This can be seen in *BW* in the case of Enoch who is seen as the righteous scribe (and prophet) who is given the divine message by the angels and from God. Similarly, in *Jubilees* 10, Noah is given knowledge by the angels in order to thwart the physical afflictions of the evil spirits. See Nickelsburg, *Commentary*, 229.

traditions from which the material has been passed down to the author. Though this approach to the documents perhaps gives the critic control over the evidence, it does not necessarily bring the reader to the right conclusions about the author's intention in writing down and bringing together these traditions in the closing centuries B.C.E. Redaction and source criticism are essential methods as one scrutinizes the text of *1 Enoch*, but they do not go far enough if one is to give serious consideration to the theological issues which the author was attempting to address in his interpretation of Genesis 6.1–4. These issues must be examined alongside the source critical theories in order to gain a clearer understanding of *BW*.

2.5 Focus of the Research

The primary focus of the research in *BW* has been an attempt to discover the source, or sources, of the tradition of the Fallen Angels and giants portrayed in *1 Enoch* 6–16.[36] There is a wide range of views concerning the author's purpose in writing *BW*, some of which will be discussed below.

Three primary foci are usually found interconnected within the research undertaken by most scholars concerning *BW*. These foci have centred on the varying cultural traditions the author of *BW* used to develop his story. First, recent research has concentrated on the origin of the sources of these traditions. The opinions surrounding this question are primarily divided into two main camps: (1) the traditions originated in Greek culture or (2) they originated in Near Eastern Semitic cultures. A third option holds that the source of the traditions found in *BW* derived more immediately from the Israelite traditions.

A second area of the research has centred on *BW*'s relationship to the story concerning the sons of God in Genesis 6.1–4. Here there are also two main camps involved (with minor disagreements in each): (1) the author of *BW* elaborated on the Genesis text and the traditions behind it or (2) the

---

[36] Adler, "Berossus"; Barr, "Enoch Fragments"; Brock, "Enoch Fragments"; Collins, "Apocalyptic Technique"; idem, "Methodological Issues"; Davidson, *Angels At Qumran*; Dimant, "Fallen Angels"; idem, "Pesher of the Periods"; idem, "A Methodological Perspective"; Greenfield and Stone, "Enoch Fragments"; idem, "Enochic Pentateuch"; Hanson, "Rebellion in Heaven"; Hendel, "Of Demigods"; Milik, *Books of Enoch*; idem, "Problemes"; Newsom, "Development of 1 Enoch 6–19"; Nickelsburg, "Apocalyptic and Myth"; idem, *Commentary*; idem, "Enoch, Levi, and Peter"; idem, "Recent Research": 210–17; Pearson, "Resurrection and the Judgment"; Reimer, "Rescuing the Fallen Angels"; Sanders, "Enoch Fragments"; Stone, "Book of Enoch and Judaism"; Stuckenbruck, "The 'Angels' and 'Giants'"; idem, "Revision of Aramaic"; Suter, "Fallen Angel, Fallen Priest"; VanderKam, "Enoch Traditions"; idem, "Major Issues"; and West, *East Face*.

redactor of the Genesis passage was relating a well established oral (or perhaps written) tradition concerning the origin of evil spirits with which his readers would have been familiar.

A third area of research has focused on how the sources of these traditions have been transmitted and adapted by the Jewish authors. This question presents the largest area of discussion regarding *BW* and has resulted in several theories concerning the author's purpose in writing the document. The question of dating *BW*, of course, plays a large role in the conclusions reached by any of these scholarly works. Several scholars have attempted to apply *BW* to a specific historical setting (e.g. Suter, Nickelsburg – the situation resulted in the composition of *BW*), while others (i.e. Hanson, Newsom, Collins, and VanderKam – the existing myth was used to explain the various situations) contend that the author wished to bring an understanding to an audience concerning the cause of their current situation in Israel. The author's purpose was to explain the origin of the evil (i.e. persecution) they were facing, to give Israel hope for the future, and to encourage them to hold fast to their faith in God despite the persecution and oppression of foreign invaders.

Excursus: Notable terms in the Book of Watchers

In order to gain a clearer understanding of major issues of debate in the research of *BW*, it is necessary to preview some of the significant nomenclature used by scholars in their presentations of the themes found in *BW*. There are five terms listed below for which I have provided a brief description of their use in *BW* and the Israelite tradition.

Watchers

BW presents the most familiar witness to a well-known subject in early Jewish literature. Generally, the Watchers are paralleled with the sons of God in Genesis 6.1–4, where they are presented without the negative connotation that is placed upon them by *BW*. The Watchers (the characters of *BW*) are thought to be angels who chose to rebel against God and heaven and entered into the human realm and mated with human women and begat giant offspring. *1 Enoch* 12.3[37] indicates that the Watchers were apparently in the same category as the archangels of heaven.[38] A slightly different story is presented in *Jubilees* (3.15). Here the Watchers are

---

[37] 12.3 "And I Enoch was blessing the Great Lord and the King of Eternity and behold the Watchers called to me, Enoch the scribe, and said to me: (4) 'Enoch, scribe of righteousness, go, inform the Watchers of heaven who have left the high heaven'"; see text in Knibb, *Ethiopic Enoch*. See Daniel 4 and Pseudo-Philo 13.6 for a positive role of the Watchers.

[38] See argument of Newsom in "Development of 1 Enoch 6–19," 317.

described as angels who are sent by God to teach humanity the ways of heaven, but are seduced by the women and produce evil offspring. The role of the Watchers in Jewish and Hellenistic writings varied. They are seen as the fallen angels, angels sent to instruct humanity in the arts of civilization, the holy ones who serve in the presence of God, the angels who keep watch over creation, protecting angels, and as intermediaries (מלאכים) between God and humanity.[39]

Shemihazah[40]

Shemihazah is an angelic leader who is associated with the Shemihazah tradition found in *BW*. He is the leader of the groups of angels in *1 Enoch* 6–16 who are considered the Watchers. These angels have been enticed by the beauty of women on the earth, *1 Enoch* 6.3–8 (cf. Gen 6.2 and *Jub* 4.15), and they all swear an oath to go down to the women and to approach them and have offspring. Shemihazah is responsible for teaching humanity (and the giants) enchantments. Because of their union with human women (*1 En* 10.12), Shemihazah and the rest of the Watchers have corrupted themselves and made themselves unclean and are bound and cast into darkness (Tartarus) until the Day of Judgment.

Azazel/Asa'el[41]

Asa'el is first encountered as one of the leaders of the Watchers who swear an oath with Shemihazah to go down to the earth and enter into relations with the daughters of men. He is introduced in *1 Enoch* 6.7 as the tenth angel identified as a leader of the group of two hundred angels. Some debate exists about whether the angel named in 6.7 is the same angel later identified as Azazel (Ethiopic) in 8.1. Here he is an angelic figure associated with the Asa'el tradition, which will be discussed in some detail below. This angel is accused of teaching humanity what is initially called the "eternal secrets of heaven" (9.6), which are later described as a "worthless mystery" (16.3). The secrets that Asa'el taught included the making of weapons of war and teaching women the art of painting their faces in order to appear more beautiful (8.1). Asa'el would be bound and cast into darkness until the Day of Judgment along with the others (10.6).

---

[39] See John J. Collins, "Watchers," in *Dictionary of Deities and Demons in the Bible*: (DDD) (ed. Karel van der Toorn, Bob Becking and Pieter W. van der Horst; 2d ed.; Leiden: Brill, 1999), 893–95. The idea of these angels is attested in multiple works, cf. CD 2.18; 4Q180; 4QEn; 1QapGen; T12P; Daniel 10–12; Hesiod, Works and Days; Philo of Byblos, Phoenician History.

[40] This tradition will be discussed in detail in ch. 4 below.

[41] This tradition will be discussed in detail in ch. 4 below.

Some scholars are of the opinion that Asa'el was connected to Azazel the demon in the desert in Leviticus 16.[42]

Giants[43]

Giants, γίγαντες, are first mentioned in the LXX in Genesis 6.1–4. γίγαντες is the Greek translation of the Hebrew terms *nephilim* and *gibborim* (Gen 6.4). These giants are thought to be the offspring that resulted from the mingling of the sons of God and the daughters of men. The origin of the word is thought to be γήγενης, born of the earth. This is derived from the Titan myth of Greek literature in which the giants are the sons of *Gaea* whom she persuades to do battle with the gods of Olympus.[44] The giants are related to the "heroes" of Greek literature who are the offspring of the relations between Zeus (and other gods) and human women. In the LXX, γίγαντες, or a form of it, is used to translate four Hebrew terms. This has created a great deal of confusion about their identity in the history of Israel. It may be understood from the Flood narrative (Gen 6–9) that all flesh, including the giants, was destroyed upon the earth, but the γίγαντες continue to appear in the text of the Greek Bible following the Flood.

The "giants" of the Watcher tradition are the offspring of the union between the fallen angels and humans (7.2). They are the cause of great turmoil and destruction upon the earth due to their appetite for blood (7.3–5). This causes God to send the Flood upon the earth to destroy the wickedness of all flesh, including the giants (10.2). The Watcher tradition relates that the spirits of the giants survive and their spirits become the evil spirits that are a cause of evil on the earth at the time of the writing of *BW* (16.1).[45]

Nephilim

The term *nephilim* is perhaps the most problematic among the designations used in Genesis 6 narrative. It is generally agreed that it is derived from the Hebrew verb נפל, to fall, in the case of the Genesis passage, "the

---

[42] Hanson, "Rebellion in Heaven." See also Lester L. Grabbe, "The Scapegoat Tradition: A Study of Early Jewish Interpretation," JSJ 18 (1987): 152–67; and B. Janowski, "Azazel," in *Dictionary of Deities and Demons in the Bible*: (DDD) (ed. Karel van der Toorn, Bob Becking and Pieter van der Horst; 2d ed.; Leiden: Brill, 1999), 128–31.

[43] This tradition will be discussed in detail in ch. 5 below.

[44] See Homer Iliad 14.279 and Apollodorus 1.1.2–4.

[45] See P.W. Coxon, "Gibborim," in *Dictionary of Deities and Demons in the Bible*: (DDD) (ed. Karel van der Toorn, Bob Becking and Pieter W. van der Horst; 2d ed.; Leiden: Brill, 1999), 345–46; and G. Mussies, "Giants," in ibid., 343–45.

fallen ones."[46] Despite its occurrence in the Genesis 6.1–4 passage, the author of *BW* chose to exclude it from the narrative, either by choice or because of a lack of knowledge of the term.[47] The *nephilim* appear only twice in the Hebrew Bible, in Genesis 6.3 and Numbers 13.3.[48] The identity of these beings is quite ambiguous, although the majority of scholars assume that they are the offspring of the relationship of the sons of God and humans.[49] *Nephilim* is translated in the LXX by the term γίγαντες, and it is from this translation that most scholars have concluded that they are the offspring of the union of the divine beings and humans.[50] Targum *Pseudo-Jonathan* identifies the *nephilim* as the chief Watchers, Shemihazah and Azazel, from the Enochic tradition.[51] Genesis 6.4a identifies the *nephilim*, if one accepts the generally accepted reading of the text, as the "heroes of old, men of renown" of verse 6.4b. This identification raises the possibility of a mythical connection with the Greek Titan myth or the Mesopotamian *Atrahasis* myth.[52]

2.6 Date, Place, and Authorship of the *Book of Watchers*

The theories concerning the date of the composition of *BW* have been greatly assisted by Milik's publication of the Aramaic fragments from Qumran. The ability of scholars to establish an approximate date for *BW* has aided efforts to locate the account of the Watchers in a historical

---

[46] See references to the Watchers and their offspring in CD 2.19.

[47] The latter proposal creates a few problems within the issue of dating *BW*. If the author was unaware of the term nephilim, then it perhaps supports the theory that *BW* predates the writing of the Genesis text. If he was aware of the Genesis tradition then why did he choose to omit such a key term in his work?

[48] The nephilim of Numbers 13.33 are the people whom the men saw when they were sent to spy out the land while Israel was in the wilderness. These beings described in the LXX present the reader with the problem of how giants survived the Flood; contra to the Watcher tradition, which conveys that all the giants were physically killed.

[49] So the problem remains as to who are the nephilim of the Gen 6.4 passage if they existed prior to the union of the sons of God and the daughters of men. The Genesis passage does not present the nephilim, or, for that matter, the offspring of the union of the בני אלהים and the women, in a negative light. On the contrary, the offspring of the sons of God in Gen 6 are considered the mighty men of old and men of renown. This in no way reflects the image of the giants presented in *BW*.

[50] See also the Watcher in *Jubilees* (6.1) for reference to the offspring as nephilim. See also *Book of Giants*, 4QEnGi[b] 3.8; and CD 2.19.

[51] As noted above, it can also be implied in CD 2 that the Watchers are the nephilim based upon the use of the verb נָפַל.

[52] J Assmann, "Nephilim," in *Dictionary of Deities and Demons in the Bible*: (DDD) (ed. Karel van der Toorn, Bob Becking and Pieter W. van der Horst; 2d ed.; Leiden: Brill, 1999), 618–20.

setting that some would suggest corresponds to the message of the composition. Such attempts have facilitated the development of several interesting theories about the sources behind *BW* and the document's function in Early Judaism. These hypotheses will be discussed below. Establishing an approximate date for the composition of *BW* will also assist in tracing the theological and anthropological themes that were developing in Early Judaism in the closing centuries B.C.E. and perhaps reveal the origin of these same themes found in later Jewish and Christian writings.

According to Milik, the *1 Enoch* Aramaic fragments found at Qumran could have been a copy of a manuscript that dates to the end of the third century B.C.E.[53] This date is based upon the palaeographic evidence of 4QEn^a which attributes the fragment to the early part of the second century B.C.E. and 4QEn^b to the mid-second century B.C.E.[54] This date includes chapters 1–36 as a single unit (although we can only assume its unity); however, traditions within *BW* may be considerably older. Milik argues that *1 Enoch* 6–11 can possibly be dated to the fifth century B.C.E. due to its relationship to Genesis 6.1–4. Milik goes so far as to argue that the Enochic material had its origin in an oral Haggadah on the Genesis 6 passage (see discussion below).

Milik states that two Qumran manuscripts, 4QEn^a and 4QEn^b, were brought from outside Qumran, but does not suggest a place for their origin. Milik contends that 4QTestLevi^a 8 iii 6–7, an Aramaic parallel to the Greek *Testament of Levi* 14.3–4, contains the earliest allusion to *BW* and dates from the second century B.C.E.[55]

Milik suggests the author of *BW* was a Judean and possibly a Jerusalemite. This argument is based on the author's view that Jerusalem is the centre of the earth and on his familiarity about the surroundings of the city. Milik considers that the author was a "modest official in the perfume and spice trade" and probably lived in the Nabataean city of Petra.[56] However, Milik's theory is highly speculative if one bears in mind that there is little in *BW* that reflects anything about the author.

---

[53] Milik, *Books of Enoch*, 24. Based on the script of the manuscript, Milik believes it is possible that 4QEn^a could have been a copy, i.e. a copy of a late third c. B.C.E. manuscript, which used scribal customs from Northern Syria or Mesopotamia; see ibid., 141.

[54] Ibid., 25–8. The terminus ante quem for *BW* is incontestably 164 B.C.E. Milik concludes that the Judean author wrote *BW* in the middle of the third c. B.C.E.; see ibid., 28.

[55] Milik argues that the Testament of Levi, based on Qumran fragments and other textual evidence, can be dated to the early third c. B.C.E. or possibly the end of the fourth century; see Milik, *Books of Enoch*, 24.

[56] Ibid., 25–6.

George Nickelsburg maintains that *BW* is made up of multiple traditions which can be dated possibly prior to the Hellenistic period, while *BW*, in its completed form (chs. 1–36), was compiled by the middle of the third century B.C.E.[57] The evidence for this dating comes from the palaeography of 4QEn[a], dated to the first half of the second century B.C.E, and also from the reference to Enoch in the book of *Jubilees* (4.21–2), which dates between 175 and 150 B.C.E.[58] The Shemihazah strand of *BW*, which Nickelsburg describes as the "primary myth," required time to generate "numerous layers of accretion" to the point of composition that is extant in the two manuscripts from Qumran.[59] Nickelsburg argues correctly that several stages of development of the Shemihazah material would allow for a date well before 200 B.C.E. in order to account for its influence on the author of the *Animal Apocalypse* in 165 B.C.E.[60]

He states that it is difficult to ascertain the provenance of *BW* due to the multi-cultural traditions that appear in the text (e.g. Babylonian, Greek, or Syria-Palestine). He implies a possible Syria-Palestine provenance due to his argument for the author's purpose in writing *BW*, which will be discussed below.[61]

Some have argued that to establish a date for the composition of *BW*, one must attempt to locate a historical context in which the tradition of *BW*

---

[57] Nickelsburg, *Commentary*, 7. I would argue that it is possible that the traditions originated in a much earlier period, perhaps as early as the late eighth c. B.C.E. due to the parallels in the Hesiod myths. Therefore, as Nickelsburg argues, the adaptation of these myths by the author of *BW* could have been as early as the end of the fourth c. B.C.E.

[58] Ibid., 293. The date for *Jubilees* is problematic. VanderKam argues that there is evidence that it was an authoritative source by the end of the second c. B.C.E. because of its alleged use by CD 16.2–4. He posits a terminus a quo of 163–161 B.C.E. and a terminus ad quem of 140 B.C.E. Therefore, it is appropriate to suggest that *BW* can be dated in the first half of the second c. B.C.E.

[59] Ibid., 169. See also Nickelsburg, "Apocalyptic and Myth," 390–91. Here Nickelsburg argues for a date around the end of the fourth century B.C.E. due in part to his theory that the Wars of the Diadochi provide the historical setting for the writing of *BW*. See also Roger T. Beckwith, "The Earliest Enoch Literature and Its Calendar: Marks of Their Origin, Date and Motivation," Revue de Qumran 10 (1981): 365–72, Beckwith follows a similar line for dating as Nickelsburg (mid-third century B.C.E.), but for slightly different reasons. He argues that *BW* is an Essene (or proto-Essene) document and was composed around 250 B.C.E. (apparently due to the beginnings of what he understands as the Essene movement mentioned in *1 Enoch* 90.5–17). Beckwith contends that *BW* has parallels to the sectarian writings of Qumran and therefore must be Essene, but this theory neither confirms nor supports a date of mid-third century B.C.E. It is possible that the document was written much earlier and was only brought to Qumran long after its composition.

[60] Nickelsburg, *Commentary*, 170. Cf. Charles, *Book of Enoch*, lii.

[61] Nickelsburg, *Commentary*, 170.

can find a proper application. In this case, Nickelsburg is open to the prospect that *BW* could have been composed much earlier than the early third century B.C.E., but recognizes that it would require one to find an appropriate historical setting for its transformation and interpretation of the Genesis 6.1–4 passage. The author, according to Nickelsburg, was probably a Jew living in Palestine.[62] However, there is no definitive evidence to support this theory.

Through a precise arrangement of connections between the Shemihazah myth and various other Enochic materials, Nickelsburg dates *1 Enoch* 12–16 to the mid-third century B.C.E., possibly between 300 and 250 B.C.E.[63] He locates the provenance of chapters 12–16 in the region surrounding Mount Hermon in northern Israel, and thus proposes that the chapters were conceived by an apocalyptic group in upper Galilee.[64] He bases his hypothesis, *inter alia*, on textual evidence that *BW* was a polemic against the Jerusalem priesthood.[65] Nickelsburg argues that the following section, chapters 17–19, has a close relationship to 12–16, but was written after them, therefore reflecting a date in the early third century B.C.E. in their current configuration.[66] According to Nickelsburg, the third and final section, chapters 20–36, should be granted a *terminus ad quem* in the late third century B.C.E.[67]

Drawing on Milik's Qumran evidence, Hanson argues that *1 Enoch* 6–11 acquired its present form by the middle of the second century B.C.E.[68] Following Nickelsburg, he contends that due to a growth process of the tradition, chapters 6–11 and the Shemihazah material should be assigned to some time during the third century B.C.E. Owing to the angelic prayer in *1 Enoch* 9.4–5, Hanson asserts that *BW* has arisen from the setting of a "protagonist group" that is suffering oppression, which resulted in the development of *BW* into a sectarian ideology. He goes on to identify this "sectarian apocalyptic group" as the Hasidim or the Essenes in the third

---

[62] See Suter, "Fallen Angel, Fallen Priests," 131. Suter implicitly connects the author of *BW* to the community at Qumran, rather than the community simply adopting *BW* for their use. He dates the myth of the Fallen Angels to the third or early second c. B.C.E., based upon the necessity of *1 Enoch* being a polemic against the Jerusalem priesthood and the document's relationship to the Damascus Document and the Testament of Levi.

[63] Nickelsburg, *Commentary*, 230.

[64] Idem, "Enoch, Levi, and Peter," 586.

[65] Idem, *Commentary*, 177. Nickelsburg contends two wordplays in verses 6.4–5 give a key to the location of the author. ירד, to descend, also the name of Enoch's father; and חרם (אחרמו) they swore upon Mount Hermon. See also Hanson, "Rebellion in Heaven," 199.

[66] Nickelsburg, *Commentary*, 279.

[67] The problem with Nickelsburg's argument for the dating of this text is that we have no fragments of chapters 20–36 within 4QEnᵃ.

[68] Hanson, "Rebellion in Heaven."

century B.C.E.[69] He argues that the Asa'el material also arose from a similar apocalyptic group, but states that details of the dates and groups involved cannot be determined.[70] Hanson does not speculate on the provenance of *BW* as a whole, but assumes, due to his sectarian theory, that it would have been in Palestine.

Devorah Dimant does not attempt to pinpoint the date of *BW*, in particular chapters 6–11.[71] She maintains that an identifiable historical setting for *1 Enoch* 6–11 cannot be established based on the text,[72] but she is willing to push the date of the sources back into the late Persian period.[73]

Alternatively, Michael Stone has identified *BW* as one of the two oldest extra-biblical Jewish religious works. He dates *BW* to the third century B.C.E., but states that it may be inferred that the sources of the work could be significantly older than the current written form.[74] He speculates that the author of *BW* was associated with "well-educated men and may possibly have been associated with the traditional intellectual groups, the wise and the priests."[75] As with others, he finds it difficult to identify an author with what little evidence there is in the text.

John Collins is less confident than others that one can, with assurance, date *BW* and its components. He does, however, follow Milik's theory that *BW*, in its present form, dates from the beginning of the second century B.C.E. He supports this argument with the work of James VanderKam, who recognizes that *Jubilees* has knowledge of *BW* in the mid-second century B.C.E.[76] Collins argues that a historical setting for *BW* cannot be established with accuracy, but he recognizes that it was multivalent and applicable to a number of situations.[77] He remarks that no evidence in the text reveals that *BW* was written in Palestine as proposed by Milik, Nickelsburg, Suter, and speculated by Hanson. He proposes instead that the author's familiarity with Babylonian traditions could possibly indicate that it was composed in the eastern Diaspora.[78] Despite understanding *BW* as an apocalypse, Collins contends that it was not necessary for it to have

---

[69] Ibid., 219–20.

[70] Ibid., 226.

[71] Dimant, "Methodological Perspective."

[72] Ibid., 331.

[73] Ibid., 338, n. 70.

[74] Stone, "Book of Enoch and Judaism," 484. Stone states the second work, the Astronomical Book (*1 Enoch* 72–82), according to Milik's evidence, dates to the end of the third century, or beginning of the second B.C.E.

[75] Ibid., 489.

[76] Collins, "Apocalyptic Technique," 95; see also VanderKam, "Enoch Traditions."

[77] See also Suter, "Fallen Angel, Fallen Priests," 131.

[78] Collins, "Methodological Issues," 321.

been composed in a time of persecution.[79] He remarks that to limit the purpose of the author in writing the Watcher tradition to an episode of a specific time of war, as Nickelsburg suggests, is difficult. Rather it could be ascribed to the feeling of oppression through much of the Hellenistic period.[80] He does not attempt to identify the author of *BW*, other than the fact that he was probably Jewish, but he does indicate that it was typical of a Jewish apocalypse to hide the identity of its author by the use of myth that relates recurring patterns in history.[81]

The issue of a date for the composition of *BW*, as can be seen above, is complicated. A scholarly consensus seems to place it (at least the extant Aramaic form) somewhere in the third century B.C.E. based on Milik's palaeography of the Qumran fragments. Milik has also pushed the date into the fourth century B.C.E. based on its relationship to the *Testament of Levi*. Several problems arise, however, with the reference in 4QTestLevi[a] 8 iii 6–7 to *1 Enoch*, which may prove it less than useful to date *BW*.[82] The first matter concerns the letters of the name of Enoch in the fragment. The inability to identify them clearly as Enoch (ךֹונ[ח] קבל אלה א[. . .] line 6) casts reasonable doubt upon the idea that this is a reference to the character spoken of in *BW*. The second arises from Milik's translation of the verb קבל. Milik translates it as "accuse," but there other possibilities to translate קבל without forcing a negative meaning onto the text. The textual evidence presented by Milik, however, can only place the fragmentss within the Qumran community at this time, but says nothing about the actual date and place of composition or authorship. Milik's theories of the date of *BW* have exercised considerable influence, sometimes negative, on scholarship attempting to determine the function of the book in Early Judaism.

It is possible to imagine that based on the Qumran material the Watcher tradition (in either oral or written form) is much older than the date suggested by Milik (and others). The various traditions that lie behind *BW* may be of some assistance in determining what influenced the author of *BW* to bring these sources together in order to present his theological message. In this determination, it may be possible to clarify further a date of origin when *BW* assumed its present form.

---

[79] Idem, "Apocalyptic Technique," 110.

[80] Ibid., 98.

[81] Ibid., 99.

[82] It should also be noted there is a lack of evidence in the later Greek material and the Cairo Geniza material. See also objections of VanderKam to the use of 4QTestLevi[a] as evidence to date 4QEn in VanderKam, "Major Issues." See also the review of Milik's reconstruction techniques in Barr, "Enoch Fragments." See also Beckwith, "Earliest Enoch Literature," 173f. Beckwith doubts the date of the Testament of Levi given by Milik and argues for a date in the second century B.C.E.

2.7 Source Critical Approach to the *Book of Watchers*[83]

The literature published since 1976 concerning *BW* has attempted to define the shape and origin of the traditions that have long been recognized as the myth of the Fallen Angels. *BW* is traditionally thought to be made up of four, or possibly five, units of text which were brought together by the author (see 2.3.0 above). There are some minor differences of opinion concerning the specifics of the division of *BW* based on the sources, which will be discussed below (6–11,[84] 6–16,[85] or 6–19[86]). Following Milik's publication, the debate concerning the sources of *BW* has resulted in several key articles which have attempted to determine the origin of the sources (i.e. Hellenistic, Near Eastern, or Israelite) and how the author used them to present the theological message of the book.

2.7.1 Milik

Milik recognizes, along with Pierre Grelot, that the material of chapters 6–19 of *1 Enoch* was an early written source for *BW* that the author incorporated into his work with very little change.[87] Milik and Grelot argue

---

[83] Some scholars suggest that Zoroastrian notions of *daēvas* may have influenced Jewish ways of thinking about spirits, demons, and angels. However, source difficulties accompany any simple acceptance of such Zoroastrian influence. First, the evidence available to us for discerning Zoroastrian beliefs in the fifth through third centuries B.C.E. is very limited: much of what we know about Zoroastrian teaching on demons can be gleaned from documents whose present form dates from no earlier than the ninth century C.E. Secondly, even if it be allowed that these late documents contain earlier material, it is far from straightforward to distinguish the earlier material from later layers of traditions. Moreover, it is not entirely clear which criteria might be used effectively to distinguish between "early" and "late" concepts. See John J. Collins, *Apocalyptic Imagination: An Introduction to Jewish Apocalyptic Literature* (2d ed. Grand Rapids: Eerdmans, 1998), 29–33. For support of early dating of the material, see Mary Boyce, "On the Antiquity of Zoroastrian Apocalyptic," BSOAS 47 (1984) 57–75. For arguments against see I. P. Culianu, *Psychanodia I: A Survey of the Evidence Concerning the Ascension of the Soul and Its Relevance* (Leiden: Brill, 1983); P. Gignoux, "L'apocalyptique iranienne est–elle vraiment la source d'autres apocalypses?" Acta Antiqua Academiae Acientiarum Hungaricae 31 (1988): 67–78. Thirdly, *BW* in particular is most probably a literary product of the Hellenistic period; indeed, we have seen how it reflects historical and ideological concerns. While some affinities with Zoroastrian thought cannot be absolutely ruled out, the evidence suggests *BW* belongs in a world where Greek tradition is more of an immediate concern to the author.

[84] See Hanson, "Rebellion in Heaven"; Dimant, "Methodological Perspective"; and Nickelsburg, "Apocalyptic and Myth."

[85] Suter, "Fallen Angel, Fallen Priests."

[86] Newsom, "Development of 1 Enoch 6–19."

[87] See Milik, *Books of Enoch*, 30–1 and Pierre Grelot, "La Legende D'Henoch Dans Les Apocryphes Et Dans La Bible: Origine Et Signification," Recherches de science

that the source of *BW* 6–19 was an oral Haggadah on Genesis 6.1–4, which later (fifth c. B.C.E.) became a written tradition by the redactors of the Pentateuch. Milik states that the "close interdependence of *1 Enoch* 6–19 and Genesis 6.1–4 is perfectly obvious," in that the two texts contain similar wording and phrasing. According to Milik, the text of Genesis 6, "deliberately refers back to our Enochic document, two or three phrases which it quotes verbatim."[88] The close relationship of *BW* and Genesis 6.1–4 is one of the central issues in the source critical arguments concerning *BW*. Milik recognizes that a Babylonian tradition is being drawn upon in reference to the names of the Watchers used by the author of *BW*. Accordingly, clear allusions can be seen to "the Babylonian model of the antediluvian kings and sages" in the hierarchical pattern of the list of angels (i.e. Shemihazah and the leaders of ten).[89]

2.7.2 Kvanvig

Helge Kvanvig demonstrates a close relationship of *BW* and Genesis 6.1–4, but he argues (contra Milik) that *1 Enoch* 6–11 is dependent on the Genesis material.[90] Kvanvig argues that Genesis 4–9 should be regarded as the source for *1 En* 6–11 based on the "high number of allusions to Genesis 4–9 and the similarity of structure." He contends despite this close relationship of the two passages, the differences in their content are very noticeable.[91] He also notes that there are several recognizable Hellenistic and Near Eastern traditions in *BW*, i.e. the *Atrahasis* myth, the *Epic of Gilgamesh*, and several from the Hittite mythology.[92] Kvanvig argues that this may be due to the presence of a mixed population in Palestine following the exile, which resulted in an adaptation of myths from other

---

religieuse 46 (1958). See also Margaret Barker, *The Old Testament: The Survival of Themes From the Ancient Royal Cult in Sectarian Judaism and Early Christianity* (London: SPCK, 1987), 18–9. See Newsom, "Development of 1 Enoch 6–19," 315, Newsom argues that chapters 6–11 were "completely independent of the Enochic tradition."

[88] Milik, *Books of Enoch*, 31.

[89] Milik, *Books of Enoch*, 29, 33, and 37–39.

[90] See Helge S. Kvanvig, *Roots of Apocalyptic: The Mesopotamian Background of the Enoch Figure and of the Son of Man*, (WMANT 61; Neukirchen-Vluyn: Neukirchener Verlag, 1988), 275–80. Kvanvig, through an elaborate process, claims he disproves Milik's assumption that *1 Enoch* 6–11 was composed prior to the final redaction of the Gen 6.1–4 passages. He also argues that this very early date is doubtful based on the idea that *1 Enoch* 6–11 suggests a later historical setting (p. 96). He notes one striking contrast of *BW* to Gen 6 is the failure of the author of *BW* to mention the Nephilim (see pp. 296–99).

[91] Ibid., 278–79.

[92] Ibid., 300–04.

cultures by the Israelites.[93] He finds it "unlikely that the Babylonian traditions first were adapted by Jewish scribes in their Babylonian form and later in Palestine were transformed into a Jewish Enochic concept." Rather he thinks that the absorption occurred in the Babylonian Diaspora and was incorporated later within Palestine.[94]

2.7.3 Collins

Collins has little doubt that the present form of *BW* is a fusion of multiple strands of tradition, but he is less convinced that it is possible to separate these strands precisely to the form of their original source.[95] He recognizes that parts of the story were independent at one point (i.e. the Shemihazah story), but were edited into the final redaction in order to be used by the author to present his message. Thus, all the units must be considered as a part of the whole story of the Watchers introduced in chapters 1–5. As Collins argues, the traditions found within *BW* (Shemihazah and Asa'el) are present in a distinct tension to help understand the function of *BW*. As to the origin of these traditions, he contends that it is possible they emerged from periods of warfare, as Nickelsburg argues,[96] but it is not a necessary conclusion. It should perhaps be considered that the traditions found in *BW* developed during the generally oppressive conditions of Hellenistic rule of the period. Collins recognizes *BW* and the myths that it contains as a paradigmatic model that could have been easily applied to other situations besides the period of the Diadochi Wars.[97] He admits the possible use of Babylonian, Greek, Persian, and Mesopotamian traditions in the journey passages in chapters 17–36.[98] Collins also proposes that allusions to biblical passages in *BW*, such as Isaiah 24.21–24, indicate that there is perhaps a Jewish tradition entrenched within the text that can be identified in canonical sources.[99]

---

[93] Ibid., 322.

[94] Ibid., 326.

[95] Collins, "Apocalyptic Technique," 95. See also Stone, "Book of Enoch and Judaism," Stone agrees that *BW* has evolved from multiple sources.

[96] Nickelsburg, "Apocalyptic and Myth," 389–91.

[97] Collins, "Apocalyptic Technique," 98. Collins states that the author has avoided clear historical references as well as the place of authorship; see idem, "Methodological Issues," 321. Collins states that it is an error to limit *BW* to one specific situation as Nickelsburg and Suter have attempted to do. Suter proposes that his paradigmatic interpretation of *1 Enoch* 6–16 "treats the actions of the angels as central," and thus draws parallels to the priesthood in Jerusalem.

[98] See Collins, "Apocalyptic Technique," 105–07; e.g. Mesopotamian: Gilgamesh, Enmeduranki and Xisouthros; Greek: Myth of Er; Persian: book of Arda Viraf.

[99] See also Barker, *Old Testament*, and Dimant, "Methodological Perspective." Dimant and Barker argue that *1 Enoch* draws on Israelite traditions.

2.7.4 Hanson

Hanson raises the question of the literary independence of *1 Enoch* 6–11 by examining the genre of the passages in relation to other works of the period. He defines this section of *BW* as an "expository narrative" based on the inability of scholars to set it in a clearly defined literary genre. Hanson argues that *1 Enoch* 6–11 is an early example of literature that would later serve as the basis for Targum, Midrash, and Jewish ethnographic historiography. The basis of this expository narrative is, as most scholars would agree, Genesis 6.1–4.[100]

Hanson contends that *1 Enoch* 6–11 was composed of two main narratives: the Shemihazah tradition and the Azazel tradition (Hanson uses Azazel rather than Asa'el for reasons that will be made clear below). According to Hanson, the Shemihazah tradition, chapters 6–11 with 7.1de, 8.1–3; 9.6, 8c; 10.4–10 removed, is the core text of *BW* and that the other material, the Azazel tradition, was used by the author as "an interpretive elaboration growing organically out of the Shemihazah narrative." It is on the basis of the Shemihazah material that he describes *1 Enoch* 6–11 as a "rebellion–in–heaven."[101] He does not regard Azazel and Shemihazah as two separate traditions brought together by the editor, but rather recognizes Azazel as an elaboration of the Shemihazah tradition.[102]

Hanson contends that the parallels within *BW* have been largely obscured by the tendencies of scholars to historicize the tradition. He suggests that the Azazel material was used by the author of *BW* to allude to sacrificial ceremonies in the Babylonian Akitu festival to the goddess of the underworld Ereshkigal.[103] He states that there may be a connection with the Greek Prometheus myth, as does Nickelsburg,[104] but claims there are some significant themes in Prometheus that do not appear in the Watcher tradition of *1 Enoch*.[105] Because of these differences, he contends that the parallels between the two traditions should be accounted for by a common source rather than a direct influence upon each other.

---

[100] Hanson, "Rebellion in Heaven." Hanson would argue that it includes, in a broader sense, Gen 4–10.

[101] Ibid., 220. Hanson also sees the Near Eastern myths behind several biblical texts: Isaiah 14.5–21 (king of Babylon), Ezekiel 28.1–10 (prince of Tyre), 11–19 (king of Tyre); 32.2–8 (king of Egypt). All of these kings, according to Hanson, follow the example of the Hurrian myth character Ashtar, the Morningstar, and characterizes them all as "rebels-in-heaven."

[102] See detailed discussion of Hanson's theory of the origin of Azazel in ch. 4, 4.3.2.

[103] Hanson, "Rebellion in Heaven," 222.

[104] See Nickelsburg's discussion on Prometheus in ch. 4, 4.3.3.

[105] Ibid., 225, n. 58. Hanson argues that two important themes that play a significant part in Prometheus are missing in *BW*: the deception of Zeus and the ravenous eagle.

Hanson suggests that the teaching of the "heavenly secrets" motif of the Watchers tradition is a later elaboration that was adapted by both the Shemihazah and Azazel material. The teaching motif found in the Watcher tradition has its origin in the ancient Near Eastern culture. This motif spread from the Near East to the Hellenistic world and shaped the "Hero" tradition. Contrary to suggestions of a direct influence upon *1 Enoch* by the Greek myths, Hanson understands that both have their origin in the Near Eastern material. He maintains that the teaching motif was first evident in the Azazel material and later taken up by the Shemihazah material.[106] He asserts that the culture-heroes were present in the Near Eastern world prior to the emergence of the Prometheus myth, as is evident in Berossos and Genesis 4. These hero myths can be traced to the third millennium B.C.E. when the heroes taught humanity divine secrets that aided in the development of civilization.[107] The instruction of the Greek heroes and the angels of the Watcher tradition both appear to be of a positive nature at their inception and only take on a negative aspect within the context of the story in *BW*, although with little explanation based upon the subjects listed in the *1 Enoch* 8 passage.

2.7.5 Nickelsburg

Nickelsburg follows the generally accepted view that *BW* is a merger of two distinct traditions about the angels Shemihazah and Azazel.[108] As with other scholars, Nickelsburg recognizes the close relationship of *BW* with Genesis 6.1–4. He argues there are multiple parallels with Genesis 6–9 in other apocalyptic works (e.g., *Testament of Moses* 5–10; *Jub* 23.12–31; *1 En* 85–90; 93.1–10; 91.11–17).[109] Contrary to Milik, Nickelsburg considers *1 Enoch* 6–11 to be dependent upon Genesis 6.1–2, 4 regardless of the original tradition of the Genesis passage.[110] He identifies the Shemihazah myth as the primary tradition found in *1 Enoch* 6–16 and through a series of expansions of the story, which included the Instruction tradition and the

---

[106] Ibid., 226f. Hanson argues that the Azazel tradition contained the teaching motif prior to its adaptation into the Shemihazah tradition based upon its similarities to the Prometheus myth, which contains the teaching of heavenly secrets motif in the ancient world.

[107] Cf. Epic of Gilgamesh. See Felix Jacoby, *Die Fragmente der griechischen Historiker, III C 1* (Leiden: Brill, 1958), pp. 378–82, text 680.F4. Hanson states that the Greek authors (Proticus and Euhemeros) transformed those who were once human into deities because of their contribution to the world.

[108] Nickelsburg, "Apocalyptic and Myth," 383. See also Suter, "Fallen Angel, Fallen Priests," 115–16.

[109] Nickelsburg, *Commentary*, 166. See idem, "Apocalyptic and Myth," 392–93.

[110] Idem, *Commentary*, 166. Nickelsburg disagrees with Milik and Barker in their separate conclusions that Gen 6.1–2, 4 refers to *1 Enoch* 6–11.

addition of the Asa'el material, we have these chapters in their current form.[111]

In chapters 6–11, Nickelsburg has identified a dependence of the *1 Enoch* material on the Greek Prometheus myth.[112] He is supported in this theory in part by Glasson, Pearson, Hengel, Delcor and Bartelmus.[113] He notes the identification in chapters 17–19 of possible comparisons to Greek and Babylonian traditions. While citing Grelot and Milik for identifying these traditions concerning the heavenly journeys of Enoch, Nickelsburg notes the evidence for these comparisons is not persuasive.[114] He further states that it is possible that *1 Enoch* echoes an exposure to the *Epic of Gilgamesh* (although this is more likely reflected in the *Book of Giants*), but the recognized allusions function differently in *1 Enoch*.[115]

2.7.6 Newsom

Carol Newsom states that *BW* has a complex redactional history between chapters 6–11 and 12–16 that includes three main elements. Chapters 6–11 contain two of those elements: (1) the Shemihazah tradition, in which the angels have intercourse with women and produce giant offspring and humans are the victims of the giant devastation; (2) the Asa'el tradition in which the angels taught forbidden knowledge and humans are seen as

---

[111] See also Newsom, "Development of 1 Enoch 6–19." Newsom is primarily in agreement with Nickelsburg in relation to the three main sections of chapters 6–16. See also Hanson, "Rebellion in Heaven."

[112] Nickelsburg, *Commentary*, 192. See here for details on the story of the Prometheus myth. Nickelsburg also draws parallels to the Titanomachia in Aeschylus's *Prometheus Bound* in *1 Enoch* 10.

[113] See T. F. Glasson, *Greek Influence in Jewish Eschatology* (London: SPCK, 1961), 65; Brooke A. Pearson, "A Reminiscence of Classical Myth At II Peter 2,4," GRBS 10; (1969): 73–4; Martin Hengel, *Judaism and Hellenism*, 1:190; Mathias Delcor, "Le Mythe De La Chute Des Anges Et De L'origine Des Geants Comme Exlication Du Mal Dans Le Monde Dans L'apocalyptique Juive: Histoire Des Traditions," RHR 190 (1976): 24; and Rüdiger Bartelmus, Heroentum in Israel und Seiner Umwelt (Zürich: Theologischer Verlag, 1979), 161–66. Dimant argues that the Enochic text is reliant on a Semitic source, possibly biblical, but also admits the possibility of a Semitic influence on the Prometheus myth, Dimant, "Methodological Perspective," 331. See also Suter, "Fallen Angel, Fallen Priests," 115, Suter does not argue for a particular cultural origin for *BW*, but cites the arguments for the Hellenistic and Near Eastern traditions.

[114] See Grelot, "Legende," 54; and Milik, *Books of Enoch*, 15–8, 33–41, 291.

[115] Nickelsburg, *Commentary*, 279. Glasson has identified a comparison of Enoch's journey to the Greek Nekyia, see Glasson, *Greek Influence*, 8–11. Further possible parallels can be found in, among others, the *Odyssey* Book 11 and Plato's *Phaedo* 113D–114C. See Nickelsburg, *Commentary*, 280. Nickelsburg also argues for the same model of journey, the Greek Nekyia, for chapters 20–36, although to a lesser degree than 17–19.

collaborators in sin.[116] Following Hanson, Newsom's third strand is the teaching of good knowledge, quite possibly an independent tradition that was taken on board by both the Shemihazah and Asa'el traditions.[117] She criticises Nickelsburg's failure to explain the distinct differences between the teaching motif found in *1 Enoch* 6–16 and the Prometheus myth.[118]

Newsom notes that there is a close association between *1 Enoch* 12–16, in particular 15.11–12, with *Jubilees* 10.1–14 and the description of the nature of evil caused by the spirits of the giants. According to Newsom, this tradition, drawn on by *Jubilees*, is possibly much older than what is found in *BW*. Unfortunately, however, she does not elaborate upon the origin of the *Jubilees* tradition.[119] Newsom does an excellent job of explaining the problematic construction of chapters 6–16 by her interpretation of the author's adaptation of the Shemihazah, Asa'el, and the teaching motif into his message.[120]

2.7.8 Dimant

Dimant follows the traditional partitioning of *BW*, i.e. chapters 6–11, 12–16, and 17–36.[121] However, her view about the source of these sections differs significantly from those discussed above. She regards chapters 6–11 as an extract from what she describes as "an independent Midrashic source." In a similar approach to Hanson and Newsom, Dimant contends the structure of 6–11 reveals evidence that these chapters consisted of "independent literary sources," primarily the Shemihazah (in which she includes the teaching material, although added at a later time)[122] and Asa'el traditions.[123]

---

[116] Corrie Molenberg argues, "The two strands of material discerned in the text of *1 Enoch* 6–11 do not represent two separate traditions but reflect changing notions of sin within some parts of the Jewish community." Corrie Molenberg, "A Study of the Roles of Shemihaza and Asael in 1 Enoch 6–11," JJS 35 (1984): 136–46.

[117] Newsom, "Development of 1 Enoch," 313. Newsom argues that the Asa'el tradition is one that is well established in the Jewish tradition and probably dates, along with the Enoch tradition, from the Mesopotamian flood story.

[118] See Newsom, "Development of 1 Enoch 6–19," 314.

[119] Ibid., 321 n. 39.

[120] See in particular her explanation of the structure of chs. 12–16; ibid., 314.

[121] Dimant, "Methodological Perspective."

[122] Ibid., 324; this is contra Nickelsburg and Hanson who include the teaching material with the Azazel tradition.

[123] Dimant describes this section as "unusual in its length, form and detailed description and is the most ancient witness to the legend of the Fallen Angels." Dimant cites the following as other sources to the tradition: Sirach 16.7; *Jubilees* 4.15, 22; 5.1–10; 7.21–25; 8.3; 10.5; CD 2.17–21; 4Q180–181; 1Q19; 6Q8; 1QapGen 2.1–5, 16; Wisdom of Solomon 14.6–7; *T. Reuben* 5.6–7; *T. Naphtali* 3.5; 2 Baruch 86.10–16; and *2 Enoch* 4; 7.

Dimant contends that the Shemihazah story is "clearly based on the biblical account of Genesis 6.1–4" established on the evidence of the parallels in *1 Enoch* 6 and 7.[124] Dimant does not agree with Hanson that the Shemihazah and Asa'el stories have a common origin because they "differ in major figure, general character, and orientation."[125] It appears, though, that Dimant has misunderstood Hanson's theory. He does not propose a common origin for the two traditions, but rather that the Azazel (Hanson's choice of the name of the angel) material was derived from Leviticus 16 and then added to the Shemihazah material by the author of *BW* as an elaboration of the themes of punishment and restoration.[126]

Dimant suggests that the Watcher tradition in *BW* is independent of the Flood narrative. She contends, however, that there is an apparent link through the Noachide Commandments, which is a basis for joining the deluge and the Watcher tradition.[127] Dimant makes this connection through the description of the sins of the angels and apparent parallels in Genesis 9.4–6. Dimant's description is problematic. Her list of Noachide Commandments in her parallel is not included in Genesis 9.4–6. Instead, she resorts to later Talmudic accretions in order to support her Flood theory.[128] Dimant admits that there was no established and accepted list of prohibitions until the third century C.E. and therefore draws on CD 4.17 and the three sins listed: fornication, property, and defiling the Temple. She argues that these three are close to those listed in the Noachide Commandments. Dimant claims that she does "not pretend to have a magic formula which will resolve all contradictions," but it appears that it would take a magic formula to make this unnecessary parallel.

Dimant argues for a Semitic influence on *BW* that perhaps originated in biblical tradition. She notes that most of the comparisons of *BW* with Greek or Near Eastern myths are ill-founded and strongly disagrees with Nickelsburg on his argument for a Greek influence, claiming that "the influence of the Greek *gigantomachia* or *titanomachia* [i.e. the Prometheus

---

[124] Note Gen 6.1–2a=*1 Enoch* 6.1–2a; Gen 6.2b, 4b=*1 Enoch* 7.1ab; Gen 6.4c=*1 Enoch* 7.2a; and Gen 6.12b=*1 Enoch* 8.2c.

[125] Ibid., 326; see also pp. 331, 336 n. 38 for Dimant's reasons for disagreement with Hanson.

[126] Hanson, "Rebellion in Heaven," 225–26. Hanson argues that the author added the Azazel material in order to give a "further biblical basis to the theology developed by the original narrative"; the origin of evil.

[127] It should be questioned as to whether or not it is necessary to make this far reaching parallel based on the inclusion of the Flood in *1 Enoch* 10.22 of the Ethiopic text. See Knibb, *Ethiopic Enoch*, 91.

[128] Dimant, "Methodological Perspective," 327–30. Cf. b. Sanh. 56b, 59a; Gen Rab. 16.6; and Exod Rab. 30.9.

myth][129] on the story of the giants is not substantiated by real evidence."[130] While Nickelsburg may be correct in his assessment, Dimant rightly states that "one must exercise the utmost caution in comparing myths from different contexts and cultural milieu . . . such an analysis must take into account the special character of the material, including its interpretative nature."[131]

As can be understood from the above presentation, no consensus can be reached about the origin of the Fallen Angel tradition in *BW*, except that it was not original to the author. The theories have varied from an origin in the biblical tradition, a Hellenistic origin, or a Near Eastern origin; based on the text of *BW*, one may argue that the Fallen Angel tradition evolved from one of these cultures or even multiple cultures. A general assumption can be made that the interaction between the Israelite, Hellenistic, and Persian cultures resulted in transference of myths, both oral and written, which resulted in the allusions and parallels that have been found in many of the literary works including *BW*.[132] Important to this understanding is that the culture of Israel did not remain isolated from that of its neighbours but assimilated aspects (in this case literary) of its occupiers', captors' and neighbours' traditions. Perhaps a more important question for the present study is how the myths behind *BW* were incorporated into the Jewish culture and used by the author to transmit his message.

2.8 The Function of the *Book of Watchers*

Scholars have attempted to ascertain the author's intention in writing *BW* as a whole (chs. 1–36). As a result, there are nearly as many opinions on the intended function of *BW* as there are articles written on the work. The

---

[129] Brackets are mine.

[130] See Dimant, "Methodological Perspective," 339 n. 74.

[131] Ibid., 331.

[132] For discussion of the possible influence of Zoroastrianism on Jewish apocalypticism, see Collins, *Apocalyptic Imagination*, 29–33. Several difficulties arise if one is to argue for the influence of Zoroastrianism on Judaism. First, the material, the Gathas and Avesta, cannot be dated precisely. They are preserved in the Pahlavi books, which are dated from the ninth century C.E. Collins argues that the influence of Persian material was not through a simple borrowing, but rather "whatever was taken over from Persian apocalypticism was thoroughly reconceived and integrated with other strands of thought." For support of Persian influence see Mary Boyce, *A History of Zoroastrianism* (3 vols.; Leiden: Brill, 1975–1991); David Winston, "The Iranian Component of the Bible, Apocrypha and Qumran," HR 5 (1966): 188–89; and R. C. Zaehner, *The Dawn and Twilight of Zoroastrianism* (London: Weidenfeld and Nicolson, 1961). For argument against the influence, see P. Wernberg-Møller, "A Reconstruction of the Two Spirits in the Rule of the Community," RevQ 3 (1961): 413–41.

complexity of the mythic story, and the possibility that multiple sources make up its current form, make it difficult to pinpoint a period in history for its authorship. The basic question that serves as a starting point of the researcher concerning *BW* is: why was there such a need for an explanation of the origin of evil spirits during this period of Israelite history? From this question, most have turned to the relationship of *BW* to Genesis 6.1–4. The correlation of these two texts creates several problems, not the least of which is the difference in perception of the action of the angels in each of the versions. In Genesis, their behaviour is not portrayed in a negative light, whereas in *BW* the behaviour of the angels is seen as unambiguously villainous. Despite the difficulty in interpreting the author's intent in writing *BW*, the task must be undertaken if one is to understand the reception of Genesis 6.1–4 and its role in the development of the theme of demonic affliction in Early Judaism.

The author of *BW* is faced with the problem of affliction that his nation must cope with on a continual basis. Who is responsible for this affliction and why is the God of Israel not coming to deliver the nation? He finds his answer in his understanding of the passage of Genesis 6.1–4 (or a tradition from which it and the Fallen Angel tradition in *BW* developed), which he has interpreted as a representation of the origin of evil spirits.

Three main theories of interpretation have been suggested concerning the function of *BW* in Early Judaism. The first theory, offered by Nickelsburg, applies the text to a period in Israelite history in which they face continual oppression by the Hellenistic kingdoms that surrounded them.[133] The second, offered by Hanson (and to a degree Newsom and Collins), describes *BW* as a narrative that reveals the origins of evil in the story of the giants, and, in addition, relates the eschatological events in which the God of Israel will judge the wicked.[134] The third, a far more problematic theory offered by Suter, identifies *BW* as a polemic against the priesthood in Jerusalem by an apocalyptic group in Israel.[135]

2.8.1 Nickelsburg

Nickelsburg contends that *BW* contains three sections within the narrative. Each of these three sections contains expansions and departures from the Genesis 6 passage.[136] The three sections describe what he understands as

---

[133] Nickelsburg, "Apocalyptic and Myth."

[134] Hanson, "Rebellion in Heaven"; Newsom, "Development of 1 Enoch 6–19"; Collins, "Apocalyptic Technique," and Kvanvig, *Roots*, 315–18.

[135] Suter, "Fallen Angel, Fallen Priests."

[136] Nickelsburg, "Apocalyptic and Myth," 386. See also Hendel, "Of Demigods," 14. Hendel discusses the problematic structure of the Gen 6.1–4 passage. He cites several scholars who describe the passage with such characterizations as "cracked erratic boulder," "a torso or fragment" (Wellhausen and Gunkel respectively). A more

the message of the author of *BW*. The first is the story of "the origins of a devastated world." One of the most conspicuous differences between the Genesis 6 passage and *BW* originates in this section of the narrative. In *1 Enoch* 6–11, the Watchers and their offspring are described in an iniquitous fashion, whereas in the Genesis 6 passage the *bene haelohim* and their offspring are described non-pejoratively. The sin of the angels in *BW* is seen as a rebellion against God (*1 En* 7.5). Their offspring are portrayed by the author as the source of evil spirits in the world.[137] They are the cause of the coming Flood that will be used to cleanse the earth of the wickedness of this rebellion. Conversely, in Genesis 6.3, 5–6, the evil of humanity is responsible for the coming Flood and the destruction of the wicked.[138]

Within the second section, "The turning point: a plea for help," Nickelsburg argues the author of *BW* draws on the story of Cain and Abel in Genesis 4.10. The destruction caused by the giants is aligned with the bloodshed motif used in Gen 4.10. In both portrayals, humanity cries out for help from heaven; however, the two responses are distinctly different. In the Genesis text (6.5), God sees the wickedness of humanity and in *1 Enoch* 9.1–3 the archangels see the bloodshed and hear the cries of humanity. The author of *BW* then inserts a prayer (*1 En* 9.5, 10–11) in which he describes the sovereignty of God in this situation, but at the same time allows for the continuation of the problem of evil by a seemingly uncaring God.[139] At the end of the prayer (9.11), the author reveals to his audience a parallel of the Genesis flood story: "And you know everything

---

interesting description is put forth by B.S. Childs. Childs describes the passage as "a foreign particle of pagan mythology" that was radically altered by the Israelite tradition (see notes 5, 6, and 7 respectively).

[137] Dimant, "Methodological Perspective," 330; Dimant argues against the concept of the emergence of demons in *BW*, stating that "this view is based on a misconception of the story itself and on overstressing a secondary element, namely, the account of the demons issuing from the dead bodies of the giants." She argues that the story is, in contrast, the myth of the "figure of the Temptor" which would emerge in later Jewish and Christian sources.

[138] Nickelsburg, "Apocalyptic and Myth," 386–87. See also Stone, "Book of Enoch and Judaism," 487. Stone argues that chapters 6–11 are interested in the origin of evil and heavenly knowledge. He understands the makeup of *BW* to be of an eschatological nature. See also Hendel, "Of Demigods," 16. Hendel argues, "the myth exists because it explains what it explains": the origin of evil; and Dimant, "Methodological Perspective," 336 n. 38d; Dimant states that in her "judgment the Shemihazah story is not 'myth explaining the origin of evil.'"

[139] The idea expressed in the closing of the prayer "you know all things," "you allow them," "but you do not tell us what to do about them," appears to be an attempt to keep God separated from the source of evil. See a possible parallel in *1 Enoch* 84 in Enoch's prayer to God.

before it happens, and you know this and what concerns each of them. But you say nothing to us. What ought we to do with them about this?" Nickelsburg argues that within the composition of the prayer the author makes a "clear and pointed statement of the problem of evil": God is in control.

The third section, "The divine resolution of the situation," reveals the coming hope for the audience of *BW*. The Flood narrative of Genesis describes the destruction of humanity and the survival of the righteous Noah. Nickelsburg notes that the author of *BW* has made an addition to the Genesis material.[140] The author's revision of the judgment theme now places the blame upon the Watchers and the giants for the corruption of the earth. This revision of the story appears on the surface to be a radical shift from the biblical text. While the need for the Flood in the biblical text lies with corrupt humanity (Gen 6.5–7), in *BW* the blame lies with the Watchers, but *1 Enoch* 10.22 describes that there will be a flood upon the earth and all sin and wickedness will be destroyed, including the wickedness of humanity described in Genesis 6.5–7.[141] The author of *BW* may be relating to his audience that the corrupt of humanity who are oppressing them will be destroyed as the corrupt of humanity were in the Genesis 6 passage. However, not only will the wicked be destroyed, but also the source of the evil. According to Nickelsburg, the author is using an *Urzeit-Endzeit* typology in which the narrative of the Genesis text is used as a prototype for what will follow in the eschaton.[142]

Nickelsburg states that the use of the Shemihazah and Asa'el myths is a key to the author's perspective. The author has described the nature of the evil at work in the world, which was a result of the rebellion of the angels against God. But beyond the origin-of-evil story, Nickelsburg argues the author is portraying a realm of evil spirits that is responsible for the evil that Israel is facing at the time. The author advises that there is no hope against these spirits without the help of God. Nickelsburg suggests the function of *BW* is to encourage the people that despite the presence of a spiritual evil, for the removal of which there appears to be no solution, there is help coming from God.[143]

Nickelsburg's understanding of the message and function of *BW* leads him to find a historical setting for the book. He places *BW* at the end of the

---

[140] Nickelsburg, "Apocalyptic and Myth," 388.

[141] It is not so apparent that the humans did not share in the blame in *1 Enoch* 6–11. There is, after all, a law at work that the humans are responsible to keep, along with the angels, the law of the cosmos. There is no evidence in the text of *BW* that the angels overwhelmed the women and took them by force, but at the same time, there is little evidence that the women knew the true nature of the angels.

[142] Ibid. See also Hanson, "Rebellion in Heaven," 195.

[143] Nickelsburg, "Apocalyptic and Myth," 389.

fourth or beginning of the third century B.C.E. in Palestine. Nickelsburg argues that he is justified in seeking a setting for *BW* and believes that it is specifically during a time of fierce military conflict, a conflict that the author considered a threat to all of humanity. He contends that the battle is the Wars of the Diadochi in the late fourth century B.C.E. He suggests that the vehicle used for the development of the story in *BW* (i.e. Shemihazah tradition) originated in the belief that the Diadochi had divine ancestry.[144] If these Hellenistic leaders had divine heritage, then it is possible that the author of *BW* recognized this, but as Nickelsburg describes, "they were not gods, but demons—angels who rebelled against the authority of God."[145] Two points should be noted in reference to Nickelsburg's suggested parallel. (1) He argues the Watchers could be paralleled to the Diadochi, but unlike the Diadochi, the Watchers did not oppress humanity. (2) He mistakenly describes the angels as demons. Nowhere in *BW* are the angels referred to as demons. This was a period of intense fighting in Israel, but did this period threaten the existence of Israel as a people?[146] Little evidence can be found, as Nickelsburg argues, to support this idea.[147] It is difficult to recognize the catastrophic effects related in the Watcher tradition to the events of these wars. No historical evidence can be suggested that describes a threat to the continued existence of the people of Israel during this period.

2.8.2 Hanson

Similar to Nickelsburg, Hanson suggests four themes develop in the narrative that lead one to believe that the purpose of *BW* is to describe a "rebellion-in-heaven," (for a thorough discussion of Hanson's theory of "rebellion in heaven," see ch. 5, section 5.2.0.)[148] The major theme depicts the cosmos in two distinct realms, heaven and earth, in which dwell

---

[144] See Nickelsburg, "Apocalyptic and Myth," 396 n. 61. Nickelsburg cites several works that have investigated this line of thought concerning the characters of the Diadochi.

[145] Ibid., 397.

[146] See discussion of the period in Bickerman, *Jews in the Greek Age*, 69–71.

[147] See also Victor Tcherikover, *Hellenistic Civilization and the Jews* [Ha-Yehudim Ve'ha-Yevanim Batekufah Ha-Kelenistit] (trans. S. Applebaum; Jerusalem: Magnes, 1959), 50–3.

[148] Hanson, "Rebellion in Heaven," 197. See Hendel, "Of Demigods." Hendel argues against the comparisons of Gen 6.1–4 and *1 Enoch* 6–11 by which both reflect a "rebellion in heaven" myth pattern. Hendel calls this pure conjecture that is unproven. Hendel's reasoning is based on two points, which, if one is to ignore the possibility of a Semitic tradition (of a Greek Myth) then he may be correct. He is correct in saying there is no sign of rebellion or condemnation in the Genesis passage alone, but if the reader considers the possibility of a far more detailed tradition (whether oral or written) behind the Genesis text, then Hendel's theory falls short.

creatures specific to each realm. But, as Hanson describes, "a rebellious inclination leads certain heavenly beings to contemplate transgressing this separation, ominously threatening the created order."[149] This rebellion has caused a defilement of the cosmos in which the author of *BW* has drawn on Genesis 6.5–12 and 8.2, describing the destruction of humanity and all other living creatures.[150]

The author of *BW* used the primordial narrative to reveal to the audience that the evil they faced originated in the giant offspring of the Watchers.[151] Hanson notes that *BW* does not present a typical pattern of *Endzeit wird Urzeit* with an exact repetition of the events of the Flood to cleanse the earth. However, there will be an elimination of evil and wickedness by the intervention of God in the eschaton, which will restore his kingdom and order in the cosmos. This pattern, according to Hanson, results in "nothing short of a radical mythologization of Israel's earlier perception of history."[152]

2.8.3 Newsom

Newsom's interpretation of *BW* suggests several interesting points in relation to the development of the theme of demonic activity in Early Judaism. The developing cosmology of the period reveals what should be construed as a shift in the understanding of the origin of evil in the Jewish world (see details below).[153] Newsom states that the events described in 6–11 are a breach of the law of the cosmos that was brought about by the sin of the Watchers. The description of the nature of the sin in 12–16 (15.2–16.1) explains the consequences of the violation of the universal order by the angels (15.4–8) and the manifestation of evil spirits from the giants. Along with a description of the consequences of the sin of the angels in these chapters, the author announces that the broken law of the cosmos will be restored in the Day of Judgment (16.1).[154]

Newsom makes a key point concerning the teachings of the Watchers in relation to enchantments and herbal lore. *1 Enoch* 15.11–12 describes the

---

[149] Hanson, "Rebellion in Heaven," 198. This "rebellious inclination" sounds markedly like the language used by Philo to describe a "force" that draws the heavenly beings to the earth and take on flesh. See Philo *De Plantatione* 14.

[150] Hanson, "Rebellion in Heaven," 199–200.

[151] Unfortunately, Hanson attempts to posit *BW* within a sectarian apocalyptic group rather than suggest it is a message for all Israel. Ibid., 219. See also Collins, "Apocalyptic Technique," 100.

[152] Hanson, "Rebellion in Heaven," 201.

[153] Newsom, "Development of 1 Enoch 6–19," 313. The difficulty with this assertion is that we have little textual evidence in the biblical and post-biblical period that supports another "origin of evil." See e.g. 4 Ezra 3.21–22.

[154] Ibid., 316.

illicit actions of the spirits of the giants; however, as Newsom notes, exactly what their activities involved is unclear in this passage. She draws on the Watcher tradition found in *Jubilees* 10.1–14 that describes the actions of the spirits against the sons of Noah. Here the spirits are accused of leading astray and slaying the children of Noah. As a result, God instructs the archangels to teach Noah about medicine and methods of healing.[155] So, it may be implied that the spirits of the giants had the ability to inflict physical harm upon humanity by the secret knowledge that their fathers the Watchers taught them.

One of Newsom's most interesting contributions to the research of *BW* comes from her interpretation of chapters 17–19. Due to its abrupt beginning and its Hellenistic elements, most commentators have argued that these chapters are an addition to *BW* that has no clear connection to chapters 6–16.[156] Thus, the material from these chapters may have developed from an independent tradition of Enoch's journeys, but it appears, as Newsom contends, that the author made an intentional connection between 17.1 and 14.25.[157] As a result, Newsom argues that chapters 17–19 are describing a counter to the mysteries of the Watchers: the knowledge Enoch receives on his heavenly journey.[158] *Jubilees* 10.12–13 may provide an allusion to the giving of knowledge by the angels, but in the *Jubilees* case, the knowledge is given to Noah. However, the knowledge given to Enoch in *1 Enoch* is not in the form of incantations or psalms of protection (as in *Jubilees*), but a tour of the residing place of God.[159] In the process, Newsom connects the journey of Enoch to yet another Mesopotamian tradition: the practice of Near Eastern diplomacy, "that of showing off the wealth and strength of one's kingdom to visiting courtiers."[160] She argues that the "royal tradition" runs throughout *1 Enoch*

---

[155] Ibid., 321.

[156] See Charles, *Book of Enoch*, 38; Charles argues these two chapters are full of Greek references (i.e. 17.5, 6, 7,8; 18.6–9, 10). See also Pierre Grelot, "La Geographic Mythique D'Henoch Et Ses Sources Orientales," RB 65 (1958): 38 n. 1; Grelot has emphasised the Mesopotamian background of the cosmic geography of *BW*.

[157] If this is the case, then this suggests that chapters 15–16 may have been an independent segment inserted in a section that included chapters 12–14 and 17–19.

[158] Newsom, "Development of 1 Enoch 6–19," 322.

[159] Newsom states that chapters 12–16 are not only a description of the sins of the Watchers, but also presents the audience with a question of God's sovereignty over his creation. Newsom elaborates further on this view in relation to the tours of a royal palace in 2 Kgs 20.13–15 and 2 Sam 14.4–24, see "Development of 1 Enoch 6–19," 325.

[160] Ibid., 324. Newsom cites several biblical passages of this practice, cf. 1 Kgs 10.4–5 and 2 Kgs 20.13–15. See also Stone, "Book of Enoch and Judaism," 484–85. Stone states that the view of Enoch presented in *BW* may be derived from Mesopotamian sources, which he may have modelled after the seventh antediluvian king. Stone also recognises this parallel in the Book of Daniel

6–19, and therefore supports, to a degree, Hanson's argument for the "rebellion-in-heaven" motif in the Shemihazah account because of its prominence in Near Eastern mythology.[161] This royal motif emphasises the dominion of God in the narrative, which in the end will destroy the evil that has been caused by the rebellion of the angels. Chapter 19 reinforces the knowledge given in previous chapters that the activity of the spirits too will end on the Day of Judgment. The knowledge revealed in the author's message in *BW* is essential for the life of the audience in the everyday world; it is an affirmation that God is still in control despite the presence of the evil spirits.[162] More important to the audience is the announcement of an eventual end to the activity of the spirits.

2.8.4 Collins

As Collins has noted, in order to understand the message of *1 Enoch* 1–36, one must decide whether to read the text from a source-critical standpoint and distinguish between separate issues (i.e. the Shemihazah and Asa'el/Instruction traditions), or to read it as a narrative in which the author is explaining the presence of evil in his time. Collins questions if it is necessary, or even possible, to separate chapters 6–11 from 12–16 or "if we are concerned with the perspective of the work, it is of fundamental importance to decide whether chapters 6–11 should be read in isolation or interpreted in the context of the entire Book of the Watchers."[163] He argues that the perceived problem of two strands of myth concerning the angels in 6–11 is not necessarily a sign of multiple sources from which the author drew. One possibility, as Collins notes, is that the problem of evil was thought to be a complicated enough issue to warrant drawing on multiple sources that were considered complimentary.[164]

In response to Nickelsburg's claim that the idea of the "angels and their half-breed offspring are the perpetrators of evil" and that "human beings are held responsible" creates a problem of incompatibility within the document,[165] Collins notes that this is only a problem if both come from the same source within a document. Not to undermine the arguments of Hanson, Nickelsburg and others, that distinct traditions exist within *BW*,

---

[161] Hanson, "Rebellion in Heaven." Newsom also cites references to the *Epic of Gilgamesh* (see 325–26).

[162] Ibid., 316.

[163] Collins, "Methodological Issues," 315.

[164] Ibid., 316. An issue that has not been raised in the research of *BW* is a question of audience. Was the author using multiple sources of the same myth because of the diversity of his intended audience? Is it possible that some of the people may have known the Shemihazah tradition while others in Israel may have only been aware of the Asa'el tradition?

[165] Nickelsburg, "Apocalyptic and Myth," 385.

Collins states this does not require these traditions to be separate documents. As a tradition, the Fallen Angel myth(s) in *BW* exists with its own particular value and function ascribed to it by the author. For this reason, Collins argues that outside *BW* we do not know of the Shemihazah tradition standing alone; therefore, it must be discussed within this context, as a part of the combined Shemihazah and Asa'el tradition.[166] Collins thus proposes that the Asa'el tradition was used by the author to form the final edition of *BW*. The sexual sin of Shemihazah is correlated to the sin of revelation by Asa'el as can be understood in chapters 7 and 16.3.[167] The improper revelation is then countered by the revelation given to Enoch on the heavenly journeys (17–36).[168]

A key issue raised concerning the message of *BW* is eschatology. What role does it play in the interpretation of chapters 6–11 and subsequently 12–16? It appears, as Collins notes, that there is a distinction between the end of the Flood and events of the eschaton. There must be a distinction between the time of the imprisonment of Asa'el in 10.4–6 and the binding of the giants in 10.12–13.[169] If these events are occurring simultaneously (or at all), as Collins argues, then it does not allow for the spirits of the giants to become the evil spirits of 15.11–12.[170] It appears that there is a cleansing of the earth during the Flood. However, a final cleansing of the earth in the eschaton is required because of the survival of the spirits of the giants and their activity (15.12; *Jub* 7.27; Gen 9–11). He states, however, that the author of *BW* is not relating all of history, and, based on a similar sequencing in *Sibylline Oracles* 1, a comparable pattern can be expected to follow in the eschaton.[171]

Collins questions if scholars do not err by attempting to place *BW* in a specific period or by assigning it to a particular event in history (e.g. Nickelsburg and Suter). Very little evidence is found in the document that can assist in determining such a situation. The message of *BW* presents the

---

[166] Collins, "Methodological Issues," 316. Collins argues that in this case, it is difficult to assume, with the little evidence available, that the myth of the Fallen Angels in Gen 6 and *1 Enoch* have the same meaning and function.

[167] Collins, "Apocalyptic Technique," 102.

[168] See also Newsom, "Development of 1 Enoch 6–19," 322.

[169] It is not clear in the text if it is actually the giants who are being bound as Collins argues, or if the phrase "and when they see the destruction of their beloved ones, bind them for seventy generations under the hills of the earth until the day of their judgment and of their consummation, until the judgment which is for all eternity is accomplished" is referring to Shemihazah and the others with him in *1 Enoch* 10.11. I would argue the Watchers who are being bound.

[170] Collins, "Methodological Issues," 317.

[171] Ibid., 319; Collins states that what follows in ch. 22 is an elaboration of the final judgment.

world of the author as one oppressed by an enemy beyond the human realm that requires the judgment of the eschaton.[172] The author has intentionally hidden the historical events within the myth in order to relieve the stress of the author's current circumstances. The solution given by the Watcher tradition can then be transmitted into the lives of the audience. The allegory of the myth detracts from the current problems facing the people and the author's use of the Watcher tradition supplies a vision for the people to see the eventual outcome of the conflict.[173]

Collins argues for the importance of the journeys of Enoch in the message of *BW*. They clearly reveal the power and wisdom of God that are needed by Israel to overcome their oppressors. The journeys are intended to arouse the emotions of the people and instil in them the knowledge that God is their deliverer.[174] Collins states that the function of *BW* is visible within its structure. Its intention is the "consolation of the righteous . . . and conversely, intimidation of sinners." However, the precise message of *BW* appears a bit ambiguous: avoid sin and practice righteousness. At the same time, a clear revelation is given to the people to have faith in things that occur in the supernatural realm.[175]

2.8.5 Suter

David Suter's interpretation of the function of *BW* proceeds in an entirely different direction than the views delineated above.[176] Suter's approach to *1 Enoch* 6–16 takes its point of departure in the issue of purity among the priests in Jerusalem during the second and third centuries B.C.E.[177] He maintains that the author of chapters 6–16 was writing a polemic against the priests for their marriages to women who were allegedly considered outside the circle of eligibility. Based on the issue of marriage between the Watchers and the women, Suter forges a parallel between the Watchers and the priests.[178] He argues for a shift in the understanding of the myth of the

---

[172] Ibid., 321.

[173] Collins, "Apocalyptic Technique," 100.

[174] Collins notes the thesis of H.D. Betz who proposes that the journey motif is also used by Greek philosophers to empower the philosophical and ethical teachings of their times; see ibid., 108, n. 88.

[175] Ibid., 110.

[176] Suter, "Fallen Angel, Fallen Priests."

[177] Collins contends that the application of "the myth of the fallen angels dates to the late third or early second century B.C.E., it is clear that its application to the Jerusalem priesthood would be all the more apt some decades later on the eve of the Maccabean revolt." Collins, "Apocalyptic Technique," 98.

[178] Suter goes to great effort to try to establish links within period documents for his theory that there is a parallel between the Fallen Angels and the priesthood in Jerusalem. His argument is a complex series of parallels, which would require an exhaustive and detailed report in order to present his theory properly, which at this point is beyond the

Fallen Angels in Early Judaism, which is generally accepted to be the creation of evil spirits through the rebellion of the angels.

Suter contends that the two approaches to understanding the myth of *BW* (as a polemic against the priests or the origin of demons) begin with the actions of the angels. But the two modes are oriented towards different results: namely, (1) the effect of those actions upon the humans and (2) the effect upon the angels themselves. Suter argues for the latter claiming the former results in "an aetiology of the origin of evil in which evil is imposed on humanity by rebellious heavenly beings – in contrast to the traditional Adamic myth, which deals with human responsibility for evil."[179] He asserts that the purity of the angels of *BW* and the effect of their actions on themselves is the focal point of the author. Secondary to this understanding is the result of their actions upon humanity.[180] This approach is difficult to understand if, as others have done, *BW* is held alongside the Genesis 6 tradition. In keeping *BW* in the perspective of the Flood narrative, one can clearly see, in Genesis 6.5, the effect the intrusion of the *bene haelohim* (6.1–2, 4) has had upon humanity. It is not obvious, as Suter has argued: "the angels and the effect of their actions on themselves are the central concern of the myth." Central to the message of *BW* are the cosmological issues at stake because of the angels' actions.[181]

Suter has ignored portions of chapters 15–16 and the issues that are apparent in these passages. The Watchers have broken the law of the cosmos by entering into sexual relations with the women and the result of their actions has brought about the emergence of evil spirits from the giants (15.8–9). Moreover, Suter fails to deal with this issue, but instead adopts a minimalist view of *BW* and remains focused on the marriage issue between the angels and women, an issue which has perhaps been taken for granted by scholars up until now (see Excursus on Marriage in Genesis 6.2 in ch. 4).

2.9 Conclusion

As can be understood from the above discussion, *BW* is a complex piece of literature from a period in Jewish history of which very little is known. It is fair to say that the date of the Aramaic composition of *BW* could be

---

scope of this thesis. For an insightful review of the complex problems of such an argument, see Samuel Sandmel, "Parallelomania," JBL 81 (1962).

[179] It should be noted that there is little mention of the Fall of Adam (i.e. in the O.T. and post-biblical literature) prior to emergence of the tradition in later Christian writings.

[180] Suter, "Fallen Angel, Fallen Priests," 116.

[181] See Newsom, "Development of 1 Enoch 6–19," 312–13.

established somewhere near the end of the third century or beginning of
the second century B.C.E or earlier. However, a question unanswered by
Milik and others is how much of what is presently found in *BW* was in
existence during the third century B.C.E. The fragments of 4QEn[a], which
date, according to Milik to the second or third centuries B.C.E., only
include fragmentary text through *1 Enoch* 12.4–6, some of which are
uncertain in identification. Unfortunately, no evidence has been uncovered
that shows chapters 1–36 existed as a whole during the period as suggested
by Milik and others. Loren Stuckenbruck has suggested that 4Q201
fragment 6 (דרג]ו[) corresponds to *1 Enoch* 13.8 based on a comparison
to 4Q204 1 vi 5 (דרגות חזיו]ן).[182] Therefore, if Stuckenbruck is correct,
then 4Q201 fragment 6 identifies the only fragment past 12.6 in *BW* to
date.[183] Despite the lack of verified fragments of all the chapters of *BW*, it
is still possible to consider that chapters 1–36 did exist as a whole during
this period. However, this does not eliminate the possibility of a much
earlier form of the tradition (pre-third century B.C.E.), whether oral or
written, to have been circulating within the region. It is difficult to make
any conclusive remarks regarding the date and place of origin of *BW* based
on the little evidence within the manuscript itself. No evidence can be
found in the text that allows one to set the work in a specific historical
situation.

Attempts to determine the author of *BW* have proven to be just as
difficult. Hanson advocates the possibility that he was a member of an
apocalyptic group, the *Hasidim* or *Essenes*, while Suter implies by his
argument that the author was in Qumran. The best we can do is stand the
middle ground and state that it is far too difficult, based on the textual
evidence, to determine the author, other than perhaps he was Jewish, but
not necessarily in Palestine.

The source of the Fallen Angel tradition found in *BW* appears to have
some basis in Genesis 6.1–4 or, as Hanson argues, Genesis 4–10. Several
arguments have been raised as to the origin of the traditions found in *BW*;
however, there is no clear consensus. Dimant clearly deems that the
tradition can be understood in the Israelite biblical tradition and is not
under foreign influence. The other opinions have varied from Greek to

---

[182] See *DJD Volume XXXVI*, 2–8.

[183] There have been fragments identified by Milik, although unverifiable, from later
chapters. These however, have been located in later manuscripts: *1 Enoch* 14.4–6 from
4QEn[b]—mid-second century B.C.E.; 13.6–14.16; 14.18–20; 15.1; 18.8–12; 30.1–32.1;
36.1–4 from 4QEn[c]—last half of the first century B.C.E., all are very fragmentary and
uncertain of verification; 22.13–24; 25.7–27.1 from 4QEn[d]–Milik gives no date but
suggests similarities to (c), all very fragmentary; 18.15; 21.2–4; 22.3–7; 28.3–29.2;
32.3,6; 33.3–34.1 from 4QEn[e]3–first half of the first century B.C.E., very fragmentary
and uncertain of verification.

Near Eastern or both. It is possible to recognize several allusions or parallels to Greek and Near Eastern myths underlying *BW*, some of which date as early as the eighth century B.C.E. (i.e. Hesiod). The early dating of the traditions, it seems, would assist in defining *BW* as an aetiology of the emergence of evil.

The central issue of discussion of *BW* has focused on the purpose and function of the text. What was the message the author intended to pass along to his audience? It is clear that aspects of *BW* can be understood as an exposition of the Genesis Flood narrative. Based on this viewpoint, *BW* can be read as an aetiology that has taken on new elements not clearly visible in the Genesis text to tell the story of the manifestation of evil spirits and the destruction they brought upon humanity. But at the same time, it describes how God will exercise his sovereignty to limit the actions of these spirits. However, as Collins and Kvanvig have pointed out, *BW* also has a paradigmatic character that allows it to be adapted to different situations; nonetheless, one should be cautious in limiting these situations to specific historical settings.

It is understood that eschatology is a part of the message of the author. Just as God redeemed humanity in the person of Noah, God again will cleanse the cosmos of the wickedness of the spirits of the giants and those among humanity who have chosen to follow the ways of corruption rather than follow the law of God. The eschaton will bring about the restoration of the law of the cosmos, the cleansing of heaven and earth, and the redemption of Israel.

The questions asked thus far in the research of *BW* reveal a great deal about the interaction of the region's multi-cultured population. How much influence did Hellenism have over the theological issues of Palestinian Judaism during this period? It is unclear based upon *BW* in itself, but a further exploration of the method and influences upon biblical interpretation of the period may help bring a clearer understanding of the theological issues. Does *BW* reflect authentic Jewish beliefs during the 2TP or is it an isolated document foreign to the Judaism of the 2TP? Were these unusual views that the author of *BW* was putting forth? Hence, are there other sources that will support such a development of demonic activity within early Judaism, either in Israel or in the Diaspora? These questions require closer scrutiny if one is to determine how the concept of demonic activity was being understood in 2TP Judaism.

In order to understand the upsurge of language about demonic activity in Early Jewish literature, the anthropological questions concerning the relationships between the Fallen Angels, the humans, and the giants, must be researched further. Why did the angels desire to procreate with humans? What kind of being was created from this union? What role does its spiritual and former physical makeup have to do with the demonic activity apparent in this period? The story told by the author of *BW* reveals a need to explain the presence of evil spirits whether as a metaphor of the Greek occupiers or as an explanation of the reality of demonic activity in Palestine. *BW* serves as an entry point for the research of these questions within 2TP Judaism.

The starting point of this journey is the biblical source for *BW*, Genesis 6.1–4. Within this enigmatic passage are the main characters of the Watcher tradition. In the biblical text, however, the *bene haelohim* lack the openly iniquitous characteristics of their counterparts, the Watchers, in *BW*. The next task, then is to attempt to uncover the biblical traditions that support such an interpretation of the Genesis passage, and thereby ascertain how the evil elements came to be associated with this passage.

Chapter 3

Strategies of Interpreting
Genesis 6:1–4

3.1 Introduction

Genesis 6.1–4 has been described by many as the strangest of all the Genesis passages because of its apparent intrusion into the larger narrative and its idiosyncratic vocabulary.[1] The passage as a whole and its

---

[1] There have been numerous studies of Gen 6.1–4 from the various aspects of its place in Early Judaism, but see specifically Philip S. Alexander, "The Targumim and Early Exegesis of "Sons of God" in Genesis 6," *JJS* 23 (1972): 60–71; Bernard F. Batto, *Slaying the Dragon: Mythmaking in the Biblical Tradition* (Louisville: Westminster John Knox, 1992); U. Cassuto, *A Commentary on the Book of Genesis*, (trans. Israel Abrahams; Jerusalem: Magnes Press, 1961); David J. A. Clines, "The Significance of the 'Sons of God' Episode (Genesis 6:1–4) in the Context of the 'Primeval History' (Genesis 1–11)," *JSOTSup* 13 (1979): 33–46; Lyle Eslinger, "A Contextual Identification of the *Bene Ha'elohim* and *Benoth Ha'adam* in Genesis 6:1–4," *JSOTSup* 13 (1979): 65–73; Hendel, "Of Demigods"; idem, "The Nephilim Were on the Earth: Genesis 6.1–4 and Its Ancient Near Eastern Context," in *Fall of the Angels* (TBN 6; ed. Christopher Auffarth and Loren T. Stuckenbruck; Leiden: Brill, 2004), 11–34; Emil G. Kraeling, "The Significance and Origin of Gen. 6:1–4," *JNES* 6 (October 1947): 193–208; Jon D. Levenson, *Creation and the Presence of Evil: The Jewish Drama of Divine Omnipotence* (San Francisco: Harper Row, 1988); Julian Morgenstern, "The Mythological Background of Psalm 82," in *HUCA* 14, (ed. Zevi Diesendruck and Julian Morgenstern David Philipson; Cincinnati: Hebrew Union College, 1939), 29–126; Pearson, "Resurrection and the Judgment"; David L. Petersen, "Genesis 6:1–4, Yahweh and the Organization of the Cosmos," *JSOTSup* 13 (1979): 47–64; Nahum M. Sarna, *Genesis*, (JPS Torah Commentary; Philadelphia–New York–Jerusalem: Jewish Publication Society, 1989); Haim Schwarzbaum, "The Overcrowded Earth," *Numen* (1957): 59–74; J. Alberto Soggin, *Das Buch Genesis Kommentar* (Darmstadt: Wissenschaftliche Buchgesellschaft, 1997); Loren T. Stuckenbruck, "Angels of the Nations," *DNTB* 29–31; idem, "The Origins of Evil in Jewish Apocalyptic Tradition: The Interpretation of Genesis 6:1–4 in the Second and Third Centuries B.C.E.," in *Fall of the Angels* (TBN 6; ed. Christopher Auffarth and Loren T. Stuckenbruck; Leiden: Brill, 2004), 86–118; N.H. Tur–Sinai, "The Riddle of Genesis Vi. 1–4," in *ExpTim* 71 (1960): 348–50; Claus Westermann, *Genesis 1–11 A Commentary* (trans. John J. Scullion; London: SPCK, 1984); John W. Wevers, *Notes on the Greek Text of Genesis* (SBLSCS 35; Atlanta: Scholars Press, 1993); and L.R. Wickham, "The Sons of God and the Daughters of Men: Genesis VI 2 in Early Christian Exegesis," in *Language and*

placement in the narrative has resulted in several studies in which authors have questioned the originality of the pericope to the larger story.[2] The obtrusive nature of the passage has led many to understand it as an addition to the Flood account in order to reveal the necessity for the destruction of humanity. However, nothing obvious in the narrative would lead the reader to understand that the characters depicted were responsible for bringing the judgment of the Flood.[3]

The purpose of this chapter is to examine the ways in which Genesis 6.1–4 was interpreted in Early Judaism. While determining the author's purpose for Genesis 6.1–4 is difficult due to the complex nature of the text, the use of the terminology in the biblical tradition may disclose how varying interpretations were possible. These interpretations may fall into one of three categories:[4] a positive, negative, or neutral understanding of the characters in the passage; that is, can we determine from the role of the characters (or their actions) whether or not the narrative had a part in bringing judgment upon the world? A positive interpretation indicates the characters had a clearly favourable role in the Flood narrative. A neutral interpretation indicates that the textual evidence reveals the characters played a relatively neutral role in bringing about the Flood. A negative interpretation indicates that evidence exists in the biblical or non-biblical traditions that the characters played a villainous role. Following this review, it may be possible to determine the likelihood that the author of *BW* had traditions to draw upon that allowed for his negative interpretation.[5]

The openness of Genesis 6.1–4 to an array of interpretations by Jewish authors (i.e. LXX, Pseudepigrapha, *DSS*, Targums, and Midrashim,) may

---

Meaning Studies in Hebrew Language and Biblical Exegesis (ed. A. S. Van der Woude; Leiden: E.J. Brill, 1974), 135–47.

[2] See Clines, "Sons of God," 33; Hermann Gunkel, *Genesis*, (trans. Mark E. Biddle; Macon, GA: Mercer University, 1997), 59; Kraeling, "Significance," 196; Petersen, "Genesis 6," 48; and Sarna, *Genesis*, 45. Petersen argues that the passage is a complete narrative in itself; although short, it is complete. See also H. Gese, "Der bewachte Lebensbaum und die Heroen, zwei mythologische Erwägungen zur Urgeschichte der Quelle J," in *Wort und Geschichte. Festschrift für Karl Elliger zum 70. Geburtstag* (ed. H. Gese and P. Rüger; Kevelaer: Butzon and Bercker, 1973), 84–5. Gese argues that Gen 6.1–4 is a passage referring to a "mythical religion," which is a particular element of ancient Near Eastern religion.

[3] See Bartelmus, *Heroentum*, 167.

[4] The category of interpretation is based primarily upon the passage's place in the Gen 6 narrative, but more importantly, in accordance with the use of the vocabulary by the author of the Hebrew text and the allusions offered to the reader.

[5] For further discussion of various interpretations, see Stuckenbruck, "Origins of Evil." Cf. *1 Enoch* 1–36, 85–90; *Jubilees*; *Damascus Document*; Wisdom of Solomon; Ben Sira; 4Q180–181; 4Q510–511.

be due in part to the rather ambiguous language used by the author. The problematic vocabulary of the text begins in verse 1 and continues through verse 4; it includes the Hebrew terms הֵחֵל (v.1), בְּנֵי הָאֱלֹהִים (v.2),[6] לְאֹ־יָדוֹן and בְּשַׁגַּם (v.3), הַנְּפִלִים and the phrase הַגִּבֹּרִים אֲשֶׁר מֵעוֹלָם אַנְשֵׁי הַשֵּׁם (v.4). Some of the difficulty of interpretation has perhaps been a result of the LXX renderings of the Hebrew בְּנֵי הָאֱלֹהִים (LXX – οἱ υἱοὶ τοῦ θεοῦ), נְפִלִים (γίγαντες) and גִּבֹּרִים (γίγαντες).[7] Why the LXX translators chose these particular Greek terms is unclear. An analysis of their use in the biblical tradition may reflect a shift in some theological and culture traditions in the course of the development of Early Judaism which resulted in the use of the Greek terms. The passage also has its own particularly complex contextual and linguistic issues, which, as will be seen below, resulted in attempts among later traditions to come to terms with those difficulties.

Recent studies concerning the tradition of the *bene haelohim* presented in Genesis 6.1–4 have endeavoured to determine if the pericope was a demythologised component of a foreign myth or a piece of Israelite mythology. David Petersen has argued that Genesis 6.1–4, as an Israelite myth,[8] is re-establishing the previous boundaries that separated the heavenly realm and the human realm, one that was breached by the *bene haelohim*. Petersen states that this accounts for the arbitrary action of God towards humanity by the use of the Flood to re-establish this boundary.[9] Likewise, Hendel argues that the passage is a genuine Israelite myth that the author has deliberately shortened because of the familiarity of the story to his audience concerning the reason for the Flood.[10] He interprets the text as expressing a negative view towards humanity; they are responsible for the coming destruction of creation. Following Petersen

---

[6] Also problematic, although perhaps secondary, in verse 2 is the phrase וַיִּקְחוּ לָהֶם נָשִׁים, "and they took for themselves women."

[7] Unless otherwise noted, LXX is the Rahlfs 1979 edition. Variants of the Old Greek tradition will be examined in further detail below.

[8] See Petersen, "Genesis 6"; Batto, *Slaying the Dragon*; Clines, "Sons of God"; Kraeling, "Significance"; and Hendel, "Nephilim." Hendel argues that Gen 6.1–4 is a myth that originated within Judaism; see Hendel, "Of Demigods," 14.

[9] Petersen, "Genesis 6," 58.

[10] Hendel, "Of Demigods," 14; Sarna, *Genesis*, 45, see also Hendel, "Nephilim." Hendel argues that the author of Gen. 6.1–4 is not suppressing material because it was a pagan myth; rather, it is short because of the prior familiarity of the author and the Israelites with the story. If verses 1–4 are an addition to the narrative, then why did the author of this intermezzo leave it in what appears to be a very ambiguous form? Was there common knowledge of the tradition that permitted the author to compress the story to its current form? Based upon the terminology (γίγαντες) used by the translators of the LXX, it seems possible that the readers were aware of a tradition on which the author of Gen 6 and later the author of *1 Enoch* 6–16 are drawing.

and Hendel, Alberto Soggin maintains the passage is an Israelite myth
that had a dual purpose in which the author is presenting (1) a polemic
against polytheistic cultures and (2) an attempt by humans to elevate
themselves to a divine level through the *bene haelohim*.[11] Emil Kraeling
argues that the passage is from a much longer, perhaps oral tradition,
which is focused on the *gibborim*.[12] In light of this, Kraeling suggests that
the passage should not be understood in the negative sense, but rather as
the story of the origin of the "heroes of old."

Following Kraeling, Claus Westermann has argued that the purpose of
the passage is to describe the origin of the *gibborim* in which he does not
interpret the author's use of Genesis 6.1–4 in a negative sense. It is
simply the story of the origin of the great heroes of history. He, however,
does recognize the multiple contextual problems of verses 3 and 4, which
have resulted in various interpretations that can be classified as negative
or neutral.[13] Haim Schwarzbaum associates the passage with foreign
myths that have been used to explain the origin of death because of
overpopulation on the earth.[14] As a result, he finds little or no negative
connotation in the Genesis passage and interprets it in a neutral sense.

In spite of the important contribution these works have made to an
interpretation of Genesis 6.1–4, they fail to reveal why the author of the
Genesis Flood story inserted this section in the narrative. However, an
examination of the literature of early Jewish authors and their Hellenistic
neighbours may contribute to a clearer understanding of Genesis 6.1–4.[15]

3.2 Interpreting the Passage – Genesis 6.1–4

ויהי כי־החל האדם לרב על־פני האדמה ובנות ילדו להם
ויראו בני־האלהים את־בנות האדם כי טבת הנה
ויקחו להם נשים מכל אשר בחרו
ויאמר יהוה לא־ידון רוחי באדם לעלם בשגם הוא בשר
והיו ימיו מאה ועשרים שנה
הנפלים היו בארץ בימים ההם וגם אחרי־כן
אשר יבאו בני האלהים אל־בנות האדם
וילדו (ויולידו) להם המה הגברים אשר מעולם אנשי השם

---

[11] Soggin, *Genesis* and Sarna, *Genesis*.

[12] Kraeling, "Significance," 196.

[13] Westermann, *Genesis*, 365–66. Westermann contends that the myth of Gen 6.1–4
is probably a Canaanite myth because of the importance of בני־האלהים in their
mythology.

[14] Schwarzbaum, "Overcrowded," 72.

[15] See Alexander, "Sons of God."

Determining the intention of an author of an ancient text can be difficult in the best of cases. However, when a passage is presented to the reader or translator in unfamiliar language and context, the task can be especially challenging. This was apparently the case with Genesis 6.1–4. Consequentially, the authors of Jewish works concerning the passage offer a variety of interpretations. As suggested above, adding to the confusion of interpreting the passage is the Greek translation of the Hebrew text in the Septuagint.[16] What part, if any, did the Septuagint play in the interpretation of the passage in the writings of the Greco-Roman period? It appears the LXX tradition may have influenced some of the writers by the emphasis its translators placed on γίγαντες in Genesis 6.4.

In what follows below, I will examine the various interpretations of Genesis 6.1–4 found in the 2TP literature and the Targums.[17] The examination will include an analysis of the key terms (Hebrew and Greek) in each of the verses that have been the focus of scholarship. Consideration will be given to the variant Hebrew readings, the translation difficulties of the LXX renditions, and the biblical, extra-biblical, and Hellenistic traditions that make up the array of interpretations. Following this discussion, a translation will be offered that will incorporate the strongest evidence from the various interpretations and traditions.

3.2.1 Verse 1

ויהי כי־החל האדם לרב על־פני האדמה ובנות ילדו להם

The openness of Genesis 6.1–4 to various interpretations begins in verse 1. Little textual evidence in the verse leads the reader to expect that anything of negative consequence will follow in the next few verses. The verse seems to indicate that humanity is simply obeying the

---

[16] The translation began in the third c. B.C.E. and continued possibly into the first c. B.C.E. See Natalio Fernandez Marcos, *The Septuagint in Context: Introduction to the Greek Version of the Bible* (trans. Wilfred G.E. Watson; Leiden–Boston–Koln: Brill, 2000), 50. See the following for possible reasons for problems of interpretations of the LXX, Bickerman, *The Jews in the Greek Age*, 107f; Marguerite Harl, ed. *La Bible D'Alexandrie La Genese*. 2d ed., (Paris: Editions Du Cerf, 1986); Martin Hengel, *Judaism and Hellenism*; Staffan Olofsson, *The LXX Version: A Guide to the Translation Technique of the Septuagint*, (Coniectanea Biblica Old Testament Series, 30; Stockholm: Almqvist &Wiksell, 1990); Emanuel Tov, *Text-Critical Use of the Septuagint in Biblical Research*, (Jerusalem Biblical Series, 3; Jerusalem: Simor, 1981); and idem, *The Greek and Hebrew Bible: Collected Essays on the Septuagint*, VTSup, 72; Leiden: E.J. Brill, 1999), 203–13.

[17] As stated in the introduction, I shall draw on exegetical traditions in the Targumim and Midrashim, which, though late, may provide some insight into ways Jewish readers were understanding Gen 6 during the 2TP.

commandment to "be fruitful and multiply." Martin McNamara argues that there is no sense in the passage that would cause the reader to think that it is declaring the corruption of humanity, but simply stating, "that the sons of men began to multiply."[18]

Two Hebrew words have received most of the attention in studies of this verse, החל and לרב. The Hebrew word החל has been generally translated in most versions as "began": "and it came about that humanity *began* to multiply upon the face of the earth."[19] The Greek translation of the LXX seems to follow the same pattern by translating החל with the aorist middle indicative ἤρξαντο (began) in the majority of manuscripts. There is only one small deviation in a few minuscules,[20] which use the third singular form of the verb ἤρξατο rather than the third plural form. It appears likely that the Septuagint translators were interpreting החל as a *hiphil* perfect third masculine singular verb – "began."[21] לרב is translated in most texts as "to multiply," while the LXX translation follows the same pattern with πολλοὶ γίνεσθαι, "became great (many) upon the earth."[22] But, evidence for different interpretations exists in early Jewish writings.

The alternative readings of this verse lend credence to the idea that 6.1–4 was the author's introduction to the degeneration of humanity and the imminent Flood.[23] The problem is how to reconcile the author's

---

[18] See Martin McNamara, *Targum Neofiti 1: Genesis* (vol. 1A of *The Aramaic Bible: The Targumim*; ed. Michael Maher, Kevin Cathcart, and Martin McNamara; Edinburgh: T&T Clark, 1992), 71. See also Clines, "Sons of God," 38–9; Clines argues that verse 1 is relatively insignificant to the narrative if it is told within a strict Jewish context, but if one sets it in parallel with the *Atrahasis Epic* (see discussion below) it then becomes significant for the narrative that follows.

[19] See Francis Brown, S.R. Driver and Charles A. Briggs, *The New Brown – Driver – Briggs – Gesenius Hebrew and English Lexicon with an Appendix Containing the Biblical Aramaic* (Peabody: Hendrickson, 1979), 320. Assumed from the root חלל which is translated "pollute, defile, and profane." See for example – Ezek 25.3; 22.16; 7.24; 22.26; 20.9, 24, 22; Isa 48.11; Lev 21.9; and 21.4. The *Hiphil* form, which is supposed in Gen 6.1, is translated as "begin."

[20] See John W. Wevers, *Septuaginta Vetus Testamentum Graecum: Genesis*, (ed. John W. Wevers; Goettingen: Vandenhoeck and Ruprecht, 1974), 108. See minuscules 18* and 408*.

[21] See also *Pseudo–Philo* 3.1. This author (possibly first c. C.E. or earlier) follows a similar line to the LXX with "And it happened that, when men began to multiply upon the earth, beautiful daughters were born to them." See Daniel J. Harrington, "Pseudo-Philo," in *The Old Testament Pseudepigrapha* (ed. James H. Charlesworth; 2 vols.; New York: Doubleday, 1983–85), 2:306.

[22] Ibid. Only one slight variation occurs in MS M but this variant does not change the meaning of the passage. Philo translates by using πληθύεσθαι (to multiply) in *Gig.* 42.1, but again this does not change the meaning of the passage.

[23] See Soggin, *Genesis*, 119. Soggin argues the passage is pursuing a double purpose: describing the degeneration process within humanity which will be countered

transition from 5.32 and the introduction of Noah, with the apparent discontent of God with humanity in 6.3, 5, and 6. Where did this corrupt humanity come from and why do verses 1 and 2 not relate this unambiguously to the reader?[24] One alternative interpretation can be found in *Genesis Rabbah* 6.1–4, which interprets הֵחֵל as 'rebelled', "and it came to pass when man rebelled."[25] The Midrash indicates three other places where this term is used in a negative sense of rebellion against God. All three occasions are found in *Genesis Rabbah* 4.26 – וַיִּקְרָא אֶת־שְׁמוֹ אֱנוֹשׁ אָז הוּחַל לִקְרֹא בְּשֵׁם יהוה, "and he called his name Enosh then he rebelled to call upon [their idols] by the name of the Lord";[26] 10.8 – וְכוּשׁ יָלַד אֶת־נִמְרֹד הוּא הֵחֵל לִהְיוֹת גִּבֹּר בָּאָרֶץ, "and Cush sired Nimrod and he [Nimrod] rebelled when he was mighty upon the earth"; and 11.6b – וְזֶה הַחִלָּם לַעֲשׂוֹת וְעַתָּה לֹא־יִבָּצֵר מֵהֶם כֹּל אֲשֶׁר יָזְמוּ לַעֲשׂוֹת, "and this they rebelled to do; and now nothing is prohibited from them which they purpose to do." Through these interpretations, one may read verse 6.1 (i.e. by reading the word הֵחֵל to mean rebel) as an introduction to the Flood. Although possible,

---

by the Flood, and the story of humanity's attempt to gain divine authority. See also Westermann, *Genesis*, 368. Westermann argues that Gen 6.1–4 is there to act as a transition from Noah to the Flood. See also Batto, *Slaying the Dragon*, 64. Batto argues that Gen 6.1–4 is an integral part of the Flood story because of its relationship to the *Atrahasis* story, which will be discussed below. For a slightly different aspect of the motif of rebellion, see Hanson, "Rebellion in Heaven," 195–223, Hanson argues from the perspective of an angelic rebellion rather than human. Sven Fockner argues that one must examine 6:1-4 along with verses 5-8 in that "Gen 6:1-8 is a carefully structured, unified section which was consciously inserted to inform the reader about the developments that led to the flood." See Sven Fockner, "Reopening the Discussion: Another Contextual Look at the Sons of God," *JSOT* 32.4 (2008): 435-456

[24] Conspicuously missing from chapter five and the generations of Adam is his son Cain. Why has the author chosen to omit Cain? Was this perhaps because Cain's line followed a line of unrighteousness not spelled out in the text but known by the author and the readers? See the discussion of the theory of the "sons of Seth" and the "sons of Cain" offered by Lyle Eslinger below.

[25] See H. Freedman and Maurice Simon, eds., *Midrash Rabbah* (vol. 1 of *Midrash Rabbah in Ten Volumes*; trans. H. Freedman and Maurice Simon; London: Soncino Press, 1939; repr., 1961), 211. The dating of this Midrash is around the period of the closing to the Jerusalem Talmud, but the tradition of Midrashim is dated to the time of Ezra in the fifth c. B.C.E. It is possible then that this type of interpretation of the text is much older than the third c. C.E. dating of *Genesis Rabbah*.

[26] Brackets are mine. See ibid., 197. An interesting note concerning Gen 4.26 is the verb הוּחַל "[the people] degraded [rebelled] to call on the name." The Midrash argues this verb is derived from "profane" and can be understood as an action performed by the victims of demons; those of humanity who became degraded in their worship, adoring men and idols more than God.

there is no clear evidence that this was the case in the centuries prior to the turn of the era.[27]

A second interpretation of the verb הֵחֵל (חלל) may be found in several other biblical passages.[28] Unlike the *hiphil* form in verse 1, by which the translators of the Septuagint understood the form of הֵחֵל, the verb also appears in a similar form הֻחַל, but is translated as a *niphal*, meaning, "to be profaned or polluted."[29] The resulting translation of the verse could read "And it happened that the *polluted part* of humanity [perhaps those who are defiling the name of the Lord] *became great* [or many] upon the face of the earth and daughters were born to them." Interestingly, the majority of these occurrences of הֻחַל in the *niphal* are concerned with the pollution of the name of the Lord. This may lend support for the translation in *Genesis Rabbah* on Genesis 4.26 – "and he called his name Enosh then they rebelled to call upon [their idols] by the name of the Lord."

It should be noted that the author of Sirach alludes to Genesis 6.1 and the multiplying of an ungodly humanity. He describes the groaning that will be caused should this occur (see 16.1–4), but more interesting is what follows in verses 5–10. In this passage (v.7 in the Greek text), he describes those who have been punished by God for their disobedience; of particular interest is the mention of "the ancient giants who revolted in their might."[30]

---

[27] *Pseudo-Philo*, which is dated in the first c. C.E. or perhaps earlier, is one possible exception. The author describes in chapter 1.20 that with the birth of Noah the earth will receive rest from those who dwell on it, because of the wickedness of those evil deeds, the earth will be visited. This suggests that the author regarded the episode of Gen 6.1–4 as the cause of the Flood.

[28] See e.g. Ezek 20.9, 14, 22, 39, 44; 24.21; 36.21, 22, 23; 39.7; Lev 18.21; 21.6, 7, 9, 14; 22.2, 32; Isa 48.11; Zeph 3.4; Neh 13.17; and Mal 1.12.

[29] It is also translated on at least six occasions (Ezek 36.21, 22, 23; 24.21; Neh 13.17 and Lev 22.32) as a *piel/pual* form. See also Soggin, *Genesis*, 120. Soggin argues that the root חלל means to desecrate by the means of transporting an object back into a secular condition – back to a beginning.

[30] See *The Apocrypha or Deuterocanonical Books NRSV* (Cambridge: Cambridge University Press, 1989), 73. The origin of Sirach, written originally in Hebrew, dates from about 190 B.C.E. and the Greek version dates from about 132 B.C.E. There is little extant Hebrew text to chapter 16. There is a marginal note that reads [. . .]בגב (*bagib[borim]*), which could be the Hebrew *Vorlage* of "ancient giants." See M. Gilbert, *Wisdom Literature*, (vol. 2 of *The Literature of the Jewish People in the Period of the 2TP and the Talmud*; ed. Michael Stone Assen–Philadelphia: Van Gorcum–Fortress, 1984), 291. See also *T. Asher* 1.3, which describes the "two ways granted to the sons of men" – good and evil; perhaps an allusion to part of humanity that chose not to follow God and rebelled against him.

The verb רב(ל) also provides a means of interpreting the passage as an attempt by the author to introduce the Flood. According to Schwarzbaum, the multiplication of humanity was leading to a problem of overpopulation of the earth and thus God introduced death to humanity in verse 6.3.[31] He argues that Genesis 6 is a myth that parallels the *Vogul* creation myth in which the deity introduced marriage into creation, which resulted in an enormous increase in the human population.[32] Therefore, the deity introduced disease and death into creation in order to reduce the population to a stable level. This course of action differs significantly from the action of God in Genesis 6. This is one of several questionable points in Schwarzbaum's thesis. His suggestion that God intended humans to be immortal prior to the Fall in the Garden is perhaps possible; however, the idea that humans gained immortality through the union with the *bene haelohim* expressed in his statement that the "privilege of immortality was once within reach of [hu]mankind in its early age, when the *bene haelohim* had consorted with the daughters of men" cannot be suggested by the text of Genesis 6. He is correct to suggest that there is no obvious objection in the text to what has occurred in verse 2 between the *bene haelohim* and the daughters of men, but it seems clear from verse 3 that there was something in their actions to which God objected.[33] Schwarzbaum states the offspring from the union of the *bene haelohim* and the women must be immortal and that the offspring are the cause of the overpopulation of the earth. This result requires God to introduce death in verse 3.[34] However, death is already in the midst of humanity prior to the events of Genesis 6.

In Genesis 3.22, God exiles Adam and Eve from the Garden fearing that they may eat from the tree of life and live forever.[35] In Genesis 5.5,

---

[31] See Schwarzbaum, "Overcrowded."

[32] Ibid., 68.

[33] On this point Schwarzbaum argues that there is no evidence for any angelic involvement in this passage, but as will be shown below, the LXX seems to point to evidence otherwise. Ibid., 73.

[34] See Kraeling, "Significance," 198. Kraeling cites two articles by Otto Gruppe (Otto Gruppe, "Aithiopenmythen," *Philologus* 47 (1889): 328–343 and "War Genesis 6.1–4 Urspruenglich mit der Sintflut Verbunden?," *ZAW* 9 (1889): 135–55) in which Gruppe argues that through the consorting of the *bene haelohim* and the women a "greater measure of spirit" was introduced into humanity through the offspring. If the offspring continued to reproduce, which Gruppe considered immortal, the population would exceed the capacity the earth could support. Thus, Gruppe argues, the Flood was sent to end this dangerous imbalance of the creation. There is perhaps an allusion to this cry of the earth in *1 Enoch* 7.6 in which, immediately following the story of the lack of food to feed the giants, the earth directs a complaint towards God about them.

[35] This verse raises some interesting questions that are outside the scope of this thesis, but should be stated. Can we assume that Adam and Eve had eternal

following the description of the genealogy of Adam, the reader is told, "all the days that Adam lived were nine hundred and thirty years, and he died." The list goes on in chapter 5 with the deaths of Seth (v.8); Enosh (v.11); Kenan (v. 14); Mahalalel (v.17); Jared (v.20); and finally, Lamech (v. 31). It appears obvious then that it was not necessary for God to introduce death into the human population in chapter 6, but what may have occurred is the necessity of the life expectancy of the offspring to be limited despite the silence of the text in this matter.[36] Schwarzbaum cites several other early Jewish sources that seem to support the idea that overpopulation was a concern of the writers in the period.[37]

Conspicuously missing from Schwarzbaum's argument is the *Atrahasis* myth. This myth describes the actions of the god Enlil who became disturbed by the noise of humanity because of the increase in population. In order to stop the disturbance, Enlil adopted desperate measures and sends the Flood upon the earth. On the surface, it appears that humanity's only fault is that they are multiplying, which seems to parallel the story in Genesis 6.1. This act would not be considered a transgression. However, there are scholars who interpret the actions of humanity in the *Atrahasis* myth as evil conduct, which would then ascribe a negative nuance to verse 6.1.[38]

The *Sibylline Oracles* also suggest that the multiplication of humanity brought about the Flood.[39] In describing the history of creation, the

---

life/immortality prior to the Fall in the Garden? If so, is this related to the "image of God" in which they were created? If eating from the Tree of Life meant immortality, does this mean that they lost this at the fall? How then do we account for souls being in Sheol in the biblical tradition? Is there a difference between a soul surviving until judgment and eternal life/immortality?

[36] It may be possible to interpret 6.3 as the establishment of a limited life span for humanity or the offspring (see below).

[37] See 4 Ezra 5.43f; *Pirke de Rabbi Eliezer* chapter 3; and also Louis Ginzberg, *The Legends of the Jews* (ed. and trans. Henrietta Szold; 10 vols.; Philadelphia: Jewish Publication Society of America, 1909; repr., 1954), 1:65. See also Clines, "Sons of God," 39f. Clines argues that the story of the Flood can be told as a story which deals with the problem of overpopulation. Clines does note that the increase of human population is not the reason for the introduction of death as Schwarzbaum states, but rather the cause of the Flood is the action of the *bene haelohim*. Cf. Westermann, *Genesis*, 370; A. D. Kilmer, "The Mesopotamian Concept of Overpopulation and Its Solution Reflected in the Mythology," *Orientalia* 41 (1972): 160–77; and R. A. Oden, "Divine Aspirations in *Atrahasis* and in Genesis 1–11," *ZAW* 93 (1981): 197–216.

[38] For a discussion on the interpretation of the actions of humanity in the *Atrahasis* myth see W. L. Moran, "Atrahasis: The Babylonian Story of the Flood," *Biblica* 52 (1971): 51–61.

[39] See John J. Collins, "Sibylline Oracles," in *The Old Testament Pseudepigrapha* (ed. James H. Charlesworth; 2 vols.; New York: Doubleday, 1983–85), 1:377–78.

author(s) portray(s) the generations of humanity in language very similar to that used by Hesiod in *Works and Days* 109–174.[40] The first generation of humanity is described in the *Sibylline Oracles* 1.75–80[41] as one of "great-hearted mortals" who become "polluted" (μιαρός)[42] with the blood of humans. The author may be referring to the generation that is discussed in Genesis 6.1. However, a more plausible understanding is that the polluted generation is the offspring of the relations between the *bene haelohim* and the daughters of men. If the description in the *Sibylline Oracles* is the generation described in Genesis 6, then, alongside the readings discussed above, Genesis 6.1 could be read as a passage that builds a bridge between Genesis 1–5 and 6.5f. Hence, it is integral to the larger narrative itself and not a foreign insertion allowing one to read verse 6.1 as an introduction to the Flood narrative.[43]

3.2.2 Verse 2

וירא בני־האלהים את־בנות האדם כי טבת הנה
ויקחו להם נשים מכל אשר בחרו

Collins argues for an early date (30 B.C.E. – pre 70 C.E.) for the Jewish section of Book 1 verses 1–323.

[40] It is noted in Philo of Byblos in fragment 2.40 of the *Phoenician History* that "The Greeks, who surpass all men in their natural cleverness, first appropriated most of these tales," (i.e. the accounts of Later Rulers) from the Phoenicians, out of which Hesiod and the highly touted cyclic poets fabricated their own versions and made excerpts of *Theogonies* and Giants' Battles and Titans' Battles." See Harold W. Attridge, Jr. and Robert A. Oden, *Philo of Byblos The Phoenician History: Introduction, Critical Text, Translation, Notes*, (CBQMS, 9; Washington, DC: Catholic Biblical Association of America, 1981), 61.

[41] See Collins, "Sibylline," 330–47.

[42] See Edwin Hatch and Henry A. Redpath, eds., *A Concordance to the Septuagint and the Other Greek Versions of the Old Testament* (2 vols.; Oxford: Clarendon Press, 1897; repr., Graz, Austria: Akademische Druck–u–Verlagsanstalt, 1975), 926; also 2 Macc 4.19; 5.16; 7.34; 9.13; 15.32; 4 Macc 4.26; 9.15, 17, 32; 10.10 and 11.4.

[43] Another point of interest concerning verse 1 is the Septuagint's inclusion of a translated Hebrew text of verse 5.32 within the corpus of 6.1 See Wevers, *Septuaginta Genesis*, 108. The inclusion of this verse in the LXX does nothing to help clear up why the ambiguous 6.1–4 (HB) has been inserted between the story of the birth of Noah's sons and the Lord's decision to destroy humanity because of their wickedness. Margarite Harl, *La Bible*, argues that the inclusion of the line of Noah in verse 1 of the LXX is an indication that the τοῖς ἀνθρώποις τούτοις in verse 3 are the men of Noah's generation. A final question concerning verse 1 is, why are the daughters of men, בנות האדם, singled out at this point in the narrative? There appears to be a deliberate contrast between the *bene haelohim* and the daughters of men. It is possible that the author was purposely making clear that the *bene haelohim* were not human, but they were some kind of superhuman or supernatural beings.

Verse 2 contains one of the most problematic expressions in the passage, בְּנֵי־הָאֱלֹהִים. The *bene haelohim* are located in three main categories in the Hebrew Bible: (1) angels, (2) minor deities, and (3) god-like men. The majority opinion concerning the interpretation with any of the three options has at least a slightly negative connotation in the interpretation even though there is no overt evidence of this type of outcome in Genesis 6.1–4. It may be suggested that these characters were well known in the culture of Israel during this time due to the lack of explanation with regard to their nature.[44]

The LXX translates בְּנֵי־הָאֱלֹהִים as οἱ υἱοὶ τοῦ θεοῦ, but several variants introduce a significant change to the translation. Multiple witnesses translate the Hebrew as ἄγγελοι τοῦ θεοῦ – "angels (messengers) of God,"[45] and in addition there are several early Jewish and Christian authors who follow the same line of interpretation.[46] A total of seven occurrences of בְּנֵי־הָאֱלֹהִים are present in the Hebrew Bible: Genesis 6.2, 4; Job 1.6; 2.1; 38.7; Psalm 29.1; 89.7; in addition, it occurs in Aramaic Daniel 3.25 (לְבַר־אֱלָהִין).[47] The LXX has translated the expression in Genesis 6.2, 4 as "sons of God" and "angels of God"; in Job 1.6 and 2.1 it is translated ἄγγελοι τοῦ θεοῦ;[48] in Job 38.7 as ἄγγελοι

---

[44] Hendel, "Nephilim,"17. At an early stage of the Zoroastrian religion, a class of gods existed, the *daēvas*, who, in time, were identified as demons, but there is no evidence that indicates these beings can be equated to the *bene haelohim*; see discussion on demons in Zoroastrianism in Boyce, *History*, 1:85–108. Boyce argues that the Watcher tradition of Azazel and Shemihazah reflects the arch-demon Aži Dahaka who was overcome by the ancient hero Thraetaona and is bound in a cavern; see ibid., 3:421.

[45] Witnessed in MS A–72, 56, 75–458, 71, 121–392, 55, 509. See also Aldina and Sixtina editions. See also Ethiopic O.T. which reads malā'ĕkta 'ĕgzi 'abḫer (angels of God). The date of extant Ethiopic texts ranges from thirteenth – seventeenth centuries C.E. See J. Oscar Boyd, ed., *The Octateuch in Ethiopic: According to the Text of the Paris Codex, With Variants of Five Other Manuscripts* (Bibliotheca Abessinica 3; Leiden: E. J. Brill, 1909–11).

[46] See in Wevers, *Septuaginta Genesis*, 108 e.g. Philo *Gig.* 6; Josephus *Ant.* I. 73; Pseudo-Philo 3.1 and others. Verse 4b also contains בְּנֵי־הָאֱלֹהִים, which is translated along a similar line as verse 2.

[47] There is one other occurrence in Deut 32.8. This passage is thought to have been altered at a later date from בְּנֵי אֵלִים to בְּנֵי יִשְׂרָאֵל. Recent discoveries at Qumran confirm the former reading בְּנֵי אֵלִ as does the LXX – υἱῶν θεοῦ. It appears that the change from בְּנֵי אֵלִים occurred prior to the mid–second century C.E. because of the evidence found in Aquila's translation of the LXX. His translation of "sons of Israel" is also affirmed in several smaller fragments; see John W. Wevers, ed., *Deuteronomium*, (Goettingen: Vandenhoeck and Ruprecht, 1977), 346–47.

[48] See Joseph Ziegler, ed., *Iob* (Goettingen: Vandenhoeck and Ruprecht, 1982), 211, 215. For Job 1.6b and 2.1b Aquila reads οἱ ἄγγελοι for οἱ υἱοί and has agreement in MS 248 (also Syrohexaplarische for 1.6b). The Latin translation of 2.1 follows the Hebrew Bible with *filii* and *Didymus Alexandrinus* reads τοῦ κυρίου for τοῦ θεοῦ.

μοῦ;[49] in Psalm 29(28).1[50] and 89(88).7 as υἰοὶ θεοῦ and υἰοῖς θεοῦ respectively; and in Daniel 3.25[51] it is translated as ἀγγέλου θεοῦ. It should be noted that in each case of the LXX translation of האלהים it is translated in the singular form God rather than a literal "'gods" or "the gods." There is one exception to this, which is the edition of Aquila, who, known for his literalness, has followed the Hebrew text word for word with οἱ υἱοὶ τῶν θεῶν – the sons of the gods. Philip Alexander notes, however, that a common literal translation of the text is not the case here. Alexander notes that Aquila often translates *elohim* in the singular as God, but where he translates *elohim* in the Greek plural, it does not mean Yahweh, but rather Aquila equates it to "false gods" (3 Kgs 14.9; Isa 37.19) or "judges" (Exod 21.6; 22.9). With this in mind, it is possible that Aquila understood בני האלהים as "sons of idols."[52]

As suggested above, some early interpreters of the Hebrew Bible understood *bene haelohim* to mean "angels." Further support for this interpretation may be found in the beginning of *BW*, which many consider an elaborate Midrash on Genesis 6.1–4.[53] Alexander argues that this concept may have originated much earlier than the second or third century B.C.E. date of the *1 Enoch* material in order to allow such an understanding to have developed. He claims that such an angelology began to develop during the exile because of the close contact with the Babylonian culture.[54] Sources from late third or early second centuries

---

[49] See ibid., 384. There is one variant for ἀγγελοὶ μου – υἱοὶ θεοῦ found in text group C. This is the only place in which this seemingly odd translation ἀγγελοὶ μου is found. There is a variant for μου – αὐτοῦ found as ἀγγελοὶ αὐτοῦ in four places; Ps 96.6 – כל־אלהים in references to idols; 102.2; 148.2 – מלאכיו; and Dan 4.24 – which appears to be a misreading of מלכא in the HB by the translator.

[50] LXX Ps 28.1 has made an addition to the HB at the end of 1b υἱοὺς κριῶν. This appears to be a contrast to the υἱοὶ θεοῦ at the end of 1(a) considering the Hebrew is clearly making a distinction of יהוה and בני אלים. See A. Rahlfs, ed., *Psalmi Cum Odis* (Goettingen: Vandenhoeck and Ruprecht, 1931), 120.

[51] See Joseph Ziegler, ed., *Susanna, Daniel, Bel Et Draco* (Goettingen: Vandenhoeck and Ruprecht, 1954), 133. LXX Daniel 3.92 has a variant in the Theodotion edition for ἀγγέλου θεοῦ] υἱῷ θεοῦ; see also *filii hominis* in Tertullian *Adverus Praxean* III.258.

[52] Cf. Alexander, "Sons of God," 64–5. See Wevers, *Septuaginta Genesis*, 108; Wevers argues that the author is drawing a contrast between the sons and the daughters and τοῦ θεοῦ and τῶν ἀνθρώπων. Also note Symmachus' reading, υἱοί τῶν δυναστευοντων (powerful ones) for האלהים. Symmachus, however, was a third c. C.E. translator who no doubt was influenced by the shift in interpretation due to the comments of R. Simeon bar Yoḥai.

[53] See Alexander, "Sons of God," 60; Geza Vermes, *Post–Biblical Jewish Studies*, (SJLA 8; Leiden: E.J. Brill, 1975), 38. Vermes' definition of a Midrash seems to fit *BW* as a Midrash on Gen 6.1–4.

[54] Alexander, "Sons of God," 61. While acknowledging that there was a tradition which identified the *bene haelohim* as angels as early as the third century B.C.E., one

B.C.E.[55] reveal a widespread understanding of this concept, which would continue until the emergence of R. Simeon bar Yoḥai in the early second century C.E.

The Targumim apparently had some difficulty with translating the expression *bene haelohim* as "angels" or "sons of God." R. Simeon bar Yoḥai began a campaign to condemn anyone who dared to call the *bene haelohim* angels or sons of God, claiming that this was blasphemous and cursed all who did.[56] Michael Maher argues that one reason for this rejection of the idea of angels was the response to esoteric groups who were granting a great deal of importance to angels during this period.[57] R. Simeon bar Yoḥai interprets the *bene haelohim* in *Genesis Rabbah* 26.5 as בני דייניא, "sons of the judges or nobles." Targum *Onkelos* interprets the passage with a reading of בני רברביא – "sons of the great ones." R. Simeon bar Yoḥai and the author of *Onkelos* were disciples of R. Akiba who was opposed to the idea of the intermarriage of angels and humans.[58] However, a contemporary of R. Akiba's, R. Ishmael, contended that the legend of the Fallen Angels was a historical fact.[59]

Targum *Neofiti* translates *bene haelohim* as בני דייניא, "sons of the judges" which follows the line of R. Simeon bar Yoḥai in *Genesis Rabbah* 26.5. Worth noting though, is a variant of a *Neofiti* marginal gloss מלכייא, "of the kings." McNamara argues that this gloss has been misread and should be translated as מלאכי, "angels."[60] Meir Zlotowitz

---

must keep in mind that Judaism was not a religion that had only one mind or one way of thinking. It is highly probably that there were various groups within Judaism, which held varying opinions on vast number of doctrinal issues. The question of who were the *bene haelohim* was probably not an exception. See also Gunkel, *Genesis*, 56. Hermann Gunkel contends that the myth found in Gen 6.1–4 is of advanced age probably originating in the Persian period. Gunkel also argues that the developing religion in Israel suppressed the myth to the shortened form which is found in the Genesis passage.

[55] See e.g. *Jubilees* 4.15, 22; 5.1; *T. Reuben* 5.6, 7; *2 Baruch* 56.11–14; Philo, *Gig.* 2.6f; and Josephus *Ant.* I.73 among others.

[56] Bernard Grossfeld, *The Targum Onqelos to Genesis* (vol. 6 of *The Aramaic Bible: The Targumim*; ed. Michael Maher, Kevin Cathcart and Martin McNamara; Edinburgh: T & T Clark, 1988), 52.

[57] Michael Maher, *Targum Pseudo-Jonathan: Genesis* (vol. 1B of *The Aramaic Bible: The Targumim*; eds. Michael Maher, Kevin Cathcart and Martin McNamara; Edinburgh: T&T Clark, 1992), 37, n.2.

[58] R. Akiba was a Tanna active during the Bar Kochba War (120–140 CE). See C.G. Montefiore and H. Loewe, *A Rabbinic Anthology* (New York: Schocken Books, 1974), 696.

[59] See *b. Yoma* 7b.

[60] Cf. Daniel 4.24. *Neofiti* also translates *elohim* in Exodus 22.7 as דייניא, "judges." See Morgenstern, "Psalm 82," 30. Morgenstern notes that all modern scholarship has rejected this interpretation, but he does remark on the division in scholarship between an interpretation of foreign kings, foreign gods, or angels.

follows a similar line of thought with the translation "sons of the rulers" (princes and judges).[61] He argues that the Targumim based the translation of *bene haelohim* as judges, rulers, and nobles on Exodus 22.7 – "and the owner of the house shall come near to הָאֱלֹהִים, 'the judges.'" Zlotowitz notes that R. Simeon bar Yoḥai's interpretation of the "sons of nobles" indicates that the sons of the nobility married the daughters of the common people who were powerless to resist.[62] R. Simeon bar Yoḥai states that these relationships came about through uncontrolled lust and signalled the moral decay of humanity. So, it appears that some early rabbinic authorities thought that not only did the בְּנֵי־הָאֱלֹהִים play a key role in the passage, but also the בְּנוֹת הָאָדָם.[63]

Targum *Pseudo-Jonathan* follows a similar line of interpretation as *Onkelos*, but adds what seems to be a clear allusion to *1 Enoch* 8.1–2: "that they painted their eyes and put on rouge and walked about with naked flesh." The reference is similar to language found in the Watcher tradition in which Asa'el is alleged to have taught humans the art of decorating the eyes.[64] Worth questioning at this point, is why the author of *Pseudo-Jonathan* would have referred to a long-standing tradition found in *1 Enoch* that clearly supports the idea that the *bene haelohim* in Genesis 6.1–4 were angels? Is this perhaps a polemic against such a myth by declaring that the characters of the Genesis passage, and therefore the Watchers of *1 Enoch*, were actually not angels at all, but merely "sons of the great ones"? This appears unlikely alongside the author's interpretation of *nephilim* in verse 6.4 as the two chief Watchers, Shemihazah and Asa'el.

It should be noted that despite the disapproval by R. Simeon bar Yoḥai in the early second century C.E. to the interpretation of *bene haelohim* as angels, some ambiguity exists in such expressions as בְּנֵי דַיָּינִא and בְּנֵי רַבְרְבַיָּא used by the authors of the Targums. *Pseudo-Jonathan*

---

[61] Meir Zlotowitz and Nosson Scherman, *Bereishis: Genesis A New Translation with a Commentary Anthologized From Talmudic, Midrashic and Rabbinic Sources* (2d ed.; New York: Mesorah Publications, 1980). The value of this particular translation is that it has taken into consideration the Targumim, Midrashim, Talmud, and other rabbinic sources.

[62] See also J. H. Hertz, *The Pentateuch and Haftorahs* (London: Oxford University, 1929), 48.

[63] See comments on Wevers' thoughts on this line in n. 53.

[64] A parallel in *Pirke R. Eliezer* 22 should be noted here, which tells of the angels who saw the *generations of Cain* walking about naked, with their eyes painted. It seems possible that there is a reference being made here back to Gen 6.1 and the "polluted part" of humanity multiplying on the face of the earth. Is it possible this was the generation, which took part in the fall of the angels in verses 2–4?

interprets *bene haelohim* in Genesis 6.2 and 4 with בני רברביא.[65] In Deuteronomy 32.8, which discusses the division of the nations according to the "angels of the nations," *Pseudo-Jonathan* uses the same expression, בני רברביא, to describe the same angels as the "princes of the nations."[66] The Targum on Psalms[67] helps to verify that *bene haelohim* were understood to be angels. *Targum Psalm* 29.1 translates בני אלים as כתי מלאכיא (band of angels) while retaining בני אלים – the passage reads, "a praise of David, Give before God praise, *band of angels, sons of God*, give before God glory and strength." The verse seems to indicate that these "sons of God" are the same beings recognized in Genesis 1.26 and Psalm 82. *Targum Psalm* 82 makes a shift from a divine interpretation of אלהים to one of perhaps human judges or at least judges. Psalm 82.1 contains the phrase בעדת־אל usually translated the "congregation of God," but the Targum has interpreted the text to read בכינשת צדיקין דתקיפין באוריתא, "in the congregation of *the righteous that are mighty in Torah*."[68]

The second part of *Targum Psalm* 82.1 is perhaps somewhat ambiguous in its choice of vocabulary and translates אלהים, usually rendered as gods or angels, as "righteous judges" (דיינין דקשוט), a similar term which is used in Targum *Neofiti* and *Genesis Rabbah* (בני דייניא) on Genesis 6.2. Psalm 82.6–7 perhaps reveals a connection to the "angels of the nations." The Hebrew reads in verse 6, אני־אמרתי אלהים אתם ובני עליון כלכם, "I, myself, said you are gods (angels) and all of you are sons of the most high." The Targum reads אנא אמרית היך כמלאכיא אתון חשיבין והיך אנגלי מרומא כולכון, "I said: As angels you are regarded, and all of you are as angels on high."[69] This translation seems to indicate some hesitancy on the part of the writer to identify the figures of the *Targum Psalm* as heavenly beings (אלהים),[70] but the same translation of verse 7 certainly seems to categorize them as something other than human. The *Targum Psalm* 82.7 reads, בקושטא היך בני נשא תמותון והיך חד מן רברבניא תפלון, "but rightly you

---

[65] Cf. *Onkelos*, בני רברביא.

[66] Unfortunately, *Onkelos* and *Neofiti* follow the reformulated HB with בני ישראל.

[67] The Aramaic text is from Paul de Lagarde, *Hagiographa Chaldaice* (Lipsiae: In Aedibus B. G. Teubneri, 1873).

[68] This view of בני האלהים as the righteous can also be found in Wisdom of Solomon 2.18.

[69] There is a question of who is speaking at this point in the Psalm, is it God, or is it someone addressing the congregation of God? One question that needs to be asked here, but is perhaps not answerable, is "why did the author use two different words for angels?"

[70] I define divine beings as a being (angel, god, spirit) whose dwelling place is in the heavenly realm.

will die as sons of men and as one of the princes you will fall." Again, this interpretation seems to point to Genesis 6.2–4 (i.e. the *bene haelohim*) and the myth of the Fallen Angels.[71] The *bene haelohim* have transgressed the natural realm where humanity dwells and, as a result, their punishment is to die as humans die.

It seems plausible that the writers were cloaking their discomfort with angels and women having sex in language that removed the idea of a heavenly being from the context. However, a possible connection with the Targum's description of the *bene haelohim* of Genesis 6.2 (בני דייניא) is found in *Targum Job* 1.21. The angels were often used in proxy for God in exceptionally problematic situations in the text. This is particularly true in Targumic traditions.[72] *Targum Job* 1.21b reads מימרא דיהוה יהב ומימרא דיהוה ובית דיניה נסיב, "the memra of the Lord gives and the memra of the Lord and his court take away"; the court in this case is the heavenly court of angels who surround God. It is plausible to imagine a possibility in which the authors of the Genesis Targumim would use such ambiguous terms as בני דייניא to describe the *bene haelohim* if they had a problem with angels having sexual relations with women.

A further interpretation of *bene haelohim* as divine beings or minor deities is derived from a Semitic tradition of which the original nuances have been lost. Apparently, during the latter part of the 2TP a merger takes place between two categories of heavenly creatures (angels and the *bene haelohim*), which were earlier thought to be separate.[73] J. Weingreen suggests the *bene haelohim* are best described as superhuman or supernatural beings. He argues איש אלהים, in the context of Judges 13.6–8, cannot mean simply a "man of God" but must be describing a supernatural being. Weingreen argues that אלהים in this case is adjectival and should be interpreted as "supernatural" or "superhuman."[74]

Nahum Sarna argues that the *bene haelohim* are divine beings that lowered themselves to a human level that resulted in the intervention of God.[75] He states that the concept of deities marrying humans is not only a

---

[71] There is also a possible parallel of angels and princes found in Daniel 10.13, 20 and 12.1. In particular Daniel 12.1 in which Michael is described as השר הגדול, the great prince, which is translated in the LXX as ὁ ἄγγελος ὁ μέγας. Of course the possibility exists that שר־צבא יהוה could be translated as "captain" Joshua 5.14–15; or in a possible messianic role – Isaiah 9.5, שר־שלום.

[72] Etan Levine, *The Aramaic Version of the Bible Contents and Context* (Berlin/New York: Walter de Gruyter, 1988), 68.

[73] See Hendel, "Nephilim," 19. Hendel cites the passage from Daniel 3.25 and the appearance of one like a *bene haelohim* in the fiery furnace; Hendel contends that this figure would have represented an angel in classical times.

[74] J. Weingreen, "Construct Genitive," *Vetus Testamentum* 4 (1954): 57–9.

[75] Sarna, *Genesis*, 45.

Greek motif,[76] but can also be found in the biblical tradition; i.e. Isaiah 14.12. Sarna claims there was an angelic rebellion by which angels lost their place in the heavenly realm. However, nothing in the Isaiah text indicates such action took place. Sarna also cites Job 4.18–19 as another passage that indicates deities intermarrying with humans, but this text only indicates the possibility of angelic rebellion, not marriage. The third passage, Ezekiel 32.27, again does not refer to marriage, only angelic rebellion. Of course, the author of these passages may have been drawing on the myth of Genesis 6.1–4 and expected his readers to understand that angelic rebellion equates to angels intermarrying with humans. Based upon Job 1.6; 2.1; and 38.7, Sarna argues that the *bene haelohim* are angels, an interpretation that is clear from the LXX variants, but not in the Hebrew. If these are angels, then why has the author of Job used the ambiguous *bene haelohim* rather than the Hebrew term מלאכים? It seems more plausible to think that in the Job passages cited by Sarna the *bene haelohim* were still understood as minor deities prior to the fusing of the two types of beings in Hebrew culture.

Jon Levenson argues that the *bene haelohim* are the divine assembly who sit at court with God.[77] He states that they are present from the beginning in Genesis 1.26 ("Let us make man in *our* image"), which, he contends, reveals a collegiality in the heavens in which God has the final word in all that occurs in the cosmos.[78] Levenson claims that this "royal court" imagery is found in Psalm 82.1: נצב בעדת־אל בקרב אלהים ישפט אלהים: "God stood in the congregation of God, in the midst of gods he shall judge" (ὁ θεὸς ἔστη ἐν συναγωγῇ θεῶν, ἐν μέσῳ δὲ θεοὺς διακρινεῖ – "God stood in the congregation of gods, and in the midst he judges gods").[79] This same imagery is also preserved in 1 Kings 22.19–23: "I saw the Lord sitting on his throne, and all the host of heaven standing by him on his right and on his left." This passage appears to have close parallels to Job 1.6–12 and 2.1–6, which reveals the heavenly court of the "sons of God."[80] This same court is identified in Psalm 82.6 as sons

---

[76] See excursus on "The Greek 'Sons of the Gods'" below.

[77] Levenson, *Creation*. See also Cassuto, *Genesis*, 293. Cassuto argues that the sons of gods in the Canaanite literature are beings that belong to the congregation of the gods. According to Cassuto, a shift occurs in Israelite tradition in which the *bene haelohim* become angels because of monotheism; Schwarzbaum, "Overcrowded," 67; and Stuckenbruck, "Angels of the Nations," 29. Cf. 4Q511 10.11.

[78] Levenson, *Creation*, 5, and also Clines, "Sons of God," 33.

[79] Levenson, *Creation*, 6. Levenson argues that this story parallels that of *Enuma Elish*, which describes the ascension to the head of the pantheon of gods by one supreme deity, Marduk.

[80] God appears in his heavenly court as judge multiple times in the Pss: 89.6–9; 29.1–2; 97.7,9; 148.2; 96.4; 95.3; 76.9; 18.8–16; 50.1–4; and 1 Chr 16.33. The HB

of God: "I declare you are gods and all of you are sons of the most high."
The story depicted here presents a variation to the monotheistic system of
Israel of 2TP Judaism. This is conceivably the reason why these *elohim*
were interpreted as angels in the Septuagint rather than minor gods.

There may be an allusion to the breach of the cosmic order that the
bene haelohim made in Genesis 6.2 in Psalm 82.5: "They do not know nor
understand, in darkness they go about; *all the foundations of the earth are
shaken*." The Hebrew verb used here, ימוטו, is also found in Isaiah 24.19
(מוט), a passage that seems to describe the judgment of the *bene
haelohim* for their actions against humanity and the cosmos.[81] In
summary, Psalm 82, in the context of the judgment in verse 1, the shaking
of the foundations of the earth in verse 5, and the loss of immortality in
verse 7, seems to affirm the idea that these אלהים are the *bene haelohim*
of Genesis 6.1–4.

The "host of heaven" is also an expression that carried a similar
meaning to *bene haelohim*. This description may further reveal the
identity of who the sons of God are in Genesis 6.1–4 and in other early
Jewish writings.[82] Deuteronomy 4.19 describes the host of heaven as a
group of heavenly beings under the command of God who are to rule over
the nations. This verse may be alluding to the angels who rule over the
nations.[83] Philo of Alexandria notes in *De Posteritate Caini* 89, 91–2 that
the nations, with the exception of Israel, were divided by God amongst
the ἀγγέλων θεοῦ.[84] In comparison to other biblical passages in which
the actions of the *bene haelohim* are described, Genesis 6.1–4 represents
the group acting autonomously, that is, outside of the directive of God.
Their independent initiative to intermingle with human women could be
construed as an iniquitous action in relation to their previous history in

---

reads בני אלהים and the LXX reads ἀγγέλοι τοῦ θεοῦ similar to the Gen 6.2
translation. Morgenstern notes that הרוח in 1 Kgs 22.21 which is translated "a certain
spirit" is also found referring to an angel in Ps 104.3–4; 148.8; 18.11; 2 Sam 22.11; Job
30.22; cf. *1 Enoch* 37; Morgenstern, "Psalm 82," 40. See also Hendel, "Nephilim," 17.
It is possible the spirit that came forward in 1 Kgs 22.21 is the figure "satan" in Job 1.6
and 2.1.

[81] *Targum Isaiah* 24.19–23 interprets the Hebrew המרום במרום על־צבא to mean
the "mighty hosts" (with a divinity in mind) perhaps indicating the angelic host.

[82] See Deut 4.19; Job 38.7; and 1 Kgs 22.19. Compare *1 Enoch* 6–16, *Animal
Apocalypse*, and *Jubilees*.

[83] See Deut 32.8. See possible origins of this concept in Plato's *Politicus* – "all the
parts of the universe everywhere were divided amongst gods appointed to rule over
them, as now gods rule over certain places." Cf. also *Critias* and *Laws*, which suggest a
similar theme; see also 1 Peter 2.25.

[84] This theme is also represented in the *T. Naphtali* 8.3f and *Jubilees* 15.31–32.

the biblical tradition.[85] The result of their independent action, revealed in Genesis 6, has a destructive affect upon the cosmos.[86]

Philo of Alexandria apparently had little difficulty in ascribing the *bene haelohim* to the category of angels. Philo states in *De Gigantibus* 6[87] (quoting Gen 6.2) that it was the custom of Moses to call angels those whom the philosophers called δάιμονας.[88] This appears to be an allusion to Hesiod's *Works and Days* 120–30 and the generation of the "golden race of mortal men." When the "golden race" died, they became pure spirits (δάιμονες), which dwell upon the earth keeping watch over humanity. This is much like Philo's view of δάιμονες. Philo's understanding is that these spirits dwell in an area of the heavens just above the earth, not on the earth as they do in Hesiod. Therefore, it is plausible that Philo is alluding to Hesiod in *De Gigantibus* 6. A full discussion of Philo's interpretation of Genesis 6.1–4 will be taken up in chapter 7.

In his work *Liber Antiquitatum Biblicarum*, Pseudo-Philo, a first century C.E. Jewish writer, retells the biblical story in a form similar to the Targumim, *Jubilees*, and the Qumran *Genesis Apocryphon*. In 3.1, the author has followed the Hebrew Bible translation of "sons of God" in reference to the *bene haelohim*. He does appear to follow a Targumic type of language in reference to the entire passage, in particular, verse 6.3.[89] Conspicuously missing from Pseudo-Philo's work is an interpretation of Genesis 6.4. This perhaps reveals his disagreement with the idea that the sons of God could have sexual relations with women, which seems to follow a conservative rabbinic line of thought in relation to the passage. Pseudo-Philo relates a negative view of the passage in general, but this is directed primarily toward the role of humanity in the Flood rather than the sons of God about whose origin he offers no comment. It is possible that

---

[85] Hendel argues that Psalm 82 describes their punishment for some previous offence, but it is possible that this Psalm is describing their punishment for their actions in the Gen 6 passage; see Hendel, "Nephilim," 19. There is no unambiguous reference to God or the angels involved in sexual exploits as in the pagan mythology

[86] See Cassuto, *Genesis*. Cassuto contends that the *bene haelohim* are depicted in the Hebrew Bible as angels, however, the beings in Gen 6.1–4 do not represent the pure and exalted character of the angels in the rest of Genesis. He therefore argues for a categorized angelology in which the angels in Gen 6 are those of a degraded class described in Deut 32.8 as the angels of the nations. He also sees the author's choice of *bene haelohim* as a general term for angels, which could indicate good or evil, very much like Philo's concept of angels and demons. See also *Jubilees*, which describes a hierarchy of angels.

[87] See also Philo *Quaestiones et Solutiones in Genesis* I.92.

[88] Philo's view of angels encompasses the ψυχαὶ, ἄγγελοι, and δαίμονες with no clear distinction between them.

[89] This will be discussed in detail in the section on verse 6.3.

what lies behind the shift of interpreting the *bene haelohim* as angels in the early centuries of the Common Era is the idea that they were identified with the gods of the other nations; hence any veneration of them would be considered idolatry.

In *Jewish Antiquities* 1.72–76, Josephus interprets the *bene haelohim* of Genesis 6.2 as "angels of God." His narrative of the angels has been inserted into a section that describes the generations of Seth from a very negative standpoint. Following seven generations of serving God (I. 72f.), the people of Seth abandoned the ways of the previous generations and chose to live lives of depravity. During this time, some of the angels of God have fallen into wickedness and consorted with human women. The offspring of their sexual relations perform deeds similar to the giants of the Greek myths. Josephus identifies what appear to be Jewish traditions concerning the gigantic offspring and their resemblance to the giants (γιγάντες) of the Greek traditions, presumably those of Hesiod's *Theogony*. This possibly could be understood as an affirmation that the two traditions, the giants of the Jewish tradition and those of the Greek myths, were seen as merging during the late 2TP. It seems likely that the nature of the offspring of the *bene haelohim* and the daughters of men could be found in the Greek mythological description of the γιγάντες. Josephus presents a very negative understanding of the function of Genesis 6.1–4 in the Flood narrative in *Jewish Antiquities* 1.72–76.

One final early Jewish source for *bene haelohim* is Daniel 3.25–28. The familiar story tells of the Israelite boys being thrown into the furnace and, while in the fire, Nebuchadnezzar saw them and a fourth with them who appeared as a "son of the gods" (דִי רְבִיעָיָא דָּמֵה בַר־אֱלָהִין וְרֵוֵה). This phrase בַר־אֱלָהִין is quite ambiguous according to the various interpretations (i.e. angel, Son of God). However, it is clear from the words of Nebuchadnezzar in 3.28 that this is an angel: בְּרִיךְ אֱלָהֲהוֹן דִּי־שַׁדְרַךְ מֵישַׁךְ וַעֲבֵד נְגוֹ דִּי־שְׁלַח מַלְאֲכֵהּ וְשֵׁיזִב לְעַבְדוֹהִי, "blessed be the God of Shadrach, Mishach, and Abed Nego who sent his *angel* [LXX – τὸν ἄγγελον αὐτοῦ] and delivered his servants." This is evidence that *bene haelohim* was being interpreted as angels as late as mid–second century B.C.E.

One of the more prominent theories raised during the early centuries of the Common Era was that the *bene haelohim* were the righteous and godly line of Seth and the daughters were from the line of Cain. This understanding of *bene haelohim* as the "line of Seth" is thought to have its origins in Christian circles beginning in the second century C.E. at the hand of Julius Africanus who attacked the view that the *bene haelohim* were angels.[90] This view was vigorously supported by several of the

---

[90] PG X. 65.

Church Fathers such as Chrysostom and Augustine.[91] It is important to address this theory even if only to eliminate it from the list of possibilities.

Lyle Eslinger argues that the identity of *bene haelohim* can be discovered through the type of sin that has been committed.[92] He begins in verse 3 by reading that the actions of God are directed towards humanity, so that the sin must have been human sin that occurred prior to verse 3. He argues that there is no violation in verse 1 because the people are only fulfilling the commandment to "be fruitful and multiply."[93] Eslinger therefore argues that the sin must be found in verse 2; since the punishment is directed against humanity (vv. 3, 5), the *bene haelohim* must be humans. He goes on to argue that verse 1 must be relating the actions of the line of Seth in chapter 5 since there are only 13 people listed in the line of Cain and no daughters. This of course is not true; there is a sister of Tubal-cain listed in 4.22, Naamah. Eslinger's second point is that there is no mention of the line of Seth taking wives, arguing that this is found only among the Cainites (Gen 4.19 by Lamech). He contends that this parallel is the sin that is found in verse 2: the breaking of the monogamous relationship established between Adam and Eve in Genesis 2.24.

At this point, the argument of Eslinger becomes quite unclear. He has argued as follows: (1) the people who are multiplying upon the face of the earth are the Sethites (based on the idea in 4.14 that Cain has been banished from the face of the earth, which should perhaps be understood to mean, as God stated in 4.12; "he is cursed by the earth"); (2) daughters are born only to the Sethites (incorrect as seen in 4.22);[94] and (3) there is no mention of marriage in the line of Seth in chapter 5. These three points cannot lead to the conclusion that the *bene haelohim* are the Cainites and

---

[91] See Chrysostom *Homil. In Genesin* 12.2 and Augustine *De Civ. Dei* 15.23. Syncellus attributes characteristics to Seth that appear to be similar to those of Enoch in *1 Enoch*; he was translated to the angels who told him of the fall of the angels, the Flood, and the coming of the Messiah. Ginzberg argues this has its origins in the apocryphal book of Seth, which is of Jewish origin, Ginzberg, *Legends,* 5:149, n. 52.

[92] See Eslinger, "Contextual Identification of the *Bene Ha'elohim.*"

[93] See Gen 1.28.

[94] Eslinger is incorrect in his assumption that the daughters are Sethites. According to *Yerahmeel* 24.10–12, the "daughters of man" are the line of Cain. See also *Pirke R. Eliezer* 22. A second view reverses the roles, the daughters are Sethites, and the sons of God are Cainites because Cain was of heavenly origin. The offspring of this union (of the Cainites) were physically strong and beautiful in appearance, but have a sinful nature. See Ginzberg, *Legends,* 5:172, n. 14. Nowhere in the literature do we find the idea that both the "sons of God" and the "daughters of men" are from the same group.

that polygamous marriage is the sin for which God will bring the Flood.[95] No evidence can be found in the Genesis 6.2 of polygamous marriages (i.e., the *bene haelohim* taking more than one woman), and by Eslinger's own argument, it is the line of Cain marrying humans (possibly from their own line, see point 2 above), which of course is not banned by God in the rebuke of Cain in chapter 4. Certainly, this is not a crime worthy of the judgment of the Flood and the destruction of humanity.[96]

The various interpretations discussed above reveal the difficulty that interpreters of Genesis 6.1–4 have had with the *bene haelohim*. It can be determined, however, that at least a part of Judaism understood *bene haelohim* as angels or some type of divine being or god. As a result, the Targumic interpretations were based upon doctrinal differences concerning angels or other divine beings. Another possibility is that the writers were attempting to protect the image of anything related to the Divine. Other early Jewish authors such as Philo of Alexandria, Josephus, Pseudo-Philo, and the authors of *1 Enoch* and Daniel had no problem interpreting the *bene haelohim* as angels. From the above discussion, the more probable interpretation for *bene haelohim* during the 2TP is they were "angels."

Excursus: The Greek "Sons of the Gods"

The "sons of the gods" are well known in Greek mythology and many have argued that they are the figures that lie behind the *bene haelohim* and the giants of Genesis 6.1–4. Hesiod describes a generation of beings in *Works and Days* 110–125 that could easily be identified as the *bene haelohim* in Early Judaism.[97] They are said to have lived ὥστε θεοί (as gods) and after the earth had covered their generation, they lived upon the earth as "pure spirits" (δαίμονες) as guardians of men and kept watch on judgments.[98] This description is similar to the Watchers who, in the *Jubilees* tradition (4.15), were sent to earth by God to watch over humanity.[99] The third generation created by Zeus is similar to the

---

[95] Eslinger, "Contextual," 73, n. 1. Clines argues that the *bene haelohim* did commit the sin of polygamy, see Clines, "Sons of God," 36, but disagrees with Eslinger's theory that they are the line of Seth, ibid., 33.

[96] See Alexander, "Sons of God," 66. Alexander deals with the various arguments of the theory that the Sethites are the *bene haelohim*.

[97] Hugh Evelyn-White translates the term μερόπων ἀνθρώπων (*Works and Days* 110) as "mortal men."

[98] Interestingly, Zeus is addressed as a δαιμόνι in direct speech by Cottus during Zeus' plea to the 3 one-hundred handers to help him fight Kronos; see *Theogony* 654.

[99] See *Works and Days* 248–255 for a description of the "watchers" of the Greek mythology.

nephilim of Genesis 6.4.[100] They are described as having great physical strength and as mighty warriors upon the earth. The fourth generation created by Zeus fits a similar description of the *gibborim* of Genesis 6.4. This was a race of "hero men" known as demigods. This race appears to have fallen to the same fate as the giants in the *1 Enoch* tradition. They are destroyed by numerous wars, in particular by the Trojan War, which as will be seen below is a possible parallel to the Flood of Semitic traditions.

Hesiod's *The Catalogues of Women and Eoiae* II 2–50, which tells the story of Zeus' plan to destroy the mortals and demigods (the offspring of the gods and humans) by raising a storm and tempest over the earth, appears to parallel the Genesis 6 story of God's plan to bring the Flood to destroy not only humanity but the offspring of the *bene haelohim* and humanity. Zeus' reason for doing so was to stop the mating of the *sons of the gods* with the mortals and for this reason he "laid toil and sorrow upon sorrow" upon the offspring of the *sons of the gods*.[101] The similarity of the Hesiod material and the Genesis passage is striking. Hesiod has depicted the gods, their relations with humans, the resulting offspring, and Zeus' displeasure with it all (although he is guilty on multiple occasions of committing the same act). The result is very similar to the displeasure voiced by Yahweh in Genesis 6.3, 5 that appear to be a part of the reason for the Flood. One problem with the comparison of the Trojan War and the Flood is the destructive effects of the Trojan War upon humanity. It appears that this would not be a devastating enough event to bring Zeus the desired results.[102]

It is possible that within Genesis 6.1–4 there is a much closer parallel to the Titan myth than previously thought. It seems that the focus of the Genesis text is the violation of the earthly realm by beings from the heavenly realm; i.e. the *bene haelohim* with the daughters of men. The Titan myth contains the same type of violation (sexual) of the earthly realm (Γαία) by the heavenly realm (Οὐρανός).[103] Although this is quite metaphorical in nature, it is plausible that this tradition was behind the thinking of the author of Genesis 6, but he chose to humanize the

---

[100] This is providing that one accepts the equality between the *nephilim* and the *gibborim*.

[101] See Hendel, "Nephilim," 31–32. Hendel states that the Trojan War brings about the destruction, but as seen above there is perhaps an allusion to the Flood in the *Catalogue of Women*.

[102] R. Scodel, "The Achaean Wall and the Myth of Destruction," *HSCP* 86 (1982): 42–3. Scodel argues that the theme of the Trojan War probably has been borrowed from the Flood myth.

[103] This interpretation must contain the idea of a rebellion of humans in the Genesis passage against the heavens, which of course is a possible reading of verse 6.1.

language for his readers.[104] The results of both stories are the same, the birth of the giants. Hendel argues, and rightly so, that the Greek tradition, which can be seen in Hesiod's works, is perhaps a component of the greater circl&of oral traditions of which Genesis 6.1–4 was a part.[105]

Despite the close similarity between the Greek myths and the Semitic material, little evidence is offered particularly for a direct parallel to the *bene haelohim* of Genesis 6. The first problem is creating a genealogical link in the Hebrew text between the *bene haelohim* and Yahweh. There is no record of a creation of *bene haelohim* as in the Greek material.[106] Missing in the Greek myth is the person of Yahweh. In the Hebrew text, heaven and earth are created out of *chaos* (ובהו תהו) by Yahweh, while in the Greek text, Γαῖα just comes into being and Οὐρανός is born to Γαῖα.[107] There is, however, no clear evidence that identifies Γαῖα and Οὐρανός as gods in the *Theogony*, but rather the Greek pantheon of gods (the Titans, among others) were born out of Γαῖα and Οὐρανός.[108] If Γαῖα and Οὐρανός are not specifically called gods (although the Orphic poems offer a possible divine identification, see below) this would exclude the Titans (and others) from the category of "sons of God" because they were born not from the gods, but rather from Γαῖα and Οὐρανός.[109]

However, the sixth century B.C.E. Orphic poems can perhaps offer a solution as to how there was a change in the adaptation of Hesiod's *Theogony* in the later centuries before the Common Era.[110] The genealogy of the gods in the Orphic poems describes Οὐρανός as the "first king *of the gods*."[111] If this was the accepted understanding of the position of Οὐρανός in the genealogy of the gods in the fourth century B.C.E., it is then conceivable that the Titans could be seen as "sons of god." *Theogony* 118 implies that Γαῖα is a god with a reference to her as the foundation of the ἀθανάτων.[112] A second possible reference to her deity is found in

---

[104] It is also possible that the Greek story was drawing upon a Semitic myth, but the author (Hesiod) chose to mythologize the content for his readers.

[105] Hendel, "Nephilim," 32.

[106] See 2 Baruch 21.6; 4 Ezra 6.41; *Jubilees* 2.2; Sirach 16.26–28; and Ps 147.4.

[107] *Theogony* 116–128. In the *Protogonos* Theogony, *Ouranos* and *Ge* come from the same mother, Night. In Homer (*Iliad* 205–07), Oceanos and Tethys are also seen as primeval parents.

[108] *Theogony* 130–50. Also born from Γαῖα and the blood of Οὐρανός are the *Erinyes*, the Giants, Aphrodite, and the Nymphs. See also *Theogony* 919.

[109] See also reference in Pindar's *Pythian Odes XI*.

[110] M.L. West, *The Orphic Poems* (Oxford: Clarendon Press, 1983), 1.

[111] Plato (fourth c. B.C.E.) appears to quote the genealogy of the Orphic poet in *Cratylus* 402b.

[112] Hesiod, LCL, 86, n.3. This line of *Theogony* is thought to be spurious.

Theogony 120 which identifies Eros as the fairest of the deathless gods in a list of emerging entities that contains Γαῖα. It seems plausible to suggest a shifting role for Γαῖα and Οὐρανός which identified them as gods and perhaps allows one to draw parallels of the Titans as sons of god with the *bene haelohim* of 2TP Jewish literature.[113]

3.2.3 Verse 3

ויאמר יהוה לא־ידון רוחי באדם לעלם בשגם
הוא בשר והיו ימיו מאה ועשרים שנה

Genesis 6.3 is perhaps the most troublesome verse for interpreters of 6.1–4 due to two very problematic Hebrew terms, ידון and בשגם.[114] The second part of the verse, והיו ימיו מאה ועשרים שנה ("and its days shall be one hundred and twenty years"), has also caused considerable confusion as to its interpretation. This phrase raises some important questions that can sway the interpretation of humanity's role in the bringing of the Flood towards a negative or a neutral conclusion. Does this phrase mean that humanity will only live for 120 years from this point on? If so, how can we account for the age of those who live extended lives after the Flood? Is this the number of years until the coming of the Flood? Or is this the length of life allotted to the offspring of the *bene haelohim* and the daughters of men?

The Septuagint offers a few variants that are significant for the interpretation of the verse. Symmachus follows the rabbinic line with his reading of οὐ κρινεῖ (shall not judge, strive with)[115] for μὴ καταμείνῃ (shall not remain, dwell with), "and the Lord God said, 'my spirit shall not judge (or strive) in these men forever because they are flesh.'"[116] The most significant detail found in the LXX, which does not appear in the Hebrew Bible, is τούτοις in the phrase ἐν τοῖς ἀνθρώποις τούτοις,

---

[113] See Josephus *Ant.* I.73; *1 Enoch* 6–36; *Jubilees*; Philo *Gig.* 16; Bartelmus, *Heroentum*, 161; Pearson, "Resurrection and Judgment"; Hendel, "Of Demigods."

[114] Kraeling argues that verse 3 originally stood after verse 4 and subsequently eliminates the contextual problems presented in verse 3. Kraeling, "Significance," 197. According to Bartelmus, verse 3 is an intermezzo, but if this were the case then why would the redactor leave it so ambiguous?

[115] Cf. Targum *Onkelos, Neofiti, Pseudo–Jonathan*; b. Sanh. 108a; m. Sanh. 10.3.

[116] There is perhaps a parallel to the phrase "he too is flesh" found in the *Epic of Gilgamesh*. See Gilgamesh I.ii; I.11, 16, 21 in ANET 73b–74a. David Clines argues that both the "sons of God" (Clines is actually referring to the offspring of the *bene haelohim*) and Gilgamesh find their life expectancy significantly reduced because they are flesh (Clines, "Sons of God," 45, n.18). See also Loren T. Stuckenbruck, "Giant Mythology and Demonology: From the Ancient Near East to the Dead Sea Scrolls," in *Die Damonen Demons* (ed. Armin Lange, Hermann Lichtenberger, and K.F. Diethard Römheld Tübingen: Mohr Siebeck, 2003), 31–38.

"in these men." Several authors have commented that this addition is directed at the generation of the Flood from which God will remove his spirit. Others have argued that "these" men are the offspring of the *bene haelohim* and God will remove his spirit from them because of their mixed nature. Other translators and interpreters do not read τούτοις from the translation; these include Symmachus, the Ethiopic version, the Vulgate, Philo (*Gig.* 19), Ambrosius (*De mysteriis* 10; *De Noe* 7), and Hilarius (*Ps* 65.5).

Sarna argues that לֹא־יָדוֹן should be read in this case as "shall not abide," but he notes that the term which follows, בְּאָדָם, is making reference to the offspring of the union if "because he also is flesh' is included. The problem with this interpretation is that until this point in the passage there is no mention of offspring, which would then direct the judgment back on בְּאָדָם.[117] If τοῖς ἀνθρώποις τούτοις refers to the offspring, that would categorize the *gibborim* and the *nephilim* as human (if two groups, *gibborim* and *nephilim*, are to be identified). A more likely scenario is this phrase refers to the generation of the Flood. This would then indicate that 3b should be read as a period of 120 years until the death of this generation in the Flood.

The Targumim have augmented the biblical text of verse 3 more than verses 1–2 and 4. This perhaps is due to the difficulty that this verse presented to the readers and the interpreters of Genesis 6. The author of Targum *Onkelos* freely interprets the verb יָדוֹן due to the anthropomorphic nature of the phrase:[118] "and God said, 'This evil generation shall not exist before me forever because they are flesh and their deeds are evil, an extension of time shall be given[119] to them of one hundred and twenty years [Grossfeld adds "to see"] if they shall repent.'" Grossfeld argues that the addition "and their deeds are evil" is to explain what the problem is: the humans are flesh – because they are flesh, their deeds are evil.[120] The closing phrase of verse 3 in *Onkelos* is perhaps the more significant addition because it points the finger clearly at humanity

---

[117] Sarna, *Genesis*, 46. Kraeling also follows the idea that the אָדָם of verse 3 is a different group than that mentioned in verse 1. But it is highly unlikely that in such a short passage the author would have intended two different meanings for the same word.

[118] Grossfeld, *Onqelos Genesis*, 52, n.2.

[119] Biblia Hebraica, Constantinople has יְהַב יִּ, "I shall grant."

[120] Ibid., 52, n.3. The idea "'humans are flesh" is otherwise foreign to the Hebrew Bible and closer to "flesh" in the *DSS*.

as the problem in creation. Unless humanity repents, the Flood will come in 120 years.[121]

Clines suggests there is evidence for two possible interpretations of the 120 years. First, the duration may mean the prime length of life granted to humans[122] or, second, it indicates a reprieve for humanity prior to the Flood.[123] A parallel to the 120 years is found in the *Atrahasis* epic. In this Flood story, the 120 years is equated to 1200 years granted as a time of reprieve prior to the Flood. Westermann suggests that the restrictive nature of the judgment in 6.3 implies a similar attempt by humanity to prolong life that is found in Genesis 3.22.[124] However, no evidence of this type of attempt by humanity is suggested in Genesis 3. God pre-empts the possible attempt by humanity to regain eternal life (by expelling Adam and Eve from Eden) rather than putting a stop to it. Only in this pre-emptive action can a parallel be drawn between 3.22 and 6.3.

Targum *Pseudo-Jonathan* expands the text even more than *Onkelos*. Similar to *Onkelos*, the word יֵדוֹן plays a key part in the interpretation of the verse for the author of *Pseudo-Jonathan*. *Pseudo-Jonathan* renders the verb as "to judge" based upon the degree of punishment that God is about to bring upon the earth in the Flood narrative to follow. Again, as the author of *Onkelos* has done, the author of *Pseudo-Jonathan* has freely paraphrased the verse:

And the Lord said in his Memra, "None of the evil generations that are to arise [in the future], will be judged according to the order of judgment applied to the generation of the Flood, [that is] to be destroyed and wiped out from the world. Did I not put my holy spirit in them that they might perform good deeds? But behold their deeds are evil. Behold I gave them an extension of a hundred and twenty years that they might repent, but they have not done so."[125]

---

[121] This follows the traditional rabbinic interpretation of the verse. Grossfeld cites Mek. Mesekhta *De Shirata* V; Avot R. Nat. Vers. A, Chapter 32; and Tanḥ. A Noah V. Ibid., 53, n.4.

[122] See Gen 50.22; Josh 24.29; Deut 31.2 and 34.7. See also Herodotus 3.23 and 1.163.

[123] Clines, "Sons of God," 42.

[124] Westermann, *Genesis*, 374. Westermann also sees a parallel to the Prometheus myth in that the *bene haelohim* are attempting to raise the status of humans as was Prometheus. Kraeling notes that the 120 years represents three generations of offspring from the union of the sons of God and the women. It is possible that this is what is alluded to in *1 Enoch* 86.4 and 87.4, which describe the offspring of the union as "elephants, camels, and donkeys." Kraeling, "Significance," 200. See also J. Klein, "The Bane of Humanity: A lifespan of 120 Years" in *Acta Sumerologica* 12, (1990), 57–70; cited in Batto, *Slaying the Dragon*, 65. Klein argues there is a similar 120-year lifespan for humanity in a Sumerian text from Emar; see D. Arnaud, *Recherches au pays d'Astata, Emar* VI.1–4, 771.19–26.

[125] Maher, Targum Pseudo-Jonathan, 38.

The theme is similar to *Onkelos* in that, although Yahweh is presented as a merciful and compassionate God who gives humanity a chance to repent, this opportunity is rejected. The same mercy of God is seen again in Targum *Pseudo-Jonathan* of Genesis 7.4 in which God said that he would give humanity one more opportunity of seven days to repent prior to the Flood, but again it is rejected.[126] The author's primary concern is to safeguard the righteous character of God. Targum *Neofiti* is similar to the translation and thought of *Pseudo-Jonathan*, but has one important addition. The author indicates that God placed his spirit in the אנשא בני (sons of men); this removes any confusion about the subject of this verse and emphatically places the guilt (or alleged guilt) upon humanity. The authors of the three *targumim* are clear about the character of humanity in this situation – even with the spirit of God in them, humans can do only evil.

No confusion is evident amongst the targumic authors about the translation of the notoriously difficult בשגם. They have all incorporated it without notice in their paraphrases of the verse. Clines suggests that בשגם should be read "My spirit shall not abide in man forever because of the *clamour of flesh*." There is no example of ש in the Pentateuch as an abbreviation for אשר. This combined with the preposition ב makes the reading difficult. Clines argues that the root of this word is שגם (Assyrian), "to howl," combined with the preposition ב. This would perhaps suggest the possibility of an allusion to the *Atrahasis* myth and the "clamouring of humanity" that results in the Flood.[127]

Alternatively, Soggin proposes that the root may be שגה or possibly שגג, meaning "to be mistaken" or "to sin instinctively." He does note, however, that this is unlikely in the context of the verse.[128] Similarly, Marguerite Harl suggests the root of בשגם should be interpreted as "to err" – "in their erring ways they are flesh."[129] Westermann contends that, more probably, the cause of the Flood was an act of sin rather than a state of creation; thus, he rejects the interpretation of בשגם as "because" man is flesh.[130] It may be suggested that "because man is flesh," his actions continue to be sinful; therefore, God must withdraw his spirit from him. Thus, it is not necessarily an "act" that is problematic, as Westermann contends; rather the condition of humanity is the problem.

---

[126] Ibid., 38, n.9.

[127] Clines, "Sons of God," 40. See also Gruppe, "Genesis 6," 146; Gruppe suggests that the "erring" is that of the sons of God. See Kraeling, "Significance," 199; Kraeling argues, contra Gruppe, that the erring is related to the humans rather than the sons of God.

[128] Soggin, *Genesis*, 121.

[129] Harl, *La Bible*, 125–26.

[130] Westermann, *Genesis*, 376.

Drawing any conclusions from the above discussion of verse 3 is difficult. The various interpretations of the early Jewish literature show that there was no problem with the difficult בשגם; the best translations remains "because" or "in that also" humanity is flesh. There is little evidence that would suggest a different translation of לא־ידון than the generally agreed upon "my spirit *shall not remain* in humanity." The only significant alteration brought about through the translation of the passage is an interpretation of the 120–year period as one that suggests a time of opportunity for humanity to repent. However, there is still evidence for the view that the 120 years is describing the expected lifespan of humans following the Flood.[131]

3.2.4 Verse 4

הנפלים היו בארץ בימים ההם וגם אחרי־כן
אשר יבאו בני האלהים אל־בנות האדם
וילדו (ויולידו) להם המה הגברים אשר מעולם אנשי השם

Genesis 6.4 contains two terms that have resulted in various interpretations of the verse. While *nephilim* and the *gibborim* are both translated γιγάντες in the LXX, it is somewhat difficult to find a philological relationship between the two terms in the Hebrew Bible. The Greek translation of the Hebrew conjures up images of the Titan myth of Hesiod and Homer's *Odyssey* and *Iliad*.[132] Why the translators chose to

---

[131] See above n. 124.

[132] The phrase "men of renown" directs our attention to Hesiod's *Theogony*. Rightfully so, there have been many theories which have attempted to read *Theogony* as the background to the Watcher tradition in *1 Enoch*. There are several points that seem to develop a parallel between the two stories. The connection to the Watcher tradition can be suggested by the following points: 1) Kronos is a son of the gods – titan; 2) he rebels against Οὐρανός (god) his father; 3) the giants are born out of this rebellion (*Theogony* 186) – the giants are associated with heroic figures of distant past; and 4) the Titans are eventually bound in Tartarus (*Theogony* 718). The following points reduce the possible connection between the two stories: 1) Kronos married his sister and becomes the father of the Olympian gods; this would then require the giants of the Watcher tradition to be the Olympian gods (*Theogony* 453–506); 2) Kronos devours all of his children (*Theogony* 462); 3) Zeus, Kronos' son, battles his father; 4) we do not know what happened to the giants born of the blood of Ouranos; and 5) note that Greek[pan] of *1 Enoch* 9.9 identifies the offspring as titans; we cannot have the Watchers *and* their offspring identified as the titans. It is possible that some of the Greek myth material has filtered down into Jewish literature, but is it legitimate to argue in a Greek to Israelite direction only? Is it not just as likely that Hesiod was drawing on a Semitic tradition that we find remnants of in Gen 6–9? Cf. P. Walcot, *Hesiod and the Near East* (Cardiff: University of Wales, 1966), 6. Walcot argues that scholars have been too quick to point out Hesiod's debt to Near Eastern motifs.

translate the Hebrew terms הנפלים and הגברים with one term,
γίγαντες, raises several questions.[133] Did the translators not understand
properly the Hebrew of the text, but knew the tradition and thus used the
Greek terms which were analogous to the characters in the Hebrew
passage? Was γίγαντες some kind of technical term that carried a
specific function in the Hellenistic culture? It appears, by comparison
with other passages in the Hebrew Bible, that either γίγαντες carried a
broad range of meaning in the Hellenistic period or there were multiple
types of giants in the land prior to and during Israel's initial entry and
occupation of Canaan.

3.2.4.1 Nephilim

In an attempt to find a correlation between the terms (i.e. הנפלים,
הגברים and γίγαντες) and to clear some of the ambiguity in the
Genesis 6.1–4 passage, it is necessary to delineate their use elsewhere in
the biblical text (Hebrew Bible and LXX). The LXX translates
הנפלים on two occasions, Genesis 6.4[134] and Numbers 13.33,[135] as οἱ
γίγαντες. Precisely who the *nephilim* are is not clear in either of the
cited passages. Most scholars have identified the *nephilim* with the
gibborim on the basis that it is the antecedent of the pronoun המה. But
this is not necessarily the case; more probable is that the antecedent is the

---

[133] This single translation for the two Hebrew expressions has possibly influenced
the translator(s) of the Greek versions of the Aramaic *BW*. The ensuing Ethiopic
translation has also either accepted the single designation (giants) for the two beings or
has understood the *nephilim* to be something else besides the giants. The translator of
Greek[sync] has likewise accepted that the *nephilim* are one category of the giant offspring
of the Watchers and the women. The terms *nephilim* and *gibborim* appear to be
synonymous in the *Book of Giants* (4Q531 5.2), גברין] ונפיל] ין, although there is little
context in the fragment that will help one understand the author's intention. See also
4Q530 2.20–21 in which Milik, Stuckenbruck, García Martínez, and Beyer reconstruct
with ו[קרו ונפיל]יא גבריא following 4Q530. Cf. also 4Q530 2.5–6 which seems to
place the *nephilim* in the assembly of the *gibborim* although this reconstruction is less
certain. See Stuckenbruck, *Book of Giants*, 109–150. Eth. O.T. translates *nephilim* as
giants (yārbĕh).

[134] Translated in ASV, NASV, NIV, and RSV as *nephilim*. Aquila's literal
translation of the LXX follows the Hebrew with the reading οἱ ἐπιπίπτοντες – "the
fallen ones" (the ones falling), this could be taken as a reference to the Fallen Angels
but it is likely that Aquila was only following his typical literal style of translation.
There is also some manuscript support for this reading; see Wevers, *Genesis*, 109.
Symmachus reads οἱ βίαιοι with minor MS support; Theodotion reads οἱ δὲ γίγαντες
with minor MS support. See also Philo *Gig.* 58.

[135] There is an interesting omission in the LXX from the Hebrew of Numbers 13.33,
the mention of the sons of Anak. The Hebrew reads ראינו את־הנפלים בני ענק מן־
הנפלים, "we saw the Nephilim, the sons of Anak from the Nephilim." The sons of
Anak are also translated as γίγαντων in Deut 1.28.

understood subject of the verb ילד, the children born to the *bene haelohim* and the daughters of men.[136] It seems that the *nephilim* were on the earth at the time when the *bene haelohim* came to the daughters of men.[137] The phrase וגם אחרי־כן appears to be a gloss added to allow for the reference to the *nephilim* in Numbers 13.33.[138] By removing the gloss, there is a clear dissimilarity between the *nephilim* and the *gibborim*. By doing so, the *nephilim* no longer stand in the role of the offspring of the union: "The nephilim were on the earth in those days when the sons of God came into the daughters of men, and they bore children to them. They were the mighty men who were of old, men of renown."

If one interprets Genesis 6.1–4 as a chronological description of the events, then the *nephilim* were already on the earth during the time when the *bene haelohim* came down to the earth and took the daughters of men to themselves as well as after the גברים were born to the *bene haelohim*. Clines argues that the *bene haelohim* are represented in the Genesis 6 passage as a generation which existed prior to the *nephilim*, but that is not obvious from the text. "The nephilim were on the earth in those days" does not suggest that this was their first appearance on the earth, but simply states that they were there when the sons of God came to the daughters of men.[139] Therefore, the *nephilim* resided upon the earth prior to these events.

The only other cognate of *nephilim* in the Hebrew Bible is a verb or participle from the root נפל.[140] The LXX translates these Hebrew references with a form of the verbs πίπτω (fall), παρεμβάλλω (set up for battle) or ἐμπίπτω (desert), primarily referring to those who have fallen in war. One instance it is used in conjunction with גברים (Ezek

---

[136] It may be suggested that the antecedent of המה is *nephilim*. This would then identify the *nephilim* as the heroic figures "the mighty men who were of old, men of renown," thus removing the "positive" image from the offspring of the sons of God and the women.

[137] Julian Morgenstern suggests that the verb יבאו expresses the idea of frequency of visits. If this were the case, then this would suggest the relationship of marriage being less likely. Morgenstern, "Psalm 82," 85, n.97. See also Clines, "Sons of God," 35; Clines proposes that the LXX translation also suggests the same, ὡς ἄν εἰσεπορεύοντο. See also Hertz, *Haftorah*, 49. Hertz argues that the *nephilim* were giants who existed prior to the union of the *bene haelohim* and the women.

[138] The *nephilim* of Num 13.33 are the people whom the men saw when they were sent to spy out the land of Canaan while Israel was in the wilderness. These beings described as γίγαντες in LXX present the reader with the problem of how giants survived the Flood, in contrast to the Watcher tradition that conveys that all the giants were physically killed.

[139] Clines, "Sons of God," 35.

[140] See cf. Deut 22.4; Josh 8.25; Judg 7.12; 8.10; 20.46; 1 Sam 31.8; 2 Kgs 25.11; Jer 6.15; 8.12; 39.9; 52.15; Ezek 32.22, 23, 24, 27; Ps 145.14; 1 Chr 10.8; 2 Chr 20.24

32.27), which is translated as γίγαντων (the mighty ones of the uncircumcised). A second instance is found in Psalm (MT) 58.9, which reads נֵפֶל (*nephel*), "like the *miscarriages* of a woman which never see the sun." Although it may be appropriate in another context (e.g. Job 3.16), this clearly does not fit the context of Genesis 6.1–4.[141]

So, the problem remains concerning the identity of the *nephilim* in Genesis 6.4, particularly if they existed prior to the union of the sons of God and the daughters of men. The Genesis passage does not represent the *nephilim*, or, for that matter, the offspring of the בני האלהים and the women, in a negative light. On the contrary, the offspring of the sons of God in Genesis 6 are considered "mighty men of old" and "men of renown." This language in no way reflects the clearly negative portrait of the offspring presented in the Watcher tradition.[142]

The *targumim* offer little about the identity of the *nephilim* in their interpretation of Genesis 6.4. Grossfeld translates Targum *Onkelos'* interpretation גיבריא as the "mighty ones."[143] This Targum interpretation lacks any elaboration upon the verse, which may indicate that none was required by the author. Targum *Neofiti's* rendition of *nephilim* follows that of *Onkelos* – גיבריה. McNamara chose to translate *Neofiti's* גיבריה with giants and notes that *Nfmg* translates *bene haelohim* of 6.4 as בניהון דמלאכיא, "sons of angels." Targum *Pseudo-Jonathan* interprets the Genesis 6.4 passage with significant changes, which indicate a strong negative interpretation of the text. The *nephilim* are identified as the angels שמחזאי ועזאל הינון נפלן מן שמיא, "Shemihazai and Azael, the ones who fell from heaven." This is a clear reference to the Watcher tradition of *1 Enoch, Jubilees*, and other early Jewish literature and offers a significantly different interpretation from the other *targumim*. Maher notes that two other rabbinic sources (*b. Yoma* 67b and PRE 22) interpret the *nephilim* as "angels who fell."[144] A similar interpretation may be found in 1QapGen ar ii 1. The *nephilim* are listed synonymously with the

---

[141] See also the interpretation of נפלים in the Manichean "Book of Giants" on Gen 6.4 as "abortions"; cf. also *Bereshith Rabbah* 26.7.

[142] See *LAE* 13.1–16.1 and *1 Enoch* 86. Morgenstern argues that the *nephilim* are Satan and his followers who were cast down from heaven because of their rebellion following the creation of humanity. God commanded Satan to give honour to Adam, but Satan refused to honour him and he was exiled from heaven, Morgenstern, "Psalm 82," 95–106.

[143] Grossfeld, *Onqelos Genesis*, 52. Note that *Onkelos* also translates *nephilim* as גיבריא in Numbers 13.33. It should be noted that the noun is in the emphatic state.

[144] Maher, *Targum Pseudo-Jonathan*, 38. See also *Midrash Rabbah*, 217 for various rabbinic opinions concerning the *nephilim*, which all have a negative connotation to them.

Watchers and the Holy Ones (i.e. the angels) in a story that seems to be connected to *1 Enoch* 106 and the story of the birth of Noah.

3.2.4.2 Gibborim

We will consider one final character that had a role in the Genesis Flood narrative, the *gibborim*.[145] The closing section of verse 4[146] contains the troublesome גבר׳ם, which is translated in the LXX as γίγαντες.[147] There are forty-one occasions in the LXX where גבר׳ם is translated into Greek as γίγας: γίγαντων (16 times),[148] γίγαντες (10), γίγαντας (3), and γίγαντος (1) γίγαντα (4) γίγας (7). There are four Hebrew terms which are translated in this manner: גבר(׳ם) (41), נפל׳ם (2), רפא(׳ם) (12), and בנ׳ ענק(׳ם) (1).[149] The term "giants" appears an additional seven times in the Apocrypha; four of them in reference to the giants of the Flood[150] and one reference in Judith 16.6 which is unclear in

---

[145] It should be noted that the work of *Pseudo-Philo*, perhaps a late first c. B.C.E. or early first c. C.E. text, which is similar in its style to *Jubilees*, has also retained the Hebrew description of "sons of God" from Gen 6.2 rather than adopting the interpretation of "angels of God" followed by Philo of Alexandria and Josephus. This text could provide a possible link to the rabbinic interpretation that the "sons of God" were mere mortals of important status in Israel. The author of *Pseudo-Philo* implies that the Gen 6.1–4 passage is dealing with strictly human characters. See Harrington, *Pseudo-Philo*, 306. See also 1QS[a] col. II 2, which identifies "men of the Congregation" as אנשת שם. See also Baruch 3.26. This text states that the giants were those "famous of old, great in stature, expert in war," but they perished because they had no knowledge and perished in their folly.

[146] ויולדו להם המה הגברים אשר מעולם אנשי השם – "And there were born to them the *gibborim* who were from the ancient days, men of renown."

[147] One manuscript (73*) omits οἱ γίγαντες and a second omission of οἱ ἄνθρωποι is noted in MSS 707 and 53. Aquila translates γίγαντες with δυνατοί (also ms 135 Syh). Symmachus translates with βίαιοι (also mss 135; 57–73; 413, 550, 130, 344, Syh). Staffan Olofsson presents a detailed discussion of why the LXX translators chose particular words in their interpretation of the Hebrew Bible. He suggests several points that shaped their translation: (1) They rendered theological terms with precision; (2) they often made implied ideas of the Hebrew explicit in the Greek; (3) they did not apply only to the immediate context, but often drew on ideas remote from the passage, e.g. the Psalms; (4) they employed favourite Greek words for multiple Hebrew words of similar meaning; and 5) it is possible that at times the translator had to guess at the meaning of a Hebrew word. See Staffan Olofsson, *Translation Technique*.

[148] Two occurrences of γίγαντων that have no equivalent in the Hebrew, 2 Sam 21.11 and 1 Chr 14.13.

[149] However, no correlation exists between the Greek terms used to translate the Hebrew. The term giant occurs only five times in the Pentateuch; Gen 6.4 (2 times), 14.5; Numbers 13.33; Deuteronomy 1.28.

[150] See 3 Macc 2.4; Bar 3.26; Sir 16.7; and Wis 14.6.

meaning.[151] In addition to the above-mentioned instances of *rephaim*, thirteen others should be noted. There are seven occurrences in which *rephaim* is simply transliterated ραφαϊν; all of the occurrences refer to the "valley of the Rephaim."[152] The same phrase is also translated in 2 Samuel 5.18, 22 as τίτανων ("of the titans"). On three occasions, Psalm (MT) 88.11 (87.10), Isaiah 26.14, and 2 Chronicles 16.12, *rephaim* is translated as ἰατροί, physicians.[153] There are also four occurrences in which *rephaim* is translated as γίγαντων in the LXX (cf. "spirits of the dead" in NASV). A final occurrence, which does not follow the preceding pattern of meanings of the Hebrew term, is found in Isaiah 26.19 in which *rephaim* is translated as ἀσεβων, the ungodly. The presence of these multiple references following the Flood narrative creates difficulty within the Watcher tradition and the survival of giants following the Flood.[154] However, there are several texts that attempt to explain the survival of the giants following the Flood that will be discussed below.[155]

The term גבור (or other forms) occurs 148 times in the Hebrew Bible. The term is used seven times in direct reference to the God of Israel being mighty.[156] In Jeremiah 26.21, גבור refers to the judges of Israel. The remaining occurrences in the biblical text refer to the *gibborim* as "men of war" or a similar phrase. Kraeling suggests that the *gibborim* were familiar characters in the history of Israel beginning in the court of David, therefore, establishing them as "mighty men." However, he argues that the term מעולם suggests that these beings were from a "previous world age."[157] Kraeling contends evidence for this is found in Ezekiel 32, which describes those who lie in Sheol as the "fallen" of an early age.[158] He also suggests that these "warriors" are described in Ezekiel 26.19 as עם עולם upon whom God brought the primeval deep, perhaps an allusion to the

---

[151] The passage refers to the "sons of the Titans" and "towering giants" who were unable to slay Ολοφέρνης, the captain of the army of Nebuchadnezzar.

[152] See 2 Sam 23.13; Deut 3.11, 13; Josh 15.8; 18.16 (reads Εμεκραφαϊν); and Gen 15.20.

[153] See also Gen 50.2 in which *rephaim* is translated as ἐνταφιασταὶ(αῖς) (2) and is read in the English as physicians.

[154] *1 Enoch* 10.2; *Jubilees* 5.

[155] *Book of Giants*; *Epic of Gilgamesh*; *Pseudo-Eupolemus* frag. 2, Eusebius, *Praeparatio Evangelica* 9.18.2 in Carl R. Holladay, *Fragments from Hellenistic Jewish Authors* (Chico, CA.: Scholars Press, 1983), 177. See Stuckenbruck, "Giant Mythology"; John C. Reeves, "Utnapishtim in the Book of Giants," *JBL* 112 (1993): 110–15; and Ronald V. Huggins, "Noah and the Giants: A Response to John C. Reeves," *JBL* 114 (1995): 103–10.

[156] See Isa 10.21; 42.13; Jer 32.18; Zeph 3.17; Ps 45.3; Neh 9.32; and Deut 10.17.

[157] Eth. O.T. describes them as "who were from the creation of the world" ('ĕla 'ĕmfĕthrata 'ālam).

[158] Hendel argues that the *nephilim* are the beings that are discussed in Ezek 32.27.

Flood. Drawing on Ezekiel 26.19, Kraeling identifies the הגברים אשר
מעולם אנשי השם as the race of warriors who lived prior to the Flood.[159]
He suggests that evidence of their existence is found in Genesis 6.11,
"And the earth was corrupt in the sight of God, and the earth was filled
with violence."[160] This would suggest that these beings were the subject of
God's remorse in Genesis 6.5–6 and would therefore identify them as
human. Their identity as offspring of *bene haelohim* does not seem to
allow this if the consensus opinion that the *bene haelohim* are heavenly
beings is accepted.[161]

The בני ענקים is perhaps the most intriguing designation. It refers to
the "giants" of the Hebrew Bible. The term occurs only six times, four of
which are transliterated into Greek, while the others are translated by two
forms of γίγας (Deut 1.28 – γίγαντων and Num 13.33 – γίγαντας).
These people are described as individuals of great stature who were in the
land of Canaan prior to the people of Israel coming out of the wilderness.
As mentioned above, the "sons of Anak" are described as "giants" in
Deuteronomy 1.28. Two other references in Deuteronomy, 2.10–11 and
2.20–21, make note of the Anakim alongside other peoples who are
described as being gigantic in stature. Deuteronomy 2.10–11 states, "The
Emim lived there [Ar] formerly, a people as great, numerous, and tall as
the Anakim. Like the Anakim, they are also regarded as Rephaim, but the
Moabites call them Emim."[162] It should be noted that neither Rephaim nor
Anakim are translated in the Greek (LXX) or English versions of
Deuteronomy 2.10–11 as giants despite the occurrences in other passages
(Deut 1.28 and Num 13.33). The second passage in Deuteronomy, 2.20–
21, states:

It is also regarded as the land of the Rephaim, for Rephaim formerly lived in it, but the
Ammonites call them Zamzummin, a people as great, numerous, and tall as the Anakim,
but the Lord destroyed them before them [the Ammonites]. And they [the Ammonites]
dispossessed them and settled in their place.[163]

---

[159] Kraeling, "Significance," 196.

[160] Aquila's usual literal translation may help define the *gibborim*. He translates
gibborim with the Greek δυνατοί, the powerful ones, which could be synonymous with
the idea of men of war.

[161] Although it is possible that these beings could appear physically to be human,
their spiritual make-up would probably be distinct from humanity.

[162] The name *Emim* is found in Job 20.25. The LXX renders it φόβοι while the
NASV translates it "terrors." This perhaps has some relation to their reputation amongst
the nations. One other reference to *Emim* is found in Jer 50.38. In this passage, it refers
to the fearful idols in the land of Babylon. See also the discussion of the origin of these
names in *Bereshith Rabbah* 26.7 in *Midrash Rabbah*, 217–18.

[163] Brackets are mine.

Zamzummin (babblers in Aramaic)[164] is also referred to in Genesis 14.5 along with Emim and Rephaim as the three nations defeated by Chedorlaomer.[165]

Numbers 13.33 perhaps provides the closest parallel to the giants of the Watcher tradition after the Flood.[166] The Israelite spies describe the inhabitants of the land of Canaan as the *nephilim*, the sons of Anak.[167] The LXX of Numbers 13.33 translates the *nephilim* as γίγαντας, the same translation found in Genesis 6.4. This is our only indication in the biblical text as to the origin of the sons of Anak. The connection is a very thin thread but one may consider that a descendent of the giants of the Watcher tradition somehow survived the Flood and lived in the land of Canaan.[168] Loren Stuckenbruck argues that the biblical text could be manipulated in a manner that suggests these giants could have survived the Flood.[169] However, their continued existence was accomplished in a manner not divulged in the narrative. Their survival is perhaps made possible in Genesis 10.8–12 by the relationship of Nimrod to Noah.[170] This connection is also made in Pseudo-Eupolemus in Eusebius' *Praeparatio Evangelica* 9.17.2–9 where he states, "the Assyrian city of Babylon was first founded by those who escaped the Flood. They were giants, and they built the tower well known in history."[171] If this is not a possibility, how then can we account for the existence of the *nephilim* on

---

[164] See *BDB*, p. 273b.

[165] This passage is attested to in 1QapGen ar XXI lines 28–29.

[166] Another biblical reference to giants is found in 1 Chr 21.1. It is possible there is an allusion in this passage to the Watcher tradition found in *Jubilees* 10.8. The passage reads וַיַּעֲמֹד שָׂטָן עַל־יִשְׂרָאֵל. What is interesting about this verse is that it follows immediately after the story of the defeat of the descendents of the Rephaim (giants, LXX) in chapter 20.4–8. Satan leads David to sin by conducting a census of Israel that was an abomination to the Lord. For this sin, David must face an angel of destruction who is controlled by God. He then uses a man, Gad his seer, to intercede to the Lord for him (21.13). It is interesting to note the multiple references (21.15, 16, 18, 20, 27, 30) to angelic beings in chapter 21, which may support the contention that there is an allusion (or echo) in 21.1 to the Watcher tradition and in particular to *Jubilees* and the tradition of Mastema.

[167] This is possibly a gloss by which the editor was trying to equate the *nephilim* of v. 33 to the Anakim in 13.28. See West, *East Face*, 117, n.65.

[168] See *b. Niddah* 61a and Tg. *Pseudo–Jonathan* to Deut 2.2 and 3.11; Tg. *Onqelos* to Deut 2.10–11. Many scholars insist that the giants of Gen 6.4 are the people involved in the building of the Tower of Babel. This of course presupposes the survival of the giants following the Flood.

[169] Stuckenbruck, "Origins."

[170] Gen 10.6–8. This possibility necessitates that Noah be a giant. See *1 Enoch* 106; Philo *Gig.* 63–66 and Josephus *Ant.* I.114.

[171] See also the possibility of Abraham tracing his lineage to the giants in *Praeparatio Evangelica* 9.18.2.

the earth prior to the Watchers' descent to the earth, or for the existence of giants after the Flood?

The Targumim have little to offer in their interpretation of גברים. All three translate the term with a similar Aramaic form, גיבריא in Onkelos and גברין in Neofiti and Pseudo-Jonathan. The secondary description of the offspring varies slightly between the three Targum; Onkelos reads גיבריא דמיעלמא אנשין דשמא, "mighty ones[172] of old, men of name"; Neofiti reads גיבריא די מן שרוי עלמא גיברין מפרשין בשמהן, "mighty ones[173] that were from the beginning of the world, mighty ones of distinguished names"; Nfmg reads גיבריא דאית מן יומת עלמא גיברין מפרשין בשמהן, "mighty ones[174] that were from the day of the world, mighty ones of distinguished names";[175] Pseudo-Jonathan reads והינון מתקריין גיברין דמעלמא אינשי שמהן, "and they were called mighty ones[176] of old, men of name."

It has been proposed that the gibborim are the Greek "heroes." If this view is accepted then it is necessary to question why the translators did not choose to use the Greek term ἥρωες for heroes rather than γίγαντες. In the Hesiod tradition, the ἥρωες were the fourth age of men who fought and fell at Thebes and Troy. The later Pindar tradition (fifth c. B.C.E.) described them as a race of beings called demigods (ἡμίθεοι) who were born of one divine parent (e.g. Herakles).[177] M. L. West suggests this is also found in the Israelite tradition, Judges 3.31 and 5.6. He argues that Shamgar, who is deemed a hero of Israel, is the semi-divine son of the Canaanite goddess Anath.[178] In the later period, the ἥρωες were considered inferior local deities under whose name a city or region was founded and would be worshipped. This is perhaps the connection to the "men of renown" in Genesis 6.4. But, again, if this is the case, why did the translators not use the term ἥρωες rather than γίγαντες? If however, verse 4 is understood in the context of the Enochic material (i.e. if the translators of LXX know the Enochic tradition), an unambiguous connection can be made to the γίγας of the Hesiod tradition that were born from a union of heaven and earth and presumably destroyed for their

---

[172] Grossfeld translates "mighty ones."

[173] McNamara translates "giants" in both cases.

[174] McNamara translates "warriors."

[175] See McNamara, Targum Neofiti, 72. This translation perhaps indicates these beings existed from the day of creation.

[176] Maher translates "heroes."

[177] West, East Face, 117. See also the Babylonian tradition which describes, in the case of Gilgamesh, a make-up of two thirds divine and one third human; Gilgamesh I ii 1, IX ii 16.

[178] Ibid., 117, n.67 and Attridge, Philo Byblos, 83, n.57.

rebellion. The death of the giants of the Hesiod myth is reflected by the infighting of the giants and the Flood in the Enoch tradition.

The giants are the dominant figures of the Greek tradition of Genesis 6.4, but they are portrayed in a relatively neutral light in the passage. However, this term brings to mind many parallels from the Greek myths. Some of these myths reflect a negative portrayal of these characters and perhaps have interacted with the Israelite traditions and helped to create the negative portrayal found in the *1 Enoch* tradition of Genesis 6.1–4. It also appears that the LXX tradition has directed other interpreters to equate the *gibborim* and the *nephilim*, but as has been demonstrated, it is possible that these are two distinct groups of beings. It may be more plausible to suggest that the *nephilim* are more closely related to the *bene haelohim* in class of being (i.e. a type of angel), but still a distinct group. Other early Jewish sources have also portrayed the *nephilim* and the *gibborim* in a relatively neutral sense.[179] The *targumim*, in particular, have

---

[179] The exception to this, of course, is the Enochic material. This tradition, along with Pseudo-Philo, fails to mention the *nephilim*. With this important character missing from these narratives, it is perhaps possible to question whether the entire verse 4a is a gloss of the author or editor of Gen 6.1–4. This would presuppose that the Enoch tradition predates the extant Gen 6.1–4 text, which of course is impossible to prove with the extant sources. A possible interpretation for the *nephilim* is found in *1 Enoch* 7.2 and *Jubilees* 7.21–22. It should be noted there is a Greek recension of *1 Enoch* 7.2 (see Greek[sync] 7.1–2) that identifies the *nephilim* as one of three different offspring from the union of the Watchers and the women. This is unattested in the Aramaic fragments and Milik's reconstruction does not include this variant. The texts of Greek[pan] and the Ethiopic have shorter versions that do not include the names of the three offspring, but refer to only the "great giants." The much longer Greek[sync] version of 7.1c–2 identifies three types of giants – "and there were born to them three offspring; the first were great giants and the giants gave birth to *Napheleim*, and the *Napheleim* gave birth to the *Elioud*." A similar description to these beings is found in *Jubilees* 7.22 – "And they begat sons the *Nâphîdîm*, and they were all unlike [Charles argues the text is corrupt here], and they devoured one another; and the giants slew the *Nâphîl*, and the *Nâphîl* slew the *Eljô*, and the *Eljô* [hu]mankind, and one man another," see Charles, *Book of Jubilees*, 68. Milik suggests that Syncellus or his predecessors, Annianus and Panodorus, perhaps adopted the motif of three offspring from *Jubilees* 7.22 or the *Book of Giants*; see Milik, *Books of Enoch*, 240. This pattern could have originated very easily within Gen 6.4. However, the text of *Jubilees* 7.22 describes the creatures as three types of one category, which does not appear to be the case in Gen 6.4. The Syncellus text follows a similar pattern; all three of the creatures are giants. A close parallel can be found with the offspring in Gen 6.4 and those listed in Greek[sync] – ναφηλειμ = נפל ים; γίγαντες = גבריא ;'Eλιουδ = (להם) ו ילדו (see discussion in Black, *Book of Enoch*, 126). *Animal Apocalypse* is also thought to be describing three categories of offspring in *1 Enoch* 86.4 – "And they all became pregnant and bore elephants and camels and asses" and also 88.2 – "And one of them drew his sword and gave it to those elephants and camels and asses, and they began to strike one another." The first of these two verses, 86.4, appears to parallel the subdued Greek[sync] 7.1–2

been especially passive in their interpretation of verse 4, which perhaps demonstrates the difficulty that these authors were having with the text in relation to their individual doctrine of angels.

3.3 Conclusion

The discussion of the interpretation of Genesis 6.1–4 has revealed a relatively neutral, or in some cases, a negative role of the characters presented in the passage in early Jewish literature. There is no convincing evidence in the biblical text itself that the actions of the *bene haelohim* are inappropriate; nor can we find any evidence in the Flood narrative that follows that they are punished. One might observe in verse 3 a negative report on the actions of humanity, but we have determined this is not necessarily the case. The passage as it stands is open to various interpretations because of its ambiguity. As a result, several interpretations of the passage can be proposed if one reads it alongside the myths that are perhaps alluded to within the narrative. By finding echoes of the Greek, Near Eastern, and Israelite myths in the story, one is in a better position to read the passage in a negative light. This type of reading allows for the characters of the narrative to be seen as destructive, thus allowing for the interpretation found in *1 Enoch* to be more plausible.

---

version, while *Jubilees* seems to have incorporated the violent nature of these creatures at their initial introduction. The support of *Animal Apocalypse* and *Jubilees* give credibility to the longer Syncellus recension, thus introducing the possibility of more than one Aramaic recension that is non-extant from Qumran. Cf. also 4Q203 8.7–8, Stuckenbruck reconstructs line 8 as "those [giants and their] son[s. . .]," suggesting the giants had offspring, see Stuckenbruck, *Book of Giants*, 87–90. If one allows for the reading of the Greek[sync] 7.2 text, then a place must be made for the fornication of the giants with women. If this is not the case, then it must be understood to mean that male and female giants existed that procreated and produced offspring. This raises some interesting anthropological questions about the dissemination of this line of being in creation. Are the giants described in the Hebrew Bible the offspring of these relationships? And if so how did they manage to survive the flood? If this is not the case, then where do these giants of the biblical text come from? Moreover, there is no evidence in the 4QEn fragments, or in the Ethiopic witnesses, which would support this reading. However, there is a reference in *Jubilees* 7.21–22, which follows a line similar to that of *1 Enoch* 86.4. Three similar categories of offspring that were born to the Watchers are described in this passage, *Naphidim, Naphil,* and the *Elyo*. It is also a possibility, as Westermann has suggested, that the *nephilim* of Gen 6.4a and those mentioned in Num 13.33 are not necessarily related, i.e. they are not the same beings; see Westermann, *Genesis*, 378. It is possible that the later designation of *nephilim* was used only to describe an exceptionally tall race of people, as were known from the Gen 6 narrative.

The exegesis of Genesis 6.1–4 by the authors of the *targumim* perhaps represents a potential understanding of the Hebrew text in the 2TP. Targum *Pseudo-Jonathan*, in particular, offers an unambiguous interpretation of the *nephilim* in its translation that correlates them to the Watchers found in *1 Enoch* and *Jubilees*, and therefore allows for an interpretation of the passage in a negative context. Josephus follows a similar interpretation in *Antiquities* I.72 in which he appears to understand the passage to contain a negative view both of humanity and of the sons of God because of their consorting with women.

Such writings as the *Atrahasis* myth, the *Epic of Gilgamesh*, and the story of the Trojan War may have played a role in an earlier and possibly much larger oral (or written) tradition of the story of the sons of God and their relationship with humans. If such background is accepted, then it is plausible to recognize that the author of Genesis 6.1–4, by his choice of vocabulary, was alluding to these various myths within the text and was indeed presenting an introduction to the Flood narrative that could relate a negative role for the characters involved.

Each verse of Genesis 6.1–4 contains difficult terms that contribute to the openness of the passage to various interpretations. Problematic in verse 1 is the Hebrew term הַחֵל. This word has been primarily translated as "began" as in "it came about when humanity began to multiply," but there are instances in other literature that allow the possibility for it to be translated as "polluted" or "rebellious" as in the "polluted or rebellious part" of humanity.[180] This particular interpretation would allow for the beginning of a negative reading of the text.[181] The multiplication of humanity in the *Atrahasis* myth may also have resulted in a negative interpretation of the passage.

Verse 2 contains the most problematic of the expressions. The phrase בְּנֵי הָאֱלֹהִים has been translated primarily as sons of God (lit. the gods). Identifying the *bene haelohim* in the story is a key to finding a plausible interpretation of Genesis 6.1–4. We have learned that the primary understanding of the term *bene haelohim* during the third century B.C.E. through the early first century C.E. (and perhaps beyond) was that they were angels. This view is re-enforced by the LXX, *1 Enoch*, *Jubilees*, Daniel, Philo of Alexandria, Josephus, Targum *Pseudo-Jonathan*, Targum *Nfmg*, and Eusebius. Two other interpretations have also been expressed

---

[180] See e.g. *Ber.* 1 c; *Exod Rab.* S. 43 – in reference "to break a vow" or "to profane"; *Deut Rab.* S. 2 – to profane; *Avot* 3.11 – those who profane sacred things; and Targum *Onkelos* on Leviticus 21.7 – to profane. The majority of use in the biblical text is in relation to being polluted or defiled.

[181] This reading possibly contributed to the interpretation of the "sons of Seth" and the "sons of Cain" in the beginning of the Common Era.

in the early rabbinic and Christian writings; the *bene haelohim* were understood as minor deities or god-like men (sons of nobles or judges). It is apparent in the posturing of later traditions that this term created great difficulty for the authors of post-biblical Judaism. Thus, one finds it difficult to categorize this verse as contributing to a negative or positive interpretation of the passage unless one considers some kind of rebellion by the *bene haelohim*.

Verse 3 gives the best possible opportunity to interpret the passage as having a negative role in the Flood narrative. However, the positioning of the verse between verses 1–2 and 4 gives the impression that it was done by a later redactor, as if to say to the reader: "Perhaps you do not know this story, but this is why the Flood occurred." The terms לֹא־יָדוֹן and בְּשַׁגַּם have created the greatest difficulties to translate or interpret the verse for early Jewish authors and they continue to produce the same difficulties for scholars today. The statement by God in verse 3, "My spirit shall not remain in humanity forever," is perhaps the only indication in the passage that the author was alluding to some kind of negative depiction of the events. The apparent conflict between the "spirit of God" and "beings of flesh," give the strongest indication that the author was using Genesis 6.1–4 as an introduction to the Flood narrative that follows. Humanity and its fleshly nature have created problems in the cosmos and God must deal with them. The result is either a 120-year period in which humans can repent, or a decrease in the lifespan of humanity.

Verse 4 has its own particularly complex contextual and linguistic difficulties. Beginning with הַנְּפִלִים הָיוּ בָאָרֶץ and continuing to the mentioning of הַגִּבֹּרִים אֲשֶׁר מֵעוֹלָם אַנְשֵׁי הַשֵּׁם, this verse presents the greatest opportunity for openness to interpretation. Adding to this difficulty is the interpretation of the verse by the translators of the LXX. The Greek translation creates the possibility of interpreting the passage in light of Greek literature such as Hesiod and Homer. From this literature, one can draw on all categories of interpretation for the roles of the characters, negative, positive, and neutral. By way of the rebellious "sons of the gods" in Hesiod, one can interpret the verse negatively. The Hebrew translation, "the *gibborim* who are from old, men of name" reminds one of the Greek heroes, which would most often depict a positive character. However, alongside the Greek literature, the LXX translator's use of the term γίγαντες for the Hebrew *nephilim* and *gibborim* reveals the passage's closest connection to the Watcher tradition in early Jewish literature. Within this tradition, the passage no doubt takes on a negative interpretation.

What, if anything, can be drawn from the textual study of the problematic Greek and Hebrew terms found in the passage and their use in other biblical texts is difficult to deduce. We have discovered that the *bene haelohim* of Genesis 6, although at times cloaked in different terminology, are found in other biblical passages, in particular the Psalms and Prophets. These texts have helped to identify the role of the *bene haelohim* in post-exilic Israel (assuming the Psalms are post-exilic) as angels or minor deities. It may be suggested that the Greek translators of the Hebrew Bible had difficulty in understanding some of the Hebrew terminology (e.g. *nephilim* and *gibborim*) and therefore translated the terms imprecisely, thus enhancing the ambiguity of the passage. Another possibility is that modern scholars have misunderstood what the Greek translators meant by their use of the term γίγαντες. It appears that more work needs to be done in order to discover the use of this term in the Greek literature prior to the translation of the LXX.[182]

Through this discussion of the biblical tradition of Genesis 6.1–4, we can offer a possible translation(s) of the passage based upon various early Israelite, Near Eastern and Hellenistic traditions that may have influenced early Jewish authors.

3.3.1 Verse 6.1

ויהי כי־החל האדם לרב על־פני האדמה ובנות ילדו להם

And it came about that humanity began to multiply upon the face of the earth and daughters were born to them.

The textual evidence is strongest for this reading, which is supported in the LXX, Philo of Alexandria, and *Pseudo-Philo*. The problematic החל does provide other possibilities that are testified to in later Jewish and Christian writings. *Midrash Rabbah* interprets the word as rebelled which would result in the following reading, *"And it came about that the rebellious part of humanity multiplied upon the face of the earth."* Another possibility of interpretation is found in other biblical passages (see above) that translate the verb as profaned or polluted. This would support the following reading, *"And it came about that the polluted part of humanity multiplied upon the face of the earth"* (see also *Sib. Or.* 1.75–80). Either of these two readings would give credence to the idea of humanity being divided into two distinct camps, the righteous, and the ungodly. The *Atrahasis* myth could have played a role in the author's mentioning of the multiplication of humanity. If this is considered, then one can read this verse from a negative perspective.

---

[182] Perhaps through this study more can be learned of the relationship of the *nephilim* in Gen 6.4 and Num 13.33.

3.3.2 Verse 6.2

ויראו בני־האלהים את־בנות האדם כי טבת הנה
ויקחו להם נשים מכל אשר בחרו

And the angels saw that the daughters of humanity were good to behold, and they took for themselves women from whomever they chose.

The interpretation of בני האלהים as angels is widely supported in the LXX, Philo, and Josephus. There is support in Hesiod and some Near Eastern (e.g. *Atrahasis* myth) for a reading of minor deities. The main argument against identifying the בני האלהים as some kind of supernatural being comes from the *targumim*. These interpreters refused to identify them as angels but chose rather to call them sons of the great ones or judges, although, as discussed above, this may be purposely-ambiguous language. It seems that the likely interpretation should be some kind of supernatural being, either angels or minor gods. In light of this interpretation, verse 2 should be read from a relatively neutral point of view.

3.3.3 Verse 6.3

ויאמר יהוה לא־ידון רוחי באדם לעלם בשגם
הוא בשר והיו ימיו מאה ועשרים שנה

And God said: "My spirit shall not remain in humanity forever in that it also [humanity] is flesh, and the days in which it [humanity] will have to repent will be 120 years."

The *targumim* offer the most significant difference in their interpretation of verse 3. These authors translated לא־ידון as "*my spirit shall not judge or strive in these men forever because they are flesh.*" It is important to note the addition of "these" also, which, some have argued, points to the offspring of the relations between the angels and women. This reading has some minor manuscript support in the variants of the LXX. The *targumim* have also directed the alleged judgment of verse 3 towards the generation of the Flood. The Targumim, along with other rabbinic writings, and the *Atrahasis* myth, interpret the 120 years to mean a period in which humanity will have the opportunity to repent. One possibility is that the 120 years will be the prime length of life for humans, but more probable, it is a period given for repentance. If one understands the 120-year period to mean a time of repentance, then the verse is declaring clearly that the condition of humanity is corrupt. Without this interpretation of the 120 years, the verse should be understood as a relatively neutral statement despite its mildly judgmental tone.

3.3.4 Verse 6.4

הנפלים היו בארץ בימים ההם וגם אחרי־כן
אשר יבאו בני האלהים אל־בנות האדם
וילדו (ויולידו) להם המה הגברים אשר מעולם אנשי השם

The Fallen Ones were on the earth in those days, and also after, when the angels went into the daughters of humanity. And there were born to them [the angels and women] the mighty men who were from the days of old, men of renown.

Despite the Septuagint's identification of the *nephilim* as giants, there is no further support for this interpretation. The Hebrew author's choice of two different expressions seems to indicate that these represent two different groups of beings. Targum *Onkelos* and *Neofiti* seem to follow the interpretation of the LXX by translating *nephilim* with גיבריא, the same word that identifies the offspring of the union. Only Targum *Pseudo-Jonathan* attempts to identify clearly the *nephilim*. The author interprets *nephilim* with the names of the two leading angels of the Watcher tradition Shemihazai and Azael. It seems that what we have in this verse is the identification of two distinct groups of angels, possibly the Watchers as the *bene haelohim* and Satan (or Mastema) as the leader of the *nephilim*. I am tempted to omit what I read as a gloss in the verse "and also after" in order to make clearer the distinction between the *nephilim* and the *gibborim*, but the lack of textual support does not permit it. The biblical evidence for identifying the *gibborim* seems to point to beings that were mighty warriors. They are identified in the Greek literature as heroes who were half-mortal and half divine. A great deal of ambiguity exists in the choice of the word γίγαντες by the translator of the LXX, which seems to reveal a difficulty in understanding the Hebrew text. Verse 4, on the surface, cannot be interpreted as stating the existence of any sinful act in the passage. It appears to carry a relatively positive outlook based on the inclusion of the *gibborim*. These figures were heroes in the history of Israel and rarely seen in a negative light.

3.3.5 Summary

The above translation represents the ambiguity of the Hebrew text of Genesis 6.1–4. It is no surprise that the ancient translators and interpreters had difficulty coming to terms with the passage. This can also be said of the modern scholars who continue to try to interpret the passage. If one relies solely on the text of the passage, then there is little indication that the events depicted in the narrative resulted in the judgment of the Flood. However, by adopting myths, whether they are Israelite or foreign, as a means of interpreting the passage, then there are suggestions within all four verses, which indicate that the author was relating the reason for the Flood. Based upon the apparent negative interpretations that appear in early Jewish writings, it appears that this understanding is the more likely scenario. The *Book of Watchers* clearly follows this scenario in its story of the origin of evil spirits. In what follows, I will attempt to uncover how the author of *BW* used the biblical traditions discussed above to present his interpretation of Genesis 6.1–4 in light of the emerging demonology and anthropology of 2TP Judaism.

Chapter 4

Reception of the "Sons of God" in the Book of Watchers

4.1 Introduction

In the previous chapter I presented various interpretations of Genesis 6.1–4 (i.e. LXX, 2TP writings, and Rabbinic material) in light of the biblical and non-biblical traditions that may lie behind the passage. In this chapter, I will discuss the reception of the Genesis text in *BW*, asking how the author drew upon it to develop his explanation for the emergence of evil spirits. It is difficult to determine the exact form of the Genesis text which the author of *BW* would have been reading, but there is no indication from textual evidence (Aramaic, Greek, and Ethiopic *BW*, or LXX) that the author used a text differing in any significant way from the Masoretic tradition. It is in fact a more risky assumption, based on the evidence presented in chapter 3, to attempt the reconstruction of a different text that is purported to have served as a basis for the author's interpretation. Indeed any attempt to construct such a text would be unnecessarily hypothetical, and perhaps misleading.

In what follows, I will illustrate how the author of *BW* adapted the main characters of Genesis 6.1-4, the *bene haelohim*, into his story of the "sons of heaven" and the daughters of humanity. I will discuss the various sources (e.g. biblical tradition and Greek myths) and the characters found in these sources from which he may have drawn the two primary traditions found in *BW*, the Asa'el and Shemihazah traditions. Each of these characters, in and of itself, may not necessarily represent a negative image within its own story, but within the context of rebellion in *BW*, their roles in the story are depicted in a villainous manner.

I will first provide a general introduction to the *bene haelohim* that will prepare the reader for the two sections that follow in which I will discuss the two main rebellious angels, Asa'el and Shemihazah. The discussion of Asa'el will centre on his role in the Instruction tradition and his possible role in the Day of Atonement motif found in Leviticus 16. The discussion of the angel Shemihazah will focus on his role as the leader of the Watcher angels and his role in the Instruction tradition. Within the multi-layered tradition of *BW*, the Asa'el and the Shemihazah material can be characterized in an iniquitous manner. Several theories have been offered about why the author has adapted these two traditions into his story. I will endeavour to identify and analyse the sources proposed for the two traditions in an effort to determine why the author composed *BW*.

4.2 Tradition of the *Bene haelohim*

The interpretation of the *bene haelohim* from Genesis 6 within *BW* (although the "*bene haelohim*" are not expressly mentioned)[1] is of primary concern if one is to understand the possible multiple messages of the author. The previous chapter in which the possible background of these angels within the biblical tradition is discussed, casts into the spotlight three possible interpretations: the *bene haelohim* are: (1) angels (2) minor deities or (3) god-like men. Of these three categories, the most plausible interpretation of the biblical text is that these beings belonged somewhere within the hierarchy of the angels. This understanding of the *bene haelohim* is, as we have seen, strengthened by the interpretation found in the Watcher tradition and various other 2TP writings.[2] The author of *BW* however, sought to clarify to which group of angels the Genesis 6 narrative refers.

Genesis 6.2 describes how the *bene haelohim* saw the "daughters of humanity" and decided that each would take for himself a woman. As one approaches this verse, there are certain aspects of the passage that were not discussed in the previous chapter, which add to the complexity of interpretation; the Genesis passage does not mention the location of the *bene haelohim*. The exclusion of this key point by the author or redactor of the Genesis text is perhaps due to an assumption about the reader's knowledge of who these beings were in the biblical tradition. This omission is perhaps responsible, in part, for later interpretations of the verse (i.e. later traditions attempt to fill in this gap of knowledge) that describe the *bene haelohim* as humans from the line of Seth. *1 Enoch* 6.2 elucidates the identity of these characters with a double description of which one part of the description, "sons of heaven," describes their

---

[1] The Ethiopic and Greek[pan] renderings read "angels, sons of heaven." Greek[sync] reads οἱ ἐγρήγοροι, the Watchers. Milik reconstructs עיריא בני שׁמיא in 4QEn[b] 1 ii.

[2] See e.g. *Jubilees* 4.15, 22; 5.1; *T. Reuben* 5.6, 7; 2 Baruch 56.11–14; Philo, *Gig.* 2.6f; and Josephus, *Ant.* I.73 among others. See also 1QH 11 iii 22 and Wis 5.5 as references to the sons of God.

dwelling place.[3] This depiction appears to be an addition to the Genesis passage by the author or redactor of *BW* because of what follows in *1 Enoch* 6.3–6. Here the Watcher account implies that these beings descended from heaven (*1 Enoch* 6) in order to take earthly women to beget children for themselves (*1 Enoch* 6.2c – "and let us beget for ourselves children"). With this description, the author is making clear from the beginning of the story that the action taken by the angels broke the Law of the Cosmos.[4] This passage may contain an underlying assumption that is made clear in *1 Enoch* 15: the angels have left the heavenly realm illegally, which would result in the destruction of humanity and their own eradication in the final judgment.[5] In the *Animal Apocalypse*, a story that allegorises *1 Enoch* 6–16,[6] the Watchers are likewise initially located in heaven. They are described as stars that fell from heaven for reasons that are left ambiguous in the story. They came down from heaven (or were thrown down from heaven) in order to have sexual relations with humans (*1 Enoch* 86.1, 3). The description in the *Animal Apocalypse* confirms the idea that the rebellious characters in the Watcher tradition were understood as beings from the heavenly realm in some Jewish circles.[7]

---

[3] "And the angels, the sons of heaven, saw and desired them." It is of course possible that the use of "heaven" by the author is an attempt to limit the use of the term "God" as a means of protecting the image of Yahweh and separating Him from any responsibility of evil in Early Judaism. VanderKam argues that this is the case in *Jubilees* (4.15). The author does not place the origin of the sin of the Watchers in heaven, but rather the evil, which has originated in heaven in *BW*, is given birth on earth, therefore keeping the origins of evil separated from the God of heaven, see James C. VanderKam, *The Angel Story in the Book of Jubilees* (STDJ 31; Leiden: Brill, 1999), 155; see Levine, *Aramaic Version of the Bible*, 68. Michael Maher suggests that this is because of the rise to prominence of angels amongst esoteric groups; see Maher, *Targum Pseudo-Jonathan*, 37, n. 2. See further use of the term "sons of heaven" in 1 Macc 3.5, 60; 4.10, 40; 9.46; 12.15; Mk 11.30; and Lk 15.18. The phrase is also used in Qumran documents for angels in general; see 1QS IV.22; 1QH^a XI.22; 4Q181 1.2; and 1QapGen ar V.3–4 (בני שמין).

[4] The angels are also breaking the elemental law of creation that each species must reproduce after its own kind (see Gen 1.11–12, 21, 24–25).

[5] Cf. Ps 82.6.

[6] See Tiller, *Animal Apocalypse*, 84. Tiller equates v. 89.1 of the *Animal Apocalypse* to 10.1–3 of *BW*, which, in his opinion, equates the fallen stars of the *Animal Apocalypse* with the Watchers of *BW*.

[7] *Jubilees* 5.1 describes the *bene haelohim* of Genesis 6.2 as angels of God. R.H. Charles suggests this represents the LXX tradition that originated from an older Jewish interpretation, which, he argues, was rejected by later Jewish interpreters; see R.H. Charles, *The Book of Jubilees or Little Genesis* (London: SPCK, 1917), 56. See discussion in chapter 3 on interpreting verse 6.2. However, *Jubilees* does not refer to where these angels are located when they look upon the daughters of men (although the *Jubilees* tradition places the angels on the earth after they had been sent by God to teach

4.2.1 Bene haelohim as the Watchers

The author of *BW* has expanded the concept of *bene haelohim* as angels in Genesis 6 by describing them as Watchers.[8] The designation leaves the impression that they had at one point the task of "watching" or being vigilant (20.1).[9] The Watchers are a class of angel that is compared with the archangels (12.3).[10] They are the "Watchers from eternity" (14.1)[11] whose place was in the "highest heaven, the holy and eternal one" (15.3). These angels once stood before the Great Lord and King of Eternity (14.23). They "do not sleep,"[12] but "stand before your glory and bless and praise and exalt" (39.12; 61.12; 71.7).[13] We can find further evidence for the meaning of this word if we consider the Greek translations of Daniel

---

humanity). *Jubilees* 10 reveals the author's use of the Enochic tradition which identifies these angels of God as the Watchers, the angelic fathers of the demonic spirits that are oppressing the sons of Noah.

[8] VanderKam (see VanderKam, "Genesis in 1 Enoch," 134) argues the author of *BW* is not merely equating the *bene haelohim* (בני האלהים) with angels; he suggests that what has been translated as "God" in Gen 5.21–24 – האלהים was understood by "ancient expositors" to mean "the angels." He states, "From this they developed their elaborate stories about Enoch's sojourns with the angels" (e.g. *1 Enoch* 12–36). There are 366 occurrences of האלהים in the MT. Twenty-one occur in Genesis, including Gen 5.21–24. This passage can be read in the manner suggested by VanderKam, but the other nineteen occasions in Genesis require one to read האלהים as God due to the context. VanderKam is likely correct in his assumption that the expositors were interpreting האלהים as angels in this instance, but it appears that this interpretation should be limited to the passages within the pre-Flood narrative.

[9] See Robert Murray, "The Origin of Aramaic *'Ir*, Angel," *Orientalia* 53 (1984) for discussion on the origins of "watcher." Murray argues that if the translators correctly defined Watcher as "one which is unsleeping" then it perhaps relates one characteristic of their nature rather than strictly a function (p. 304). *Jubilees* 5.16 has taken up the tradition that the Watchers were sent by God to the earth to watch over creation. See excursus on *The Watchers and the Holy Ones* in Nickelsburg, *Commentary*, 140–41.

[10] This comparison requires identifying the Watchers named in *1 Enoch* 12.3 (the angels who are still in heaven and have been discussed in the previous verses, 10.1f) as the archangels. Cf. 20.1f "And these are the names of the holy angels who keep watch"; also 82.10 which describes one of the tasks of the four archangels as those "who keep watch that they [stars] appear at their times," translation from Knibb, *Ethiopic Enoch*, 106, 189.

[11] Ibid., 95.

[12] This motif, in an ironic way, emerges in relation to the giants in the *Book of Giants*. See e.g. 4Q530 II 3–6 and 4Q531 17.1, 10. Stuckenbruck argues that the dream visions that the giants had prevented them from any further sleep; see Stuckenbruck, *Book of Giants*, 137, 162–67.

[13] Knibb, *Ethiopic Enoch*, 127. *1 Enoch* 71.7 appears to place the Watchers in the same class as the *Seraphim*, the *Cherubim*, and the *Ophannim*, which are described as ones who "keep watch over the throne of his glory" (ibid., 166).

4.10, 14, 20.[14] The Aramaic עִיר (and וְקַדִּישׁ)[15] has been translated ἄγγελος in the old Greek translations.[16] Theodotion has transcribed the term to produce ιρ καὶ ἅγιος ("watcher and holy one") Aquila and Symmachus have apparently connected the Aramaic עִיר to the root עוּר "to wake up." Both Aquila and Symmachus translated עִיר with the term ἐγρήγορος – "the wakeful." This is the same term used in the extant Greek manuscripts of *BW*.[17] Similar phrasing to that found in Daniel is also found in two Qumran documents 4Q534 col. ii 18 and 1QapGen ar ii 1. The text of 4Q534 col. ii.18 reads [. . .]וְעִירִין] קַדִּישׁ.[18] It is likely, though, that this is not referring to the evil watchers of *1 Enoch*,[19] but rather to the

---

[14] Cf. Black, *Book of Enoch*, 106. Black suggests the origins of the idea of watchers can be traced to Ezekiel 1 – the eyes of the Cherubim; or to Zechariah 4.10 – "the 'seven' who are 'the eyes of the Lord.'"

[15] As Murray suggests, it is likely that both of these terms denote angels. קַדִּישׁ is related to the Hebrew קָדוֹשׁ, through which the connection can then be made to the heavenly court of watchers of Ps 89. Cf. also 1QS 11.8 קְדוֹשִׁים וְעִם בְּנֵי שָׁמַיִם, "holy ones and with the sons of heaven," this text appears to be describing the angelic court to which the righteous will become a part.

[16] The word ἄγγελος can be used to describe either the nature of these beings (i.e. heavenly, immortal, holy, divine) or as their function in the divine realm (i.e. a messenger of God – the Hebrew term usually used for messenger is מַלְאָךְ, which refers to a heavenly being, but can also refer to a human messenger, guardian [see Isa 62.6], or a member of the court of God). See *BDB*, 521. Both the nature and the function of ἄγγελος can be understood in the biblical tradition that is behind the *bene haelohim*.

[17] See *1 Enoch* 6.2 (against ἄγγελος by Syncellus; no Qumran Aramaic fragment, but Milik has reconstructed in 4QEn[b] 1 ii עִירִיא בְּנֵי שָׁמַיָּא – "Watchers, sons of heavens"); 10.7 (no Aramaic frag) in which angels and watchers are paralleled (Syncellus reads ἐγρήγορος for ἄγγελος in the first part of the verse); 10.9 (4QEn[b] 1 iv contains עִירִיא), 10.15 (no Aramaic frag, but Milik has reconstructed רוּחַת עִירִיא – spirits of the Watchers); 12.4 (no Aramaic frag); 13.10 (no Aramaic frag); 14.1 (Milik has reconstructed עִירִיא in 4QEn[c] 1 vi; 14.3 (no Aramaic frag); and 16.2 (no Aramaic frag). Knibb has translated Ethiopic *1 Enoch* 6.2 "And the angels, the sons of heaven," while the remaining instances are read Watchers. Based on the reading of fragment of 4QEn[b] 1 iv – עִירִיא, it is plausible to state that the Watchers were understood as angels during the time of the writing of *BW*. The Watchers, עִירִיא, are possibly found in related passages in CD 2.18; *Jubilees* 4.15, 22; *T. Reuben* 5.6–7; *T. Naphtali* 3.5; 4Q180 1.2; and 1QapGen ar ii 16. Each of these passages describes the Fallen Angels of the Flood narrative. For a summary of the use of term, see Joseph A. Fitzmyer, *The Genesis Apocryphon of Qumran Cave 1*, (BibOr 18A; Rome: Biblical Institute Press, 1971), 80. The Greek translation of Dan 4.13, 17, 23 translates the term עִירִיא as a general description for angels. See Charles, *Book of Jubilees*, 53. This phrase can also be reflected in the Enochic *Book of Parables* – 39.12, 13; 40.2; 61.12; 71.7 – "those who do not sleep."

[18] Text is from Stuckenbruck, *Book of Giants*, 227.

[19] Ibid., 216.

group related to the archangels. The text of 1QapGen ar ii 1 reads באדין
חשבת בלבי די מן עירין הריאתא ומן קדישין ה[י]א ולנפיל[י]ן הא
("so then I thought in my heart that the conception was from the Watchers
or from the Holy Ones, or due to the nephilim"),[20] which appears to be
directly related to the Watchers of *1 Enoch*. This passage describes the
birth of Noah, which his father feared was brought about by the fallen
Watchers.[21] A final passage that helps identify the original plans and
function of the Watchers is *1 Enoch* 15.2. The task of the Watchers in 15.2
is clear: "You ought to petition on behalf of men, not men on behalf of
you." The Watchers are intercessors according to this passage, a function
that aligns them with the four archangels of *1 Enoch* 9.1. One of the tasks
of the "holy ones of heaven" (Michael, Gabriel, Suriel, and Uriel) is
alluded to in 9.3, "and now, to you O holy ones of heaven, the souls of
men complain, saying: 'Bring our suit before the Most High.'"[22]

4.2.2 Bene haelohim as the Angels of the Nations

A second understanding of *bene haelohim* in the Enochic tradition may be
derived from Deuteronomy 32.8. In general terms, as seen above, they are
angels that possibly belong to a class of angels similar to the archangels.
One characteristic of the Watchers that stands out is their autonomous
attitude.[23] For whatever reason, these angels have a distinct nature from
other angels represented in the biblical tradition; accordingly, they seem to
hold a specific place in the organization of the cosmos. It is possible that
Deuteronomy 32 describes their position prior to their fall in *1 Enoch*,
although, chronologically, this presents some difficulty. Some MSS of
Deuteronomy 32.8, which has its textual problems, describes the occasion
when God divided the nations "according to the *bene elim*."[24] The
Septuagint translates the *bene elim* as ἀγγελοὶ θεοῦ (also υἰοὶ θεοῦ),
paralleling them to the *bene haelohim* of Genesis 6.2, 4. Deuteronomy
32.8, along with Psalms 29.1; 82.6; 89.7; LXX Job 2.1; LXX Daniel 3.92

---

[20] Text is from Fitzmyer, *Genesis Apocryphon*, 50.

[21] Cf. also *1 Enoch* 106–107.

[22] Cf. 1Q19 II; Milik has suggested that this is a fragment from a work about Noah
which may have been incorporated into *1 Enoch* (possibly 106–07); see Milik, *Books of
Enoch*, 59. See also discussion in Stuckenbruck, *Book of Giants*, 219–20. See also C.
Brekelmans, "The Saints of the Most High and Their Kingdom," *OTS* 14 (1965): 305–29
and L. Dequeker, "The 'Saints of the Most High' in Qumran and Daniel," *OTS* 18 (1973):
108–87, for a discussion of the "holy ones of heaven."

[23] See Cassuto, *Genesis*, 292. See also Hanson, "Rebellion in Heaven," 198. Hanson
argues the Watchers are possibly a parallel to Hesiod's "minor deities" – υἰοὶ οὐρανοῦ.

[24] The MT reads בני ישראל, but has variants that correspond to the LXX and 4Q44
(on Deut 32.7–8), בני אלים, בני אל.

(MT Dan 3.25), describes an assembly of gods under the leadership of Yahweh (Deut 32.9). Psalm 82, in particular, describes these angels, *bene elim*, as a divine council whose task it is to rule over the nations and dispense justice. The same task is given to the Watchers in *Jubilees* 4.15: "And he called his name Jared, for in his days the angels of the Lord descended on the earth,[25] those who are named the Watchers, that they should instruct the children of men, and that they should do judgment and uprightness on the earth."[26] It is possible through these texts to understand the Watchers in *BW* as the "angels of the nations," who, when they were upon the earth, saw the beauty of the daughters of men and desired them.[27]

4.2.3 Bene haelohim as the Host of Heaven

A third understanding of the *bene haelohim*, which can be found in the Enochic tradition, is their association with the "host of heaven." Assuming that the *Animal Apocalypse* is drawing on *BW*, *1 Enoch* 86.1 describes the angels of *BW* as stars. In its description of the descent of the *bene haelohim* (Gen 6.2 = *1 Enoch* 6.2), the *Animal Apocalypse* makes less ambiguous the existence of the "two Watcher traditions" within *BW*. Tiller equates the first star that descends in *1 Enoch* 86.1 with the Watcher Asa'el in *1 Enoch* 8.1.[28] This two-tiered distinction of the *bene haelohim* in the *Animal Apocalypse* does not correspond to the story in *BW* (6.6), which only describes the descent of a single group of stars, perhaps the group

---

[25] Cf. *1 Enoch* 6.6.

[26] Translation is from Charles, *Jubilees*, 53. Cf. Sir 17.17; *Jubilees* 48.9, 16–17. Stuckenbruck suggests that the "prince of the Mastema" is one of these "celestial rulers" who is at times acting autonomously, but in the context of *Jubilees* 48 one must assume that *Mastema* is the angel assigned over Egypt if he is to fit into the role of a celestial ruler, angel of the nations, but *Jubilees* 10 does not seem to identify him in this manner; see Stuckenbruck, "Angels of the Nations," 30. *Mastema* is the chief of the spirits that have come out of the giants following their death (although he is not a spirit of a giant). It is unclear whether the angels of the nations בני אלים continue their task after the Flood. It is possible that the spirits now under the authority of *Mastema* took up the work of these angels (see *Jubilees* 15.31).

[27] An interesting question in relation to this hypothesis is whether the angels took on human form while performing their task of watching over the nation. If so, this may prove an interesting connection to Philo of Alexandria's thought of those spirits who take on bodily form, but are unable to control the lusts of the flesh, cf. *Cher.* 3.13 and *Gig.* 3.12 (see chapter 7 for discussion). Secondly, if this is the case, it may present the possibility of a demotion of the gods of other nations by the author; or perhaps more plausibly, it is an allusion to idolatry.

[28] Tiller, *Animal Apocalypse*, 84. Tiller comes to this conclusion by way of the description given in 88.1 of the binding of the first star, which he equates to *1 Enoch* 10.4–8.

described in 86.3.[29] This is just one of what Tiller describes as "significant differences" between the two accounts. Tiller suggests that the *Animal Apocalypse* grants the first star special status in that he did not change to a bull – meaning he did not take on human form as did the second group of stars (Shemihazah and the Watchers). According to Tiller, there is no evidence in the *Animal Apocalypse* that Asa'el is thought to have mated with human women (see 86.4; cf. 90.21). However, *1 Enoch* 86.4 implies the transformation of the second group of stars (Shemihazah and others) to animal form, which would be understood as taking on human form in the *Animal Apocalypse*.[30]

The description of the Watchers as stars in the *Animal Apocalypse* perhaps finds its source in several Old Testament passages that discuss the "host of heaven."[31] Psalm 148.2 establishes that an analogy can be drawn between מלאכים (angels) and צבא (host) – הללוהו כל־מלאכיו הללוהו כל־צבאו. The LXX reads αἰνεῖτε αὐτόν, πάντες οἱ ἄγγελοι αὐτοῦ· αἰνεῖτε αὐτόν, πᾶσαι αἱ δυνάμεις αὐτοῦ.[32] There are sixteen occasions in the MT which make reference to צבא השמים (host of heaven), six of which appear to follow the parallel in Psalm 148.2 (2 Kgs 17.16; 21.3, 5; 23.4, 5; 2 Chr 18.18). In five other references (1 Kgs 22.19; 2 Chr 33.3, 5; Jer 8.2; 19.13), the LXX renders צבא השמים with στρατιὰν τοῦ οὐρανοῦ (army of heaven). The latter translation identifies the angels as those who do battle for the Lord (see Judg 5.20).[33] A clear reference is found in Job 38.7 that parallels the "morning stars" (כוכבי בקר) with the *bene haelohim* (בני אלהים). The passages noted above identify a parallel between the stars and the angelic host. This concept

---

[29] It is possible if one considers the presence of metal forging in Gen 4.22 as an implied presence of Asa'el prior to Gen 6.4.

[30] Other significant differences include no mention of other Watchers' teaching in the *Animal Apocalypse*. There are three types of offspring defined in the *Animal Apocalypse* compared to the single offspring in Ethiopic *BW* (Gr^sync retains the three types – giants, *Naphilim, Elioud*); the leadership role of Shemihazah is ignored in the *Animal Apocalypse* and Asa'el is apparently set apart from the two hundred Watchers who descend with Shemihazah.

[31] Cf. *1 Enoch* 80.2–6.

[32] Cf. *1 Enoch* 20.1; the archangels are described as ἄγγελοι τῶν δυνάμεων.

[33] Interestingly, the majority of the above references are in some way related to idolatry. The author of the *Animal Apocalypse*, by his use of stars as an analogy to the Watchers, may be alluding to the tradition of the Watchers leading men to idolatry. *1 Enoch* 19.1 indicates that the Watchers were leading humanity to sacrifice to demons as gods. *Jubilees* 8.3 describes the teaching of the Watchers as observing "the omens of the sun and moon and stars in all the signs of heaven." *Jubilees* 12.16–20 alludes to the idea that evil spirits were attempting to lead humanity to worship the stars. Cf. Amos 5.26 and Obadiah 1.4, which identify stars as objects of idolatry.

perhaps influenced the author of the *Animal Apocalypse* to use "stars" as an analogy to the Watchers of *BW*.[34]

The *bene haelohim* have been clearly identified as angels in *BW*, more explicitly as the Watcher angels. In doing so, the author has removed their origin from the earthly realm and established them as heavenly beings that can be compared to the archangels (*1 Enoch* 12.3). They are identified as a group of angels who stood before the Lord always without sleep. Their task is to act as intercessors for humanity, but with an autonomous nature that is distinct from other angels in the biblical tradition. This characteristic helps identify them as the "divine council" which rules over the nations, possibly the angels of the nations in Deuteronomy 32.8. One final identity can be drawn from their role in the *Animal Apocalypse* as the host of heaven. By identifying the *bene haelohim* as heavenly beings, the author has set the stage to characterize their actions as rebellious toward God and the law of the cosmos.

The following two sections of this chapter will present the author's expansion of the biblical tradition that surrounds the *bene haelohim*. In an effort to identify possible sources that may have influenced *BW*'s interpretation of Genesis 6.1–4, I shall speak of only two traditions present within *BW*, the Shemihazah tradition of the Fallen Angels and the Instruction/Asa'el tradition. My reasons for not identifying a separate Asa'el tradition will become apparent in the following discussion.

4.3 The Asa'el/Instruction Tradition

1 Enoch 6–16 identifies two major characters that play a leadership role within the group of Watchers, Asa'el (8.1) and Shemihazah (6.3). Most scholars acknowledge that two separate streams of tradition have been brought together within *BW*, each related to one of these two angels.[35] However, it should be noted that the two traditions are woven into the different layers of chapters 6–16 (e.g., 6–11; 12–16; or possibly 15–16 as a separate section). Despite the opening focus on the larger group of the Watchers (6.1–3), Asa'el (or the Instruction tradition) seems to receive the focus of the blame for the iniquity that is taking place on the earth in chapters 6–9. The Aramaic, Greek, and Ethiopic traditions are not unanimous concerning Asa'el's precise nature and function in relation to the rest of the Watchers. This section will attempt to identify the author's

---

[34] A connection may exist for the author's use of stars to represent the angels to the Hellenistic concept found in the writings of Philo; cf. *Somn.* I.134.

[35] For a source–critical discussion of *BW*, see chapter 2 section 2.7.0.

purpose in using the Instruction tradition in his interpretation of Genesis 6.1–4.

As Nickelsburg has proposed, it is possible that the Instruction tradition has its origins in the Greek myths, i.e. the Prometheus myth.[36] The author's (or redactor's) purpose in including two traditions concerning the corruption of humanity could be due in part to the changing notions of the origin of sin within Judaism, as suggested by Molenberg. But it should also be considered that the Instruction tradition was a possible polemic against Greek philosophical instruction that may have been penetrating Judaism during the third through the second centuries B.C.E.

In an attempt to incorporate the Instruction tradition into a "Midrash" on the Israelite tradition of Genesis 6.1–4, the author or redactor has adapted some of the names of the angels that belong to *1 Enoch* 6.7.[37] Asa'el has been chosen in particular to head up the Instruction tradition because of the creative nature of the name (see below).[38] He is likely listed first due to the particularly destructive nature of his instruction in the arts of war, the results of which could be seen and experienced on a regular basis by Israel due to the wars that took place in and around the land.[39]

It can be suggested that the Instruction tradition of *1 Enoch* is closely connected to the Watcher tradition found in *Jubilees* (i.e., the *Jubilees*

---

[36] See a detailed discussion in Nickelsburg, *Commentary*, 191–93 and idem, "Apocalyptic and Myth," 399–404. Cf. also Glasson, *Greek Influence*, 65 and Bartelmus, *Heroentum in Israel*, 161–66.

[37] *1 Enoch* 8.1 presents the reader with a potential obstacle if he or she is to attempt to follow the majority opinion in scholarship that *1 Enoch* 8 reveals the convergence of an Asa'el and Shemihazah tradition within *BW*. If the name Asa'el in 8.1 is representative of the tenth angel on the list in 6.7 (as suggested by the Greek[sync], "First Azael the tenth of the leaders taught to make instruments of war and body armours and all instruments of war . . ."), why then is he listed first and followed by what Knibb describes as the leader, Semyaza? It appears, as Knibb suggests, that the Ethiopic and Greek (both [pan] and [sync]) are a corruption of the name Asa'el, apparent in 4QEn^a I iii 9 – עשׂאל עסירי֯ן לה and 4QEn^c I ii 26 – עש]אל. The author of chapter 8 may have listed the tenth angel first because of the severity of damage that would be attributed to the instruction that he gave to humanity. This possible interpretation does not nullify the idea that there are two traditions, which have been brought together by the author or editor of *BW*, but it does perhaps allow for a continuous narrative in chapter 8. Cf. Dimant, "Fallen Angels," 83. Dimant argues that there is no need for Asa'el to be a leader of the angels, but rather he is the one who acted first in the instruction (cf. p. 66).

[38] See Knibb, *Ethiopic Enoch*, 73, n. 10. Knibb suggests the name can be translated "God has made," thus implying the creative nature of the task of the angel. It should be noted that this is not possible with the Ethiopic name Azazel.

[39] There is limited support in Leviticus and Deuteronomy of the practice of listing the nature of sin in a descending order based on their severity; see Lev 20.9–21; 24.16–20; Deut 4.6–21; 22.21–29. Cf. *Jubilees* 5.11. Cf. also Gal 5.19–22; 1 Cor 6.9–10.

Instruction tradition). *1 Enoch* 8.2 states, "And there was great impiety and much fornication [not necessarily among the angels and women], and they went astray, and all their ways became corrupt."[40] This clearly describes the corruption of humanity due to the teachings of the angels. A parallel to this verse can be found in *Jubilees* 5.10, which states, "when judgment is executed on all those who have corrupted their ways and their works before the Lord." *Jubilees* 5.2–10 tells the story of the corruption of humanity due to the teaching of the Watchers, which resulted in the Flood. By drawing the Instruction tradition into *BW*, the author found a way to integrate the Flood narrative of Genesis (6.11–12) into the story.[41] By assimilating the *Jubilees* 4.15 "Watcher" tradition (Instruction tradition) into *BW*,[42] the author has integrated a connection to both the Flood narrative in Genesis and the alluring of the angels of the Shemihazah tradition by the "beautified" daughters of humanity in *Jubilees*.[43]

We may also consider that the author used the Instruction tradition to link the teachings of Asa'el in *1 Enoch* 8.1 back to Genesis 4.22.[44] The skills attributed to *Tubal-cain* concerning the forging of implements of bronze and iron appear to have a close similarity to the instruction given by Asa'el: "Asa'el taught the men to make instruments of war and weapons and shields and body armour, lessons of angels, and showed them the metals and works of them" (8.1).

---

[40] Brackets mine, translation is from ibid., 81.

[41] There is similar corruption language in Gen 6.11–12 to that found in *Jubilees* 5.2–10 and *1 Enoch* 8.2, "now the earth was corrupt in the sight of God, and the earth was filled with violence. And God looked on the earth and behold it was corrupt; for all flesh had corrupted their way upon the earth."

[42] Although this does not necessitate that the *Jubilees* tradition existed first, rather both may have drawn on a common tradition, or *Jubilees* adapted the Instruction tradition for its own purposes.

[43] It is possible that the emphasis of the beauty of the daughters in Gen 6.2; *1 Enoch* 6.1; and *Jubilees* 5.1 was a result of the teaching of Asa'el concerning the painting of eyes and the wearing of jewellery. Cf. also the Greek[sync] reading of *1 Enoch* 8.1; "First Azael the tenth of the leaders taught to make instruments of war and body armours and all instruments of war, and the metals of the earth and the gold, how to work and to make decoration of the women and the silver. And he taught them the shining and the beautifying of eyes and the precious stones and the dyes. And the sons of men made for themselves and their daughters, and they led astray the holy ones."

[44] See Nickelsburg, "Apocalyptic and Myth," 399. See also a reference to *nephilim* with weapons of war in Ezek 32.27. The Greek translation reads "the fallen giants of old," perhaps a reference to Gen 6.4.

4.3.1 Asa'el versus Azazel

Previously scholars have discussed the two (or three) traditions, which can be discerned within *BW* concerning the leaders of the angels; however, little work has been done on the distinction between the angels "Azazel" and "Asa'el." It is the consensus of scholarship that there is an independent Asa'el tradition within *BW*, which focused on the teachings of the angel Asa'el as a distinct tradition of sin and corruption in the world. Two main proposals have been advanced in an effort to discover the origin of the Asa'el tradition. The first proposal by Hanson posits the Azazel material as taken from the story in Leviticus 16 concerning the two goats of atonement. The second proposal, put forward by Nickelsburg, suggests that the Asa'el material is related to the Prometheus myth in Hesiod's *Theogony*.

Prior to examining these two proposals, I will first present the linguistic data for the name Asa'el (Azazel) that is found in the Aramaic, Ethiopic, and Greek extant material of *1 Enoch*. From a linguistic perspective, the angel Asa'el originated within the Shemihazah tradition (*1 Enoch* 6.7), but was, at some point, taken up by the author to introduce a second pattern of sin and corruption: the Instruction/Asa'el tradition.[45]

4.3.1.1 Origin of the Name of Asa'el

Two possible explanations for the name Asa'el are preserved in the Ethiopic translations. The first suggests the scribes transmitted the name corruptly[46] and the second suggests it was adapted by the author of *BW* from Leviticus 16.[47] The initial appearance of the name (i.e. Asa'el) occurs in *1 Enoch* 6.7 where it is applied to the tenth angel amongst the leaders of the group that belongs to the Shemihazah tradition. There is agreement in all three versions of the verse (i.e., Aramaic, Ethiopic, and Greek) that the name of the angel was Asa'el. The Aramaic fragment lists him as עׂ(שׂ)אֵל; the Greek[pan] lists him as Ασαηλ (the Greek[sync a] contains what appears to be a corrupt transmission of the name which reads Αζαλζηλ);

---

[45] The Greek[sync] reading makes the origin of the angel Asa'el in *1 Enoch* 8.1 from the Shemihazah tradition quite plausible; "First Azael the tenth of the leaders taught to make instruments of war and body armour and all instruments of war, and the metals of the earth and the gold . . ."

[46] See Molenberg, "Roles of Shemihazah and Asael," 141; Knibb, *Ethiopic Enoch*, 73, 79; and Black, *Book of Enoch*, 121.

[47] Hanson, "Rebellion in Heaven"; cf. Grabbe, "Scapegoat Tradition," 154–55; Nickelsburg, "Apocalyptic and Myth," 401–03; Dimant, "Methodological Perspective," 336 n. 38; Nickelsburg and Dimant disagree with Hanson's theory of a connection with Leviticus 16 for varying reasons.

and the Ethiopic text reads Asa'el ('sā'ĕl). The extant Aramaic texts from Qumran provide adequate evidence[48] that the name which began as Asa'el in the Ethiopic *1 Enoch* 6.7 ('sā'ĕl), but was transcribed as Azazel ('zāzĕl) in all the occasions which follow (cf. 8.1; 9.6; 10.4; 10.8; 13.1; 54.5; 55.4; and 69.2 – this is assuming it is the same angel), probably remained as עש(ס)אל throughout Aramaic *1 Enoch*. The following chart details the occurrences of the name throughout *1 Enoch*.[49]

Verse	Ge'ez	Knibb Ge'ez	Greek^sync a	Greek^sync b	Greek^pan	Aramaic
1En 6.7	'sā'ĕl	ኣሳኤል Asa'el	Αζαλζηλ[50]	Not Extant	Aσαηλ	עסאל[51] עשאל[52]
1En 8.1	'zāzĕl	ኣዘዜል Azazel	Αζαηλ[53]	Not Extant	Αζαηλ	עסאל[54] עשא[ל][55]
1En 9.6	'zāzĕl	ኣዘዜል Azazel	Not Extant	Αζαηλ	Αζαηλ	Not Extant
1En 10.4	'zāzĕl	ኣዘዜል Azazel	Αζαηλ	Not Extant	Αζαηλ	עסאל[56]

---

[48] Although there has been legitimate questioning of Milik's reconstruction of the Qumran fragments, the fragments in question appear to have been reconstructed based upon firm evidence within the various fragments.

[49] Greek^pan is the Akhmim Manuscript (Codex Panopolitanus), which contains *1 Enoch* 1–32 and is thought to date from the sixth c. C.E. Greek^sync is a ninth c. C.E. manuscript by George Syncellus who appears to have based his text on fifth c. C.E. chronographic works by Pandorus and Annianus (see Nickelsburg, *Commentary*, 12). The Ethiopic text is dated sometime between the fourth and sixth centuries C.E. and probably translated from Greek. However, the oldest Ethiopic manuscript available is from the fifteenth c. C.E., see Knibb, *Ethiopic Enoch*, 27.

[50] It is likely that Αζαλζηλ is a corruption of Αζαηλ.

[51] See 4QEn^a I iii 9; see Milik, *Books of Enoch*, 150.

[52] See 4QEn^c I ii 26; see ibid., 188 – Milik reconstructs as עש[א]ל – Knibb argues this means "God has made" – cf. 2 Sam 2.19–23, 32; 3.30; Ezra 10.15. See also Nickelsburg, *Commentary*, 194. Knibb suggests that Greek^sync a and Eth 69.2 confuse the name Asa'el with Azazel – cf. 8.1; 10.4, 8; 13.1; see Knibb, *Ethiopic Enoch*, 73.

[53] Nickelsburg contends that Greek^sync is preferred over the reading of the Ethiopic and Greek^pan; see Nickelsburg, *Commentary*, 188, n.1a.

[54] See 4QEn^a I iii 23 – Milik reconstructs as [עסאל אלף לאנשא ל[מעבד . . .]; see Milik, *Books of Enoch*, 150.

[55] See 4QEn^b I ii 26 – Milik reconstructs [עשא]ל. All the characters are questionable; see ibid., 168.

[56] See 4QEn^a I v – Milik reconstructs [ולרפאל אמ]ר[אנ]זל נא רפאל ואסר ידין; רמא] ורגלין;לעסאל, see ibid., 162. There is no extant text of Asa'el in 4QEn^a I iv.

Verse	Ge'ez	Knibb Ge'ez	Greek^sync a	Greek^sync b	Greek^pan	Aramaic
1En 10.8	'zāzĕl	Azazel ኣዛዝኤል	Αζαηλ	Not Extant	Αζαηλ	Not Extant
1En 13.1	'zāzĕl	Azazel ኣዛዝኤል	Not Extant	Not Extant	Αζαηλ	Not Extant
1En 54.5	'zāzĕl	Azazel ኣዛዝኤል	Not Extant	Not Extant	Not Extant	Not Extant
1En 55.4	'zāzĕl	Azazel ኣዛዝኤል	Not Extant	Not Extant	Not Extant	Not Extant
1En 69.2	'sāĕl[57]	Azazel[58] ኣዛዝኤል	Not Extant	Not Extant	Not Extant	Not Extant

The Greek texts appear to have followed the Aramaic fragments in their transliteration of the name עז(שׁ)אל with a minor linguistic change that can be accounted for by similar occurrences with proper names in the LXX. The following serve as examples in which the translator of the LXX has transliterated the šin or sin as a *zeta*: 1 Esdras 9.14 (=Ezra 10.15) translates עשׂהאל as ἀζαήλος;[59] 2 Esdras 23.23 (=Nehemiah 13.23) translates אשׁדוד as Ἀζῶτις;[60] 2 Esdras 20.12 (=Nehemiah 10.13) translates שׁריה as ζαραβια;[61] Genesis 46.13 translates שׁמרון as ζαμβραν;[62] 2 Chr 29.13 translates שׁמרי as ζαμβρει;[63] and 3 Kgs 16.34 translates שׂגוב as ζεγουβ.[64] It seems possible that the translator of the Aramaic text to Greek was following a transliteration of the Aramaic rather than attempting to infuse the Leviticus idea of Azazel, as is found in the Ethiopic. The above discussion reveals that there is little textual evidence to connect the angel Asa'el to the "Azazel" allegedly found in the Day of Atonement tradition in Leviticus 16, which will be discussed below.

---

[57] Knibb argues that the Ethiopic reading 'zāzĕl (Azazel) is probably a corruption of 'sāĕl (Asa'el) – cf. 6.7. It is generally recognized that the angel list of 69.2 is a secondary supplement from 6.7. In doing so, as Knibb and others have argued, the transcriber has made several mistakes while copying the list; see Knibb, *Ethiopic Enoch*, 159.

[58] Azazel – the 10th angel of the list of leaders – cf. 6.7. The second Ethiopic name of a 21st angel 'zāzĕl, but Knibb argues this is likely a corruption of 'rāzĕyāl – cf. 6.7 – 20th angel.

[59] See Hatch and Redpath, *Concordance to the Septuagint*, 7c.

[60] Ibid., 8c; see various others of the same Hebrew: Josh 13.3; 1 Kgs 5.3 2 Esdras 14.7 (Neh 4.1); 1 Kgs 5.1, 5, 7; 6.17; 2 Chr 26.6; Amos 1.8; Zeph 2.4; Zach 9.6; Isa 20.1; Jer 32.6 (25.20).

[61] Ibid., 65b.

[62] Ibid., 65a; see variant in MS A – ζαμβραμ.

[63] Ibid., 65b.

[64] Ibid., 66b.

4.3.2 Asa'el and the Atonement Motif

The proposal offered by Hanson that the "Azazel" tradition was taken up by the author of *BW* from Leviticus 16 should be examined on several points. First, no linguistic evidence exists within *1 Enoch* that can date the adoption of this name prior to the early centuries of the Common Era.[65] No textual evidence can be found that this name existed as such in the extant Greek versions, which the majority of scholars agree were derived from an Aramaic (or Hebrew) original. Second, there is no textual evidence that the name existed in the Aramaic versions of *BW* found at Qumran. Third, one should consider that if the author of *BW* was attempting to draw the "atonement motif" of Leviticus into his work, why would he choose to use the name Asa'el rather than simply the term Azazel?

In defence of Hanson, there are fragments of the *Book of Giants* (4Q203 7.6 – 4QEnGiants^a), which contains the name לעז[ז]אל ("for Azazel"), but there is no clear reference in the fragment to the atonement ritual.[66] The name עזאזל in 4Q203 7.6 does apparently correspond to the spelling found in Leviticus 16 (the א is difficult to read and the second ז is reconstructed by Milik, לעז[ז]אל, but there is little within the context of the fragment that would correspond to Leviticus). It is possible that what is represented by the name עזאזל in 4Q203 7.6 may be the beginning of the inclusion of the Asa'el motif into *BW* in order to interpret the Day of Atonement motif in Leviticus. But based on the difficulties of dating the fragments of *BG*, it is problematic to interpret the presence of the name עזאזל as evidence for the Leviticus atonement motif within a possibly much earlier *BW*.[67] Based on this type of evidence (i.e. that discussed

---

[65] See above for the dating of the Ethiopic versions. This can also be said of Hanson's use of Targum *Pseudo-Jonathan* as support for the interpretation of the atonement motif in *1 Enoch*.

[66] See Stuckenbruck, *Book of Giants*, 78. Stuckenbruck argues that the spelling of the Aramaic Azazel in this fragment is following the biblical tradition of Lev 16.8, 10, 26. An obvious genetic link exists between *BG* and *BW*; e.g. a list of names given to the Watchers in *BW* and a list of names given to the giants in *BG*; however, the dating of the Qumran *BG* fragments to the first c. B.C.E. implies there was considerable time between the writing of the two traditions; i.e. 6Q8 – end of the first c. B.C.E.; 1Q23 – 100–50 B.C.E.; 4Q203 – last third of first c. B.C.E.; 4Q530 – first half of first c. B.C.E. However, Stuckenbruck suggests a date for the composition of *BG* in the mid-second c. B.C.E. See idem, "Giant Mythology and Demonology."

[67] Milik has concluded by a very complicated process that *BG* was written between 128 and 100 B.C.E. See discussion in Stuckenbruck, *Book of Giants*, 28–29. Stuckenbruck argues that Milik has erred in the dating of *BG* in several points: (1) Milik's dating of *Jubilees* to a post–129 B.C.E. date; (2) the lack of reference to *BG* in *Jubilees*; and (3) Milik's reliance on CD col. ii 11.18–19 and the reference to the giants "whose bodies were as mountains." Stuckenbruck cites VanderKam's dating of *Jubilees*

above), the present-day interpreter must use caution when attempting to apply traditions or interpretations of a later text to an earlier text.

The Hebrew text of 4Q180 frag 1.7–8 contains a similar name to that found in 4Q203 7.6 – עזזאל (God is powerful). The spelling of the name עזזאל in this Hebrew fragment does not correspond to that of the Hebrew text of Leviticus 16 (לעזאזל), therefore leaving some doubt as to the connection between the two. Stuckenbruck suggests that the author of 4Q180 perhaps borrowed the figure of Azazel from the Leviticus story and related it to the birth of the giants, but there is little in 4Q180 that suggests similar language to that of *1 Enoch* 10.8, although this is not necessary.[68] He suggests that the author of 4Q180 (see frag 1.7–10) may have been following the tradition found in *1 Enoch* 10, the binding of Asa'el and allocating all sin to him, thus linking him to the atonement ritual of Leviticus 16.[69] However, within what little context there is of the fragment, there is no clear indication in the text that there is any allusion to Leviticus 16.[70] Stuckenbruck correctly states that an "expiatory role" for Azazel in

---

pre-161 B.C.E. as more accurate (see ibid. 30, n. 112). R.H. Charles dated *Jubilees* in the last half of the second c. B.C.E.; see Charles, *Book of Jubilees*, xxxiii. Stuckenbruck argues for a literary dependence of *BG* on *BW* and a possible dependence of Dan 7 on *BG*, therefore positing a date for the writing of *BG* "between the late third c. and 164 B.C.E."; see Stuckenbruck, *Book of Giants*, 30–31. Stuckenbruck is no doubt correct about the literary dependence of *BG* on *BW*, but this does not require the use of Klaus Beyer's hypothesis that *BG* "would have been copied alongside other Enoch literature as 'das jüngste Stück des hebräischen Henochs' in the third century B.C.E." See Klaus Beyer, *Die aramäischen Texte*, 259. It is clear the content of both Dan 7.9–10 and 4Q530 II.16–20 hold a common tradition, but, as Stuckenbruck suggests, "It is not necessary to conclude from the observations made here that *BG* as a whole antedates Daniel 7" (see Stuckenbruck, *Book of Giants*, 121–23). Rather it is possible that they both preserve a common theophanic tradition.

[68] See Stuckenbruck, *Book of Giants*, 79, n.52. There is some correspondence to the language of *1 Enoch* 10.8–9 – "And the whole world has been ruined by the teaching of the works of Asa'el, and *against him write down all sin*" and that found in 4Q180 1.8 – "And concerning Azazel [is written . . .] [to love] injustice and *to let him inherit evil* for all [his] ag[e . . .]." The difficulty that arises from trying to make this connection is twofold; (1) the language of *1 Enoch* 10 appears to be a language of responsibility for the corruption of the world rather than a language of atonement which is seen in the "Azazel" goat of Leviticus 16; (2) it seems almost inconceivable that the community of Qumran would consider adopting the sacrificial type language of Leviticus 16 concerning the "Azazel" goat if, as later traditions appear to suggest, there was any idea of having to placate a demonic being.

[69] Cf. 4Q181 2.4; this fragment appears to parallel line 9 of 4Q180 1 but makes the subject plural rather than singular, blame being placed upon עזזאל.

[70] There are several documents at Qumran concerning Leviticus – 1Q3; 2Q5; 4Q23 (frag of Lev 16.15–29 – *DJD* 12 – 153–76) 4Q24; 4Q25; 4Q26; 4Q26a; 4Q26b; 6Q2; 11Q1; 11Q2; unfortunately there are no fragments from Lev 16.8, 10. 11Q19 XXVI 13

Ethiopic *1 Enoch* 10.4, 5, 8 cannot be discounted. However, the corresponding Aramaic fragment of *1 Enoch* 10.4 does not use the name Azazel; instead, the name has been reconstructed by Milik to read Asa'el. Stuckenbruck suggests the presence of the biblical form Azazel in the Ethiopic witnesses may be, "a deliberate connection to the Yom Kippur ritual," however; its presence in the Ethiopic text does not mean that was the original author's intention.[71]

Although documents dated later than Aramaic *BW* contain the Leviticus Azazel motif, to use these documents to support the reading of this tradition back into *BW* as Hanson and Grabbe have suggested is untenable.[72] Further, to suggest the same type of support for the *Book of Giants* (4Q203) by drawing parallels to it from the *Midrash of Shemhazai*

(the *Temple Scroll*) contains a description of the sacrifice of the two goats on the Day of Atonement. Line 13 contains a similar spelling of Azazel to that which has been established in 4Q180 I 7–8, עזאזל. This text does not, however, identify עזאזל as a demon, but only as a place in the wilderness and therefore does not assist in determining a clearer interpretation of עזאזל.

[71] Stuckenbruck suggests correctly that Grabbe is overstating his interpretation of 4Q203 7 by concluding that the fragment "clearly states that punishment for all the sins of the fallen angels is placed on Azazel." See Grabbe, "Scapegoat Tradition," 155.

[72] The *Apocalypse of Abraham* 14.5–6 appears to parallel the tradition of Asa'el. This document is possibly dated around 80 C.E. originally written in Hebrew and later translated into a literal Greek, which was later translated into Slavonic. Verse 5 describes the angel Azazel *who gave away the secrets of heaven*. His heritage is with the Stars (Watchers?) and with men born of the clouds (men to whom the clouds gave birth=giants?), of whose portion he belongs. It is possible that this is a reference to Asa'el as one of the *nephilim*; if so, this would place into question whether or not the *nephilim* were the offspring or the *bene haelohim*. It is possible that the translator of the Greek to Slavonic has read the Greek νεφέλαι (from what Rubinkiewicz calls a very literal Greek translation) that could possibly be a literal transliteration of the *nephilim* of the Genesis 6 tradition. The end of verse 6 seems to indicate that the "men born by the clouds" are the offspring of Asa'el, which would be the giants of the Watcher tradition – "indeed they exist through your being." Unfortunately, there are no extant Greek manuscripts of the *Apocalypse of Abraham*, but evidence in the Slavonic manuscripts reveals that there is a Greek text behind the Slavonic. See R. Rubinkiewicz, "Apocalypse of Abraham," in *The Old Testament Pseudepigrapha* (ed. James H. Charlesworth; 2 vols.; New York: Doubleday, 1983–85), 1:686. See also *T. Sol* 7.7 which describes Αζαηλ as one of the archangels who has the power to thwart the demon *Lix Tetrax*. *T. Sol* is late first or second c. C.E., but it is certainly consistent with first-century Jewish thought. It is possible that it is a collection of incantations that were composed and used by Solomon against the demons, see D.C. Duling, "Testament of Solomon," in *The Old Testament Pseudepigrapha* (ed. James H. Charlesworth; 2 vols.; New York: Doubleday, 1983–85), 1:940–41. See also the *Sib. Or.* ii 215; a variant reading includes Azael in a list of the archangels of God. See also 2 Ezra 9.14.

and 'Aza'el is again unwarranted.[73] Authors and translators in first century B.C.E. and beyond likely knew of the angel Asa'el in *1 Enoch* and began to connect him to the story in Leviticus 16, but there is no evidence that this was the intention of the author of *BW*.[74]

A second difficulty arises in accepting Hanson's suggestion that the name Asa'el would invite a comparison with the Yom Kippur story in Leviticus.[75] This comparison would require first of all the personification of the term לעזאזל from Leviticus 16.8.[76] Jacob Milgrom suggests that there are three main readings of this term in connection with Yom Kippur.[77] The first interpretation of לעזאזל is derived from the LXX translation (16.8) τῷ ἀποπομπαίῳ – "for the one carrying away [the evil]." A similar understanding is read in 16.26, τὸν χίμαρον τὸν διεσταλμένον εἰς ἄφεσιν – "the goat, the one dispatched for remission."[78] The second interpretation regards the term לעזאזל as a "rough and

---

[73] See Milik, *Books of Enoch*, 321–39 and Stuckenbruck, *Book of Giants*, 82, n.59. See also Émil Puech, "Les fragments 1à 3 du *Livre des Géants* de la grotte 6 (pap 6Q8)," *RevQ* 19 (1999): 227–38. Puech criticises Stuckenbruck for relying too much on the *Midrash of Shemhazai and 'Aza'el*.

[74] Cf. Dimant, "Fallen Angels," 84. Dimant argues that it is unnecessary to connect the fall of Asa'el with the story of Satan (i.e. Azazel of Lev 16) at this early stage of the tradition. Cf. also *Jubilees* 5.17–18 (and *Jubilees* 34.18–19) which describes the Day of Atonement with no mention of the Azazel goat.

[75] See Hanson, "Rebellion in Heaven," 221, n.47. Hanson argues for an Ethiopic original ('azāz'ēl) over the Greek based on the need for a connection to the Lev 16 motif. He suggests that if the Greek was original then the implied connection to the Leviticus text still exists. Hanson is correct in that later readers may have made the connection to the Leviticus story through *1 Enoch* 10.4–8, but, again, there is little proof this was the author's intention. Hanson suggests the Azazel material was added to the Shemihazah material in order to parallel the need to atone for the sins of Israel and the cleansing of the earth. Cf. Molenberg, "Roles of Shemihaza and Asael," 143, n.34. Molenberg disagrees with Hanson's conclusions of a connection to the atonement motif.

[76] Hanson does present somewhat convincing parallels of Babylonian and Akkadian literature that appear similar to the Day of Atonement ritual of Leviticus 16, see Hanson, "Rebellion in Heaven," 220, n.46.

[77] See Jacob Milgrom, *Leviticus 1–16: A New Translation with Introduction and Commentary* (AB; 3 vols.; New York: Doubleday, 1991), 1.1020

[78] In the later traditions that adopt the idea of the personification of Azazel as a demon in the desert, the sins of Israel are laid upon the scapegoat not upon Azazel; the goat is then removed from the camp. The tradition presents the idea that the scapegoat is being made a sacrifice to the demon Azazel in the desert. Hanson argues (see "Rebellion in Heaven," 221) that "the biblical source for the Azazel material supplies no accusation against the hapless scapegoat; rather he is to atone for the sins of others," however, this would seem to indicate that Hanson is equating the scapegoat to Azazel, which is wrong. Azazel cannot play the part of both the goat that the sins are laid upon and the demon to which it is being sent.

difficult place" which is a description of the destination of the goat. This interpretation is found in later Jewish texts such as Targum *Pseudo-Jonathan*; *b. Yoma* 67b; *Sifra, Ahare* 2.8. Some textual evidence exists (i.e. the presence of לעזאזל) in the *Temple Scroll* (11Q19 26.11–13) that this was a possible understanding of לעזאזל in the Qumran community – ". . . and will confess over its head all the sins of the children of Israel with all their guilt together with all their sins; and he shall place them upon the head of the he-goat and will send it to Azazel, [to] the desert [לעזאזל המדבר], from the hand of the man indicated."[79] The third interpretation of לעזאזל identifies it as a deity. The evidence for this interpretation primarily comes from Midrashim; e.g. *3 Enoch* 4.6; *Pirqe R. Eliezer* 46. Milgrom suggests this idea is supported by the parallel structure of Leviticus 16.8 in which a goat is dedicated to the Lord and one dedicated "for Azazel." This, Milgrom argues, designates a divine name, i.e. a demon.[80] Thus, he suggests that Azazel is referring to a demon to which the goat has been dispatched in the wilderness, the habitation of demons.[81] This suggestion by Milgrom requires an interpretation of *1 Enoch* 10.4–5 that betrays the text. He argues that the angel Raphael is ordered to bind the *demon* Asa'el and banish him to the wilderness.[82] Initially, Milgrom's comment appears to be a legitimate parallel; however, nowhere in *BW* is Asa'el actually designated as a demon.[83] Only in *1 Enoch* 15.8 is there a

---

[79] Brackets are mine. Translation is from García Martínez/Tigchelaar, *Dead Sea Scrolls*, 2:1249.

[80] See also Hayim Tawil, "Azazel The Prince of the Steepe: A Comparative Study," *ZAW* 92 (1980): 43–59. Tawil argues that Azazel is the epithet of the Canaanite god Môt, i.e. a demon. A question may be raised here concerning whether or not there is a theological development within 2TP Judaism that is making room for the personification of certain themes such as Azazel as the personification of evil or a human Messiah as personification of God's salvation. Unfortunately, the limitations of this work do not allow further development of the issue.

[81] See Isa 13.21; 34.14; Bar 4.35, and Tob 8.3. Part of *1 Enoch* 19.1 ("and led them astray to sacrifice to demons (δαιμονίοις)") suggests that the Israelites were in fact offering the second goat on the Day of Atonement as a sacrifice to Azazel in the wilderness.

[82] A few texts indicate that demons dwelled in the desert; cf. Isa 31.21; 34.11; Tob 8.3; and Eth. *1 Enoch* 10.

[83] Cf. Nickelsburg, "Apocalyptic and Myth," 402. Nickelsburg argues that in *1 Enoch* 10 Asa'el is "clearly a demon," which is an interpretation of the passage that can only be made by application of the later Christian tradition of the Fallen Angels as demons. The Eth. of *1 Enoch* 19 describes how the spirits of the Watchers led men astray and caused them to sacrifice to demons, but it does not identify the angels as demons. The extant Greek text is less clear as to whom or what led the humans astray. The text perhaps hints that it is the spirits of their offspring at work until Judgment Day – "and their spirits, becoming many forms, violently maltreated the men and led them astray to sacrifice to

reference to what one might consider demons and these are the evil spirits that come from the giant offspring, not from the fallen Watchers.[84] The Septuagint offers further evidence that around the time of the writing of Aramaic *BW* the Azazel motif in the Leviticus 16 passage was yet to be embodied as a demon.

16.8 And Aaron shall cast lots upon the two he-goats one lot to the Lord and one lot to the one sent away.[85] 9. And Aaron shall offer the goat, upon which the lot for the Lord fell, and offer it up concerning sin. 10. And to the he-goat, upon which the lot of the remission fell he will set it living before the Lord to make atonement and to send it out for the remission,[86] he shall send it to the wilderness. 26. And the one sending out the he-goat, the one separated for forgiveness,[87] will wash the garment and will bathe his body in water, and afterwards, he will re-enter into the camp.[88]

The Greek translators of the Hebrew text have failed to personify עזאזל in their Greek translation. Although this is an argument from silence, it challenges the idea that Azazel was personified in the second to third centuries B.C.E., perhaps casting doubt that this was a motif expressed by the author of *BW*.[89]

4.3.3 Asa'el and the Prometheus Myth

Nickelsburg has suggested a theory of the origin of the Asa'el tradition, which goes outside the bounds of Judaism and into the mythological world of the Greeks. Nickelsburg's proposal, which suggests the author of *BW* has adapted the Instruction tradition from the Prometheus myth, needs to

---

demons (δαιμονιοις)." This passage, if it is describing the angels, contradicts what we have been told in *1 Enoch* 10.12 in which the Watchers are bound up under the hills of the earth until Judgment Day.

[84] A possible alternative reading that would allow an understanding of Asa'el as a demon would require incorporating the Greek concept of demon as just another name for an angel or spirit, see Philo's *Gig.* 16.

[85] See Wevers, *Septuaginta Leviticus*, 186, n. on verse 8. Variant *azazel* in Latin codices 91, 92, 94, 95.

[86] For variants see ibid., 186, n. on verse 10.

[87] For variants see ibid., 192, n. on verse 26.

[88] 16.8 καὶ ἐπιθήσει ᾽Ααρὼν ἐπὶ τοὺς δύο χιμάρους κλῆρον ἕνα τῷ κυρίῳ καὶ κλῆρον ἕνα τῷ ἀποπομπαίῳ. 9. καὶ προσάξει Ααρὼν τὸν χίμαρον, ἐφ᾽ ὃν ἐπῆλθεν ἐπ᾽ αὐτὸν ὁ κλῆρος τῷ κυρίῳ, καὶ προσοίσει περὶ ἁμαρτίας· 10. καὶ τόν χίμαρον, ἐφ᾽ ὃν ἐπῆλθεν ἐπ᾽ αὐτοῦ ὁ κλῆρος τοῦ ἀποπομπαίου, στήσει αὐτὸν ζῶντα ἔναντι κυρίου τοῦ ἐξιλάσασθαι ἐπ᾽ αὐτοῦ ὥστε ἀποστεῖλαι αὐτὸν εἰς τὴν ἀποπομπήν· ἀφήσει αὐτὸν εἰς τὴν ἔρημον. 26. καὶ ὁ ἐξαποστέλλων τὸν χίμαρον τὸν διεσταλμένον εἰς ἄφεσιν πλυνεῖ τὰ ἱμάτια καὶ λούσεται τὸ σῶμα. αὐτοῦ ὕδατι, καὶ μετὰ ταῦτα εἰσελεύσεται εἰς τὴν παρεμβολήν.

[89] See Grabbe, "Scapegoat Tradition," 154–55.

be examined.[90] As discussed above, a parallel to the Instruction/Asa'el motif may be found in Genesis 4.22,[91] a somewhat ambiguous reference in the biblical tradition. Nickelsburg suggests that we must look outside the biblical tradition for the source of the Instruction tradition. This source, he contends, can be found in Hesiod's *Theogony* 507–616 and *Works and Days* 42–105.[92] The story identifies Prometheus as a Titan who is characterized as an advocate of humanity. He stole the mechanical arts of Hephaestus and Athene,[93] along with fire (apparently the mechanical arts could not have been acquired nor used without fire), and then he gave them to humans. Thus, humanity had the wisdom necessary to support life. Glasson argues several of these arts can be identified within the teachings in *1 Enoch* 8.1–3 (e.g. humans soon developed articulate speech and names; and they constructed houses, made clothes, shoes, and beds, and drew sustenance from the earth). But it is unclear that any of these can be understood as part of the instruction in *1 Enoch* 8.1.

The account in Hesiod focuses primarily on the issue of the provision of fire to humanity and the punishment of Prometheus. Unlike the suggested purpose of the fire in *BW* (i.e. to forge weapons of war), the account in Hesiod reveals that Prometheus gave the fire for cooking food. Therefore, it is difficult to see a direct link from the *Theogony* in which Prometheus can be said to have taught humans the arts of war, to the instruction of Asa'el found in *1 Enoch* 8.1.[94]

The account of Aeschylus, on the other hand, which describes in far greater detail the myth of Prometheus, attributes several teachings to Prometheus that parallel the Instruction tradition in *BW* (e.g. potions for illness, the art of divination, interpreting dreams, the mining of ores – "all

---

[90] Cf. also Glasson, *Greek Influence*, 65; Hengel, *Judaism and Hellenism*, 1.190; Pearson, "Classical Myth," 73–4.

[91] Glasson argues that the Instruction tradition found in *BW* is "without the slightest biblical basis," Glasson, *Greek Influence*, 67. Nickelsburg argues that based on Euhemeristic traditions, which relate that humanity was instructed by the gods on the arts of civilization, the Instruction/Asa'el motif is unlikely to be connected to Gen 4, see Nickelsburg, *Commentary*, 192. However, this theory is a possibility if one considers Asa'el to be one of the *bene haelohim* in perhaps the broader sense of a minor deity.

[92] See also Aeschylus' *Prometheus Bound* (437–508) and Plato's *Protagoras* 321 and *Politicus* 274 C. For further discussion of Prometheus myth see K. Bapp, "Prometheus," in *Ausführliches Lexicon der griechischen und römischen Mythologie* (ed. W.H. Roscher; Leipzig: Teubner, 1902–09), 32, 3032–3110.

[93] See Plato's *Protagaras* 321 C–D.

[94] There is a line in Aeschylus's *Prometheus Bound* that alludes to the idea that humanity developed further gifts from the use of fire, e.g. forging of metals. This document is from ca. 430 B.C.E.

manner of arts of men").[95] Hesiod implies in *Theogony* (561–84) that the theft of the fire by Prometheus brought about the corruption of the earth through Zeus' creation of the woman Pandora. *1 Enoch* 8.2 describes a similar result to the teachings of Asa'el, "And there was great impiety and much fornication, and they went astray, and all their ways became corrupt."[96] That is, the act of Prometheus and the act of Asa'el both brought about the same result, the corruption of the earth. Noticeably missing from *BW* is language that describes Asa'el as a benefactor of humanity. This deficiency however, could be possible if the Instruction tradition is the "beneficial" type of instruction originally intended by God, as it is understood in the Watcher tradition in *Jubilees*. The *Jubilees* tradition (4.15) states that the original commission given to the Watchers was to instruct humanity and do judgment and uprightness on the earth.

A more impressive parallel between *BW* and the Prometheus myth (especially in Aeschylus) is found in the punishment motif of the two main characters with which we are concerned. For his crime of rebellion against Zeus and for the stealing of the fire, Prometheus is bound with chains and entombed by Zeus in Tartarus.[97] Similarly in *1 Enoch* 10.4, Asa'el is bound (cf. 13.1) hand and foot, thrown into the darkness of Dudael (=Tartarus?), and covered over with jagged and sharp stones. Both characters remain entombed until they are brought out: Asa'el on the day of eschatological judgment (10.6) and Prometheus to face the judgement of Zeus. Asa'el is judged and punished by God. Prometheus is judged by Zeus and is impaled with a stake and hung on a cliff (*Theogony* 507–543). Zeus sends an eagle that attacks him and proceeds to devour his liver. The account varies between Hesiod and Aeschylus. Hesiod's *Theogony* (there is no account of the punishment story in *Works and Days*) has Prometheus rescued from the punishment of Zeus by Heracles, while Aeschylus' account ends with Prometheus sinking into the abyss of Tartarus. The Aeschylus account demonstrates a closer parallel of the demise of Prometheus to that of Asa'el and the type of instruction that was betrayed by the two characters.[98]

Nickelsburg's proposal that the redactor of *BW* used the Prometheus material appears attractive and, if accepted, reveals a major infusion of

---

[95] *Prometheus Bound* 442–505.

[96] Translation Knibb, *Ethiopic Enoch*, 81.

[97] See *Sib. Or.* 1.101, 119, and *T. Sol* 6.3.

[98] Hanson argues that it is unnecessary to look to Hellenistic material to account for the Instruction tradition of *BW* since "it is possible to derive all aspects of the Azazel episode from Semitic sources", see Hanson, "Rebellion in Heaven," 225, n.58. Newsom questions why there are only certain elements of the teaching of Prometheus included in the Instruction tradition of *BW*; see Newsom, "Development of 1 Enoch," 314.

Greek mythology into early Jewish literature. Nickelsburg correctly advises caution in coming to any conclusions about which material the author or redactor of *BW* was drawing upon.[99] Some of the material may have come from an oral tradition that circulated in both Semitic and Hellenistic cultures, or that the Greek myths have their origins in a Semitic source that predates *BW* and is no longer extant.

4.3.4 Summary of the Instruction/Asa'el Tradition

I have suggested that the author of *BW* incorporated the Instruction tradition into his writing in order to integrate a reading of the Watcher tradition that is clear in *Jubilees* (4.15); this is not to suggest the Instruction tradition is original to *Jubilees*. Through this connection, the author of *BW* has established a link between the Flood tradition and the actions of the *bene haelohim*. By incorporating the Instruction/Asa'el tradition, he has introduced the corruption of humanity through the arts of war and the beautifying of the women.

We have discovered that Hanson's suggestion for a connection with the atonement motif of Leviticus 16 lacks the documentary support in the extant Aramaic and Greek texts. This is not to suggest that this connection of the Leviticus Atonement motif (i.e. Azazel as a demon) to the Enochic material was not adopted in a later period, but there is little evidence that this was the author's intention at the time of the writing of Aramaic *1 Enoch*.

A more impressive parallel is suggested by Nickelsburg. He argues for a connection between the Instruction motif of *BW* and the Greek Prometheus myth. Nickelsburg's theory suggests an infusion of Greek mythology into Jewish literature. This idea is appealing but perhaps unnecessary. As we have argued above, identifying the origins of the Prometheus myth is difficult. Hesiod could have been influenced by a Semitic tradition that was known by both the Greeks and the Jews, and through this common tradition, the author of *BW* has introduced the Instruction tradition.

Any definite conclusions about the source of the Instruction/Asa'el tradition are difficult to delineate, but even less confidently can one draw any clear conclusions about the author's purpose in using the motif. One option is that he was attempting to involve the *bene haelohim* of Genesis 6.1–4 in the corruption of humanity and bringing about the Flood. Alternatively, the author may have been trying to deflect some of the blame from the Watchers and maintain a connection to the Adamic concept of human responsibility for evil in the world. The Instruction motif makes room for a division of responsibility for evil between the angels and

---

[99] See Nickelsburg, *Commentary*, 193.

humans. This theme suggests that humans may have persuaded the angels to seek out sexual relations with the women. Without this human influence, the angels are fully responsible because of their rebellion for the events that follow.

4.4 The Shemihazah Tradition

The Shemihazah myth is made up of several layers of tradition that have been combined over a lengthy period of time probably during or prior to the Hellenistic period. The original myth, likely based on Genesis 6.1–4 or possibly an oral tradition,[100] was supplemented by the author with the Instruction tradition (*1 Enoch* 8), the punishment and eschatological material (*1 Enoch* 12–16), and perhaps, finally, the visionary material of chapters 17–36. The fragments from Qumran reveal that all these different layers were likely brought together as *BW* by the late third or early second centuries B.C.E. This could push the date of composition of the Shemihazah myth to an earlier period, possibly early third or late fourth centuries B.C.E.

In this section, I will attempt to show how the authors of *BW* used and expanded the biblical tradition of the *bene haelohim*. It becomes apparent that by including these characters, the author recognized a need to tell the story of the rebellion of the Watchers and the consequences of their action.[101] The *bene haelohim* have been described as a rebellious group of angels who, led by their chief Shemihazah, have broken the law of the cosmos and produced offspring. These offspring became the giants in *BW* whose spirits would represent evil.

---

[100] Milik and others have argued for a Genesis dependence on the Shemihazah tradition of *1 Enoch* based upon the "abridged and allusive" formulation of the Genesis text; see Milik, *Books of Enoch*, 30–32. Milik contends that the author of Genesis has deliberately paralleled the *1 Enoch* text in a common stylistic form, which he argues the author of *BW* has referred to in the *Astronomical Book*. Similarly, the author of the *Epistle of Enoch* summarizes a more detailed account of the birth of Noah in *1 Enoch* 106–7. This hypothesis, however, does not prove the direction of dependency between the two traditions. See Nickelsburg, *Commentary*, 166.

[101] There are several possible reasons why the author told this story. For example: the origin of evil spirits, the cultural clash between Judaism and Hellenism, or a religious clash between different groups within Judaism; for all of which a case could be made that it was the purpose of the author.

4.4.1 Who is Shemihazah?

The first major expansion of the Genesis text in *BW* occurs with the appointing of a group of leaders over the *bene haelohim*[102] of which Shemihazah is the chief.[103] In *1 Enoch* 6.3, he is described as the leader of the angels, the sons of heaven, who saw the daughters of men and desired them.[104] The text indicates that Shemihazah, as the leader of the Watchers, is the angel primarily responsible for the actions of the entire group. No such leader is named in the Genesis narrative. To this end, *BW* differs from the biblical text by naming the Fallen Angels and assigning them a leader, but it is difficult to identify why the author relates this information (or as Milik might have suggested, why the author of Genesis omitted it). Although there is some doubt whether or not Asa'el should be considered the chief of the Watchers,[105] several scholars have conjectured that the

---

[102] The names of these leaders found in 6.7 (cf. 69.2) vary between the Aramaic, Greek, and Ethiopic listings, but most of the problems can be resolved. See Knibb's explanation of the difficulties in Knibb, *Ethiopic Enoch*, 69–76 and Black, *Book of Enoch*, 116–24.

[103] Job 1.6 and 2.1 present a similar hierarchy amongst the angels. Shemihazah could be equated with השׂטן although it is difficult to determine in the Job passages if השׂטן is the leader of the *bene haelohim*.

[104] A similar motif is found also in the biblical tradition. Beginning in Gen 1.26, several references place angels in leadership roles: "Let us make man in *our* image" (See Levenson's argument chapter 3, p. 68f.). It has been argued that the angels were part of a heavenly court that Yahweh ruled over. Job 1.6 and 2.1 describe the sons of God as a type of court that continually presents itself before the Lord. Ps 82.1, 6 describe them as a group of beings that have dealt unjustly with the people given into their care by God. Ps 89.5–7 describes them as "the assembly of holy ones" who are the council of the Most High. Dan 12.1 describes the angel Michael as "the great prince who stands over the sons of your people." There is a similar leadership role ascribed to the *bene haelohim* of Gen 6.2 in *Gen Rab.* 26.5 and Targum *Onkelos* and *Neofiti*. However, the authors of these later Jewish writings appear to be ascribing these leadership characteristics, at least on the surface, to humans rather than angels, i.e. R. Simeon bar Yoḥai – "sons of judges or nobles"; *Onkelos* – "sons of the great ones"; *Neofiti* – "sons of the judges." See my discussion in the chapter 3, which suggests that these authors were alluding to angels by their choice of terminology.

[105] There is no reference in *BW* that identifies Asa'el as the chief of the Watchers. He is only singled out in 8.1 and 10.8 because of the type of instruction that he gave to humanity. Only in later traditions do we find that he was ascribed some sort of chief role in the tradition. This role could have its origins in the *Animal Apocalypse* in which Tiller has identified the first star to fall from heaven as Asa'el. Tiller has dated the *Animal Apocalypse* to approximately 165 B.C.E.; see Tiller, *Animal Apocalypse*, 78–9. This does not specifically attribute the role of a chief of the Watchers (i.e. Shemihazah), but rather only ascribes to him a significant role in the history of Israel.

roles of two chief angels are paralleled in the model of the Babylonian antediluvian kings and sages; Shemihazah is a king and Asa'el is a sage.[106]

Others have attempted to draw a parallel between Shemihazah and the Watchers on the one hand, and the Titans of Hesiod's *Theogony*, on the other. Glasson argues that in *BW* we have a Jewish borrowing of material from Hesiod's *Theogony*. He cites two sources for this parallel. The first is Judith 16.6, which, he proposes, provides a possible Hebrew parallel (of which there is no extant Hebrew text) that identifies the giants of Genesis 6.4 as the sons of the Titans.[107] Glasson suggests that the Titans can be identified as the Watchers, that is the *bene haelohim* of Genesis 6. The second source is the *Sibylline Oracle* 2.228f., which, Glasson argues, identifies the Titans and the giants as those who were overtaken by the Flood. Glasson also suggests that the authors of Jude 6 and 2 Peter 2.4 were influenced by the words of Hesiod; however, the language cited by Glasson (Tartarus, chains, gloom) could have been adopted through Jewish traditions such as *1 Enoch* or other works.[108] It thus seems unnecessary to agree fully with Glasson's conclusion. The general use of the term γίγας (or a form of it) in the Septuagint seems to indicate that this was a common synonym for *gibborim* (see discussion above, ch. 3, 3.2.4.2).

4.4.1.1 Origin of the Name of Shemihazah

The Aramaic fragments from Qumran (4QEn[a] I iii 6 [*1 Enoch* 6.7]; 4QEn[a] I iv 1 [*1 Enoch* 8.3]) write the angel's name as either שמיחזה (6.7) or שמי חזה (8.3). The name may be translated "my name has seen," "he sees the

---

[106] See Milik, *Books of Enoch*, 29. Milik equates these two figures with the human figures Noah (king) and Enoch (sage).

[107] "For their mighty one did not fall by the hands of the young men, nor did the sons of the Titans strike him down, nor did tall giants set upon him; but Judith daughter of Merari with the beauty of her countenance undid him." It is possible that the Titans (τιτάντων) and giants (γίγαντες) could be paralleled in this passage, but there is nothing to identify the tall giants as the *gibborim* of Genesis 6.4.

[108] See Glasson, *Greek Influence*, 63–4. See also Pearson, "Resurrection and Judgment," 36. Pearson argues that post-biblical Jewish authors saw a clear connection between the giants of the Hebrew Bible and the Titans of Greek mythology. See also Stuckenbruck, "Angels and Giants," 370; idem, "Giant Mythology and Demonology." Cf. Dimant "The Fallen Angels," 48, who argues "there is no need to suppose that in every case in which the translators used this word (γίγαντες) they intended to convey the full mythological meaning of the concept"; see *Odyssey* 7.59, 206; 2 Sam 5.18; Jud 16.6 for (γίγαντες) in non-mythical uses. See also Nickelsburg, *Commentary*, 221; and Hendel, "Of Demigods," 18–9. There can also be a close association found between *1 Enoch* 88.2–3 and *Theogony* 675, 713–26. The *Animal Apocalypse* material describes Michael as "hurling stones and earth quaking"; similar imagery to that found in the *Theogony* material.

name" or "vision of God."[109] Nickelsburg suggests that the name is given in "anticipation of the motif of God seeing the sins committed on the earth" in verses 9.1, 5, 11 (cf. Gen 6.5, 11, 12).[110] Martin Noth has argued that the initial part of the name, שם, is the Phoenician god *Esmun* and is associated with theophoric appellations: אשמרם, and שמשלך found in Elephantine and the biblical examples שמידע (Josh 17.2); אשימה (2 Kgs 17.30) and אשמת שמרון (Amos 8.14); and שמואל (1 Sam 1.20).[111] Following the pattern of the names of the angels in 8.3 (cf. also *1 Enoch* 20) in which the name of the angel is made to represent the type of instruction he taught, this may also be the case with שמיחזה.[112]

Although we cannot be sure if the Greek translators of *1 Enoch* had direct use of a Semitic Vorlage, two possibilities exist for a reading of the name. The first option is that the name could be read as שמיאזה which could account for the Greek[pan] reading of Σεμιαζά and possibly the Greek[sync] reading of Σεμιαζᾶς.[113] However, it appears the Greek translators were generally writing η for the Aramaic א,[114] with the exception of 4QEn[a] I iii 9 in which the reading of the name עסאל is transcribed in the Greek[pan] as Αοεαλ (cf. 4QEn[a] I iii 23 – עסאל – [Milik's reconstruction], which the Greek[pan sync] translators have read as Αζαηλ). A second possibility, and a more likely one, is that the translators read (Milik's reconstruction) ה as ה – שמיהזה. The common transliteration of the ה is the Greek α.[115]

---

[109] See Knibb, *Ethiopic Enoch*, 2:67–8. For a summary of the various ways to translate the names, see Nickelsburg, *Commentary*, 178. He identifies the *yod* as a first person singular suffix – *my name*; see Knibb, *Ethiopic Enoch*, 2:70; Sokoloff, "Notes on the Aramaic Fragment of Enoch," 207; and Joseph Fitzmyer, "Now This Melchizedek," *CBQ* 5 (1963): 305–21. Black rejects this proposal and suggests the *yod* is a case ending that denotes genitival relationship between the two parts of each name – "vision of God."

[110] Nickelsburg, *Commentary*, 179. This is an interesting thought, but perhaps Black's suggestion of vision of God is more plausible considering the visionary material that follows.

[111] See Martin Noth, *Die Israelitischen Personennamen im Rahmen der Gemeinsemitischen Namengebung* (Stuttgart: Kohlhammer, 1928), 33–4. Noth suggests that the name Shemihazah possibly originates in the name אשמן who was a god of vegetation in Palestine and Syria thus allowing the connection to the "cutting of roots" in his instruction.

[112] One possibility of Shemihazah's task prior to his fall was to be a messenger of visions or prophetic type deeds.

[113] If this is the case, it would appear to be a misreading by the scribe, as אזה is not attested in Hebrew or Aramaic.

[114] Loren Stuckenbruck, in a personal conversation, suggests this may simply be evidence for the collapse of guttural sounds.

[115] If this reading is accepted, then the name Shemihazah could be translated as "my name has dreamt" or "he has dreamed my name" possibly referring to Enoch's dream

Nickelsburg further suggests that the name could have originally read Šĕmayyāhăzāh, "Heaven has seen," which indicates a possible circumlocution for God by the use of the word heaven. Considering the use of "sons of heaven" for sons of God in verse 6.2, this should be given consideration. However, Nickelsburg notes two problems with this reading: (1) the use of the *yod* as first person suffix; (2) the spelling needed to attain this reading would have required the elimination of an *aleph* or the assimilation of a *nun* by the *ḥet*, both of which are unlikely. The Greek texts are no help in this question, as they appear to be simply a transliteration of the Aramaic, one that seems to have presented some difficulty to the translators. The following chart outlines the occurrences of the name Shemihazah in the extant documents:

Verse	Ge'ez	Knibb Ge'ez	Greek[sync a]	Greek[syncb]	Greek[pan]	Aramaic
1 En 6.3	Sĕmyāzā	ሰማያዛ Semyaza	Σεμιαζᾶς	Not Extant	Σεμιαζά	שמיחזה[116]
1 En 6.7	Sĕmyāzā	ሰማያዛ Semyaza	Σεμιαζᾶς	Not Extant	Σεμιαζά	שמיחזה[117] ®שׄ[מיחזה [118]
1 En 8.3	'mezarāk[119]	ኣመዛሬh Amezarak	Σεμιαζᾶς	Not Extant	Σεμιαζᾶς	שמי חזה[120] שמיח[זה]ה[121]
1 En 9.7	Sĕmyāzā	ሰማያዛ Semyaza	Not Extant	Σεμιαζᾳ̂	Σεμιαζᾶς	שמי חזה[122]
1En 10.11	Sĕmyāzā	ሰማያዛ Semyaza	Σεμιαζᾶν	Not Extant	Σεμιαζᾳ̂	שמ[יחז]א[123]
1En 69.2[124]	Sĕmyāzā	ሰማያዛ Semyaza	Not Extant	Not Extant	Not Extant	Not Extant

visions that would follow. However, this is not attested in biblical Aramaic; therefore, it is likely the better reading is as suggested above "my name has seen" or "he sees the name."

[116] Milik makes a curious reconstruction in 4QEn[b] I i 5 with שמיחזא without explanation. Knibb suggests the Aramaic was the same as that found in 6.7 and 8.3 – שמיחזה.

[117] See 4QEn[a] I iii 6; see Milik, *Books of Enoch*, 150.

[118] Reconstruction by Milik – 4QEn[c] I ii 7; ibid., 188.

[119] Knibb argues this is an inner Ethiopic corruption of Semyaza; see Knibb, *Ethiopic Enoch*, 2:82.

[120] 4QEn[a] 1 iv 1; Milik, *Books of Enoch*, 157.

[121] Reconstruction by Milik – 4QEn[b] I iii 1; ibid., 170.

[122] Reconstruction by Milik – 4QEn[a] I iv 21; ibid., 158.

[123] Partial reconstruction by Milik – 4QEn[b] I iv 9; ibid., 175.

Little in the extant texts concerning the construction of the name can help to clarify the role of Shemihazah other than he was the chief angel. As their leader, he convinced the other Watchers to transgress the laws of the cosmos, which resulted in the emergence of evil spirits.

4.4.2 Shemihazah's Role in the Instruction tradition[125]

1 Enoch 8.3 describes Shemihazah's role in the Instruction tradition within a list of several other Watchers whose instruction is known through their names.[126] This angel appears to take up a position under the leadership of Asa'el at this point. But as noted earlier, this is perhaps due to prominence ascribed to Asa'el because of the harmfulness of the instruction given by him to humanity rather than due to an actual shift of the responsibility of leadership. Shemihazah (8.3) was to teach the magical arts, שמיחזה אלף [. . . שרשין ומקטע חבר]ו (4QEn^a1 iv 1 – *1 Enoch* 8.3), a teaching that may have been in practice during the composition of *BW*.[127] The text of

---

[124] The list of Watchers in 69.2 is considered a later supplement copied from the Eth. 6.7. The differences are considered scribal errors. For discussion of the errors, see Knibb, *Ethiopic Enoch*, 2:159.

[125] The instruction of the angels in 8.3 is part of the larger Instruction tradition of 8.1–4, which has long been considered an interruption to the Shemihazah story. It appears possible that a similar interpolation was made at the end of 7.1 – "and they taught them sorcery, enchantments, and roots and they made known to them the herbs." Cf. Hanson, "Rebellion in Heaven"; Nickelsburg, "Apocalyptic and Myth"; Newsom, "Development of 1 Enoch"; Molenberg, "Roles of Shemihaza and Asa'el"; Dimant, "Methodological Perspective"; Collins, "Methodological Issues."

[126] This list helps explain the possible instruction of all twenty of the Watchers described in 6.7. The list of names provided in verse 6.7 relates little about whom these angels are, but their names seem to be related to some part of the heavens or act of nature. For discussion on the complexity of the list of names in 6.7; 8.3; and 69.2 see Knibb, *Ethiopic Enoch*, 69–76. See also *Sib. Or.* 1.87–103 which may contain a parallel to the teachings of the Watchers. Line 97 seems to reflect the idea that their names indicated the task with which they accomplished – "Different ones devised that with which they were concerned." There have been no explanations offered as to why we are given only a small portion of the duties of the twenty leaders. It would seem appropriate that if the two hundred angels have been divided into groups, then each group would have assigned tasks, which would be designated by the name of their leader. It is, however, difficult to determine the teachings of the other twelve Watchers from the Shemihazah tradition.

[127] See Milik, *Books of Enoch*, 157; Milik reconstructs "and cutting of roots." Nickelsburg argues, "the point of the passage is that various kinds of magical and divinatory practice have their source in an angelic rebellion"; see Nickelsburg, *Commentary*, 197. It is unclear if these practices were connected to the demonic during the author's time. Nickelsburg states, "The magical arts and certain kinds of manticism represent a tradition that is demonic in origin." I would argue this is going beyond what

Greek[pan] states, "Semiazas taught enchantments and cutting of roots," while Greek[sync] reads, "And still also the first of them Semiazas taught [how] to be impulsive according to the mind and the roots of the plants of the earth."[128] The Ethiopic reads, "Amezarak taught all those who cast spells and cut roots." All versions appear, at least, to agree that the teaching of Shemihazah involved casting spells of some kind.[129]

A question should be raised about the negative consequences of the instruction given by the angels listed in *1 Enoch* 8.3.[130] Two points should be highlighted. First, some fragments of the Dead Sea Scrolls contain instructions that allow for legitimate use of incantations, the casting of spells, and the use of herbs for healing. Especially important in this regard are the following texts: 4Q510 1.4–5; 4Q511 35.6–8; 48, 49, 51 (speaks of the sage subjugating evil spirits by declaring the splendour of God); 4Q560 (the casting out of spirits); 4Q444 (speaks of the suppression of demonic

---

the text relates about the Watchers; they are responsible for evil spirits, but they themselves are not demons.

[128] Greek[sync] reads ἔτι δὲ καὶ ὁ πρώταρχος αὐτῶν Σεμιαζας ἐδίδαξεν εἶναι ὀργὰς κατὰ τοῦ νοός, καὶ ῥίζας βοτανῶν τῆς γῆς. This reading is very difficult to translate. According to Black, it perhaps implies "sooth-sayers"; see Black, *Book of Enoch*, 128. Black suggests it is "an irrecoverable corruption"; if correct, this would imply a longer recension than we have available in the Qumran fragments. Knibb suggests that "these variants should be attributed to the editorial activity of Syncellus"; see Knibb, *Ethiopic Enoch*, 82. Greek[sync] is in close agreement with 4QEn[a]1 iv 1–5 and 4QEn[b] I iii 1–5 concerning the number of angels involved in the instruction of 8.3. The Aramaic texts have identified the teaching of the third through the eighth angel by his name that is closely transliterated in the Greek[sync] text.

[129] The question that is remains unanswered is; who or what were these spells being cast against? It is possible that *1 Enoch* 9.7 implies that Shemihazah made the spells known to the angels with him, who then used them against the humans. See *T. Reuben* 5.6 in which women were deceived by the appearance of the Watchers.

[130] Cf. the instruction of the Watchers in *Jubilees* 4.15 which has no negative connotation to it. Dimant suggests that the text does not mention a negative effect of the instruction of Shemihazah (and others of 8.3) upon humanity, see Dimant, "Methodological Perspective," 324. The task of the other angels in 8.3 is one that can be primarily related to astrology. *Praeparatio Evangelica* 9.17.3 states that Abraham "excelled all in nobility and wisdom; he sought and obtained the knowledge of astrology." This statement seems to imply that the instruction of the angels concerning the sun and moon and stars was not looked upon negatively. Cf. *1 Enoch* 65.6, which addresses the negative adoption of the angelic teachings by humanity, but does not necessarily present the teachings in a negative light – "and a command has gone out from before the Lord against those who dwell upon the dry ground that this must be their end, for they have learnt all the secrets of the angels, and all the their secret power." *1 Enoch* 65.6–8 appear to communicate the Instruction tradition of 8.1–3. See also *Sib. Or.* 1.87–103, which appears to be a parallel of the teaching of the Watchers and Genesis 4. According to *Sib. Or.* 1.88, these Watchers appear to be human. They are apparently punished for some deed as they are bound up in Tartarus and made as retribution to Gehenna – 10.13. It is possible that we have here an allusion to the Prometheus myth.

spirits – spirits of the bastards – רוחות מ[מזרים . . .]); 11Q11 2
(Solomon subjugated the spirits and the demons); and 11Q5 27.9 (songs
sung by David over those possessed by evil spirits).[131] However, when
considering this evidence one must realize the problems connected with
assuming that similar practices were taking place when *BW* was being
composed.

Second, in light of the presence of these fragments, and the possible
practice by members of the community, the teachings listed in *1 Enoch* 7.1
and 8.3 were not necessarily condemned throughout 2TP Judaism. The
instruction ascribed to Shemihazah (and the angels with him in 7.1)
appears to be inconsequential compared to the act of intercourse.[132] In the
charge against Shemihazah and the others in 10.11, their teachings are not
identified as a reason for their punishment. In 9.7, the author notes the
issue of the teaching of spells,[133] but this is only from the address of the
archangels to the Lord concerning the complaints from the earth. Verses 6
and 7 address the punishment of Asa'el and Shemihazah, but verse 7
perhaps indicates that Shemihazah did not teach humanity how to cast
spells, but rather taught the angels under his authority. It could be argued
that 7.1c describes the angels teaching the skills to the women, but this text
seems to be incongruous in the Shemihazah tradition. However, 4QEnᵃ I iii
15 (ול אלפה אנין חרשה ו]), "and they teach them sorcery and . . ." (see
also Greekᵖᵃⁿ version of 7.1c) suggests the angels taught spells and

---

[131] Cf. also the seventh c. B.C.E. Hebrew incantation against night demons found in
Assyrian town of Hadattu; see H. Torczyner, "A Hebrew Incantation Against Night-
Demons From Biblical Times," *JNES* 6 (1947): 18–29.

[132] Newsom argues that Shemihazah's role in the Instruction tradition is in relation to
the seduction of women or the teaching of the giants (7.1; 9.8; 10.7); see Newsom,
"Development of 1 Enoch," 314. A further negative implication may be applied to this
instruction when one considers that this instruction was taught to the giants. However,
there is no evidence within *1 Enoch* that the giants used the instruction of 8.3 in their
oppression of humanity. It perhaps may be implied in *Jubilees* 10.12 that the spirits of
the giants used the magical aspects of the instruction to seduce and corrupt humanity, cf.
also *Jubilees* 11.8.

[133] Cf. Greekᵖᵃⁿ and Greekˢʸⁿᶜ of which neither has "Shemihazah has made known
spells." See *1 Enoch* 10.7b – this verse is sandwiched between the punishment of Asa'el
and the blame for all sin to be placed upon him. The verse states, "For I shall restore the
earth, so that not all the sons of men shall be destroyed through the mystery of everything
which the Watchers made known and taught to their sons." The difficulty here is who are
the Watchers. Is it referring to Shemihazah and those with him? If so, this would qualify
the instruction from 7.1 and 8.3 as destructive. A second interpretation could be that this
instruction was something that the Watchers gave specifically to their offspring and is
not the same type of instruction that is referred to in 7.1 and 8.3.

enchantments to the humans. Nonetheless, it is not necessary that we read negative connotations into this practice.[134]

Hanson suggests that the teaching motif was first evident in the Instruction/Asa'el tradition and later taken up by the Shemihazah tradition. He states that the culture-heroes were present in the Near Eastern world prior to the emergence of the Prometheus myth, as is evident in Berossos and Genesis 4. These hero myths can be traced to the third millennium B.C.E. in which the heroes taught humans divine secrets, which brought about the development of civilization.[135] At its introduction, the instruction of the Greek hero myths and the Watcher tradition appears in a positive light and only takes on a negative aspect within the context of the story. Based upon the topics listed in *1 Enoch* 8.3, these teachings do not suggest they should be construed in a negative light. Hanson states that the Greek authors (i.e. Proticus and Euhemeros) transformed those who were once human into deities because of their contribution to the world. This leads to the question: did the author of Genesis 6 know of this practice of the Greek authors? If so, this may account for the identification of these heroes as *bene haelohim*.

How then may readers and hearers in the second century B.C.E. have understood this material, given that the content of the instruction in *1 Enoch* 8.3 is not regarded as harmful in nature *per se*?[136] The particular subject of the instruction (i.e. sorcery, power of spell-casting, astrology) may help place the Instruction tradition in a historical context, i.e. around the time of Babylonian exile. It may be suggested this particular section of *BW* could very easily bring to mind Isaiah 47, that is, the prophets rebuke of Babylon for its practice of sorcery and divination (see e.g. verses 9, 11, 12, 13).[137] However, a second suggestion implies sorcery and divination were accepted practices in early 2TP Judaism. This approach, however, would require a change in practice of divination that is strictly prohibited in the biblical period (Deut 18.10–12):

---

[134] See discussion on 7.1–8.3 in Knibb, *Ethiopic Enoch*, 76–84.

[135] Hanson, "Rebellion in Heaven," 228. Cf. *Epic of Gilgamesh,* and the story of *Xisouthros* preserved in Berossos, which is found in Eusebius, *Praeparatio Evangelica* I. X. 35c. See Jacoby, *Die Fragmente der griechischen Historiker*, 378–82, text 680.F4.

[136] *1 Enoch* 1.2b – "And I heard everything from them, and I understood what I saw, but not for this generation [the generation of Enoch], but for a distant generation which will come [generation of the author]" indicates that what would follow in the elaboration of Genesis 6.1–4 would be understood by those who read and heard the interpretation, brackets mine. See Devorah Dimant, "1 Enoch 6–11: A Fragment of a Parabiblical Work," *JJS* 53 (Autumn 2002): 223–37 (232) for discussion on the language of *BW*.

[137] It is possible that these practices had been taken up in the post–exilic period in Israel and resulted in apostasy within Israel.

There shall not be found among you anyone who makes his son or his daughter pass through the fire, one who uses divination, one who practices witchcraft, or one who interprets omens or a sorcerer, or one who casts a spell, or a medium, or a spiritist, or one who calls up the dead. For whoever does these things is detestable to the Lord. (NASV)

There is evidence that these practices were common in Israel prior to the exile to Babylon. Nevertheless, it is not clear if they were accepted within the sphere of the righteous. In 2 Chronicles 33.6 (2 Kgs 21.6), we are told that King Manasseh practised all these things and that he was regarded as evil in the eyes of the Lord. Jeremiah 27.9 implies that King Zedekiah of Judah used diviners and soothsayers to prophesy to him, but Jeremiah calls them prophets of lies.[138] It is not clear if these rituals were in and of themselves evil, or if it was dependent on the person who was using them, i.e. the righteous could perform these rituals for appropriate reasons. In an effort to establish that divination was in practice during the second and first centuries B.C.E., we need only look to the *DSS*.[139] The presence of "magical" texts at Qumran implies that some within the community might not have had difficulty with this particular practice of the Watchers. Again, one must keep in mind that because texts concerning this custom were found at Qumran, it does not mean that it was being carried out when *BW* (6–11) was composed.

---

[138] Cf. 1 Sam 28.3b – "And Saul had removed from the land those who were mediums and spirits," also 2 Kgs 23.24. See 1 Sam 28.8 where Saul uses a spiritist to conjure up Samuel when he is not able to hear God through the prophets. See also Lev 19.31; 20.6, 27 – prohibitions against the practice of spiritists or mediums; 20.27 in particular – "Now a man or a woman who is a medium or a spiritist shall surely be put to death." (NASV)

[139] The language in 4Q201 iv 1–4 does not appear particularly offensive or damaging in the case of Shemihazah, "Shemihazah taught incantations," however, certain aspects of the teachings of the other angels, which are related to astronomical reading, may have been interpreted as offensive. The *Animal Apocalypse* (*1 Enoch* 86.1–2) seems to imply that because of contact with the single star (Asa'el) that fell from heaven, the bulls (humans) changed their way of life, perhaps after being influenced by the instruction of Asa'el. The *Animal Apocalypse* does not refer to instruction concerning Shemihazah and the angels with him, but rather it makes explicit the sexual sin with quite graphic language (86.4), "all of them let out their private parts like horses and began to mount the cows of the bulls [daughters of men]." The only actual instruction comes from one of the archangels to Noah (89.1), "And one of those four went to a white bull and taught him a mystery." The language of "mystery" here seems to apply to knowledge of the revelation of coming events (apocalyptic) much the same as in the biblical prophetic literature, cf. *1 Enoch* 10.2 and the instruction given to Noah in *BW*, "and reveal to him the end which is coming." Translation is from Knibb, *Ethiopic Enoch*, 2:199, and 87. Cf. *Jubilees* 12.16–20 where God admonishes Abram for seeking signs in the heavens.

A subsequent development of the Instruction tradition is found in *Jubilees* 10.12–13.[140] This story describes the archangel Raphael instructing Noah how to counter the diseases and seductions that the evil spirits of the giants were attempting to inflict upon his family. Verse 13 implies that it is an instruction which involves the use of the herbs of the earth, that is, the very thing in which Shemihazah is seen to have instructed the humans prior to the birth of the giants. The Shemihazah tradition perhaps marks the starting point in which the mysteries of heaven (*1 Enoch* 9.6; 16.3[141]), used in a negative manner, played a role in the story of the origin of evil in the 2TP.

4.4.3 Shemihazah Tradition and the "Origin of Evil"

The Shemihazah tradition and the account of the origin of evil are found in *1 Enoch* 6–11. It is a story that describes, in greater detail than Genesis 6.1–4, the union between the *bene haelohim* and the daughters of men. The birth of giant offspring of this union was the starting point of the destruction of creation. The resulting expansion of the Genesis 6.1–4 myth in *1 Enoch* 6–11 introduces a secondary motif of the origin of evil (i.e. in addition to the Adamic myth)[142] and more importantly provides an explanation for the Flood narrative in Genesis 6.5f.[143] The origin of evil in this case is the breaking of the law of the cosmos by a group of archangels who were, in some capacity, in the service of God prior to the act. Although the transgression of the angels is not stated explicitly in the Genesis narrative, the sin of the Watchers is made clear in the introductory chapters of *BW, 1 Enoch* 1–5. Chapter 1 verse 5 clearly states that the Watchers will come under the wrath of God in the future. The sin of the Watchers is defined by implication in chapter 2 verse 1: they have transgressed the law of the cosmos.[144] Chapter 5 verse 4 states that those

---

[140] See Charles, *Book of Jubilees*, 80, n. 4.

[141] *1 Enoch* 16.3 is considered a problematic text. For discussion, see Knibb, *Ethiopic Enoch* 102.

[142] It should be noted that the Adamic myth is not a prominent theme in the 2TP. Apart from the Hebrew Bible there is little mention of it. There is perhaps an allusion to it in *1En* 32.6.

[143] VanderKam argues that chapters 6–11 represent the core of the myth of *1 Enoch*, James C. VanderKam, *Biblical Interpretation in 1 Enoch and Jubilees* (JSPSup14; Sheffield: JSOT Press, 1993), 103. This is true to the degree that it is the primary expansion of the Genesis narrative, but it seems it would be warranted to include chapters 15–16 within the core message of *1 Enoch*.

[144] "Contemplate all the events in heaven, how the lights in heaven do not change their courses, how each rises and sets in order, each at its proper time, and they do not transgress their law," translation is from Knibb, *Ethiopic Enoch*, 60–1. Cf. also Pss. Sol. 18.10–12 and *T. Naphtali* 3.5 – "Likewise the Watchers departed from nature's order."

(Watchers and humans) who have broken the law of the Lord "will not have peace," a phrase that is found on several instances in chapters 12–16 referring to the Watchers (e.g. 12.5, 6; 13.1; 14.4; 16.4). It is reasonable to assume that the chief aim of *1 Enoch* 1–16 is to demonstrate and accentuate the nature of the sin of the angels and, secondarily, humans.

Several motifs within the Shemihazah tradition are alluded to in the Genesis narrative. The author of *BW* has interpreted the action described in Genesis 6.2 as a "great sin" that the angels have done, a characteristic missing from the Genesis story, "the sons of God saw that the daughters of men were beautiful; and they took wives for themselves, whomever they chose." This "unlawful sexual act"[145] is then identified in *1 Enoch* 6.3 as the great sin for which Shemihazah does not want to be solely responsible,[146] perhaps an allusion to the punishment of Asa'el in 10.8 – "and against him write down all sin."[147] The language within the Shemihazah tradition (i.e. language of defilement, cf. *1 Enoch* 15) demonstrates that the angels had violated boundaries that had been set by God to govern the cosmos (see *1 Enoch* 15.4–7; 2.1). *1 Enoch* 7.1 states: "and they took to themselves women; each one of them chose for him a woman. And they began to go into them and they were defiled by them."[148]

Cf. *1 Enoch* 21.6; seven stars are equated to the Watchers, possibly the seven who are accused of instruction in 8.1–3. Verse 5.4 also accuses them of being "hard of heart" a phrase that is also attributed to them in 4Q266 II 2.17–18. Compare also *Jubilees* 7.21 – "For owing to the three things came the flood upon the earth, namely owing to fornication wherein the Watchers against the law of their ordinances went a whoring after the daughters of men." See Collins, "Apocalyptic Technique," 96, Collins argues that the Law of the Lord is not the Sinai Law but the Law of Nature which guides the actions of the beings within the realms of the universe.

[145] See Greek^pan 6.3; cf. 1 Thess 4.4–6.

[146] It is implied in *1 Enoch* 6.2 that Shemihazah has proposed this action that the angels create their own offspring – "Come let us choose for ourselves women from the men and we shall beget for ourselves children," but *1 Enoch* 6.4 indicates it was a group decision.

[147] Translation is from Knibb, *Ethiopic Enoch*, 2:88; cf. Greek^pan and Greek^sync – "and upon him will be written all sins."

[148] Greek^sync reads "And these all of the remaining ones in the one thousand, one hundred and seventy years of the world took to themselves a woman, and they began to corrupt themselves with them." Cf. also 9.8, 9; 10.7, 11; 12.4; 15.3. Each of these passages establishes a negative result from the mingling of the spiritual *bene haelohim* and the flesh of humans, a result that would require the cleansing of the earth; see 10.22. It is possible that Greek^sync 6.2 assigns blame for the incident to the women, "and the Watchers lusted after them and they were seduced by them." This motif appears likely to have been a part of the Watcher tradition found in *Jubilees* 5.1, which states that God sent the angels to the earth prior to their sinful act. Cf. 4Q530 2.7; 3.11 in which it may be implied that the Watchers were gardeners who came down from heaven to watch over

Shemihazah and those with him are well aware of the consequences of their actions inasmuch as they swear an oath that binds them with curses to carry out the act (6.4–5), perhaps sealing their fate to destruction. It is clear that Shemihazah is the leader of the angels who had intercourse with the women, but it is unclear why the author chose to single out his role considering there is no hint of a leader of the *bene haelohim* in the Genesis 6 passage.[149]

The issue of cosmological defilement of the Watchers is reasonably straightforward in *BW*. It concerns the result of the actions of the angels in *1 Enoch* 7.1b. According to the Greek[pan] version of 7.1b ("and they began to go into them and they were defiled by them") and the Greek[sync] version ("and they began to be corrupted by them until the Flood"), the angels were defiled because of their contact with the women.[150] The text of 7.1 (also 9.8) does not describe specifically how the Watchers were defiled. Several have suggested that the menstrual blood of the women corrupted the Watchers; this, however, is not clearly supported in the Greek or Ethiopic versions of *BW*.[151] There are four possible reasons for the defilement of the angels by their intercourse with women:

---

the earth. See discussion in Stuckenbruck, *Book of Giants*, 113–16. The seductive powers of the women could have been brought about by the instruction of Asa'el (8.1).

[149] The punishment of the Watchers, described in 10.11–14, is a corporate punishment, with Shemihazah singled out by name, which is likely due to his leadership status among the angels. His leadership role in the Watchers is verified again in 6.7 (see also 9.7) in which he is described as the leader of the twenty angels who are suggested as the leaders of groups of ten angels, "And they were two hundred, the ones who descended in the days of Yared to the peak of Mt. Hermon" (Greek[sync] 6.6). A variation of the Watcher tradition found in *Jubilees*, which is believed to be a later and much narrower expansion of the Gen 6.1–4 tradition, does not identify any of the angels by name, but does, however, identify the name of the "chief of the spirits" Mastema (*Jubilees* 10.8). See also *Jubilees* 4.15, 22; 5.1, 9; 7.21; 8.3; and 10.5.

[150] However, there is a difficulty with the Ethiopic, perhaps resolved, as Knibb suggests, by a misreading of μιαίνεσθαι as μίγυνεσθαι, Knibb, *Ethiopic Enoch*, 76–77. Knibb argues for what he describes as a more plausible answer; "a confusion within the Aramaic between שמט "to be mixed up" [lit. "to sink"] and (י)שמא 'to be defiled.'" This of course would require a direct influence of the Aramaic on the Ethiopic. Unfortunately, there is no Aramaic fragment for this passage. See also 9.8.

[151] See Suter, "Fallen Angel, Fallen Priest," 118–19. Suter argues the angels were defiled by the women's blood. Nickelsburg argues the angels slept with the women during their menstrual period, Nickelsburg, *Commentary*, 271. VanderKam interprets the blood described in *1 Enoch* 15.4 as menstrual blood, which resulted in a violation of Lev 18.19, VanderKam, *Angel Story in Jubilees*, 165. Cf. Dimant who argues that to suggest menstrual blood would be a stretch of the text, Dimant, "Methodological Perspective," 324.

1. The angels had sex with menstruating women – 10.11 (ἀκαθαρσία)[152] – the problem with this approach is how did the women become pregnant if they had sex during their period?[153]

2. The angels had sex with virgin women (בתולה) – the problem with this is that the blood of a virgin was not seen as unclean.[154]

3. The angels had sex with adulterers – the text of Greek[pan sync] 10.9 indicates that the partners of the angels were adulterers and fornicators; meaning they were having sexual relations with the angels outside of marriage (see excursus "Marriage in Genesis 6.2" below).[155]

---

[152] Milik reconstructs 4QEn[b] 1 iv [בטומאתהן] לנשׁ[י]א לאסתאבה בהן "with women to defile themselves in their uncleanness," Milik, *Books of Enoch*, 175.

[153] There are six times in which ἀκαθαρσία, or a form of it (ἀκαθαρσίας or ἀκαθαρσίαις) is used in the LXX to render the Hebrew נדה, the word usually related to menstrual blood or impurity, see Lev 15.24, 30; 18.9; Ezek 22.10; 36.17; and Ezra 9.11. Four times the word ἀφέδρου (or ἀφέδρῳ) is used to translate more precisely the Hebrew נדה. Three of these refer to menstrual impurity, Lev 15.25, 26; *Pss. Sol.* 8.12; and once in 2 Chr 29.5 in which נדה refers to those things which must be removed from the Temple. *1 Enoch* 15.4 appears to be the only sticking point for uncleanness other than through blood – "through the blood of the women you were defiled." There is no Aramaic fragment available; Knibb argues the Ethiopic is corrupt, "you became unclean upon the women." This, however, does not require it to be menstrual blood (likely ἀφέδρῳ for נדה). The blood of the women may indicate what is coming in the rest of the verse – that offspring would be born to the angels through "flesh and blood," which seems to be a reflection upon the mortality of humanity and now the angels.

[154] The angels may have taken for themselves virgins from the daughters of men. If this is the case, a later written tradition, *m. Niddah* 1.3, states that the blood of a virgin (בתולה) is clean and therefore does not defile the participants; this being the blood from first–time sexual intercourse. R. Eliezer states that a virgin is only unclean during the time of her flow – also R. Joshua. See also the discussion in *b. Niddah* 11a–b.

[155] In *Bereshith Rabbah* 26.2 on Genesis 6.2, Rabbi Judan states that the line "and they took them wives" means they took married women. The *T. Reuben* 5.6 states that "while the women were cohabitating with their husbands, they [the Watchers] appeared to them," see Howard C. Kee, "Testaments of the Twelve Patriarchs, in *The Old Testament Pseudepigrapha*, (ed. James H. Charlesworth; 2 vols.; New York: Doubleday, 1983–85), 1:775–828 (782–85). Secondary support for this theory identifies the offspring of the union as bastards. The Ethiopic and Greek[pan] appear to transcribe the Aramaic ממזרא. Greek[sync] has identified the offspring as γίγαντες perhaps due to the inability to identify the word it was trying to translate. See also 4Q202 iv 5; 4Q204 v 2; 1QH xxiv 12 and possibly 1QH xxiv frag 6.3; 4Q511 frag 2.3; frag 35.7. Cf. also *1 Enoch* 12.4 in which angels were defiled κατὰ τῶν γυναικῶν; and 15.3, "and lain with the women and become unclean by the daughters of men and you took to yourself women" – does this mean they had more than one? Cf. Gen 4.19 in which Lamech takes two women for himself. See also Sir 23.22–26 in which the bastard children of an adulterous relationship shall not take root, i.e. shall be killed before the assembly.

4. The angels were defiled because they crossed the line between eternal immortal beings and "flesh and blood" (2.1; 15.4–7). *1 Enoch* 10.22 states the earth shall be cleansed from all ἀκαθαρσία, perhaps describing the result of the union of the angels and humans. The act of fornication not only defiled the angels, but brought ἀκαθαρσία upon all creation.[156]

Point four seems the most likely reason for the defilement of the angels and the earth if one considers the language that follows in *1 Enoch* 7.4–6: "And the giants turned against them [humans] in order to devour men. And they began to sin against birds, and against animals, and against reptiles and against fish, and they devoured one another's flesh and drank the blood from it. Then the earth complained about the lawless ones."[157] The corruption of the angels by the blood of the women may be considered if we are only to take into account the effect this action had upon the angels alone, as Suter has argued.[158] However, the events that follow their defilement by sexual intercourse are the focus of *BW* 6–16, the defilement of the earthly creation. The offspring of these unions is shedding blood upon the earth causing the creation to become ritually impure and thus requiring the Flood to act as a ritual immersion to cleanse the earth of the defilement caused by the Watchers' rebellion against heaven and the crossing over into the realm of human mortality.[159]

---

[156] Cf. *Jubilees* 7.21 which states that the angels through the fornication with women caused the beginning of uncleanness on the earth.

[157] Translation from Knibb, *Ethiopic Enoch*, 78–79.

[158] See Suter, "Fallen Angel, Fallen Priests." Suter's main argument concerns the issue of the purity of the angels (who are, in his view, the Temple priesthood). It appears though the central issue of *1 Enoch* 6–16 is not the purity of the angels, but the corruption of humanity by the giants because of the actions of the angels and the emergence of evil spirits. Suter argues the central concern of the tradition is the effect upon the angels when it is clear from *1 Enoch* 15–16 that the results of their actions upon humanity is the key issue as it is in the Hellenistic tradition. See Glasson, *Greek Influence*, also Hesiod, *Theogony*, and *Catalogues of Women and Eoiae*, and Apollodorus, *Library*. See also the *Odyssey*, Book 7.55, 205; 11.315. The tradition of *BW* is concerned with the giants and their effect upon humanity as Nickelsburg has rightly pointed out. See Nickelsburg, "Apocalyptic and Myth," 384.

[159] *Jubilees* 4.23–4 – Enoch writes down all the corruption of the children of men for which God brings the Flood. *1 Enoch* 89.5 describes the destruction of the Watchers and their offspring by the Flood, but it does not mention specifically the cleansing of the earth, but perhaps implies it in 89.8, "and the darkness departed and light appeared," translation from Knibb, *Ethiopic Enoch*, 2:201. See also *Sib. Or.* 1.150–56. This passage describes Noah preaching to humanity prior to the Flood, although he is addressing humans, the actions are similar to those of the giants in *BW*. Also, *T. Naphtali* 3.5 implies that the earth required cleansing (by the Flood) because of the actions of the Watchers. The Greek verb used in *1 Enoch* 6.11 μιανθῆναι is used in other literature in reference to cultic ritual impurity; see Josephus *J.W.* 4.25, 201; *Ant.* 11.300; and 1 *Macc* 1.63.

1 Enoch 6–11 offers two reasons why the Flood occurred following Genesis 6.1–4. Firstly, the union of the angels and women resulted in the birth of the giants who destroyed the earth and thus needed to be punished.[160] Secondly, because of what humans learned from the angels, they committed evil and brought destruction to the earth. A connection may exist in the biblical tradition (Gen 6.12–13), which places blame upon the giants for their role in the punishment by the Flood (cf. *Jub* 5.2).

There is some likelihood that the author of *BW* understood the reference to "flesh" in Genesis 6.3 refers to the giants, "Then the Lord said, 'My spirit shall not dwell with humanity forever, because it is also flesh.'" *1 Enoch* 10.9 states that the giants will be destroyed from the midst of humanity, "for they will not have length of days" which could be understood as an allusion to Genesis 6.3. *Jubilees* 5.7–8 makes the connection even clearer, "and against their sons [the sons of the Watchers] went forth a command from before his face that they should be smitten with the sword and be removed from under heaven. And he said, 'My spirit will not always abide on man; for they also are flesh and their days shall be one hundred and twenty years.'"[161] Verse 9 follows with a similar description of the destruction of giants found in *1 Enoch* 10.9.[162]

Most of the previous research on *BW* has concluded that the *bene haelohim* (the Watchers) married the daughters of men in Genesis 6.2 (*1 Enoch* 6.2). It has been suggested these unions resulted in the contamination of the angels by the menstrual blood of the women. This conclusion has resulted in the suggestion that the focus of *BW* is the corruption of the angels, rather than the affect the union had on creation. It also has been suggested that *BW* is a polemic against the priesthood in Jerusalem and their marriages to foreign women. In what follows, I present possible textual evidence that may cast some doubt that the angels and women were married, and thus casting doubt on this hypothesis.

Excursus: Marriage in Genesis 6.2

The idea that the *bene haelohim* married the daughters of humanity in Genesis 6.2 has been the consensus of scholarship for some time, but an examination of early Jewish sources seems to leave room for a different

---

[160] *Jubilees* 7.21, which clearly ties the Flood to the acts of the Watchers, states: "for owing to these three things came the flood upon the earth, namely, owing to fornication wherein the Watchers against the law of the ordinances went whoring after the daughters of men."

[161] Brackets are mine.

[162] See comments on Gen 6.3 in Sarna, *Genesis*, 46.

interpretation of the verse, one that reveals relationships outside the boundaries of matrimony.

Targum *Pseudo-Jonathan* has elaborated considerably on verse 2 with allusions that seem to point to *BW*. Michael Maher translates נשין as wives and reads verse 2 as "The sons of the *great ones* saw that the daughters of men were beautiful [טובות], that *they painted their eyes and put on rouge, and walked about with naked flesh. They conceived lustful thoughts* and they took *wives* to themselves from among all who pleased them."[163] The addition of "they [the *bene haelohim*] conceived lustful thoughts," has resulted in considerable comments in rabbinic literature. The verse has been interpreted in *Genesis Rabbah* 26.5 to mean that the daughters were טובות, virgins; the phrase "and they took wives" equates to the *bene haelohim* taking married women; and "whomsoever they chose" equates to the taking of males and beasts. R. Huna states that the generation of the Flood was blotted out because they produced marriage agreements between men and beasts.

Targum *Onkelos* makes no additions to verse 2 and Grossfeld translates, without comment, נשין in *Onkelos* as wives.[164] Targum *Neofiti* offers some interesting comments on verse 2. The interpretation of *bene haelohim* as judges results in R. Shimon b. Yoḥai commenting that the "sons of the judges," as a result of their position in society, took daughters of the common people by force.[165] The Aramaic text of Targum *Neofiti* has אנשי, which has been expanded by the editor in the text to read אנשין which could be the result of an error in transmission. The other option is that it could be read as men or husbands. Grossfeld argues that there are two other possible meanings besides an error for אנשי; 1) that אנשי is the subject of the verb clause; or 2) it is the direct object of the clause which would read "and they took for themselves males" which would follow the rabbinic accusations against the generation of the Flood of the practice of homosexuality.[166] It seems plausible from the readings of the Targum that there were other possible interpretations of נשין in the 2TP period.[167]

---

[163] Maher, *Targum Pseudo–Jonathan: Genesis*, 38.

[164] Grossfeld, *Targum Onqelos to Genesis*, 52.

[165] This is also the view of Ibn Ezra, Ramban, and Rashi. Sarna notes that ויקחו להם נשים is the normal language of marriage and does not indicate any type of violence, see Sarna, *Genesis*, 46. See also Cassuto, *Genesis*, 295.

[166] See Bernard Grossfeld, *An Analytic Commentary of the Targum Neofiti to Genesis: Including Full Rabbinic Parallels* (New York: KTAV, 1992); *Gen. Rab.* 26.5; *Tanh.* b 33.

[167] There is perhaps an allusion being made by Jesus to the doctrine of angels marrying women in Matt 22.30 and Mk 12.25. Although it is in reference to the

Josephus' interpretation of Genesis 6.2 in *Antiquities* 1.72–76 reveals a clearer alternative to the relationship that occurred between the *bene haelohim* and the women. The first is found in *Antiquities* I. 73.2 and Josephus' description of the angels consorting with women, πολλοὶ γὰρ ἄγγελοι θεοῦ γυναιξὶ συνιόντες.[168] Josephus makes no mention of the angels marrying women, but only coming together with them to produce offspring. This is a significantly different interpretation of the incident than those encountered in the *targumim* and other rabbinic literature and presents the possibility that Genesis 6.2 was interpreted in this manner.

J.T. Milik has offered the restoration of line 4QEn[a] 1.iii 13 (*1 Enoch* 7.1, the parallel to Gen 6.2), which reads כלהן נסבו להן, "all of them took to themselves," followed by what Milik argues should be read wives, נשין.[169] He claims the wording in this line follows "word for word" the text of Genesis 6.2 (ויקחו להם נשים)[170] and its reference to the angels entering into marriage with the daughters of men. However, the Hebrew of Genesis 6.2 does not follow the pattern of text construction required to read, "all of them took to themselves *wives*," suggested by Milik and others. According to the textual evidence, for the Hebrew to be read in this manner, one would expect a *lamed* (ל) prefix attached to נשים, "women." There are fifty-seven cases in the Hebrew Bible, fifteen in Genesis, which describe this particular situation.[171] Five of the occurrences in Genesis follow the verb לקח (take), which would be similar to the reconstruction of Milik in 4QEn[a]1.iii line 8.[172] It appears that for a similar idea to be conveyed by the Genesis 6 passage, the verb לקח should be followed by לאשה or לנשים, rather than נשים, in order to extract the idea that there is

---

resurrection, he states, "For in the resurrection they neither marry, nor are given in marriage, but are like angels in heaven."

[168] See Josephus, *Ant.* 1.73.2.

[169] Milik, "Problèmes de la littérature," 349.

[170] The passages in HB and LXX both follow Milik's suggested "word for word" phraseology. The extant Greek texts of *1 Enoch* 7 do not follow the "word for word" pattern as one might expect.

[171] See Gen 12.19; 25.20; 28.9; 34.4, 8 using לקח; 16.3; 29.28; 30.4, 9; 38.14; 41.46 using נתן; 20.12; 24.67; 34.12; 41.45 using תהי לי.

[172] Further, Milik offers no explanation for his use of the verb נסב to convey his meaning of "to take" in line 13 and 4QEn[a] 1.iii line 13 and En[b] 1.ii line 18. There is no reason for him to choose this verb over לקח except to impose his presuppositions of a marriage. It appears that לקח was readily available to the author of *1 Enoch* as is evidenced in its use in biblical Hebrew and in later Targum literature. See Marcus Jastrow, *A Dictionary of the Targumim, the Talmud Babli and Yerushalmi, and the Midrashic Literature* (New York: Choreb, 1926), 717.

a marriage taking place between the angels and the daughters of men.[173] It seems that similar language would be needed in *1 Enoch* 7.1 if we were to understand that a marriage took place between the two parties.

Targum *Onkelos* offers multiple instances of the use of לאיתו (to be a wife), which confirm this understanding, one of which appears to imply a legal marriage contract.[174] This case is especially important as it discusses the marriage between Shechem and Dinah after Shechem has raped her. *Onkelos* on Genesis 34.4 reads "and Shechem said to Hamor his father, saying, 'Take this young one for me to be a wife'" (ואמר שכם לחמור אביו ית עולימתא הדא לאיתו למימר סב לי).[175] This appears to indicate some sort of a legal contract as can be seen in verses 8 and 9 where by the two families will enter into a covenant. It would seem then that similar language would be needed in Genesis 6.2 and *1 Enoch* 7.1 if we are to presume a marriage took place between the two parties. It may be better understood that the נשין should simply be read as women, which is entirely possible with the evidence of the extant Greek witnesses' of *1Enoch* use of γυναῖκες.

Milik's reconstruction of 4QEn[b] 1 iv also helps support the argument against a marriage between the angels and the women. However, Milik's reconstruction of line 9 must be taken into consideration first. Milik's addition of the phrase בטומאתהן ("in their uncleanness") indicates that the defilement of the angels was caused by the women rather than by the angel's decision to cross the species line of creation. Although the extant Greek texts of *1 Enoch* contain the same phraseology, it is not clear where the uncleanness originates other than in the actual act itself. Milik's insertion of ל[נשיא as the object of אתחברו verifies that the sexual union with the women brought defilement to the angels. It should be noted here that there is no mention of the blood of the women but only the union between the two beings as the cause of the defilement.[176]

The language of Genesis 6.2 is unclear whether marriages actually took place between the *bene haelohim* and the daughters of men. Up to this point in Genesis, we have no mention of marriage based on the formula

---

[173] נשים is used primarily in the Hebrew bible as the plural of אשה. See BDB, p.61a. It is used in later Targum Aramaic for the same purpose; the plural form, נשין, of נשא. Franz Delitzsch contends that לקח אשה "is everywhere used for the contraction of actual and lasting marriages." However, as stated above, this is not the case, see Franz Delitzsch, *A New Commentary on Genesis* (Clark's Foreign Theological Library 36; 2vols.; trans. Sophia Taylor; Edinburgh: T & T Clark, 1888), 225.

[174] See also *Neofiti*.

[175] Cf. MT, ויאמר שכם אל־חמור אביו לאמר קח־לי את־הילדה הזאת לאשה.

[176] Nickelsburg, *Commentary*, 184.

discussed above. The occurrences of אשתו,[177] usually translated "his wife" could just as easily be translated "his woman." Only in Genesis 4.19 is language similar to that in Genesis 6.2b actually found, but there is no indication in 4.19 that a marriage actually took place, but rather ויקח־לו למך שתי נשים could be translated and understood as "Lamech took to himself two women."[178]

4.5 Conclusion

The author of *BW* has expanded the biblical tradition of the *bene haelohim* by identifying them with Shemihazah and his followers for reasons that are not made fully explicit. Several possible sources of the tradition have been offered, but no clear-cut origin can be traced. The Aramaic form of Shemihazah offers little help about why the author would have used this particular name, or why he chose to give the *bene haelohim* a leader in the first place. The concept may have originated with the role of the accuser who is associated with the *bene haelohim* in Job 1.6 and 2.1, a possibility advanced with the *Mastema* tradition of *Jubilees* (although he is not the same class of being that he is leading). Multiple attestations of the *bene haelohim* as members of a heavenly court can be found in the biblical tradition, but only in Job do we find a group of angels that, in the slightest sense (i.e. in relation to שטן), could be construed as villainous.

The author of *BW* has used the Shemihazah tradition as the core of the Watcher narrative, but in addition has included the Instruction/Asa'el motif found in *1 Enoch* 8. This motif remains an even greater mystery concerning its inclusion in the story, as there is little with which to relate it in the biblical tradition surrounding Genesis 6. A possible link to Genesis 4 is offered through a parallel to the Greek myth of Prometheus, but again this may be an unnecessary connection to material outside of the Israelite tradition. The type of instruction found in *BW* can be found in the biblical tradition of Israel, which may imply that the use of this motif reflects a polemic by the author against the use of this type of instruction for purposes apart from God's purposes.

The historical events of the author's time that brought about the embracing of the Shemihazah myth (if in fact there were such events) can only be hypothesized by modern scholarship. Some scholars have argued that the characters within *BW* (and the myth in general) are fictional and

---

[177] See Gen 3.20; 4.1, 17, 25.

[178] It is possible that what we see in 4.19 and again in 6.2 is the breaking of monogamous relationships.

purely symbolic which allows for reinterpretation in various settings. This in part may be due to a worldview that does not allow for the events depicted in the Shemihazah myth to be interpreted in any other way than as symbols for a crisis that Jews were facing at the time the story was written. Likewise, some 2TP Jewish groups may have understood *BW* as an analogy for the difficulties the nation was facing in the third through first centuries B.C.E., but this does not eliminate the possibility that others understood *BW* as a story about the origin of evil spirits (see discussion of the reception of *BW* in ch. 6).[179]

The author of *BW* has interpreted the Genesis 6 story with the Shemihazah tradition in order to strengthen his view about the existence of evil spirits in his world. The Genesis text has provided him the opportunity to give authority to his view that the *bene haelohim* crossed the boundaries of the cosmos, which resulted in the corruption of the world and everything in it. The sin of the Watchers has resulted in their demise, the demise of their offspring, and the demise of humanity, all of which is a result of their rebellion.

---

[179] The *Animal Apocalypse* and *Jubilees* record the descent of the Watchers within the history of Israel from the beginning of creation through the early Maccabean period, which is considered to be the era in which the author lived; see Nickelsburg, "Apocalyptic and Myth," 94, where Nickelsburg states, "the fall of the angels is an event in primordial history and is not the cause of human woe here and now." See also VanderKam, *Biblical Interpretation*, 115. Milik argues that the Battle of Beth-Zur (164 B.C.E.) is reflected in *1 Enoch* 90.13–15; see Milik, *Books of Enoch*, 42–44. The placement of the myth early in the chronology perhaps represents the author's thoughts concerning the authenticity of the myth.

Chapter 5

The Rebellion Motif
in the Book of Watchers

5.1 Introduction

The previous chapter introduced in some detail the traditions from which the author of *BW* interpreted the story of the *bene haelohim* in Genesis 6.1–4. The complexity of the tradition required first a general introduction to the possible interpretations of the *bene haelohim* by the author in light of the biblical tradition. This was followed with a discussion of the two main traditions recovered within *BW*, the Shemihazah tradition and the Instruction/Asa'el tradition. Each of these sections provided a pathway for what will follow in this chapter, a discussion of the crux of *BW*, the rebellion of the Watchers.

The conduct of the *bene haelohim* in Genesis 6.1–4 has been interpreted in early Jewish literature, in general, as a less than provocative act, with the exception of the Watcher tradition. We read of no obvious condemnation of the episode by the author of the story in Genesis, but the events that follow this passage seem to indicate that the actions described play some part in bringing the Flood. The interpretation found in *1 Enoch* has led several scholars to propose that the rebellion motif already served as a reason for the angels' behaviour in Genesis 6. This chapter will discuss several theories about the origin of this rebellion motif and its effect upon the angels, their offspring, humanity, and the rest of creation.

5.2 Rebellion of the Angels

There is no unambiguous concept of angelic rebellion within Genesis 6.1–4. Nevertheless, the author *1 Enoch* 6.3–5 has interpreted the biblical tradition of Genesis 6.1–4 as some sort of rebellion against heaven.[1]

---

[1] Cf. also *1 Enoch* 12.4 (15.3) – "Watchers of heaven who have left the high heaven and the holy and eternal place"; 12.5 – "they will have on earth neither peace nor forgiveness of sin"; 16.3 appears to be the strongest support for a rebellion of the angels

Several scholars have set out possible theories concerning the motive of the rebellion of the Watchers in *1 Enoch* and, in so doing; they identify a connection between Genesis 6.1–4 and the Flood. Hanson and Julian Morgenstern have put forward two theories of particular interest.[2]

Hanson suggests that Genesis 4–10 provides the origin of the myth of the Watchers in *BW*.[3] He contends *BW* is comprised of four stages of a "mythic pattern around the theme of rebellion-in-heaven." The four stages are identified as rebellion, devastation, punishment, and restoration.[4] He maintains that these four developments in the Shemihazah tradition have their origins in the Genesis narrative, though the tradition should be considered an elaborate Midrash of the Genesis account.[5] The first stage of Hanson's "mythic pattern" is the plot by "astral deities" to rebel and their descent to earth (*1 Enoch* 6.2–8 = Gen 6.2). Hanson offers three points that he finds in *BW*, which, he contends, corroborate his theory of a rebellion motif in Genesis 6.2. The first point is the introduction of a hybrid

---

in *BW* – "You were in heaven, but [its] secrets had not yet been revealed to you and a worthless mystery you knew. This you made known to the women *in the hardness of your hearts.*" See also the *Book of Parables* 64.2 – "these are the angels who came down from heaven on to the earth and revealed what is secret to the sons of men and led astray the sons of men so that they committed sin." See also in the *Animal Apocalypse* 86.3 – "and again I saw in the vision and looked at heaven, and behold, I saw many stars, how they came down and were thrown down from heaven to that first star and amongst the heifers and bulls." Both of these references show the influence of *BW* on this very point. Knibb suggests "and threw themselves down" perhaps implies rebellion, see Knibb, *Ethiopic Enoch*, 2:197. Cassuto argues that the traditional rabbinic interpretation that the action of the *bene haelohim* was in "opposition to the world order approved by the Lord" does not fit the language of the Genesis passage. He suggests that the language "and they took them wives" is a normal idiom for marriage and therefore sees no rebellion in the actions of the angels. If we consider that this is not the case with the idiom, we have a possible rebellion motif in the Genesis passage. See Cassuto, *Genesis*, 294.

[2] See Hanson, "Rebellion in Heaven" and Morgenstern, "Psalm 82."

[3] Contra Milik, "Problemes," 349.

[4] See Hendel, "Of Demigods," 17, n.17. Hendel argues that Hanson's theory has a two-fold problem: (1) the *bene haelohim* are not seen as rebels in Gen 6; and (2) the sexual mingling is not condemned. Hendel suggests the Genesis passage serves as a preface for the Flood narrative in that it introduces the evil behaviour of humanity and God's displeasure with them. Hendel draws on the Babylonian Atrahasis myth and the Greek Trojan War myth. The basis of the Flood story in the Atrahasis myth is an imbalance in the cosmos, i.e. the overpopulation of humanity which brings the Flood as a result. Hendel describes the Trojan War as a parallel to the Flood as it serves as a division of two ages; ibid., 18, n.22. Furthermore, Hendel finds a close parallel in Hesiod's *Catalogue of Women* frag 204 M–W to Gen 6.1–4. The Hesiod text describes the destruction of humanity in order to prevent the sons of the gods from mating with mortals. The mixing of the two beings has brought about the creation of the demigods: men of renown (seen also in the Prometheus myth). See ibid., 16–7.

[5] See Hanson, "Rebellion in Heaven," 199 and Alexander, "Sons of God," 60.

offspring into the divine creation, which clearly transgresses the separation of the two realms (*1 Enoch* 6.2, 7.2). The second point is the fear of retribution by God for their act (*1 Enoch* 6.3), followed by the third point, a formal oath of conspiracy (*1 Enoch* 6.4–5). All of these elaborations of the Genesis narrative heighten the tension of the narrative produced in *BW*.

The second stage of Hanson's "mythic pattern" is identified in the union of the angels and women, the birth of their giant offspring, the destruction caused by the giants, and the plea of the earth (*1 Enoch* 7.1–6; 8.4 = Gen 6.4; 5–12; and 8.2). This step in the rebellion has unleashed chaos, which in turn brings about the defilement of the creation and the collapse of the divine order. Hanson argues that the author of the Shemihazah tradition has gone far beyond standard midrashic elaboration by transforming the original message into an account about the primordial origins of evil and the future judgment of the Fallen Angels and the unrighteous of humanity.[6]

Hanson contends the third stage involves the intercession of the archangels, the deliverance of Noah, and the punishment of the Watchers and the giants (*1 Enoch* 9.1–10.15 excluding 9.6, 8c, and 10.4–10 = Gen 6.12–13). Whereas the Genesis passage states God is looking down on the earth and sees the destruction, Hanson suggests that the parallel verses in *BW* are an attempt to distance God from evil by substituting the archangels for God in verse 9.1.[7] Furthermore, he suggests *BW* is stressing God's foreknowledge of coming events, a common theme in 2TP literature.[8] Hanson argues this theme is understood through the deliverance of Noah and the punishment of the rebels.

The fourth stage of Hanson's "mythic pattern" is discovered in the restoration of God's kingship and the divine order (*1 Enoch* 10.16–11.2 = Gen 9.8–17; also 8.17, 22; and 9.1). Hanson contends the author of this section of *BW* has plunged all of history into the "ominous chaos of the deluge," thus achieving the final purging of evil from the cosmos in the eschaton.[9]

---

[6] Based on this principle, Hanson argues for the influence of Gen 4–10 upon the author of *1 Enoch* 6–11 which is *contra* Milik's view in which he argues that *BW* served as the source of the Gen 6.1–4 narrative.

[7] Hanson argues that the author was attempting to exonerate God as the one responsible for the evil of the world in Early Judaism. In early Israelite religion, other deities were excluded from a role in the directing of the cosmos. Hanson argues that it was necessary to find an alternate view that allowed for the origins of what appeared to be an uncontrolled evil. See Hanson, "Rebellion in Heaven," 203.

[8] See ibid., 200. See e.g. *Jubilees* 1.4, 26; 1QH 1.7–9, 19–20, 23–24, 28; 15.13–14, 17, 22; CD 2.7–10; and 1QpHab 7.13–14.

[9] Several difficulties arise with Hanson's description of *BW* as a "rebellion-in-heaven," not the least of these is the story line of the Asa'el tradition of the *Animal Apocalypse* and the story of the Watchers in *Jubilees*. The story in these two traditions

Hanson argues that *1 Enoch* 6–11 reveals how scripture was being used in third through second centuries B.C.E., in particular, in an apocalyptic author's explanation of the origin of evil spirits in the world. By following this interpretation, the author has adopted what Hanson calls the theme of "rebellion-in-heaven." This idea, Hanson contends, "can be traced in an unbroken continuum on Near Eastern soil from the mid-second millennium down to the time of the composition of the Shemihazah narrative" in *1 Enoch.*[10] The adaptation of mythopoeic thought by the author of the Shemihazah tradition has transformed the message of Yahwism, which attributed all acts in the divine order to Yahweh (including those with the appearance of evil), into one that, in relation to the origin of evil, attributes this theme to the rebellious Watchers.[11]

Julian Morgenstern contends that *BW* and the *Animal Apocalypse* depict similar accounts of rebellious actions of the *bene haelohim* in Genesis 6.1–4.[12] His contention is based on the term *nephilim* in v. 4, which he argues,

---

describes the angels as already being on the earth; the Watchers were sent there by God and ultimately were led astray by the women. The Shemihazah tradition seems to imply the angels were on the earth when they swore the oath to commit the sin (*1 Enoch* 6.4–6.6). Perhaps a better description might be a "rebellion towards heaven," which would, however, remove some of Hanson's parallels to the earlier Greek and Near Eastern traditions.

[10] Ibid., 232. Hanson understands a consistent stream of Near Eastern influence on the myths that appear in the Watcher tradition, i.e. *Kumarbi* and *Illuyanka* texts. See examples of Hurrian myths that Hanson understands as parallels to *BW*; ibid., 204–06. He argues against a direct Hellenistic parallel to the Shemihazah tradition and goes as far as to contend that there is a Near Eastern myth behind Hesiod's *Theogony*. Despite Hanson's argument for a Near Eastern origin of the Watcher tradition, he uses terminology that can be tied to the Hellenistic traditions, i.e. Hesiod's *Theogony*. The angels are described as οἱ ἄγγελοι υἱοὶ οὐρανοῦ (Ethiopic *malā'ekt weluda samāyāt*), which Hesiod used to describe the gods, in particular the offspring of the gods, in the *Theogony*. Hanson also describes the angels as "astral deities," which seems to grant them a very Greek representation. He does, however, argue that there are direct lines of influence upon Jewish writings from Greek literature; ibid., 204. The problem with the N.E. examples is that the rebellious agent is a deity and not an angel as in the Watcher tradition.

[11] Ibid., 198. Hanson's use of the term "rebellious inclination" (unfortunately he does not elaborate on this expression) implies that there is some kind of sinful nature in the angels and perhaps gives a clearer understanding of how it was possible for them to cross the line between heaven and earth. If this sinful nature is the case, then this raises several questions as to the origin of a "sinful nature" in humanity. Primarily, is there such a thing in humans? And if so, is it possible for it to be in the flesh or of the spirit?

[12] Morgenstern, "Psalm 82," 96. Morgenstern would draw a parallel between *1 Enoch* 86.1 and *1 Enoch* 6. Cf. also the Watcher tradition in *Jubilees* 4.15; 5.1; 7.21, which follows a similar pattern of angelic rebellion found in the *Animal Apocalypse*, although, it is implied the angels were seduced by the women with similar results.

does not represent the same beings as the *gibborim*.[13] He suggests the identity of the *nephilim* can be found in the parallel to the Watcher tradition in *1 Enoch* 86.1f. He argues the language implies that the first star (Asa'el) either fell from heaven by mistake, or more probably, he states, is "that it was cast out of heaven, its original abode, by the Deity."[14]

Morgenstern draws on another version of the Watcher tradition in *2 Enoch* 18.1–6, which, he argues, identifies the star/angel of *1 Enoch* 86 as *Satanail*. He contends this work, possibly dated in the first century B.C.E. or C.E., describes two groups of angels who both rebelled against the deity, but at different times. One group of angels, described as the *Grigori*, rebelled against God along with the angel *Satanail* (*2 Enoch* 29.4–5).[15] Morgenstern maintains *Satanail*, which he identifies as the star in *1 Enoch* 86.1 (cf. *1 Enoch* 6.2), is the leader of the *nephilim* in Genesis 6.4. He then identifies the second group of stars/angels in *1 Enoch* 86.3 as the *bene haelohim*, that is, the angels of the Shemihazah tradition in *1 Enoch* 6.2 who came down from heaven, or were thrown down from heaven after the initial descent of the first star/angel *Satanail*/Asa'el. Morgenstern identifies a line of tradition of angelic rebellion that he argues emerged in the fifth century B.C.E. or earlier and was elaborated upon by the authors of *1 Enoch*, in particular in chapters 6–16.

---

[13] See ibid., 95.

[14] However, the language of 86.1 does not seem to suggest that this is the case, but rather the "star" seemed simply to come to earth and settle in. "And again I looked with my eyes as I was sleeping, and I saw heaven above and behold, a star fell from heaven, and it arose and ate and pastured amongst those bulls"; translation from Knibb, *Ethiopic Enoch*, 2:196.

[15] Morgenstern, "Psalm 82," 98f. Morgenstern argues that the myth of Satan and his rebellious attempt "to supplant God as ruler of the universe has all the indications of great antiquity." It is possible that a motive for this rebellion will be alluded to in the Satan tradition found in the *LAE*. It is here that we find the adoption of a jealousy motif similar to what can be found in *BW* (chs 15–16). The tradition in *LAE*, however, takes on a slightly different twist than the one found in *BW*. *BW* does not attribute the actions of the Watchers to jealousy, but rather the jealousy relates to the activities of the spirits of the giants. Their violent and carnivorous behaviour towards creation implies they have great animosity towards humans, perhaps because of their previous existence as fleshly beings, or as some have suggested, because of the survival of humans after the Flood. *LAE* 12–16 frames jealousy in a very different context: Satan was jealous of the creation of Adam and desired to create his own creature alongside God's. See especially 12.1–2 – "and the devil sighed and said, 'O Adam, all my enmity and envy and sorrow concern you, since because of you I am expelled and deprived of my glory which I had in the heavens in the midst of the angels and because of you I was cast out onto the earth.'" See comments of Dimant, "Fallen Angels," 35–6; she suggests the author of *BW* interpreted 6.2 to mean the *bene haelohim* wanted to father children for themselves, thus adding to the "full measure" of the transgression of the angels. The destructive nature of the offspring affirms the negative implications of this desire and action.

The theories discussed above present some possible traditions that explain the actions of the *bene haelohim* of Genesis 6; however, none of these suggestions offers a clear motive for why the angels rebelled against God. One could only offer mere speculation about the reason why the angels came to earth other than what is offered in Genesis 6.2 ("and the sons of God saw the daughters of humans that they were good to behold"). Nonetheless, *1 Enoch* 6.2–6 indicates that the action of the angels was clearly rebellious: they bind each other with a curse to insure that each one would follow through with the plan (6.4–5). The results of the interaction of the angels and the women brought about catastrophic consequences, not only for themselves but also for the rest of creation.

5.3 Interpreting the Consequences

The consequences of the angelic rebellion in *BW* and Genesis are described in relation to the effect upon humanity and the rest of creation. The first aspect of the consequences is described in Genesis 6.5 (cf. Gen 8.21) which declares that humanity has grown completely evil following the descent of the *bene haelohim* and the birth of their offspring: "Then the Lord saw that the wickedness of humanity was great on the earth and that every inclination (יֵצֶר) of the thoughts of their hearts were only evil continually."[16] The author of *BW* states the theme of this verse in the Instruction motif in *1 Enoch* 8.2: "and there was great impiety and much fornication, and they went astray, and all their ways became corrupt."[17]

Little else is disclosed in either account about the actions of humanity. Genesis 6.6 states that the Lord was sorry that he had created humans and decided to remove them from the face of the earth (v.7), perhaps implying that humans were to blame (v.5) for the previous events in 6.1–4. *BW* interprets these events from a completely different viewpoint. Although humans have a role in the rebellion, they are passive victims of the oppressive behaviour of the angels. If humanity is seen as corrupt (8.1), the author links their corruption directly to the sexual encounter with Shemihazah and the other angels in 7.1 and to the teachings of Asa'el in 8.1. The author makes no mention of blame being placed directly upon humanity (see 7.6; 9.2, 3, 10). Humans are left at the mercy of the giant

---

[16] Cf. *1 Enoch* 8.2, 4. See also *Jubilees* 7.24 (also 5.3) – "and every imagination and desire of men imagined vanity and evil continually." See also *Pseudo-Philo* 3.3, "And God saw that among all those inhabiting the earth wicked deeds had reached full measure; and because they were plotting evil all their days." Translation from Harrington, "Pseudo-Philo," 1:306.

[17] Translation from Knibb, *Ethiopic Enoch*, 2.81.

offspring who bring about the destruction of humanity and the corruption of the earth, both of which are described in the Genesis narrative. In addition to these aspects, the author of *BW* introduced three major elaborations to the Genesis 6 story: that is the role of the *bene haelohim* in the bringing of the Flood, the judgment and punishment of the angels and their giant offspring, and the introduction of evil spirits into creation.

5.3.1 The Corruption of the Earth

The first major elaboration of the Genesis narrative is the angels' involvement in the cause of the Flood. Genesis 6.11 states that the earth had become corrupt (שׁחת – be ruined, be led astray); this included the corruption of all flesh (ותשחת הארץ לפני האלהים ותמלא הארץ חמס, "the earth was corrupted before God, and the earth was full of violence").[18] This verse conceivably makes a direct connection of the violence and corruption of the earth to the angels of Genesis 6.2, 4. The Hebrew of 6.11, האלהים, translated "God," could follow the same suggested pattern of interpreting Genesis 5.24 – ויתהלך חנוך את־ האלהים "and Enoch walked about with the angels." If this is the case, the text of Genesis 6.11 could be read this way: "and the earth was corrupted *by* (*in*) *the presence of the angels* (i.e. *bene haelohim*) and the earth was filled with violence," thus implicating the angels (Watchers) as a cause of the Flood. The author of *BW* identifies this particular theme beginning in *1*

---

[18] Cf. 1 *Enoch* 9.1, 9–10; 10.7–8, 22; 16.3. See a similar description in 4Q556 (Puech designates 4Q533) frag 6.1–3 (cf. 4Q206 3; 4Q201 IV 7; 4Q202 III 8 – Stuckenbruck, *Book of Giants*, 189–90 – Stuckenbruck suggests the end of line 2 may have read "were spoken":

1. לש[ט]קרה[ן ב]ארעא כל[ן
2. דם]הוה מוחפך וכדבי[ן הוו מנ]מלל ין(?)
3. [ ] ובֹל על ארע]א

1. to de]ceive the earth. All/every [
2. blood] was being shed, and lies were being *m*[
3.] And everything upon [the] earth[

See also *Jubilees* 7.21 – "and they made the beginning of uncleanness"; 7.23 – "and everyone sold himself to work iniquity and to shed much blood, and the earth was filled with iniquity." See also *Sib. Or.* 1.77–78, "They were polluted, sated with the blood of people and they made wars"; also 1.154–56 (Noah speaking to humanity prior to the Flood), "Be sober, cut off evils, and stop fighting violently with each other, having a bloodthirsty heart, drenching much earth with human blood." The *DSS* and the N.T. both identify demonic activity within the realm of uncleanness. The Watchers, giants, and their evil spirits all fall into the category of "unclean." Philip Alexander argues that "objects or beings that are out of their proper sphere and in the wrong place" within a society's norms are considered unclean within 2TP Judaism. See Philip S. Alexander, "The Demonology of the Dead Sea Scrolls," in *The Dead Sea Scrolls After Fifty Years A Comprehensive Assessment*, (ed. Peter W. Flint and James C. VanderKam; Leiden: Brill, 1999), 2:348–50. This is certainly the case with the angelic characters of *BW*.

Enoch 9.9 (cf. 9.1) in which a scene of massive violence is described by the author and attributed to the giants ("and the women bore giants and thereby the whole earth has been filled with blood and iniquity").[19] The author of *BW* clearly understood that the responsibility for the corruption of humanity and the earth was the fault of the angels.

Genesis 6.12 states that, for some unstipulated reason; all creatures (i.e. flesh) had fallen into ruin. The author of *1 Enoch* 7.5 picks up this theme in his description of the action of the giants: "and they [presumably the giants] began to sin against birds, and against animals, and against reptiles and against fish, and they devoured one another's flesh[20] and drank the blood from it."[21] By doing so, the author was presumably connecting the reason for the Flood directly to the action of the *bene haelohim* (i.e. the birth of the giants) through his interpretation of Genesis 6.5, 11, and 12. He has not only explained the Flood in antiquity, but he has also identified a reason for the oppression that Israel was facing during his time: evil spirits. Strangely lacking in the Genesis narrative is any direct reference to the *bene haelohim* in 6.5 and following. The author of *BW*, however, by describing their punishment in *1 Enoch* 10.4–15, specifies that they (the Watchers) are responsible for the catastrophic events that are about to take place in the coming Flood.

5.3.2 The Judgment of the Watchers

The second elaboration of the Genesis 6 narrative in *BW* is the description of the judgment and punishment of the angels. The author reveals to the reader the events that followed the disobedience of the angels towards God and his laws that govern the cosmos. *1 Enoch* 10.4–15 describes the punishment of the Watchers for their crimes against God and His creation. Asa'el is first to face his punishment for his role in the Instruction motif of *BW* (10.4–6, 8). He will be bound and cast into the darkness where he will be entombed until the Day of Judgment at which time he will be destroyed in the fire. The angels from the Shemihazah tradition face a similar punishment in 10.11–14. They will first view the death of their offspring (10.12) and secondly, they will be bound under the earth until the day of

---

[19] The Shemihazah and Instruction/Asa'el traditions attribute the destruction of the earth to the actions of the angels.

[20] One may question here whether the giants turned to cannibalistic practices because of the lack of food. The text seems to be referring back to the giants, but it is possible that what we have here is the beginning of prey and predator instincts in the animal kingdom.

[21] Brackets are mine. See *Jubilees* 7.24 (also 5.2), "and after this they sinned against the beasts and birds, and all that moved and walked on the earth." There is perhaps an allusion to the giants devouring humans found in Ps 14.4, "Do all the doers of evil not know, the ones eating my people *as* they ate bread, and the lord they do not call"?

their judgment (10.12). The judgment occurs after seventy generations of entombment at which time they will be cast into the fire where they will be destroyed (10.13–14).

The author of *1 Enoch* 15 offers a further explanation for the punishment of the Watchers by contrasting the angels and Enoch.[22] *1 Enoch* 15.6 (also 15.4) describes the former condition of the Watchers prior to their violation of the law of the cosmos: "but you formerly were spiritual, living an eternal, immortal life for all the generations of the world." The punishment of the angels was the loss of their immortality and they would not dwell in the high heaven (13.5).[23] The Watchers have exchanged their dwelling place in heaven, among the council of the holy ones (15.10),[24] for a prison under the earth till the Day of Judgment (10.4–5, 12).[25] In contrast, the *Epistle of Enoch* states that Enoch would take up a place in the heavens with the angels (106.7). These contrasts perhaps corroborate the theory that the Watchers crossed the line of their place in the cosmos, which ultimately produced the giant offspring. This leads to a third expansion of the Genesis 6.1–4 narrative in *BW*, one which is perhaps the most difficult to locate within early Jewish literature, the giant offspring and their evil spirits.

5.4 The Nature of the Gibborim

There is little argument amongst scholars that the offspring of the union of the Watchers and women were creatures of gargantuan stature. *1 Enoch* 7.2 makes clear that the offspring were physically huge, "and their height was three thousand cubits."[26] Because of their stature, the giants are said to

---

[22] (1) The Watchers have sent Enoch to petition on their behalf (15.2) which was formerly their task; (2) they had left the high, holy, and eternal heaven to dwell on the earth (15.3); Enoch was now walking with the angels in the heavens (*1 Enoch* 14; 17–36; Gen 5.22); and (3) they exchanged their immortality for mortality; Enoch exchanged his mortality for immortality in heaven.

[23] The author of *BW* may have been drawing on Ps 82.7, which appears to describe the fate of the Watchers because of their great sin: "nevertheless you will die as men and as one of the princes you will fall."

[24] "And the dwelling place of spirits of heaven is in heaven," see also Ps 82.6, 89.6–7.

[25] See also *Jubilees* 5.6, "And against the angels whom he had sent upon the earth, he was exceedingly wroth, and he gave commandment to root them out of all their dominion, and he bade us to bind them in the depths of the earth." Compare also *Sib. Or.* 1.100–103, "they were mighty of great form, but nevertheless they went under the dread house of Tartarus guarded by unbreakable bonds, to make retribution to Gehenna of terrible, raging, undying fire." Translation from Collins, "Sibylline Oracles," 1:337.

[26] See Ethiopic and Greek[pan]. See also 4Q201 3 16. It is possible that the giants were indeed superhuman "heroes," not necessarily gigantic in physical size, but in spiritual

have devoured all the sustenance that humanity produced until the supply
ended and they ultimately turned on the humans themselves. Thus, the
author of *BW* has turned the seemingly heroic *gibborim* of Genesis 6.4 into
a group of bloodthirsty cannibals with little inducement from the Genesis
passage.[27] The author's description of the giants and their actions is quite
graphic in *1 Enoch* 7.4. They are described as murderers and cannibals.
The Aramaic fragment of 4QEn[a] 1 iii 18, 19 reads והוו גבריא] קשרין
לקטלה לאנשא ו֯לֹלמכל אנון, "but the giants] conspired to kill men and
[to devour them."[28] Moreover, it is possible that *1 Enoch* 7.6 describes
them as "lawless ones," though it is unclear whether the verse refers to the
giants or the Watchers. In the immediate context, it would appear that the
expression has the giants in view; this could then imply that the author
understood they are in violation of numerous Levitical laws concerning
blood. Leviticus 3.17; 7.26, 27;[29] 17.10, 12, 14;[30] and 19.26[31] all proscribe

---

size. The Greek[pan] of *1 Enoch* 15.8 identifies the spirits of the giants as πνεύματα
ἰσχυρά, "strong spirits" (Greek[sync] reads πνεύματα πονηρά, "evil spirits"). This may
help identify the spiritual nature of the giants. The spiritual power that resides in the
spirit of an angel now occupied a human body, thus pushing the limits of the human flesh
that attempted to contain it, thus Gen 6.3. *1 Enoch* 15.7 states that God did not allow
angels to reproduce with women because of their spiritual nature; their place was to
reside in the heavens not in human flesh.

[27] The violent nature of the giants creates difficulty if we are to try to make a point of
contact with the offspring of the sons of god (and Zeus himself) and mortals in the Greek
tradition. The offspring of the Greek myths were good and evil, not evil in a sense of
destroying creation as the giants of *BW* nearly brought about, but rather for the
preservation and continuation of it. It is possible; however, if we take into consideration
the implied evil activity of humanity prior to the descent of the *bene haelohim* and its
increase after, the giants may have played a similar role of bringing about the
preservation and continuation of the earth.

[28] See Milik, *Books of Enoch*, 150–51. Milik has reconstructed the beginning of the
verse (supported in the Ethiopic and Greek), "but the giants" and the ending, "to devour
them." Cf. 4QEn[b] 1 ii 22–23 in which Milik reconstructs the entire verse similar to that
found in 4QEn[a] 1 iii 18, 19. His reconstruction is supported in the Greek[pan] of *1 Enoch*
7.4. There is a possible parallel to the giants in *Sib. Or.* 1.104–08, see Collins, "Sibylline
Oracles," 1:337. This passage refers to a generation who were "mighty in spirit, of
overbearing terrible men appeared who performed many evils among themselves. Wars,
slaughters, and battles destroyed these continually, men of proud heart," see *1 Enoch*
10.9 and 14.6. Interestingly, this generation immediately follows the mention of the
Watchers.

[29] Lev 7.26 and 27 make specific reference to drinking the blood of birds and animals,
which the giants are accused of violating in *1 Enoch* 7.5.

[30] Lev 17.14 presents two interesting questions about the action of the giants. The
verse states, "For the life [נפש] of all flesh is its blood, it is its life [נפש]. And I said to
the sons of Israel, 'You shall not eat blood of any flesh for [the] life of all flesh is its
blood; anyone who eats of it shall be cut off.'" First, we should perhaps ask if there is
any significance in why the giants drank the blood of the animals. One possible answer is

eating (or drinking) the blood of an animal, an injunction which is broken by the giants in *1 Enoch* 7.5.[32] The punishment for this sin, articulated in Leviticus is that the person shall be cut off (נכרתה) from his people.[33] The result of this sin is described in *1 Enoch* 10.15, "and destroy all the spirits of lust and the sons of the Watchers, for they have wronged men."

The death of the giants reveals something about the nature of their spirits. They are considered evil spirits because they were born on the earth; they are a mixed product of a spiritual being (Watcher angel) and a physical, and a somewhat spiritually undefined human.[34] The resulting entities are identified in *1 Enoch* 15.8 as "strong spirits," "evil spirits," which come out of their bodies at their death.[35] The spirit of the giant is in a class similar to the spirit of a Watcher, but with distinct differences.

There are two main points that identify important characteristics of the nature of the giants' spirits in relation to the angelic Watchers. First, we find no evidence that upon the death of their physical body, the spirits of the giants are able to transform themselves into human form[36] in order to

---

that they were seeking immortality through the drinking of blood. Second, were the giants cut off from the people? Anyone in violation of the law of Lev 17.14 was to be cut off from the people, which would occur in the case of the giants (*1 Enoch* 10.9).

[31] Lev 19.26 describes the eating of blood alongside the sin of the practice of divination and soothsaying, two practices that could be tied to the Instruction of the Watchers in *1 Enoch* 8.2.

[32] See also the concern of the author of *Jubilees* over the issue of eating or drinking blood in relation to the evil spirits in *Jubilees* 7.

[33] The verb נכרתה is defined as cut off, removed, or destroyed. See David J. Clines et al., eds., *The Dictionary of Classical Hebrew* (vol. IV; Sheffield: Sheffield Academic, 1998), 465.

[34] We get no real sense of the spiritual nature of the Watcher's offspring other than they are strong or evil spirits. There are references outside of Hebrew tradition that describe the nature of the offspring of somewhat similar unions. Hesiod's *Catalogue of Women* frag 1.6 describes the offspring of relations between women and the gods as ἡμίθεοι, "half–gods," perhaps indicating a 50/50 mix of human and divine. The *Epic of Gilgamesh* I ii 1, IX ii 16 describes the Sumero-Babylonian hero, who is the son of the goddess *Ninsun*, as two-thirds divine and one-third mortal. The latter description may better suit the spirits of the giants, as they seem to take on more of the angelic influence following their death than the human side, i.e. they are able to roam the earth. See also West, *East Face*, 117. There is a possible Israelite heroic figure identified in Judg 3.31 and 5.6; he is Shamgar the son of a Canaanite goddess called Anat,

[35] See above n. 26. There are no extant Aramaic fragments of *1 Enoch* 15.8. *Jubilees* 10.1–3 identify them as unclean demons, wicked (unclean) spirits.

[36] For reference to angelic transformation see *1 Enoch* 17.1 – "And they took me to a place where they were like burning fire and when they wished, they made themselves look like men." This verse is describing the action of the angels with whom Enoch is touring heaven, but the Watchers were likely in the same class. *1 Enoch* 19.1 – "And Uriel said to me: 'The spirits of the angels who were promiscuous with the women will stand here and they, assuming many forms, made men unclean and will lead men

have intercourse with the women, as did their fathers.[37] The second point involves the necessity for the Watchers to be bound in Tartarus in order to halt their activity, while the spirits of the giants, following the death of their physical body, are allowed to roam freely upon the earth.[38] The ability to roam about the earth links the nature of the evil spirits of the giants to the spiritual nature of the Watchers prior to their fall. What is not clear is why these beings are given that freedom. However, the Watcher tradition in *Jubilees* indicates that this semi-freedom was required in order for them to operate within the divine economy.

Jubilees 10, in describing Noah's complaint about the spirits of the giants who were leading astray and corrupting humans, states that in order for their (the evil spirits) actions to be stopped, they must be bound up and held fast (i.e. from moving about freely on earth) in the place of condemnation, similar to the fate of their fathers (*Jub* 10.5, 11). However, Mastema asks the Lord for some of the spirits to remain free in order that he may execute his task upon the earth, perhaps an elaboration of a similar theme in *1 Enoch* 15.11–12.

---

astray.'" See also 4Q204 frag 5 col. II 18–19 – "they transgressed [the word of the Lord . . . they si]nned and trans[gressed ... and] they changed [th]eir [nature] to g[o] 19 [unto women and sin with them ...]"; *T. Reuben* 5.6 – "then they (watchers) were transformed into human males." These texts seem to indicate that angels had the ability to transform into humans (at least in part), which is an attribute clearly missing from the nature of the spirits of the giants. The inability to transform themselves into human form may have implications in the evil spirit's desire to re-inhabit a human body.

[37] 4Q203 frag 8.7–8 states that the sons of the watchers had wives and sons of their own. Stuckenbruck reads the fragment:

7. ‏ועובדכון ודי נש [. . .]‎

8. ‏אנון [ו]בני[הון ונ[נ]שיא ד]ני כולהון‎

7. your activity and that of [your] wive[s and of your children and of
8. those [giants and their]son[s and] the [w]ives o[f all of them.

See Loren T. Stuckenbruck, *The Book of Giants From Qumran, Texts, Translation, and Commentary* (TSAJ 63; Tübingen: J. C. B. Mohr, 1997), 87–90. Cf. Florentino García Martínez and Eibert J. C. Tigchelaar, eds., *The Dead Sea Scrolls Study Edition* (Leiden/Grand Rapids: Brill/Eerdmans, 1997–98), 1:411.

7. ‏ועובדכון ודי נשישון [. . .]‎

8. ‏אנון [ו]בני[הון] ונשיא ד]ני בניהון [. . .]‎

7. and your deeds and those of you wives [. . .]
8. they [and the]ir sons and the wives o[f their sons . . .].

This would imply that the giants had sexual intercourse with human women (or female giants?).

[38] See Lk 11.24–26, which suggests unclean spirits inhabit a human body and when they are not, they wander the earth. Philip Alexander suggests that the free roaming spirits of the giants (lot of Belial) are found in 1QM 1.5 and 9.5–6. See Alexander, "Demonology of the Dead Sea Scrolls," 2:339.

A further description of the character of the giants is given in *1 Enoch* 10.9. The author of this verse may have been trying to connect the corrupt nature of the offspring of the angels and women to Genesis 6.3. Any allusion to Genesis 6.3 is curiously omitted in *1 Enoch* 6, but is possibly alluded to in 10.9–10. The author of 10.9 may be identifying the characters of Genesis 6.3 as the giants: "Proceed against the bastards[39] and the adulterers[40] and against the sons of the fornicators, and destroy the sons of the Watchers from amongst humanity. Send them into a war of destruction, for they will not have length of days."[41] The term "bastard" is defined in

---

[39] Cf. also Greek[pan] *1 Enoch* 10.15 which identifies the spirits of the giants as "bastards" (τὰ πνεύματα τῶν κιβδήλων) while the Ethiopic refers to them as "souls of lust and sons of the Watchers," translation from Knibb, *Ethiopic Enoch*, 90. See also 3 Macc 2.4; Sir 16.7; and Wis 14.6, which claim the giants died in the Flood because of their arrogance or revolt.

[40] Does this imply the giants also had sexual relations with married women? Based on the references to the three layers of offspring in Greek[sync] *1 Enoch* 7.1c–2, 86.4; and *Jubilees* 7.22 it seems possible that the giants fathered their own offspring. Alexander argues, based on "a sterile race of the Giants," that there is a fixed number of demons on the earth; see Alexander, "Demonology in DSS," 340. In addition, he suggests that since *1 Enoch* 6.6 states that there were only two hundred Watchers at the start of the rebellion, and "unless they were extremely promiscuous and their partners very fertile, we should not be thinking of countless myriads of demons." Alexander is correct in his assumption that there is a limited number of demons at work on the earth, but the number could be quite large, based on (1) the Watchers could have been with more than one partner; (2) the giants could also have had sexual relations with human women (or other female giants); and (3) there is a possible 120 year span of time before the Flood in which all this could have repeated itself.

[41] Cf. *Jubilees* 5.6–11 which describes, in similar terms, the destruction of the giants, "And against their sons went forth a command from before his face that they should be smitten by the sword and removed from under heaven." The author of *Jubilees* 5.8 has, similar to *1 Enoch* 10.9, made a connection between the physical giants and Gen 6.3. The *Jubilees* author has in fact quoted the passage, "My spirit will not always abide on man for they also are flesh and their days shall be one hundred and twenty years." Cf. also *1 Enoch* 88.2, "and one of them drew his sword and gave it to those elephants and camels and asses and they began to strike one another," see also *1 Enoch* 12.6, "for they will not rejoice in their sons. The slaughter of their beloved ones they will see, and over the destruction of their sons they will lament and petition forever," see Knibb, *Ethiopic Enoch*, 2:92; also *1 Enoch* 14.6. The story of the death of the offspring is slightly different in the *Animal Apocalypse*. Unlike their deaths prior to the Flood in *BW*, the author of the *Animal Apocalypse* (89.6) states that the death of some of the offspring will occur during the Flood. It appears that not only do we not have the survival of the physical giants, but also there is no reference to the survival of the spirits of the offspring. However, the author may have allowed for the survival of the spirits of the giants in the form of the seventy shepherds. The actions of the shepherds (under the influence of the spirits?) in *1 Enoch* 89.59–90.25 perhaps allude to the actions of the spirits in *Jubilees* 10.8, while 90.25 could represent the final destruction of the spirits on the Day of Judgment (16.1).

the biblical texts as either a person of questionable birth (Deut 23.3) or a person whose lineage is pagan (Zech 9.6). The giants no doubt fall into the category of questionable birth as the children of illegitimate sexual relations between the angels and humans.[42] There are several attestations of ממזר in the Qumran literature. It refers to people who are refused entry to the community at Qumran in 4Q395 39 and 4Q174 III 4. 1QH[a] XXIV 16 perhaps hints that ממזרים are demonic spirits if we consider the document's dualistic nature.[43]

The statement, "for they will not have length of days," indicates that the giants will not live a long "human" life. At the same time, however, it does not say anything about the issue of their continued spiritual existence. The Watchers have petitioned for the lives of their offspring in hope that they may live a long life (ζωὴν αἰώνιον), but the answer is no.[44] Their children shall be destroyed in front of them (cf. *Jub* 5.10). The authors of *Jubilees* and *BW* have identified the giant offspring as the characters of Genesis 6.3, thereby reflecting the link already established in Genesis 6.1–4.

The character of the *gibborim* of Genesis 6.4 has been clearly elaborated upon by the author of *BW*. They no longer carry the heroic image that is implied by the language of the Genesis narrative. They have emerged as a hybrid creature that wreaks havoc upon the earth while it is in its physical form. Without the intervention of God to end their physical existence, they would have destroyed all of humanity. They caused the corruption of the earth that required its purification by the Flood and a new beginning for humanity through Noah. Nevertheless, the physical death of the giants did not bring the end to their existence. Following their deaths by fratricide, the author of *BW* introduces the crux of the problem of the union of the Watchers and women: the emergence of evil spirits from the bodies of the giants.

5.5 Aetiology of Evil Spirits

BW's depiction of the origin of evil spirits describes the beginning of an ongoing problem with evil spirits in the 2TP. It is evident from a number

---

[42] For discussion of "Mamzerim," see article of Ben Zion Schereschewsk, "Mamzer," *EncJud* 11:840–42. See also J. Hastings, "Bastard," in *Dictionary of the Bible*, 91.

[43] See Armin Lange, "Spirit of Impurity" in *Demons: The Demonology of Israelite–Jewish and Early Christian Literature in Context of their Environment*, (eds. Armin Lange, Herman Lichtenberger and K.F. Diethard Römheld; Tübingen: Mohr Siebeck, 2003), 254–268.

[44] Petersen has suggested that Gen 6.1–4 is a text which "sets Yahweh's limitations on human life in the primeval period, a time when the world was being moulded," see Petersen, "Genesis 6," 54–5. Petersen argues, "The mortality of humanity, the absolute boundary, was established in Genesis 3. Genesis 6.1–4 serves to preserve and set specific limits on that temporality."

of references in early Jewish literature that these spirits had taken up a place in the theological worldview of at least a portion of Early Judaism.[45] This may explain, or be explained by, the aetiological use of Genesis 6 in the development of evil spirits in *1 Enoch* 15–16.

Before exploring the aetiology further, it is important to consider an objection raised by Devorah Dimant. She has argued, "From the viewpoint of the story's structure and content, there is no place for demons or evil spirits."[46] She goes on to suggest that "if one assumes that evil spirits emerge from the bodies of the dead giants, there is no reason for the punishment of destruction imposed on the giants because the spirits continue to cause evil for humanity." She argues that the destruction of the giants does not fulfil its purpose, claiming that with the emergence of the evil spirits from the bodies of the giants, there is no need for the command to Gabriel and Raphael to cleanse the earth from evil (10.16). She contends that by allowing the evil spirits to exist, the command to cleanse the earth is not fulfilled.[47] However, Dimant's objection should be refuted, and three points may be made. (1) The punishment of the giants is enacted on their physical bodies and in response to concern that all of humanity would be lost. (2) They must be stopped from reproducing with the humans (or perhaps other giants).[48] (3) A second judgment is promised (*1 Enoch* 10, 16) in which the evil spirits will be destroyed.[49]

Dimant contends that the introduction of evil spirits in *BW* is from a different haggadic version of the story, which was combined with the story of the offspring as physical giants. She states two strands that bear distinctive emphasis describe the evil inflicted upon humanity: (1) the women gave birth to physical giants who attack humanity; and (2) the

---

[45] See e.g. 4Q560; 4Q510; 4Q511; 4Q230; 4Q231; 11Q11; 1QapGen; 4Q544; 4Q429; and 4Q444. The evil spirits are designated as πνεύματα πονηρά, which are usually spirits that lead people to sin or they cause illness. A possible origin is found in the O.T. in 1 Sam 16 and 18. It is also found in literature of the immediate period; see e.g. *T. Simeon* 3.5; 4.9; *T. Judah* 16.1; *T. Levi* 5.6; 18.12; Tob 6.7; and in Gospel accounts of Lk 7.21; 8.2; 11.26; and Matt 12.43.

[46] See Dimant, "Fallen Angels," 62.

[47] John Collins and others suggest that this command to the archangels could easily be an event that will occur in the eschaton, as is suggested in *1 Enoch* 16.1. See John J. Collins, "Methodological Issues in the Study of 1 Enoch: Reflections on the Articles of P. D. Hanson and G. W. Nickelsburg," in *SBL Seminar Papers* (ed. Paul J. Achtemeier; Missoula: Scholars Press, 1978), 318–19.

[48] See n. 40 above.

[49] See Paolo Sacchi *Jewish Apocalyptic and its History* (trans. William J. Short; JSPSup 20; Sheffield: Sheffield Academic, 1990), 54. Sacchi suggests that "already and not yet" eschatology is a characteristic of 2TP Jewish apocalypticism,

women gave birth to evil spirits. The inclusion of evil spirits who are not destroyed and who inflict distress upon humanity is "closer to a world view that explains the source of evil in the world and not a story about frightful sinners."[50] She states that this view of the myth of the Fallen Angels is unfounded and is based on an emphasis of the account of the evil spirits.[51]

Dimant seems to have misunderstood the author's intent; whether there are one or two or many different sources within *BW* is irrelevant, what does matter is that this story appears as a whole in the third to second centuries B.C.E and therefore should be read and interpreted in that form because of the wide-ranging influence it no doubt exerted on 2TP Judaism.[52] Support for such a reading is readily available in the Qumran material, which provides evidence of a well-developed and widely received Watcher tradition in the third through the first centuries B.C.E. No matter what sources the author used, he was concerned with a story about the past (the origin of evil spirits), his present (the continued oppression of Israel by the spirits), and the future (the ultimate destruction of the spirits).

In *1 Enoch* 15.6 God declares to Enoch the extent to which the Watchers have disrupted the cosmos. They were spiritual beings that were never meant to cross the line of their heavenly existence and become part of the fleshly world (15.7). The continued existence of the angels did not require the act of procreation for which God gave women (θηλείας) to men. Therefore, by procreating through the women, the Watchers have created an unauthorized new being, one that is a mix of the heavenly nature of angels and the body and flesh of humans: "they will be called evil spirits" and they will dwell amongst humans (15.8). *1 Enoch* 15.9 helps to clarify further the spiritual nature of the giants. "Evil spirits came out from their bodies[53] because they originated from above,[54] and out of the

---

[50] Ibid., 63.

[51] Idem, "Methodological Perspective," 330. See also p. 338, n. 66 for a list of those who share this opinion with her.

[52] See Collins, "Methodological Issues," 316.

[53] Greek^syne reads, "They will be evil spirits, the evil spirits which have come out from the bodies of their flesh."

[54] Greek^syne reads, "they originated from men" which is followed by Black, *Book of Enoch*, 34. The Greek^pan and Ethiopic reading "from above" seems to make better sense. Knibb argues that "the clause explains why *spirits* came out of the flesh of the giants, not why *evil* spirits came out," but it seems this is precisely the explanation; see Knibb, *Ethiopic Enoch*, 2:101. The spirits of the giants originated within the Watchers, but became eternal spirits of impurity. Nickelsburg suggests that we should not compare the spiritual make-up of the giants with the spiritual make-up of humans, see Nickelsburg, *Commentary*, 272f. The spirit of a giant is a result of the Watchers spawning their substance onto the earth.

holy Watchers; [this is] the origin of their creation and their foundation. They will be called evil spirits."[55] The author of *BW* has made it clear in 15.10 that, as spirits, the former giants are no threat to the heavenly realm; they are spirits born on the earth, who are confined to the earth. Conversely, they are perceived as a threat to humanity (15.11).

Similar to Genesis 6.5–7.24, there is no clear textual evidence in the Watcher tradition that permits the survival of the physical giant offspring from Genesis 6.4.[56] On the contrary, their physical destruction seemed certain in each development of the tradition (*1 Enoch* 15.12, 89.6 and *Jub* 7.25).[57] However, equally certain is the survival of the evil spirits that came out of their bodies upon their death (16.1). The giants, like their human counterparts, were composed of two elements; they each had a fleshly body, which could die, and they each had an immortal spirit (in the sense that its existence continued following a physical death).[58] The spiritual element of the giants, however, had a slightly different nature to that of the human spirit. The giants' spirits, unlike the human spirit, were able to roam the earth unseen (*1 Enoch* 15.11), a trait inherited from their fathers. Alexander suggests an important difference that exists between the giants and angels; the former, as evil spirits, are able to invade the human body.[59] This characteristic, it seems, goes beyond the description of their task as evil spirits upon the earth in *1 Enoch* 15.11–12: "And the spirits of the giants, the nephilim,[60] inflicting harm, being corrupt, and attacking, and

---

[55] Greek[sync] 9e–10 reads, "They will be evil spirits upon the earth."

[56] Stuckenbruck suggests there were sufficient grounds for the readers of 2TP literature to imagine that these giants had survived the Flood. He proposes two likely scenarios: (1) they escaped on the ark with Noah's family, either as part of it or otherwise (see *1 Enoch* 106–07; 4Q205 frag 5 ii; and 1QapGen 2); and (2) the author of the biblical text omitted the specifics of how they survived the deluge, but from the many references in the biblical narrative, one may surmise their possible survival, see Stuckenbruck, "Angels and Giants," 356. See in particular the story of Nimrod as a γίγας in Gen 10.8–11. Nimrod's connection to Babylon is perhaps alluded to in Eusebius' *Praeparatio Evangelica* 9.17.2–3. The city of Babylon is founded by the giants who escaped the Flood, who then built the tower of Babel (Gen 10.10; 11.3–4); see R. Doran, "Pseudo-Eupolemus," in *The Old Testament Pseudepigrapha* (ed. James H. Charlesworth; 2 vols.; New York: Doubleday, 1983–85), 2:880 (see discussion pp. 100–01).

[57] This is also the case in several of the *DSS* fragments, 4Q370 1.6; 4Q202 iv 5–6; vi 8–10; 4Q203 frag 5; 4Q204 v 2; vi 15–16; 4Q531 frag 4.5.

[58] 4Q531 14 indicates a self-description by the giants that they are neither "bones nor flesh," a form from which they will be blotted out, implying they are spiritual beings; see discussion in Stuckenbruck, *Book of Giants*, 159–60. See also *T. Sol* 5.3, which identifies the demon Asmodeus of *Tobit* as the son of an angel with a human mother, identifying him as a giant (cf. also *T. Sol* 17.1).

[59] See Alexander, "Demonology in *DSS*," 339.

[60] Unfortunately, there are no Aramaic fragments of this passage. All three extant versions, Ethiopic, Greek[pan], and Greek[sync] appear corrupted and seem very disjointed.

fighting, and dashing on the ground,[61] and they cause sorrow; and consuming nothing, but abstaining from eating and do not thirst, and they strike spirits."[62] Nonetheless, as Alexander notes, this list of characteristics does not eliminate the possibility that the spirits are also capable of "possessing" a human body.

Jubilees 10 describes a similar situation concerning the actions of the spirits of the giants following the Flood. We are told that the unclean spirits began to lead astray humanity and to destroy them, "impure demons began to mislead Noah's grandchildren, to make them act foolishly, and to destroy them."[63] This ability of the evil spirits to lead humanity astray may be premised on the Watchers' teaching their sons the mysteries of heaven. This idea is found initially in *1 Enoch* 10.7, "not all the sons of men shall be destroyed through *the mystery of everything which the Watchers made known and taught to their sons.*"[64] *1 Enoch* 19.1 may suggest what exactly the humans were led to do that would destroy them, " . . . [the spirits of the angels] who lead men astray so that they sacrifice to demons (δαιμονίοις) as gods."[65] Several passages in the Hebrew Bible (see e.g. Deut 32.17 and

---

Black presents a good mix of the Greek versions; see Black, *Book of Enoch*, 34. See discussion of the corrupt nature of this portion of the text in Knibb, *Ethiopic Enoch*, 2:101

[61] Greek[pan] reads here πνεύματα σκληρὰ γιγάντων – "hard [harsh] spirits of [the] giants."

[62] See Greek[pan], καὶ προσκόπτοντα πνεύματα – "striking spirits." Knibb has suggested "and are not observed," ibid., 2:102; Black suggests "and produce hallucinations" (from Greek[sync]), Black, *Book of Enoch*, 34.

[63] Translation from James C. VanderKam, *The Book of Jubilees*, (CSCO 511 Lovanii: Aedibus E. Peeters, 1989), 58. *Jubilees* 10.1, 2 identifies the spirits of the giants with the term "demon," which is not a term used in *BW* to identify the spirits.

[64] Italics mine. Translation Knibb, *Ethiopic Enoch*, 2:88. This, again, is a very corrupt text that Knibb suggests was altered by Syncellus or his sources. *1 Enoch* 16.3 explains that the instruction, which the Watchers taught humanity and their sons, was a "worthless mystery" that caused evil to increase on the earth. *1 Enoch* 16.3 also implies that it was for malevolent reasons (perhaps jealousy?) that the Watchers taught these mysteries, "in the hardness of your hearts."

[65] There are suggestions in the Watcher tradition that imply the spirits of 19.1 may be the spirits of the giants. Nickelsburg suggests this can be found in 15.11 by reading νιμόμενα ("pasturing") for the Aramaic רעין, corrupt for תעין (lead astray) or for רעעין (shatter) in 11a; see Nickelsburg, *Commentary*, 268, 273. This idea is elaborated upon in *Jubilees* 7.27; 10.2, 7–13; 11.4; 12.20. The spirits, by implication, would carry on the activity of the giants and their fathers the Watchers based on 10.7. The Watcher tradition in *Jubilees* makes it clear that it is the spirits of the giants who lead humans astray (10.2), "and the sons of Noah came to Noah their father and they told him concerning the demons which were leading astray . . ." *Jubilees* 10.4 implies it is these same spirits which lead humans to make idols and to worship them, "and malignant spirits assisted and seduced them into committing transgression and uncleanness." The difficulty with the extant forms of 19.1 is that it challenges the interpretation of the

Ps 105.37) state that humans were sacrificing to demons.[66] According to these two examples, the people were led to sacrifice to demons (Hebrew, שֵׁדִים) as gods.[67] Although we cannot assume that these texts influenced the author of *BW*, it seems the author was aware of the practice in Israel's history.

The author of *BW* introduced an answer to the evil in his day that the Genesis Flood narrative does not address. The Genesis narrative implies that all corrupt flesh will be destroyed in the deluge (Gen 6.13). This throws the spotlight on the figure of Noah, in whom both biblical narrative and *BW* are theologically invested. What does complete annihilation through the Flood mean in relation to Noah?[68] As the rest of the story of Genesis shows, sin continues after the Flood.[69] Genesis simply implies that sin survived through Noah and his family, whereas the Watcher tradition recounts the survival of the evil spirits as an explanation of why evil persists in the author's day. However, the author does not leave the reader without hope concerning these evil spirits. In *1 Enoch* 16.1, he describes their unabated oppression and affliction of humanity, but he reports that there is a limit to their dominion. The great Day of Judgment will end their powers over humans and they will be judged and punished along with the Watchers and human sinners.

Jubilees presents a slightly different view of the post-deluge actions of the evil spirits. It is a perspective that perhaps brings the actions of the surviving evil spirits in line with the limited demonic activity we find in the Hebrew Bible. *1 Enoch* 15.12 states that the spirits of the giants "will

---

judgment scene of the Watchers in chapter 10 of *BW* and *Jubilees* 5. If we interpret the story as pre-Flood, and there is nothing to tell us otherwise, it looks back to the time before the confinement of angels, when during their time on earth they led humanity to sacrifice to idols. Therefore, it may be plausible for one to suggest that the spirits of the giants are leading humanity to sacrifice to idols; ibid., 287.

[66] These demons (δαιμονίοις) should not be understood as the evil spirits of the giants, but rather as the spiritual powers of the principalities and nations (cf. Deut 32.8 and Sir 17.17).

[67] The Greek[pan] text of *1 Enoch* 16.1 states that these evil spirits will corrupt humanity without judgment until the great judgment. The Ethiopic text differs significantly from the Greek texts in this verse. Siam Bhayro has suggested in a personal correspondence that the Greek[pan] text is likely the most reliable in comparison to the Aramaic original of *BW*. The Ethiopic makes no mention of the continued destructive work of the spirits of the giants until the Day of Judgment. Another significant variant occurs in 16.3 in which the Greek describes the mysteries that the Watchers revealed were "mysteries of God", whereas the Ethiopic reads "worthless mysteries".

[68] Noah's prayer in *Jubilees* 10.3 implies that he is very much aware of his sinful nature and is thankful for the mercy and grace that God has shown to him.

[69] *Jubilees* 10.8 states that following the Flood "great is the wickedness of the sons of men."

rise against the sons of men and women because they came forth from them."[70] The context of this verse, established in 15.11, seems to indicate little restraint is placed upon the activity of the giants' spirits; their end will come only in the eschaton. The author of *Jubilees* 10 further develops this element of the Watcher tradition by limiting the autonomy of the evil spirits. It is possible from Charles' reading of 10.6, that up to this point, the spirits had free reign over humanity (similar to what we find in *1 Enoch* 15.11–12), "for you [God] alone can exercise dominion over them. And let them not have power over the sons of the righteous."[71] God then orders the archangels to bind all the evil spirits (10.7), but the chief of the spirits, Mastema, implores the Lord to leave some of them with him in order to carry out his task against humanity. This is a major shift from the role of the evil spirits in *BW*; there they have no apparent leader, and there is no mention of the figure of Satan (Mastema in *Jubilees*). The notion of a leader over the realm of evil spirits seems to have been taken up in some of the *DSS* that express a demonological interest. The figure in the *DSS*, identified as *Belial*, may be connected to *Mastema* in *Jubilees* (see below).

Excursus: Mastema and Belial[72]

The term *Mastema* originates from the Hebrew root שׂטם (satam) which is a derivative of שׂטן (satan).[73] The origins of this personification are found in the Hebrew Bible.[74] *Mastema* appears in Hosea 9.7–8 as a noun that is translated "hostility." It has likely evolved from the concept of hostility or

---

[70] This verse seems to imply the reason for the spirits' oppression of humanity is simply that they were born out of their flesh. This could indicate a need for the spirit to reoccupy flesh, i.e. possession. Alexander suggests that "as disembodied spirits roaming the world, like the human 'undead,' they particularly seek embodiment, with all its attendant problems for the one whom they possess," see Alexander, "Demonology in DSS," 339.

[71] Nickelsburg, *Commentary*, 287, n. on 10.6. Nickelsburg argues that Charles has emended the Ethiopic without due cause, and that it should read; "for you alone know their punishment; and may they not have power over the sons of the righteous."

[72] See J. W. van Henten, "Mastemah," in *Dictionary of Deities and Demons in the Bible (DDD)* (2d ed.; eds. Karel van der Toorn, Bob Becking and Peiter W. van der Horst; Leiden/Grand Rapids: Brill/Eerdmans, 1999), 553–54 and David S. Sperling, "Belial," in ibid., 169–71.

[73] See P.L. Day, *An Adversary in Heaven: Śāṭān in the Hebrew Bible* (HSM 43; Atlanta: Scholars, 1988).

[74] The LXX uses the term διάβολος to translate the Hebrew השׂטן thirteen times as a proper name – Job 1.6, 7(2), 8, 9, 12(2); 2.1, 2(2), 3, 4, 6, 7; Zech 3.1, 2(2); and 1 Chr 21.1. In these instances, it could be implied that השׂטן is a member of the *bene haelohim*; however, it could be understood that he has been singled out, thus leaving room to recognize him as some other type of being. The Hebrew שׂטן is transliterated three times (1 Kgs 11.14, 23, 25) and is translated as ἐπίβουλος (adversary) in 1 Kgs 5.18. In these four instances, שׂטן is portrayed as a human adversary.

adversarial conduct to the personification of this concept in post-biblical Judaism in the figure of Satan, *Mastema* (*Jubilees*), *Belial* (*DSS*)[75] and other designations in the New Testament.[76] In *Jubilees* 10.8, he is seen as the "chief of the spirits" and is identified as Satan in 10.11.[77] It seems likely that the origin of *Mastema* as the leader of the demonic realm began in *Jubilees* and the Qumran literature. The Watcher tradition in *1 Enoch* makes no mention of this figure as a part of the group of angels who descended to earth, nor does it allow for any of the Watchers to have the freedom to act as an adversary following their encounter with humanity; all of them have been bound up until their judgment (*1 Enoch* 10.4–6, 12). It seems unlikely that he is the fallen angel of later Christian tradition,[78] but rather an angel or entity that did the work of God in the area of the punishment of the enemies of God and testing the faith of the people of God (see Job 1.6; 2.1).[79] The Qumran literature introduces a shift in his role of an instrument in the economy of God to the leader of those beings who are the enemies of God's people.[80]

The concept of *Belial* is thought to have originated in the Hebrew Bible, possibly 2 Samuel 22.5 (cf. also Ps 18.5), which reads "the torrents of *Belial*" (נחלי בליעל).[81] This phrase stands in parallel with "waves of death," which Sperling suggests implies a personification of wickedness

---

[75] See e.g. 4Q390 1.11; 4Q387a 3.3.4; and 4Q388a 1.2.6 – angels of enmity, מלאכי המשטמות, God abandoned Israel to these angels to serve other gods. 4Q390 2.1.7 – angels of enmity, מלאכי המשטמות, who lead people astray from God (same task as *Jubilees* 10); also paralleled to "dominion of *Belial*," ממשלת בליעל. 1QM 13.10–12 – *Belial* is equated to an angel of enmity that is equated to *Mastema*. Spirits of his lot are angels of destruction, מלאכי חבל. 1QM 13.4 – *Belial* has a plan of enmity, משטמה. 1QM 14.9 – משטמה is equated to works of *Belial*; see also 4Q286 7.2.1–3 for similar comparison. See CD 16.5 – angel of enmity, מלאך המשטמה, follows after the enemies of God (*Jubilees* 15.32?).

[76] Michael Mach, citing Exod 4.24 and *Jubilees* 49.2, suggests that *Mastema*, the "prince of demons," developed from the angel of the Lord who was assigned to inflict punishment on those who opposed the Lord; see Michael Mach, *Entwicklungsstadien des Jüdischen Engelglaubens in Vorrabbinischer Zeit* (Tübingen: Mohr Siebeck, 1992), 81, 96.

[77] Syncellus uses ὁ διάβολος to identify *Mastema*, the chief of the spirits in *1 Enoch* 10.8. The Ethiopic of 10.11 reads sayĕtan. For Satan in the *DSS*, see 11QPsᵃ 19.15 – appears to be identifying Satan as the *Mastema* figure of *Jubilees* 10 along with the evil spirits of the giants, "Let not Satan [שטן] rule over me, nor an evil spirit . . . " 1QSᵇ 1.8 identifies the enemy of holiness as שטן in a general manner.

[78] See Alexander, "Demonology in DSS," 341.

[79] It is possible that the figure of Satan became personified in an effort to protect the image of God and to deflect blame for his wrathful actions towards humanity.

[80] See in particular the *War Scroll*.

[81] See a parallel in 1QHᵃ col. XI 29, 32.

alongside a personification of death (משברי־מות).[82] The figure of *Belial/Beliar* is prominent in 2TP literature.[83] He plays a leading role in the ongoing struggle between good and evil in the sectarian documents of Qumran in which there are significant parallels or allusions between *Belial* and the figure of *Mastema*.[84] *Belial/Beliar* is clearly a leader of a group of

---

[82] Sperling correctly suggests a possible origin of personification of *Belial* in 2 Sam 22.5 with a parallel in Ps 18.5, but his suggestion that most of the occasions of בל יעל in the Hebrew Bible are serious crimes against the Israelite religion is exaggerated with one exception, Deuteronomy 13.14, which describes a person who is leading others to idol worship, see Sperling, "Belial," 169. Of the approximately twenty-four Hebrew passages which contain בל יעל, the majority are simply describing a person of a debased nature [Deut 13.13; 15.9; Judg 19.22; 1 Sam 1.16; 2.12; 10.27; 25.17; 25.25; 2 Sam 16.7; 1 Kgs 21.10, 13; 2 Chr 13.7; Job 34.18; Ps 41.9; 101.3 (perhaps identifies an idol); Prov 6.12; 16.27; 19.28; Nah 1.11, 15; 2.1]. It is possible that we can interpret Nahum 2.1 as a personification of wickedness or evil. The Greek translation does perhaps carry a rendition that is closer to Sperling's interpretation of the action being contrary to the law.

[83] Some thirty-six references to *Belial/Beliar* are found in *T12P* (this number is likely to fluctuate considerably due to the number of existing versions); see Kee, "Testaments of the Twelve Patriarchs." *T. Levi* 19.1 – sets the works of *Beliar* in opposition to the Law of the Lord; *T. Simeon* 2.7 – Prince of Error, a personification of the spirit of jealousy; 3.5 and 4.8 imply possession – "stirs up his soul and fills his body with terror"; *T. Judah* 1–3 – suggest sexual promiscuity, love of money, and idolatry separate you from the Law which would imply these are "works of *Beliar*"; *T. Issachar* 6.1 – personifies *Beliar* as an enemy of God; *T. Dan* 1.7 – the physical possession of Dan by a spirit of *Beliar* which spoke to him to kill Joseph – spirit of anger; *T. Gad* 4.7 – a spirit of hatred works by Satan through human frailty; *T. Naphtali* 8.6 – he who does evil will be inhabited by the devil as an instrument; *T. Asher* 1 – two-spirits at work in men; good and evil inclination; *T. Benjamin* 3.3 – spirits of *Beliar* seek to oppress humans; *T. Reuben* 2–3 – suggests there are multiple spirits at work in his world. See also *Martyrdom and Ascension of Isaiah* 1.8 – he appears to be an agent of *Beliar* who causes Manasseh to do evil; and 2.1 – the appearance of Sammael Malkira as a wicked angel who dwelt in King Manasseh; see also 3.13; 5.15; 7.9; and 11.41. See Michael A. Knibb, "Martyrdom and Ascension of Isaiah," in *OTP* (ed. James H. Charlesworth; 2 vols.; New York: Doubleday, 1983–85), 2:143–76.

[84] See e.g. 1QS 1.16–2.8 – he is personified as the leader of the wicked; 1QM 14.9 – notes the empire of *Belial*; 4Q390 2 1 4 – dominion of *Belial*, ממשלת בליעל; CD 4.12–15; 5.8; 1QM 1.4–5; 13–16 – there is an eschatological war against the army of *Belial* who is the leader of the sons of darkness; 4Q386 I 2.3 – notes that a son of *Belial* (darkness) is a person under the influence of *Belial* who tries to oppress Israel; 1QM 13.4–12 equates *Belial* with *Mastema* and all the spirits of his lot are wicked; 11Q11 IV 1.12 – identifies *Belial* as Satan, prince of enmity, ruler of the abyss of darkness (I 11.5–6), ruler of the earth (III 1.9). Line 12 describes these spirits as מלאכי חבל, which Alexander has argued correctly, should be interpreted as "agent of destruction" rather than angel, see Alexander, "Demonology in DSS," 334. A second possibility is that the מלאכי חבל was the role of the Watchers prior to their fall. This may be the reason they are found appearing along with Satan in Job 1, 2 (cf. *Jubilees* 17.16). Is it possible then that not all of the Watchers rebelled, but some of them remain in the service of God's economy? *Mastema*'s request for the spirits to remain and help him to corrupt humanity,

spirits in 2TP Judaism who is attempting to lead astray the people of Israel from following Yahweh and his commandments. Even so, he may still be operating as an agent of God during this period. It is possible that in the *DSS* we find the authors of several fragments implying that the spirit of *Belial* or the spirits with him are oppressing humans. This is clearly a parallel to the work of *Mastema* and the spirits in *Jubilees* 10.[85]

The author of *Jubilees* (10.8) has followed a similar pattern of expanding the story concerning the evil spirits in the Watcher tradition as the author of *BW* had done with the *bene haelohim* in Genesis. *Mastema* is introduced in a leadership role over the evil spirits similar to the role of Shemihazah over the Watchers. In addition, he has limited the autonomy of the evil spirits. The author of *BW* makes no mention of the spirits being under a leader or as a part in the economy of God (*1 Enoch* 16.1). *Jubilees* has placed the evil spirits within in the economy of God and under a central leader who, in the biblical tradition, must answer to God. Each author has presented his version of the Watcher tradition, a motif which introduces the reason for the continued battle of good and evil in 2TP Judaism. Each has presented it in a way that to one degree or another separates God from the responsibility for the evil that Israel sees around it.

5.6 A Developing Anthropology

The demonology that was developing in various 2TP Jewish writings offers an analogy between demonic and human spirits. While comparing the description of the two categories of spirits, one is able to recognize a developing anthropology that allows for the affliction and possession of humans. As the sources show, the understanding of human nature is bound up with perceptions of evil. This is already suggested in *1 Enoch* 15–16, which, at the same time, leaves a number of questions about human nature unanswered. Fortunately, some authors of the *DSS* and other early Jewish literature have taken up *BW*'s account about evil spirits to formulate an anthropology that reveals more fully the effects of the interaction of these spirits with humanity.

The author of *BW* presents a basic picture of his anthropology in chapter 15 by offering a comparison of the human makeup to that of the Watchers

---

leads to the question; what was he using for help prior to this? It seems possible that his request for some of the spirits of the giants to help him to corrupt humans would imply that he needed prior help.

[85] See also the parallel in *Jubilees* 1.20 of *Beliar* and Satan of Job 1.6. From this, and the reference in *Jubilees* 10, which connects *Mastema* and Satan, we can conclude that *Beliar* and *Mastema* can be considered different names for the same being.

and the giants. *1 Enoch* 15.5 states that humans are physical beings and require physical reproduction in order to continue their species. They are described as having souls (see 9.10; 22.3) that cry out to heaven from the place of the dead following their demise at the hand of the giants.[86] It is implied in 15.10 that because they were born on the earth they have spirits (cf. 20.3; 22.3, 5).[87] The angels on the other hand are immortal beings (15.6) who do not need to reproduce, as their immortality is a given (15.7). For them to reproduce, therefore, was to contravene the law of the cosmos. Whether through rebellion against God, or sinful lust, the Watchers fell and lost their immortality. This did not involve a change in nature; rather it meant that they would be destroyed in eschatological judgment.

The author also presents a basic picture of his giantology in chapters 15–16. The giant offspring are a mixed nature. They are similar to humans in that they are born of flesh and blood, and so, unlike their fathers the Watchers, they could die a physical death. They also shared the nature of angels; they are immortal spirits that emerged from their physical bodies at the point of death and are able to remain active on the earth (15.9). The physical and spiritual nature of the giants described in *BW* reveals some key distinctions between the giants (and ultimately their evil spirits) and humanity. These distinctions are apparent in the notion of spirit and soul, which will be discussed below. However, we shall first consider the general use of "spirit" and "soul" in the biblical tradition.

5.6.1 Spirit in the Biblical Tradition

In the biblical tradition, it is difficult to discern a clear distinction between spirit and soul with reference to the nature of humans (e.g. Isa 26.9 soul // spirit). Genesis 2.7 states the soul comes from the breath of God, which is imparted to humans in the "breath of life," (*nephesh*, נֶפֶשׁ). The spirit on the other hand is not clearly identified. It is thought to be a force that is external to the body that operates in or through the body. Ezekiel 37.5–10 identifies the spirit as something that is also given to the human body by God.

---

[86] An important point to note here is the omission of any existence of the human soul or spirit outside of the "places of the dead." I am unaware of any instances in the Hebrew Bible that describes the body and soul together in Sheol. There are several passages which state the soul (*nephesh*) will be brought up out of Sheol; see 1 Sam 28:14; Ps 30.3, 49.16 (MT), 86.13, 89.49 (MT); and Prov 23.14. *1 Enoch* 22.3–5 states that all the souls and spirits of the dead are gathered to these places until the day of their judgment. This is a clear contrast to the spirits of the angels and giants that either have to be bound under the earth (angels) or be free to roam the earth (giants).

[87] These passages seem to make no clear distinction between the human soul and spirit. They are perhaps two distinct parts of the human composition, inseparable from each other, but not from the human flesh.

The LXX translates the Hebrew רוח (*ruah*) primarily with the Greek πνεῦμα with a few exceptions (e.g. Gen 41.8, Exod 35.21, ψυχή). Πνεῦμα is used to identify several things. It may refer to the human spirit, a spirit sent by God, the spirit of God, and the spirit of holiness.[88] The LXX has followed a similar pattern of consistency with *nephesh*, for which ψυχή serves as the primary translation with a few exceptions.[89] However, it is difficult to discern whether *BW* has followed a similar consistency in the use of רוח and נפש due to the lack of Aramaic fragments of the lines in question. Therefore, it is impossible to distinguish when the Greek translators of *BW* were using πνεῦμα for רוח and ψυχη for נפש with reference to humans. However, we find in *BW* (Greek[pan]) a consistent use of πνεῦμα(τα) when referring to the spirits of the giants or the angels.[90] The Greek[pan sync] versions of *BW* (as well as the Ethiopic) describe the humans as having both a soul (ψυχή)[91] and spirit (πνεῦμα(τα)).[92]

Two other biblical texts that characterize the human soul are Leviticus 17.11 and 14, which states the soul (נפש, ψυχή) of any living creature is in its blood. We can assume that this text is talking about animals and humans, although the author of *BW*, if he knew this passage, may have thought this referred to the giants as well.[93] If the author of *BW* knew this passage, then it may have informed his anthropology and quite possibly his giantology. From the Leviticus text, one might infer that since the giants were both spirit and flesh (*1 Enoch* 15.8), then they too must have spirit and soul, but the author does not make this clear. In fact, we should keep

---

[88] See e.g. in LXX Num 5.14, spirit of jealousy; Num 11.25, spirit of prophecy; Gen 41.38, spirit of God; Ps 30.6, spirit of a human; Ps 50.13, the Holy Spirit.

[89] See e.g. Lev 17.4; the Hebrew האיש (the man) is translated ψυχή and Deut 6.6 the Hebrew לבב (heart) is also translated ψυχή. Of note is Lev 16.29, which indicates that to practice physical self-denial is to "afflict the soul." This expression may indicate a connection between the physical body and the soul.

[90] There is one exception to this in *1 Enoch* 16.1. This text is considered corrupt and there is no Aramaic text with which to compare the Greek or Ethiopic. The Greek texts identify the spirits of the giants as the ones that came out of their souls and their flesh. The Ethiopic reads, "the spirits have gone out from their bodies" which makes better sense; cf. Knibb, *Ethiopic Enoch*, 102. Milik has made a questionable reconstruction of 13.6 with נפשת[הון (see 4QEn[c] vi 1, plate XII), which refers to the spirits of angels.

[91] See *1 Enoch* 9.3, 10 – souls of those crying out; 22.3, souls of the dead and souls of men; and 4Q530 col. II 1 – concerning the death of our souls.

[92] See *1 Enoch* 20.3, spirits of men; 22.3, spirits of men; spirit of Abel; 22.9, spirits of the dead and of the righteous; 22.11 (2), spirits of the dead; and 22.13, spirits of the righteous.

[93] Milgrom suggests that Leviticus mutes the demonology within Israel during the pre-exilic period and he argues that the demons have been expunged from the world and man is now responsible for the demonic activity. See Jacob Milgrom, "Israel's Sanctuary: The Priestly Picture of Dorian Gray," *RB* 83 (1976): 390–99.

in mind that the author of *BW* does not correlate the nature of the giants with the nature of humans. *1 Enoch* 15.10 states that spirits that were born on the earth must dwell on the earth, something that obviously applies to humans and, in the case of *BW*, the giants. Whereas the author of 15.8 implies that the spiritual origin of the giants is from the Watchers, he does not clearly articulate the spiritual origin of human beings.

5.7 Giantology Versus Anthropology

In *BW*, while the physical giants are still alive they are confined to the earth, as are humans. The spirits of the giants, though heavenly in nature, are confined to the earthly realm, unable to approach the heavens as spirits after the death of their physical bodies. *BW* states that at the point of death, humans, as spirit and soul, are removed from upon the earth to the "places of the dead" (22.3).[94] The giants however, upon their death are not confined to the places of the dead, but rather their spirits roam freely upon the earth.[95] A clear difference between the anthropology and giantology of the author of *BW* emerges: there is no evidence that the giants' spirits linger in the places of the dead, nor do human spirits roam freely upon the earth.[96] This may imply that for the author of *BW*, the giants are composed of angelic spirits (cf. 15.10), not of human souls *per se*, and that this difference perhaps allows them the freedom to roam the earth.

This giantology of *BW* raises some interesting questions concerning the nature of the giants, and in particular, about their relationship to humans. Was there an innate incompatibility between the angelic spirit of the giant and his flesh? Is this the reason they had such a violent nature?[97] It seems

---

[94] *1 Enoch* implies all souls go to Sheol to await the judgment, 102.5 – the righteous, and in 102.11 the wicked. The wicked human spirits are destroyed in the fire (98.3); 99.11 – "they will be killed in Sheol – they will not have peace."

[95] *Jubilees* 10.7, 11 state that in order for the evil spirits of the giants to stop oppressing humans they must be bound in the place of condemnation, i.e. with the Watchers.

[96] This could lead to the understanding that the spirit and soul are inseparable. If we assume the giants do have souls then they will likely follow a similar composition to humans; the spirit and soul will be inseparable upon the death of the body.

[97] It should be noted that the violent behaviour of the giants is strikingly similar to the type of action found in some of the pericopes of demonic possession in the Gospels. See e.g. Mk 1.23, 26; 5.2–8; 9.20–25; Lk 4.33–35; 8.29. Mk 5.4–5 perhaps betrays the influence of the giantology of *BW* in its description of the actions of the demoniac. The presence of the unclean spirit within his body results in violent and destructive behaviour, although it is toned down considerably from the actions of the giants. This may be directly related to the "angelic" nature of the unclean spirit that is now confined to a human body.

the spirits of the giants were not able to exist within a physical body without bringing about violent behaviour because they are illegitimate and not properly constituted.[98] By contrast, God created humans both physically and non-physically. This is a key distinction between humans and giants: God has no part in the creation of the giants (*1 Enoch* 15.7–12).[99]

We have two very distinct created beings present in *BW*. The Watchers, who are only spirit, have mated with humans who are spirit, soul, and flesh. The resulting hybrid has, according to the story, only spirit and flesh. The spirit of the giant is a corrupted spirit that has evolved from the angels (15.9). The human spirit in *BW* is created directly from God; we must assume that although the author does not mention the spiritual origin of humans, the anthropology of *BW* does not undermine the Jewish belief that the spirits of humans are created in the image of God (see *T. Naphtali* 2.5). We are presented with what may be understood as two created images of human beings, one with the corrupt spirit of the giants and the other with the spirit of God. What we have then in *BW* is a possible "origin of evil" in early Judaism.[100] The spirit of God (רוּחַ[a]) within humans results in the existence of "good" within creation, while the spirit of the Watchers (רוּחַ[b]) within the giants results in the origin of evil which would rise to prominence as a result of the desire to exonerate God from any responsibility for evil amongst Jews (and Christians) in the coming centuries.[101] If we recognize this as a possibility, the giantology we recover

---

[98] If Gen 2.7 were brought into consideration, God would have played no part in the creation of these beings, as they would not have received the "breath of life." Against this background, the giants were without the *nephesh*.

[99] *Jubilees* 5.7–10 may create some difficulty in keeping God separated from any role in the creation of the giants. In the context of discussing the Watchers and the destruction of their sons, Gen 6.3 ("my spirit shall not always abide on man; for they also are flesh and their days shall be one hundred and twenty years") is inserted into the story in reference to the slaying of the giants by the sword. The author of *BW* makes it clear that the spirits of the giants are illegitimate and therefore do not come from God, which would appear to negate any connection of the giants to the Gen 6.3 verse. The only explanation to offer is that the *Jubilees* tradition is a later interpretation that equated this verse to the giants. See discussion of the interpretation of Gen 6.3 above, ch. 3, 3.2.3.

[100] See John Collins, "The Origin of Evil in Apocalyptic Literature and the Dead Sea Scrolls," in *Supplements to Vetus Testamentum Congress Volume Paris 1992* (ed. et al., J.A. Emerton; Leiden: E.J. Brill, 1995), 25–38. Collins argues the story of the Watchers "provides a paradigm for the origin of sin and evil" in humanity.

[101] If accepted, this anthropology/giantology may be responsible for later demonic motifs such as possession and exorcism. It is possible that the giantology of *BW*, later adopted as a dualistic anthropology, understood the giants as humans possessed by evil spirits that required the exorcising of these spirits in order to restore the individual to the community of God.

in *BW* becomes, perhaps, the origin of, or at least a step towards, the developing ethical dualism attested in the *DSS* (and *T12P*).

5.8 Conclusion

BW has represented the sons of God of Genesis 6 as Watcher angels, who have, for reasons not fully explained, rebelled against God. The story of the rebellion has parallels in Hellenistic and Near Eastern sources, but the myth may have originated in the Israelite tradition. The author of *BW* has taken up the Genesis narrative (or possibly a common source) and expanded the myth of the *bene haelohim* to incorporate the story of the origin of evil spirits and their continued existence during the post-deluge period.

The focus of the author of *BW* is the lasting effect the action of the angels had upon themselves, their offspring, and humanity. The intrusion of the angels into the human realm resulted in the birth of the giants and the destruction of humanity. More importantly, it has brought about the existence of evil spirits. Within the framework of this story, the author of *BW* begins the development of an early Jewish anthropology that is further defined by certain authors of the *DSS* and incorporated into the anthropology and theology of early Judaism. The evolution of this anthropology alongside the giantology of *BW* would contribute to the emerging demonology (i.e. affliction of humanity by evil spirits) in early Jewish literature and in the later New Testament where it seems to be more coherent. The reception and development of this demonology in early Jewish literature is most visible in the incantation prayers and prayers of protection in the *DSS*, which contain parallels or at least allusions to the Watcher tradition in *1 Enoch*. As will be seen below the authors of several of the *DSS* texts embraced the Watcher tradition and advanced the demonology and anthropology within their dualistic worldview.

Chapter 6

Reception of the Watcher Tradition
in the Dead Sea Scrolls

6.1 Introduction

The Watcher tradition in *1 Enoch* describes the rebellion of a group of God's angels and the consequences of their actions. The author's interpretation of Genesis 6.1–4, by which he presented his giantology, introduced the reader to the emergence of evil spirits. As will be seen below, demonology would become a significant theme in Palestinian Judaism around the turn of the Era.[1] Alongside these evil spirits, the early stages of an anthropology can be seen that characterizes humanity as susceptible to the attacks of the evil spirits.

We can only assume from the presence of *BW* amongst the *DSS* that the evil spirits introduced in *BW* had some influence upon the developing demonology recovered in the Scrolls.[2] The lack of a clear anthropology in *BW* perhaps minimizes the influence it had upon the anthropology of the Scrolls; however, similar to *BW*, some *DSS* fragments betray some form of susceptibility within humans to attack by evil spirits (cf. *1 En* 15.12).[3] Therefore, it seems plausible to suggest that the demonology and anthropology of the Watcher tradition provided a conceptual basis on

---

[1] See Sacchi, *Jewish Apocalyptic*, 58. Sacchi argues that Jewish apocalyptic ideology originated in *BW* and the thought of *BW* was inserted (taken up) as much as possible into the traditional context of Jewish thought.

[2] For discussion of the influence of *1 Enoch* on the author of 4Qinstruction see Stuckenbruck, "4Qinstruction and the Possible Influence of Early Enochic Traditions: An Evaluation" in *The Wisdom Texts From Qumran and the Development of Sapiential Thought* (*BETL* 159; ed. C. Hempel, A. Lange and H. Lichtenberger; Leuven: Peeters, 2002), 245-61. Due to the dating of the relevant *DSS*, it should not be assumed that the fragments that contain episodes of the demonic in the *DSS* had any influence upon the author of *BW*.

[3] These concepts are found primarily in scroll fragments that depict the harassment of humans by the spirits of Beliar. See e.g. 1QH[a] 5 20; 4Q417 2 II 12; 4Q370 I 3; 4Q280 1 2; 1QM 13; 4Q286.

which the authors of some of the *DSS* could further develop their demonology and anthropology.[4]

The *DSS* contain three main themes that underscore the reality of evil spirits in the worldview of 2TP Judaism. The first theme is the idea of the good and evil inclination in humanity. The good and evil inclination is an intricate part of the second motif, the work of Belial and his efforts to test and tempt people to turn from God and to neglect His commandments. The third theme is found in the "incantation prayers" in several fragments. These prayers reveal an understanding within Judaism of a need for protection against evil spirits that appear to find their origin in the Watcher tradition. I will discuss each of these motifs in detail in an effort to attest to the taking up of the Watcher tradition in Early Judaism as a mechanism to explain the problem of evil. First, I would like to offer an excursus that presents the various "dualisms" that might be understood in the major documents under discussion below.

Excursus: Dualism in Relevant Qumran Fragments

It is difficult to identify a single concept of dualism in the relevant Qumran material. It can be proposed that there are three primary "dualisms" present in the worldview of the community. The first, "cosmic dualism," establishes that two opposing forces of good and evil exist within both the cosmos and humanity. However, the forces, i.e. spiritual beings, involved are neither causal nor coeternal. The second is understood as an "ethical dualism" that separates humanity into two distinct groups based upon the presence of virtues or vices at work in the lives of the group's members. The third category, "psychological dualism," depicts the struggle of an individual with two internal inclinations (e.g. יצר הטוב and יצר הרע) that are being influenced by the opposing forces within the cosmic dualism to follow or not follow God.[5]

---

[4] See e.g. 1QS 3.24 – describes the spirits who lead humanity to iniquity, *1 Enoch* 15.11; 19.1; 4Q387a frag 3 III 3f – Israel is abandoned to the messengers of enmity and the worship of other gods, *1 Enoch* 19.1; 4Q511 frag 3 5 and frag 10 11 use language found in *1 Enoch* 1–5 and 12–16 – "you shall have no peace"; 11Q11 V – mentions demons who are perhaps the offspring of humans and angels, *1 Enoch* 15.12; 4Q560 frag 1 I – describes an evil spirit that penetrates human flesh, *1 Enoch* 15.11; 4Q266 frag 6.I.5f – describes the healing from leprosy which is caused by a spirit, *1 Enoch* 15.11; possibly 4Q417 frag 2.I.16f – Enosh did not follow after the "spirit of the flesh," *1 Enoch* 15.12; and 1QH[a]8.19–20 – spirit of a just man (Noah), *1 Enoch* 10.1.

[5] For a thorough discussion of the dualisms present in the Qumran material, see Jörg Frey, "Different Patterns of Dualistic thought in the Qumran Library. Reflections of their Background and History," in *Legal Texts and Legal Issues: Proceedings of the Second Meeting of the International Organization for Qumran Studies, Cambridge 1995, Published in Honour of Joseph M. Baumgarten.* (STDJ 23; eds. Moshe Bernstein, Florentino García Martínez and John Kampen; Leiden: Brill, 1997), 275–336.

In what follows, I will discuss briefly and attempt to categorize the dualistic characteristics within the text of various fragments found in the Qumran library. There are numerous fragments that could fall into this category; therefore, I will focus on just a few in order to give an overall picture of the dualistic worldview presented in the material; however, it is not my intention to present them in any particular order of importance to the community or in chronological order.

1QS–Rule of the Community[6]

1QS 3.13–4.26 should be considered a multi-faceted dualistic document that contains three possible categories: cosmic, ethical, and psychological.[7] It is probable, as Frey and others have argued,[8] that this section of text is an older text used by the community and added to the covenant liturgy 1.1–3.13 for specific reasons. The additional sections, 1.1–4.26, were then added to the Community Rule 1QS 3.13–4.26 is characterized as a sapiential document with its primary instruction providing wisdom for individuals in the community to be able to discern good and wicked (see 4.24). 1QS 3.18–19 introduces a psychological dualism that declares God has "created for him [i.e. humanity] two spirits to walk in until the appointed time of his visitation, that is the spirits of truth and wickedness" (cf. 4Q186).[9] These two spirits would serve as the point of conflict within

---

[6] The manuscript 1QS is a collection of different literary units that were collected or redactionally combined in the manuscript. There are four main sections which include the opening liturgy 1.1–3.13 (an Essene or Sectarian writing); the second section includes the Doctrine of Two Spirits 3.13–4.26 (according to Frey a sapiential text, likely pre-sectarian, formed prior to the establishment of the community of the *Yahad*); this is followed by the Rule of the Community beginning in 5.1 (sectarian); the final section is a closing hymn which is likely sectarian. Cf. 4QS which primarily parallels 1QS from 5.1ff. For thorough discussion of 1QS see Sarianna Metso, *The Textual Development of the Qumran Community Rule*, (STDJ, 21; Leiden: Brill, 1997).

[7] Frey describes the dualism of 1QS as "creation founded and eschatalogically confined cosmic dualism with a subordinate ethical dualism." See ibid., 294.

[8] See Frey, "Different Patterns," 295–96 and Armin Lange, *Weisheit und Prädestination. Weisheitliche Urordnung und Prädestination in den Textfunden von Qumran*. (STDJ 18; Leiden E.J. Brill, 1995): 6–20. Cf. arguments for a community origin in A.R.G. Leaney, *The Rule of Qumran and its Meaning*, (London: SCM, 1996) and Devorah Dimant, "Qumran Sectarian Literature" in *Jewish Writings of the Second Temple Period* (CRINT 2/2; ed. Michael Stone; Assen: van Gorcum, 1984), 483–550.

[9] My brackets. 4Q186 is a document that describes a human as a being that is divided into nine parts of spirit some of which belong to the House of Light and others to the Pit of Darkness. The distribution of the nine parts into light or darkness is likely determined by which spirit (of the two spirits of 1QS) has the upper hand (psychologically?) and the individual has chosen to follow. A second possibility is that the division is based upon cycle of the Zodiac in which the individual is born (see 4Q186 1 col. II lines 7–9; III 5–6 and 4Q186 2 col. II lines 6–9).

an individual by which the two opposing spiritual beings on a cosmic level, the Prince of Light (Angel of Truth) and the Angel of Darkness, would battle for the souls of the sons of righteousness. The two angelic spirits operate under the sovereignty of God within the human realm where the lives of individuals are directed by one of the two spirits. A major difference between the two beings is that the Angel of Darkness has the assistance of a group of evil spirits (see col. 3 line 24 – Frey mistakenly calls them evil angels[10]). Frey argues that we can assume that there is a "corresponding entourage of good angels" but he may be reading into the text something that is not needed. The text of col. 3 line 24 stipulates that the Angel of Truth is assisted only by the God of Israel to bring the Sons of Light to truth and light. However, in defence of Frey's suggestion 1QM 13 10, which some argue is a sectarian document,[11] asserts that the Prince of Light (שַׂר מָאוֹר) has under his dominion (בממשלתו) all the spirits of truth (suggesting a cosmic dualism). This phrase could lead one to interpret the line to mean the Prince of Light has a group of spirits working with him, while at the same time it could be referring to the spirits of humans who have chosen to obey the spirit of truth within him/herself.

1QS col. 4 provides the reader with an ethical dualism that divides humanity into two distinct groups based upon a list of virtues and vices. Again it appears that psychological dualism plays a role in determining to which group an individual belongs. The resulting struggle to follow one of the two spirits (inclinations) within the individual is manifested in the evidence of virtues and vices in his or her life (line 23).

An important concept that helps to shape a dualistic worldview in 1QS is predestination.[12] Column 4 line 26 suggests that God has predetermined to which group, that is the sons of light or sons of darkness, each human shall belong: "And he allots them to the sons of man for knowledge of good [. . . and thus] dec[id]ing the lots for every living being, according to his spirit . . .," *his spirit* referring to the spirit(s) of the person.[13] Similarly, 4Q181 1 5 suggests a casting of lots by God to determine the place of an

---

[10] See Frey, "Different Patterns," 292–93.

[11] .ושר מאור מאז פקדתה לעוזרנו ובֹן[   ]לֹ ובול רוחי אמת בממשלתו
Frey argues that 1QM is a later development of 4QM which presents the sectarian reception and redaction of the War Rule. See ibid., 308. See also J. Duhaime, "Dualistic Reworking in the Scrolls from Qumran," *CBQ* 49 (1987): 32–56.

[12] See Eugene H. Merril, *Qumran and Predestination: A Theological Study of the Thanksgiving Hymns*, STDJ, 8 (Leiden: Brill, 1975).

[13] Translation from Elisha Qimron and James H. Charlesworth, *The Dead Sea Scrolls: Hebrew, Aramaic, and Greek Texts with English Translations*: *Rule of the Community and Related Documents* (vol. 1 of *The Princeton Theological Seminary Dead Sea Scrolls Project*; ed. James H. Charlesworth; Tübingen/ Louisville: Mohr Siebeck/ Westminster John Knox, 1994), 18.

individual either in the holy congregation or in the community of wickedness. The content of this fragment may be referring to the Watchers of *1 Enoch* as the wicked lot, although Allegro's reconstruction is quite speculative.[14]

1QH^a – Thanksgiving Hymns

The *Thanksgiving Hymns* (identified by Frey as a sectarian text[15]) suggest some categories of thought that fall under an ethical dualism, i.e. the division of humanity into two lots – the wicked and the righteous. Within this dualism, the author affirms in 1QH col. 1 lines 7–9 a clear belief in predestination: "And before you created them you knew all their works . . . and nothing is known, but only in your will, you formed every spirit . . . and judge all their works." Further, the ethical dualism is articulated clearly in col. 15 lines 14–15 (creation of the righteous) and col. 15 lines 17–19 (creation of the wicked): 14) "Only you [created] 15) the righteous, and from the womb you established him for the appointed time of favour . . . And you created the wicked (ones) for the [periods of your wrath]." The language used here seems to demonstrate a belief in two divisions within humanity that were predestined to fall into their lot of either the righteous or the wicked.

4QAmram–Visions of Amram

4QAmram has survived in seven copies (4Q543–4Q549) possibly dating from the first half of the second century B.C.E.[16] It has been identified as a priestly pre-Essene document, which contains language that would allow one to place it in the category of cosmic dualism.[17] Milik has suggested that the vision of the two angels seen by Amram were of the group of angels known as the Watchers of *1 Enoch*. However, this is only through optimistic reconstructions by Milik in two fragments, 4Q544 col. 3 line 12 (עירא) and 4Q547 col. 3 line 9 (עירין). The text identifies two angelic beings that have been given authority to rule over humanity (מלכי רשע –

---

[14] See John M. Allegro, *Qumrân Cave 4 I (4Q158–4Q186)* in *Discoveries in the Judean Desert 5* (ed. Emanuel Tov; Oxford: Clarendon, 1968).

[15] See Frey, "Different Patterns," 333–334.

[16] See discussion in Émile Puech, *Qumrân Grotte 4, XXII, Textes Araméens Premiére Partie 4Q529–549* in *Discoveries in the Judaean Desert XXXI* (Oxford: Clarendon, 2001), 289–405. Frey ("Different Patterns," 320, n. 173) suggests only six manuscripts (4Q543–548), while Davidson (*Angels at Qumran*, 264) suggests only five fragmentary copies.

[17] See Frey, "Different Patterns," 320 and Davidson, *Angels at Qumran*, 265. Davidson argues that because of similar language and concepts to those found in 1QS, 1QM, and CD, 4QAmram "should be regarded as a Qumran sectarian document or else a work very closely allied to the sect's writings."

4Q544 frag 2 col. 3 line 13; the name for the angel over the light has been reconstructed as מלכי צדק – as suggested by Davidson and Kobelski[18]); however, humanity has the power to choose which dominion he or she wishes to fall under. Certainly the language of 4QAmram suggests a cosmic dualism with hints of psychological dualism implied in the concept of human choice.

11Q11(Apocryphal Psalms)

The *Apocryphal Psalms* perhaps date from a pre-Essene period as early as the third or second century B.C.E., although the extant material is dated to the Herodian times. 11Q11 demonstrates an apparent increased awareness of a very active demonology within a cosmic dualism. However, the cosmic dualism of this manuscript differs considerably from those discussed above. The battle in this case is primarily between the Prince of Enmity (reconstructed שׂ]ר המשׂט[מה – likely Belial) in col. 2 line 4 and יהוה – col. 1 line 4, col. 3 lines 3, 9, 10, 11; col. 4 line 4; and col. 5 line 8. There is only one obvious reference to an angel of God being involved in the battle in col. 4 line 5 (מלאך תקיף). There is an allusion to an ethical dualism in col. 6 line 3 – בני בל]יעל – this could indicate that there are two groups of humans involved in the picture – the sons of Belial and the sons of Light. This reference in the text to one of the two possible groups, and the assumption that there is a group of individuals who are given these prayers to defend themselves against Belial, suggest the document has an ethical dualism operating within a cosmic dualism. However, due to lack of reference to the second group of the "sons of light" this is only speculation. 11Q11 will be discussed below in greater detail in section 6.4.0 concerning the prayers of protection at Qumran.

4Q510 and 511 – Songs of the Maskil

The *Songs of the Maskil* present a distinct cosmic dualism in comparison to those documents discussed above. These sectarian fragments are perhaps the adoption and the expansion of the pre-Essene demonology of 11Q11.[19] There is a distinct group of individuals called the Sons of Light (4Q510 1 8 – בני אור[ר]) who are members of the lot of God (4Q511 frag 2 col. 1 line 8 – גורל אלוהים), members of the covenant (frag 63 col. 3 line 5 – אנשי ברית) who serve alongside the angels of the luminaries (frag 2 col. 1 lines. 8–9, מל]אכי [מאורות כבודו). However, a seemingly more powerful enemy (or enemies) of the lot of God is now identified with a

---

[18] See Davidson, *Angels at Qumran*, 268 and Paul J Kobelski, *Melchizedek and Melchireša*, (CBQMS, 10; Washington, D.C: Catholic Biblical Association of America, 1981), 36.

[19] See Frey, "Different Patterns," 328.

string of names that includes the spirits of the destroying angels, spirits of the bastards, and various other demonic creatures (4Q510 1 5–6). There is still a well-defined ethical dualism present which sets at odds the sons of light and the sons of iniquity (frag 1 col. 1 line 8 – בני עולה), but the focus of the songs shifts to doing battle against a cosmic enemy, the demonic beings listed in 4Q510 1 5–6.

CD – Damascus Document

The *Damascus Document* contains an ethical dualism based on the predestined knowledge of God concerning human choice. However, there is no unambiguous identification of the sons of light, rather they are described as covenanters/Sons of Dawn (see MS A col. 13 line 14; cf. 4Q298 frag 1 line 1 – בני שחר, here the Maskil is addressing a group that he encourages to seek the virtues of the Essenes[20]). The opposing group of people are described as the "Sons of the Pit" (col. 6 line 15) and the "congregation of the lie" (col. 8 line 13). The list of virtues and vices for these two groups of humans as a criteria for defining ethical dualism is missing, however, in its place is a list of characteristics of God which will be manifested in the two groups; long forbearance and multiplied forgiveness to those of the remnant (the lot of God–col. 2 line 11) and great wrath and fiery flames for those who depart from the Way and despise the Law (lines 5–6). There are obvious references within CD that also point to a strong cosmic dualism. Manuscript A col. 2 lines 18–19 make a clear reference to the Watcher angels and their intrusion into the human realm – a "breaching of the cosmos" – while the customary battle of the Prince of Lights and Belial is described in col. 5 line 18. There is also an indication of psychological dualism present in CD. Column 2 line 16 warns that those in the covenant should "walk perfectly in all his ways and do not stray in the thoughts of *guilty inclination* (יצר אשמה) and eyes of whoring" (עני זנות – possibly interpreted as idol worship). The use of inclination here could indicate the author is aware of the concept of good and evil inclination represented in the treatise on the two spirits found in 1QS.[21]

11Q5 Column 19 – Plea for Deliverance

The *Plea for Deliverance* scroll offers a post-biblical perspective on prayers of protection that are taken up by the Qumran community. The free use of the Tetragrammaton suggests a non-Qumran origin, although a

---

[20] See also Joseph M. Baumgarten, "The 'Sons of Dawn' in *CDC* 13:14–15 and the Ban on Commerce among the Essenes," *IEJ* 33 (1983): 81–5.

[21] See also 4Q417 frag 1 col. 2 line 12: "Let not the thought of an evil inclination mislead you."

sectarian authorship should not be ruled out based solely on its presence in the document.[22] 11Q5 col. 19 alludes to two forms of dualism, cosmic and psychological. Line 15 certainly describes half of the cosmic duo of angelic beings found in the texts discussed above: "Do not allow Satan to lord over me nor an unclean spirit." This line describes the possible actions of Satan, but the Psalm lacks any mention of an angel of God; it informs us that any help the individual seeks will come directly from God. The second form of dualism, psychological, is found in lines 15–16: "Do not allow pain and evil inclination to dwell (possess?) in my body [bones]." The psychological dualism may be further supported if one is to read רוח אמונה ודעת (spirit of faith and knowledge) in lines 14–15 in the sense that this is one of the two spirits described in 1QS 3–4.[23]

Summary

From the preceding discussion we can put forward the suggestion that at least three distinct, although at times integrated, forms of dualism exist in the Qumran material. Whether the material is of sectarian origin or not is perhaps insignificant. What is clear is that the existence of the documents in the Qumran library demonstrates that at least a portion of the members of the community embraced on some level a dualistic worldview. The dominant theme is demonstrated in a conflation of cosmic and ethical dualism. There are at times two distinct groups of individuals, the sons of light and the sons of darkness; however, these groups are the focal point of the larger battle between the cosmic forces of the Angel of Light and the Angel of Darkness (Belial). The central focus of Qumran dualism, perhaps demonstrated in 1QS 2, is the division that has been established between the insiders and outsiders of the community. The covenant members are in the realm of the light while those who have failed to enter the covenant community walk in darkness. 1QS 3–4 and the Doctrine of the Two Spirits lies behind this sectarian dualism; however, it is no longer the struggle in one's heart,[24] rather, the text is now interpreted within the understanding of

---

[22] See Armin Lange, "The Essene Position on Magic and Divination," in *Legal Texts and Legal Issues: Proceedings of the Second Meeting of the International Organization for Qumran Studies, Cambridge 1995, Published in Honour of Joseph M. Baumgarten.* (STDJ 23; eds. Moshe Bernstein, Florentino García Martínez and John Kampen; Leiden: Brill, 1997), 380, n.8 and 381, n.14.

[23] J.A. Sanders suggests that "spirit of faithfulness" has replaced "spirit of truth" and that Satan and evil inclination have replaced Belial and spirit of wickedness which are more common to Qumran sectarian documents. See J. A. Sanders, *The Psalms Scroll of Qumran Cave 11 (11QPsᵃ)* (*DJD* 4; Oxford: Clarendon Press 1965), 76.

[24] Although we do not see the internal struggle of an individual found in 1QS 3–4 in other Qumran texts, we cannot rule out that members of the community held to the

the election and predestination of the members of the community and the rejection of those on the outside.

It is unclear if the dualistic worldview of these documents and their presence in the Qumran library resulted in the community adopting the *Book of Watchers* or the community's knowledge and perhaps possession of some form of the Watcher tradition resulted in the writing of this material. What is apparent is that these documents, i.e. their concepts and characters, assumed significant roles in the development of Qumran demonology, angelology, and anthropology.

6.2 Incorporation of a Dualistic Worldview[25]

Some of the fragments found at Qumran depict a community that espoused the idea that humanity was engaged in a spiritual battle, a battle that set at odds the wicked spirits of Beliar and the sons of righteousness. 1QH[a] 4.17 and 1QS 3.18 acknowledge that God has placed "two spirits" in humans, by which some people do acts of injustice by a *spirit of deceit* and the others walk in righteousness by a *spirit of truth*.[26] The nature of humanity in these documents is conceived along the lines of an ethical dualism that allows for a duality in the anthropology of some of the Scrolls.[27] A possible origin of this dualism can be understood in concept found in the Hebrew

---

understanding that they still faced the struggle of inner turmoil and temptation. It is likely they realized that pious people could sin and go astray.

[25] Sacchi suggests that Qumran dualism was developed from traditions found in Job, Chronicles, and *BW*. See Sacchi, *Jewish Apocalyptic*, 62.

[26] Sacchi suggests that 1QS 3.18 implies that God created people good and bad and that those who are bad by nature cannot be cleansed: see Sacchi, *Jewish Apocalyptic*, 69. Cf. 1QH[a] 8.19–20 – "I have appeased your face by the spirit which you have placed [in me] to lavish 20) your kindnesses on [your] serv[ant] for[ever] to purify me with your holy spirit, to bring me near by your will according to the extent of your kindnesses." Translation from García Martínez/Tigchelaar, *Dead Sea Scrolls*, 1:157. Cf. also 4Q473 frag 2.

[27] It may be suggested that in 1QM 13.10–12 God instituted dualism as a part of creation. "From of old you appointed the Prince of Light to assist us, and in {his} ha[nd are all the angels of just]ice, and all the spirits of truth are under his dominion. You made Belial for the pit, angel of enmity; in darkness is his [dom]ain, his counsel is to bring about wickedness and guilt"; see trans. García Martínez/Tigchelaar, *Dead Sea Scrolls*, 1:135. Cf. trans. of Jean Duhaime in *The Dead Sea Scrolls: Hebrew, Aramaic, and Greek Texts with English Translations* (vol. 2 of *The Princeton Theological Seminary Dead Sea Scrolls Project*; ed. James H. Charlesworth; Tübingen: J.C.B. Mohr (Paul Siebeck) Louisville: Westminster John Knox, 1995), 122–23. "The commander of light, long ago, you entrusted to our rescue *wb*ᵒ[. . .]*q*; all the spirits of truth are under his dominion. You have made Belial to corrupt, a hostile angel. In the darken[ss. . .]*tw*, his counsel is aimed towards wickedness and guiltiness."

Bible of a good[28] or evil inclination[29] of the human spirit.[30] Some of the Qumran documents use the "good inclination" to refer to the works of Yahweh in an individual. These works are reflected in the keeping of the Law.[31] An example that may describe these individuals is found in 1QS 3.20f, which states that the sons of justice are guided by the Prince of Light, שר אורים, into the paths of truth and light.[32]

The biblical motif of "evil inclination" is found in Genesis 6.5 (cf. Gen 8.21), "Then the Lord saw that the wickedness of man was great on the earth and that every inclination (יצר) of the thoughts of his heart was only evil continually."[33] The theme is picked up in several Dead Sea documents

---

[28] See 1 Chr 28.9 (וכל יצר מחשבת) and Isa 26.3 (יצר סמוך תצר שלום). See also 4Q417–418.

[29] See Gen 6.5 and 8.21 – יצר רע.

[30] Although an O.T. origin for the Qumran dualism could be considered (see e.g. J. Barr, "The Question of Religious Influence: The Case of Zoroastrianism, Judaism and Christianity," JAAR 53 (1985): 201-235), it is possible, as Collins and others have suggested, that the dualism has been passed down from Zoroastrianism. See Collins, "Apocalyptic Imagination," 153, n. 31. Collins argues that the Two Spirits of Light and Darkness in the community documents are clearly rooted in Zoroastrian Dualism. *Gathas*, the oldest part of the Zoroastrian text *Avesta* states the humanity must choose between two spirits, holy and destroyer (*Yasna* 30). Zoroastrian dualism, much like Qumran dualism, is not seen as an equality of two objects, but rather two objects that are opposed to each other. Similar to Judaism, Zoroastrianism has one supreme deity (*Ahuramazda*) with a host of entities called *mainyu* (possible origin of *bene elohim*?). Two of these *mainyu*, *Spenta Mainyu* (virtuous spirit) and *Angra Mainyu* (deceitful spirit), fall directly under the authority of *Ahuramazda*. *Angra Mainyu* is understood to be in direct opposition to the *Spenta Mainyu* and not the supreme deity. Some argue these two *mainyu* can be understood as an "angel of light" and an "angel of darkness (e.g. Collins). The Qumran Community dualistic worldview is delineated in 1QS, Testament of Amram, and the War Scroll in which the doctrine of the two spirits can be explained as a development of Sapiential thought within the developing second c. B.C.E. angelology (see Frey "Different Patterns," 300). Mary Boyce argues for heavy influence of Zoroastrianism upon writings in the Pseudepigrapha and *DSS*, see Boyce, *History*, 3:415–36. For Zoroastrian texts and translations see Mary Boyce, ed. and trans., *Textual Sources for the Study of Zoroastrianism* (Manchester: Manchester University, 1984). However, one should keep in mind that dating the Zoroastrian material is difficult (eleventh or sixth c. B.C.E.) along with determining the possible influence it had upon developing Judaism; see Boyce, *Textual Sources*, p. 33, n. 83 for discussion of the date.

[31] See 4Q417 frag 1.i.16f (4Q418 43, 44, 45.1.13). Man (Enosh?) is formed (יצר) in the pattern of the holy ones (righteous); this is in opposition to the spirit of the flesh that cannot discern the difference between good and evil. If humans are like angels their task is described in 4Q418 55.9f (69.10–11), "pursue all the roots of understanding and keep watch over all knowledge and their inheritance is eternal life."

[32] 1QS 4 2–8 describes the characteristics of what could be understood as the "good inclination" (spirit of truth), spirit of meekness, patience, compassion, goodness, etc.

[33] In Genesis 6–9, humanity takes the brunt of the blame and punishment in reference to the action that occurred in Gen 6.1–4. *1 Enoch* 7.3–5; 8.2; 15.9 and *Jubilees* 7.22, 27;

and identified as the work of Belial.[34] 1QS 3 20–23 maintains those who walk in darkness, sons of injustice (עול), are led by the Angel of Darkness (מלאך חושך) into the paths of injustice and darkness.[35] The Angel of Darkness described here is perhaps responsible for a later tradition of Satan as one of the Fallen Angels.[36] However, within the Scrolls, he likely falls into a similar category of "the leader of the spirits," which includes Mastema, Beliar, Belial, and others (although these figures stand vis-à-vis God, while the Angel of Darkness stands vis-à-vis the Angel of Light in 1QS; see the contrast in 1QM 13.10–12). However, one may draw a parallel between the Angel of Darkness and Belial in 1QM 13.10–12. Belial is seen in opposition to the Prince of Light who in turn is seen in opposition to the Angel of Darkness in 1QS 3 20–21.[37]

Other images of the dualistic worldview are reflected in 1QH[a] 5.20f., which describes the "spirit of flesh" as one born of a woman. It is "a structure of dust fashioned with water. His counsel is the [iniquity] of sin, shame of dishonour and so[urce of] impurity, and depraved spirits rule over him."[38] Here, the "spirit of flesh" in humans is ruled by the evil inclination, which results in the person seeking after the desires of the

---

10.1–9; 11.4–5 relate a similar story. In the case of *BW* and *Jubilees*, humans play a more passive role as the victims of the disobedience of the Watchers and the violence of the giants [it may be implied that through the instruction of Asa'el, the humans had a more active role in the bringing of the Flood (see *1 Enoch* 8.1–2; 19.2 and *Jubilees* 4.23)]. In both accounts, a corrupt humanity is due in part to the introduction of a debased culture through the instruction of the Watchers. The effects of the instruction continue after the binding of the Watchers, either through the actions of humanity or the spirits of the giants.

[34] See e.g. 4Q417 frag 1.ii.12; 4Q370 I 3; and possibly 4Q280 frag 1.2. Cf. 1 QM 13 11, which states that the task of Beliar is to bring about wickedness and guilt to humanity.

[35] 1QS 4 9–14 describe characteristics that could be understood as the "evil inclination" (spirit of deceit), greed, injustice, wickedness, falsehood, pride, etc.

[36] It is possible to translate מל אך simply as messenger rather than angel.

[37] Alexander argues that 1QS 3.25–26 allows Qumran to stay within the boundaries of theism and avoid an absolute dualism; see Alexander, "Demonology in the DSS," 343.

[38] The occurrences of "spirit of flesh" in the *DSS* may be alluding to the spirits of the giants. The spirits of the giants are identified in this manner in *1 Enoch* 15.12, "and these spirits will rise against the sons of men and against the women because they came out from them," i.e. the spirits of the giants came out of the flesh of humans; thus, a giant = "spirit of flesh." 4Q418 could be referring to the giants with the designation "spirit of flesh." These references mention the spirit of flesh alongside the sons of heaven concerning their judgment and destruction. See 4Q418 frag 2.4–5; frag 2.12–13.4; frag 81 1–4. This fragment discusses, in holiness language, the separation of the righteous from every "spirit of flesh." Translation García Martínez/Tigchelaar, *Dead Sea Scrolls*, 1:151.

flesh.[39] It is evident that some of the Dead Sea documents thought opposing moral powers to be active in two arenas, called, respectively, flesh and spirit. If the human spirit, led by the will of the "spirit of truth," is strong, Beliar is unable to gain control. If the human spirit is weak and is led by the will of the "spirit of flesh," Beliar controls that person's actions. Several of the Dead Sea documents, which refer to those who are under the control of Beliar as the "sons of Beliar," further magnify the duality of good versus evil.[40] The evil spirits that emerged in *BW* are given a place in the plan of God in the *DSS*. These spirits are not to be confused with the human "spirit of flesh"; rather, they are external to them. Their task is to lead astray those people who are not led by the "spirit of truth" and thus follow God.

The ethical dualism of the *DSS*, in an effort to delineate a more precise anthropology, draws boundaries that distinguish two classes of individual. The first group of individuals, the "sons of light," is identified by their membership in the community, their obedience to the Law, and their purity. Those who find themselves outside of the boundaries delineated by this ethical dualism, the "sons of darkness" or "sons of Beliar," are in danger of affliction from the array of evil spirits that emerged in *BW* and are now a part of the divine economy in the Scrolls.

---

[39] 4Q417 2.2.12 warns, "Let not the plan of evil inclination mislead you" (יצר רע). See possible parallel in 4Q418 frag 12.3.1.

[40] See for example 4Q386 1.2.3f – "YHWH said: 'A son of Belial will plot to oppress my people, but I will prevent him, and his dominion will not exist.'" 4Q387a 3.3.3f – "and I will abandon] the country in the hand of the angels of enmity" (*Mastema* = *Belial*); cf. 4Q388a 1.2.6. 4Q390 1.11 – "and over them will rule the angels of destruction"; 2.1.3f – "and [there will co]me the dominion of Belial upon them to deliver them up to the sword." 4Q390 2.1.6f – "And I shall deliver them [to the hands of the an]gels of destruction and they will rule over them." 4Q286 7.2.1–3 – "And afterwards [t]he[y] shall damn Belial and all his guilty lot … And cursed be all the spir[its of] his [l]ot in their wicked plan." 1QS 3.20–23; 1.16–2.8; 1QM 13.10–12 – "You made Belial for the pit, angel of enmity; in dark[ness] is his [dom]ain, his counsel to bring about wickedness and guilt." 1QM 14.9f – "…during the empire of Belial. With all the mysteries of his enmity, they have not separated us from your covenant." 1QM 1.5 – "And th]is is a time of salvation for the nation of God and a period of rule for all the men of his lot, and everlasting destruction for all the lot of Belial." 1QM 1.13 – "the army of Belial will gird themselves in order to force the lot of [light] to retreat." 13.4 – "And in their positions they shall bless the God of Israel and all the deeds of his truth and they shall damn there Belial and all the spirits of his lot." CD 16.4f – "And on the day on which one has imposed upon himself to return to the law of Moses, the angel of Mastema will turn aside from following him, should he keep his words"; cf. CD 4.12–15; 5.8 and 1QH^a 11.19f.

6.3 Demonic Possession in the *DSS*

Although there are a few references that indicate actual physical possession of the human body, the language of demonic possession in the Scrolls suggests the evil spirits were influencing humans rather than taking physical possession of the body.[41] The concept of demonic possession in the *DSS* may have its origins in the motif of "evil inclination."[42] 1QH[a] 15.3 states, "for Belial is present when their (evil) inclination becomes apparent" (כי בליעל עם הופע יצר הוותם);[43] however, this does not necessarily mean physical possession by an evil spirit. It could simply imply the influence of Belial over the human inclination. Similarly, 1QH[a] 5.21 conceives of a person with a "spirit of flesh" who is ruled over by an evil spirit.

However, some of the *DSS* do offer examples of physical possession. It could be understood from 1QS 3 20 that the sons of injustice were afflicted by evil/unclean spirits (physically possessed as were the giants) and thus required an exorcism of the spirit. 1QS 4 20–21, although in eschatological and cosmic language, perhaps suggests such an exorcism. These lines describe, in very graphic language, the removal of the "spirit of injustice" from the structure of a man. García Martínez translates the verse "ripping out all spirit of injustice from the *innermost part of his flesh*" (italics mine). The spirit of injustice can be related to the unclean spirit that causes defilement (see line 22), but the question that remains is: what is the *innermost part of his flesh*? It may be possible that this phrase is alluding to Leviticus 17.11, 14 with the understanding that the human soul is in the blood, which, if I may suggest, could be understood as the "innermost part of his flesh." This would imply then that the influence of an evil spirit

---

[41] See e.g. 4Q560 frag 1 1 – possession by an evil visitor; 11Q5 19 13 – fear of possible possession (= 11Q6 frags 4–5); 1QS 10 21 – "man shall not retain Belial in his heart." Alexander argues the demonology of the *DSS*, in particular the community documents, appears to be linked to the issue of impurity, Alexander, "Demonology in DSS," 348f. There are a few documents that mention an unclean spirit, רוח טמאה, in relation to demonic possession language of the Scrolls (e.g. 1QS 4 21–22; 11QPs[a] 19.15; 4Q444 1 i 8; 4Q230 frag 1 line 1; and possibly 4Q458 2 i 5). Through this purity language (cf. 1QS 3 8–9), the Scrolls reflect an image within the demonology of Qumran that equates demonic possession to impurity, but at the same time does not limit impurity to demonic possession. This term occurs in the Greek (πνεύματα ἀκάθαρτα) twenty-two times in the demonic pericopes of the Gospels in which "unclean spirits" are seen as responsible for physical possession and affliction of individuals, ibid., 349, n. 51.

[42] There is little indication of such an act in *BW* with the possible exception of the Greek version of *1 Enoch* 15.12. This verse indicates that the spirits of the giants strike against spirits (human?), which could imply an act of bodily invasion.

[43] Text and translation from García Martínez/Tigchelaar, *Dead Sea Scrolls*, 1:176–77.

might be upon the soul or upon the intellect of the individual.[44] Demonic possession in the *DSS* then could be understood as something that affects the ethical behaviour of an individual rather, than in a strict sense, denoting an invasion of the physical body.[45] 4Q510 frag 1.6 suggests that the evil spirits lead astray the mind of the individual, "And those who strike unexpectedly to lead astray the spirit of knowledge"[46] rather than occupying the body.[47] These texts offer evidence of a further progression of the demonology of 2TP Judaism.

From this discussion, it is clear that the nature of evil spirits and human spirits is kept strictly separate in the Scrolls. What we do see is a desire, or purpose, of the evil spirits to afflict humans for reasons that are left somewhat ambiguous. The possibility disclosed by *BW* that logically, the spirits of the giants may wish to invade humans to regain what they have lost, a physical body, is not explicitly followed up in the Scrolls. However, the ability of evil spirits to affect the ethical behaviour of an individual in an effort to separate him or her from God and his law is a primary theme in the demonology of the *DSS*. In what follows, the Scrolls reveal an effort by Jews to set out prayers of protection against the activity of evil spirits that may contain echoes of the Watcher tradition in general.

---

[44] See J. Keir Howard, "New Testament Exorcism and its Significance Today," *ExpTim* 96 (1985): 105–09. Howard discusses the symptoms of the individuals in six demonic pericopes in the Gospels in light of a modern medical diagnosis. He concludes that all of them can be attributed to some form of mental illness or physical symptoms related to mental illness.

[45] Cf. *T12P*.

[46] והפוגעים פתע פתאום לתעות רוח בינה. Text from Maurice Baillet, *Qumrân Grotte 4 III (4Q482–4Q520)* (DJD VII; Oxford: Clarendon, 1982), 216.

[47] Alexander argues the Scrolls indicate "evil spirits were leading the sons of light to err through attacks on their intellect." If this is the case, since the giants of *BW* were partially human, then it makes sense to attack them psychologically, which is seen as an effective method in 4Q510–11. See Alexander, "Wrestling Against Wickedness in High Places: Magic in the Worldview of the Qumran Community," in *The Scrolls and Scriptures Qumran Fifty Years After* (ed. Stanley E. Porter and Craig A. Evans; Sheffield: Sheffield Academic, 1997), 324. This image may be partially reflected in Mk 5.15 and Lk 8.35. The demoniac is found to be in his "right mind" following the removal of the unclean spirit by Jesus. However, the Gospel pericopes seem to indicate a physical possession by the spirit of the man's body, but it seems possible the same behaviour could have been caused by mental affliction. See the most recent discussion of possession and exorcism in the New Testament in Eric Sorensen, *Possession and Exorcism in the New Testament and Early Christianity*, (WUNT 2 157; Tübingen: Mohr Siebeck, 2002). See also discussion of the unclean spirits in Clinton Wahlen, *Jesus and the Impurity of Spirits in the Synoptic Gospels*, (WUNT 2 185; Tübingen: Mohr Siebeck, 2004).

6.4 Prayer at Qumran

A large corpus of material amongst the Scrolls has been identified as containing some form of prayer or hymn. Esther Chazon notes that the Qumran material offers over two hundred previously unknown hymns and prayers along with portions of approximately one hundred and twenty–five biblical psalms. These texts disclose a facet of the spiritual life and religious practices of Early Judaism.[48] This group of documents contains several prayers that perhaps fall into the category of incantation or prayers of protection.[49] Although these prayers do not necessarily enhance our understanding of the developing anthropology, they do reveal how humans contended with evil spirits in Judaism during the 2TP. The language of the prayers indicates a possible influence of the Watcher tradition upon the authors.

Incantation prayers are one of the two main categories of magical texts found in the Scrolls.[50] The first group of texts includes those which are concerned with divination, omens, and foretelling (e.g. 4Q186; 4Q561; and 4Q318). The second group is concerned with prayers that request or enforce a defence against evil spirits (e.g. 4Q510; 4Q511; 4Q444; 4Q560; 11Q5; and 11Q11). The prayers of the second group of texts can be subdivided into possibly three forms. In the first, the person addresses the spirit directly by invoking the Divine Name. In the second (although this prayer may be categorized as a hymn of thanksgiving), the person makes a direct plea to God for his protection from the evil spirit. And in the third, the person invokes the praise and glorification of God in order to stop the activity of the evil spirits in his or her life. We will examine briefly an example of each of these types of prayers.

---

[48] See Esther Chazon, "Hymns and Prayers in the Dead Sea Scrolls" in *The Dead Sea Scrolls After Fifty Years A Comprehensive Assessment* (ed. Peter W. Flint and James C. VanderKam, 2 vols. Leiden: Brill, 1998), 1:244–70. It is possible that some of the prayers and hymns encountered in the Qumran material will reflect similar prayer traditions found in the later rabbinic period. In both cases, lack of the Temple edifice, due to the community's voluntary separation and the Temple's destruction in 70 C.E., may have spurred similar responses to the need for a substitute for sacrificial worship. This may be what is alluded to in 11Q5 18 9–11. The author states "the person who gives glory to the Most High is accepted like one who brings an offering, like one who offers rams and calves, like one who makes the altar greasy with many holocausts."

[49] The term "incantation," if it is to be given a technical definition, must carry with it some key concepts. First, the person must be operating under some kind of authority, whether it is by divine name or a word of power. Second, it requires a repetition of what can be defined as a certain formula of words given to the person by a figure who is connected with the authority, i.e. a prophet, diviner, etc. These words must then be spoken directly to the spirit in question or the divinity in question.

[50] See Alexander, "Wrestling Against Wickedness," 318–337.

6.4.1 11Q11 (11QPsApᵃ): Invoking the Divine Name

The first form of incantation prayer is found in 11Q11.[51] This document
dates from early first century C.E. and contains six columns of text in a
very fragmentary condition. J. P. M. van der Ploeg has identified within
11Q11 cols. 1–5 three incantations against evil spirits followed by a
version of Psalm 91 in column 6.[52] Van der Ploeg, followed by Émile
Puech, has suggested that the prayers from 11Q11 are the four prayers
mentioned in 11Q5 col. 27 which describe four prayers that David prayed
over the possessed.[53] Puech concludes the prayers are from an ancient
Israelite ritual and were adopted by the Qumran community for
prophylactic and incantation purposes.[54]

According to van der Ploeg, the prayer begins in column 2 lines 2–4
with the mention of David's son Solomon.[55] These lines may allude to a
tradition in which Solomon has the ability, through the wisdom of song, to
exorcise demonic spirits (see Josephus, *Ant.* 8.45; *Wis* 7; *T. Sol*). Although
the fragmentary nature of the text resists a precise interpretation, it seems
to suggest that one is told to invoke the name of the Lord (יהוה) against

---

[51] Cf. also 4Q560 frag 1 2 in which the person addresses the evil spirit directly. It is
difficult to discuss this text in any detail due to its very fragmentary nature and the lack
of the presence of the Divine Name. For a thorough discussion, see Douglas L. Penney
and Michael O. Wise, "By the Power of Beelzebub: An Aramaic Incantation From
Qumran (4Q560)," *JBL* 113 (1994): 627–50. Penney and Wise argue the presence of
these incantation prayers in the *DSS* is due to the intense spiritual battle going on within
Judaism with spiritual forces outside of the community.

[52] See J. P. M. Van der Ploeg, "Le psaume XCI dans une recension de Qumran," *RB*
72 (1965) 210–17.

[53] The idea that these are prayers said over the possessed is based on the word
הפגועים in col. 5 line 2. See Émile Puech, "11QPsApᵃ: Un ritual d'exorcismes. Essai
de reconstruction," *RevQ* 14 (1990): 377–408.

[54] Van der Ploeg suggests 11Q11 cols. 2, 3, and 4 contain a series of prayers against
evil spirits that invoke the Divine name. The term "invoke" is a key to understanding
these psalms as incantations. Puech and later García Martínez/Tigchelaar reconstruct col.
2 line 2 (col. 1 for Puech) with ויקר]א.

[55]

[שׁם]	[1.
]ה שלומה] [ויקר]א	[2.
הרו[ו]חות] [והשדים]	[3.
[אלה [הש]דים ו]מ]ר המשט]מה	[4.

1. ?
2. [ ] Solomon, [ ] and he shall invo[ke
3. [the spi]rits, [ ]and the demons, [
4. [ ] These are [the de]mons. And the p[rince of enmi]ty.

evil spirits.[56] Unfortunately, based on the fragmentary nature of the text, we must assume the presence of the Divine Name in this particular column. This is followed in lines 10–12 by words that glorify God for his works, although much of this text is reconstructed.[57]

Column 3 (again fragmentary) continues with a reminder of the creative works of God (lines 1–4); this is followed by a call to all creation to witness against those who sin against God (lines 4–7).[58] It is due in part to these lines that one may question if these columns are a series of three prayers, as suggested by van der Ploeg, or a pair of incantations (found in cols. 4 and 5) that are introduced in columns 2 and 3 with a reminder to the reader, or hearer, of the effect these prayers had in the life of Solomon.

The fragmentary nature of the document makes it extremely difficult to determine what may have been original. Some of the difficulties are revealed by observing the attempts at reconstruction and translation of column 3 lines 4–5 by Puech and García Martínez and Tigchelaar.[59] García Martínez and Tigchelaar read, "(YHWH) who summons all [his] a[ngels] and all [the holy] se[ed] to st[a]nd before [him . . .]." Puech reads, "He adjures every ang[el to help] all of the ho[ly seed] who are st[a]n[d]ing

---

[56] One might ask if 11Q11 contains יהוה, does this require it to be classified as a non–sectarian document. See Alexander, "Wickedness," 325.

[57]

10.]ביהוה אלוהי אל׳ם אשר עשה[את השמים
11.]ואת הארץ ואת כול אשר בם א[שר הבדיל]בין[
12.]האור ובין החושך. [. . .]עד[. . .]

10. [on YHWH, God of gods, he who made] the heavens
11. [and the earth and all that is in them, w]ho separated
12. [light from darkness . . .] . . . [. . .]

The reconstruction is based on the use of the verb הבדיל in Gen 1. Other possible uses are separation of Israel from the nations in Lev 20.24. In Qumran literature: 1QS 5 1; CD 6 14, the separation of the community from Israel and CD 6 17, separation between pure and impure. García Martínez suggests it could be related to demons in the sense of impurity. See Florentino García Martínez, Eibert J. C. Tigchelaar and Adam S. Van der Woude (*DJD* XXIII; Oxford: Clarendon, 1998), 192.

[58]

4. עשה את ה]אלה בגבור[תו משביע לכול מ]לאכיו[
5.]וא[ת כול זר]ע הקודש]אשר התן׳[צבו לפנ׳]ו וי׳עיד א[ת
6.]כול הש[מ]ים ו]את כול[הארץ]ן בהם]אשר ישש]ו]על
7.]כול א׳[ש חטא ועל כול א]דם רשע ו[הם יודעים

4. (*YHWH*) made t[hese through] his [streng]th, who summons all [his] a[ngels]
5. and all [the holy] se[ed] to st[a]nd before [him, and calls as witness]
6. [all the he]avens and [all] the earth [against them] who committed against
7. [all me]n sin, and against every m[an evil. But] they know.

[59] See Puech, "11QPsAp[a]" and García Martínez/Tigchelaar, *Dead Sea Scrolls*, 2:203.

before [Him . . ."].[60] These two translations represent two very different
understandings of one event. García Martínez and Tigchelaar reconstruct
with language that is characteristic of a scene of judgment (i.e. a summons
to stand before the Lord) going as far as to suggest a possible reading of
"(God) adjures the bastards and the seed of evil to appear before him."[61]
Puech, meanwhile, uses language that is representative of the
commissioning of a task based on the idea that angels are often told to
assist the righteous.

It is possible that 11Q11 col. 3 is alluding to the tradition of the
judgment of the Watchers in *1 Enoch* 10.13 for their rebellion against God,
which we may also find in Psalm 82.6–7. The author of 11Q11 has set this
story before the incantation that follows in column 4 as a reminder to the
reader or hearer of the fate that awaits the spirits that afflict him or her.
This may suggest that the incantation will not bring about the immediate
destruction of the evil spirit; that destruction must wait for the eschaton. In
the meantime, however, the incantation will provide immediate protection
against these afflicting spirits.

The text that follows in column 4 describes the incantation that is
spoken by the individual or group who invokes the Divine Name against
the spirits.[62] This prayer is a direct speech used to terrify the spirit with a
description of its fate.[63] The punishment is described in lines 7–9 ("who
will [bring] you [down] to the great abyss, [and to] the deepest [Sheol.]
And . . . [. . .] . . . And it will be very dark [in the gr]eat [abyss."). This is
similar to the description of the punishment of the angels described in *1
Enoch* 10.4–5 – "Bind Azazel . . . throw him into the darkness . . . cover
him with darkness . . . over his face that he may not see light"[64] (cf. also
col. 5 lines 8–10).[65] It is difficult to determine direct influence of *BW* on
this prayer, but the similarity in language suggests the possibility.

---

[60] Puech's reconstruction and translation is based on the idea in 1QS 3 24 – "the God
of Israel and the angel of his truth assist all the sons of light"; and 1QM 13 10 – "from of
old you appointed the Prince of Light to assist us."

[61] משביע לכול מ[ומזרים [וא]ת כול זר[ע הרשע [אשר התנ]י[צבו לפני], see
DJD XXIII, p. 194, note on line 4–5.

[62] It can be argued that the end of the incantation in col. 5 line 3, "Amen, Amen,
Selah" (usual in Jewish magical incantations) indicates the prayer was recited in a public
setting.

[63] Cf. perhaps *Book of Giants* – 4Q530 col. 2 20–24. The giants and *nephilim* became
frightened when they heard of their fate.

[64] Translation Knibb, *Ethiopic Enoch*, 2:87–8.

[65] "YHWH [will bring] you [down] [to the] deepest [Sheo]l, [he will shut] the two
bronze [ga]tes through [which n]o light [penetrates.] [On you shall] not [shine the] sun . .
."

A second incantation prayer in this document is found in column 5. This prayer is a direct address to an evil spirit in which the person invokes the Divine name, יהוה (see line 4). This is the only prayer of the three suggested by van der Ploeg and Puech that can be clearly attributed to David. There are several allusions to *BW* in this particular prayer. The threat levelled against the evil spirits in line 6 resonates with the interaction between God and the evil spirits in *BW*. Although there is some argument over the reconstruction of 11Q11 col. 5 line 6,[66] it is possible the author was alluding to the spirits of the giants in *BW* – מי אתה [הילוד מ]אדם ומזרע הקד[ש]י[ם] ("who are you [oh offspring of] man and of the seed of the ho[ly one]s?").[67] This line may be describing the hybrid offspring of the angels and humans in *1 Enoch* 7.2 and 15.8–9. In 11Q11 col. 5 lines 6–10, the evil spirit is told of the punishment that awaits it at the hand of the chief of the army of the Lord[68] in the darkness of Sheol, similar to what is found in col. 4, lines 7–8. Again, the description of the fate of the evil spirits in this text seems to be informed by the Watcher tradition in *1 Enoch*.

6.4.2 11Q5 (11QPsa) Column XIX: Plea for Deliverance

J. A. Sanders proposed that 11Q5 19[69] originally contained about twenty-four verses beginning in column 18.[70] The text of the psalm is considered

---

[66] There have been two other proposed reconstructions of the lacunae [oh offspring of]. Van der Ploeg reconstructs it with מי אתה [ותירא מ]אדם following an example in Isaiah 51.12 ("Who are you that you fear men?"). García Martínez suggests this is too long for the space and does not make sense syntactically. The second reconstruction, from Puech, is מי אתה [ארור מ]אדם ("Who are you cursed of man?"), which he contends corresponds to the curses of Belial and the spirits in other *DSS*; see 1QS 2 4–7; 1QM 13 4–5; CD 20 8; and 4Q175 23. García Martínez argues that translating ארור as a jussive is unwarranted. See *DJD* XXIII, 198–201.

[67] "Holy ones" (קדשים) identifies the angels in the biblical psalms (Ps 89.6, 8; cf. Zech 14.5 – "God comes with his holy ones"). Dan 8.24 identifies the destruction of "holy people," קדשים.

[68] Cf. Josh 5.14–15; Dan 8.11.

[69] Line (8) "My soul cried out to praise your name, to give thanks with shouts (9) for your compassionate deeds, to proclaim your faithfulness, to the praise of you there is no end. I was near death (10) for my sins and my iniquities sold me to Sheol, but you (11) YHWH, did save me, according to your abundant compassion and abundant righteous acts. Also I (12) have loved your name and I have found refuge in your shadow. When I remember your strength, my heart is strengthened (13) and upon your mercies I lean. Forgive my sin YHWH (14) and cleanse me from my iniquity. Grant me a spirit of faith and knowledge. Let me not stumble (15) in transgression. Let not Satan rule over me, nor an evil spirit; let neither pain nor evil inclination take possession of my bones." A second copy of the prayer is suggested in 11Q6 frags 4–5. This very fragmentary text contains only small sections of thirteen of the sixteen lines that are thought to correspond closely with 11Q5 XIX, see *DJD* XXIII, 43–44.

incomplete with possibly the first five lines missing. The incantation section of the prayer is found in column 19 lines 13–16, in which the person is making a direct plea to God (using the Divine Name, יהוה) for his forgiveness, strengthening, and protection from Satan and evil spirits.[71]

The psalm follows a biblical model in the way of form, content, and the vocabulary.[72] Sanders argues certain vocabulary used in 11Q5 19 differs from other Qumran documents relating to the spiritual battle of the community, i.e. the use of Satan and the evil inclination rather than Belial and the spirit of wickedness.[73] Sanders opts for a closer connection to rabbinic literature because of the presence of Satan and evil inclination, but these terms are also found in the Hebrew Bible (Job 1.6; 2.1 and Gen 6.5). A connection to rabbinic literature, while insightful, should not suggest that the document is dependent on rabbinic ideas, but rather the language of the document may represent a developing tradition that is documented in rabbinic literature.

The prayer begins with an acknowledgment of the greatness of God in lines 1–12. Within this praise, the author recognizes God's sovereignty, mercy, loving kindness, and great deeds. This is followed by the acknowledgement by the author of his sin and the need for forgiveness and purification, perhaps recognizing a reason for the affliction of evil spirits. This is followed in lines 15–16 with a request for God's protection against

---

[70] See Sanders, *Psalms Scroll.*

[71] David Flusser identified a close affinity between 11Q5 19 and the Aramaic *Testament of Levi* found at Qumran (4Q213ᵃ frag 1 I); see David Flusser, "Qumran and Jewish 'Apotropaic' Prayers," *IEJ* 16 (1966): 194–205. 11Q5 19 line 15 contains a similar phrase (אל תשלט בי שטן) to that which is found in Aramaic Levi line 17 אל תשלט בי כל שטן). See also the use of Satan in 1QH frag 4 6; frag 45 3 and 1QSᵇ 1.8. This of course does not require a literary dependence in either direction (although both may be drawing on Ps 119.133), but perhaps supports the idea of a developing tradition within Judaism of personal incantations against evil spirits in the late second c. B.C.E. There are also three later prayers in *Berakhoth* 60b that have parallels to the Scroll material. Flusser argues it is possible that the apotropaic prayers of the Scrolls and later rabbinic literature can be traced back to Ps 51. However, one major difference between the biblical psalms and the Scroll material is the demonization of sin in the Scroll texts. The biblical psalms offer no counterpart to the Holy Spirit or willing spirit. Flusser suggests this is evidence for a late development of a belief in demonic powers as a parallel to positive spiritual powers inside and outside of humans and the dualistic movement at Qumran. See ibid., 204.

[72] In their reconstruction of 11Q5 frag E iii, García Martínez/Tigchelaar contend the document contained Ps 147.14–17 in the missing lines 1–4 and verses 18–20 make up lines 5–7. They also suggest the rest of the psalm is directly related to Ps 105.

[73] These characteristics would suggest a non-Qumran authorship; however, at least three Qumran documents include the phrase "evil inclination" – 4Q435, 4Q370, and 4Q422. Sanders suggests the psalm has possible parallels to 1QS col. 3–4 (cf. also *1 Enoch* 84 for a similar type of prayer).

Satan and unclean spirits. It may be assumed from these two lines that unclean spirits are responsible for physical affliction and the manifestation of the evil inclination in humanity. The term "unclean spirit" may characterize further the developing anthropology of Early Judaism. The term can only find definition if it is set against the human spirit, which then must be defined as a clean spirit, or an undefiled spirit.

The "Plea for Deliverance" closes with a further praise of God and recognition of his grace. The author acknowledges his near-death experience due to his sins and iniquity. He also recognizes his inclination to sin and the ability of evil spirits to lead him in that direction, a characteristic of Qumran demonology. He therefore asks for a spirit of faith and knowledge to be strong against their attacks. This prayer should perhaps be categorized a prayer of thanksgiving for deliverance rather than an incantation.

6.4.3 4Q510 and 4Q511: Songs of the Maskil

The third form of incantation prayer is found in 4Q510 and 4Q511, the "Songs of the Maskil."[74] These two texts are quite fragmentary and contain some uncertainties in their reconstruction.[75] 4Q510 is made up of two fragments of which there are fourteen lines, nine on fragment one, and five on fragment two. A much larger portion of text has survived from 4Q511 that includes twenty-three fragments of (approx.) 130 lines. Similar language found in the two texts has prompted Nitzan and Alexander to suggest that 4Q510 and 511 are two copies of the same text by different scribes.[76]

The surviving text of 4Q510 frag 1 begins with four lines of praise directed towards the glory of God without using the Divine Name

---

[74] Armin Lange and Esther Chazon suggest a parallel to these two documents in 4Q444 (Incantation). I disagree with Lange's proposal that the beginning of 4Q444 should parallel 4Q510 frag 1 4–5. 4Q510 1.4–5 is clearly set out as words of praise to terrify the demons. There is not the sense in 4Q444 that this is an incantation in the same sense that which is found in 4Q510–11, but rather it seems to be closer to the wisdom text of 4Q417–18, which describes a spirit that is granted to the person in order to rebuke spirits which are trying to lead him or her away from God's Law. See e.g. 4Q444 frag 1 line 2, "and they became spirits of dispute in my understanding of the statute," ויהיו לרוחי ריב במבנתי חוק. Cf. CD 16.4f; 4.12–15; 5.8 and 1QH[a]11.19f.

[75] See M. Baillet, *Qumran Cave 4*.

[76] See Alexander, "Wrestling Against Wickedness," 319 and Bilhah Nitzan, *Qumran Prayer and Religious Poetry* (trans. Jonathan Chipman; STDJ 12; Leiden: Brill, 1994). Arguably, this is a possibility, but it is also possible that 4Q510 is a single incantation out of a collection of prayers, a recipe book, of which 4Q511 may have served as the main body.

יהוה (instead, אלהים is used).[77] Alexander suggests these apotropaic lines of thanksgiving are sectarian in origin based upon the "siege mentality" and the "distinctive language of the Qumran group" contained in the hymn (i.e. "sons of light" – 4Q510 frag 1, 1.7; and "men of Covenant" – 4Q511 frags 63–64, 2 1.5).[78] The apparent failure to use the Divine Name (יהוה), which is found in other incantation texts, may be due in part to the author's recognition of the sanctity of the name and his fear to use it as a magical charm. However, as Nitzan suggests, the text may have contained adjurations with יהוה that were subsequently lost.[79] The use of a divine name would follow the normal pattern of incantation prayers in which the name of the deity (in this case יהוה) is used as the word of power, rather than the words of glorification and praise of God, which we find in 4Q510–11.[80]

Nitzan suggests each of the "Songs of the Maskil" can be divided into three primary components: a word of power, banishment of the demons, and the time in which the prayer will be effective.[81] These components can be identified in 4Q510. The "word of power," which Nitzan identifies as the *praise and glorification of God* rather than the Divine Name, is found in lines 4–6.[82] In this instance, they are used to terrify and scatter the evil spirits – "and I, a Sage, declare the splendour of his glory in order to frighten and terrify all the spirits." The second component is the identification of all the spirits by the Sage which are turned away by the

---

[77] See also 4Q290 for the use of אל as the name of God in prayer for protection. The opening lines of 4Q510 and fragments of 4Q511 may have been an allusion to *1 Enoch* 9.4–5, 11, which contain the prayer of the archangels concerning the evil that was being done by the Watchers and their offspring. The idea that the angels were worshipping alongside the covenanters may have influenced the author in adopting this method of prayer.

[78] See also Chazon, "Hymns and Prayers."

[79] This theory, however, may perhaps be questioned due to the presence of אלהים.

[80] See ibid., 248–250.

[81] Ibid., 244.

[82]

4. ואני משכיל משמיע הוד תפארתו לפחד ולב[ה]ל[

5. כול רוחי מלאכי חבל ורוחות ממזרים שדאים לילית אחים ו[ציים. . .[

6. והפוגעים פתע פתאום לתעות רוח בינה ולהשם לבבם בקץ ממשל[ת]

7. רשעה ותעודות תעניות בני או[ר]

4. And I, a sage, declare the splendour of his glory in order to frighten and terr[ify]

5. all the spirits of the corrupting angels and the bastards spirits, demons, Lilith, owls and [jackals]

6. and those who strike suddenly to lead astray the spirit of knowledge, to make their hearts devastated. And you have been placed in the era of the rul[e of]

7. wickedness and in the periods of humiliation of the sons of lig[ht].

incantation (lines 5–6): the spirits of the corrupting angels, bastard spirits, demons, Lilith, owls, jackals, and those which strike suddenly. A description of several of these evil spirits is found in *BW*, again offering a possible influence upon 4Q510 by the Watcher tradition (see *1 En* 19.1; 10.9).[83] The third component of Nitzan's formula (the time of effective prayer) is found in lines 6–8.[84] Nitzan suggests this is a warning to the spirits that their time is limited, but that their activity is permitted through Divine decree until the Day of Judgment (see *Jub* 10).[85] It is through this prayer of glorification of God that the people will find an immediate end to the demonic activity and a promise of an eschatological punishment of the spirits.

4Q511 is more complex than 510. The fragmentary nature of the text does not seem to allow the psalm to fit into Nitzan's formula of components listed previously. Nevertheless, the document is clearly an incantation against evil spirits. Fragment 35 line 6f. identifies the task of the Maskil to exalt the name of God (?) and to (terrify) the spirits of the bastards[86] (see *1 En* 10.9; and 4Q511 frags 48, 49, 51 lines 2–3[87]). The text also contains scattered words of praise and glorification of God (frag 2 col. 1; frags 28, 29, 30, 52, 54, 55, 57–59, 63–64). Fragment 10 appears to be the end of the list of demons that is given in 4Q510 frag 1 5–6. A point of significant difference in 4Q511 is the numerous promises of protection by God in what appears to be eschatological language. Fragment 1 describes a region in which there are no evil spirits. Fragment 2 column 1 states that God has removed the chief of dominions (cf. frag 3). Fragment 8 describes the protection of the person in the secret (place) of El Shaddai amongst the holy ones (cf. Ps 91.1). These promises of protection perhaps enforce the idea of an immediate deliverance from the affliction of the spirits while at the same time reminding the people of the final destruction of the spirits in the eschaton described in *BW*.[88]

---

[83] See also Isa 13.21 and 34.14.

[84] A second possible interpretation of these lines is that the Maskil is addressing the people. It is not clear who the "you" is in the word *natatem* (you have been placed in the era of the rule of wickedness). If it is the people then it could be understood as a word of encouragement that the rule of the wicked is ending. They are told that their lives will not come to everlasting destruction during the period of humiliation.

[85] Cf. 4Q511 frag 35 8–9.

[86] ‏ואני מירא אל בקצי דורותי לרומם שם דב]. . . ולפחד] בגבורתו כו]ל [‏ רוחי ממזרים‎ – "And as for me, I spread the fear of God in the ages of my generations to exalt the name [. . . and to terrify] with his power al[l] spirits of the bastards." See García Martínez/Tigchelaar, *Dead Sea Scrolls*, 2:1032.

[87] "And through my mouth he startles [all the spirits of] the bastards, so to subjugate [all] impure [sinners]."

[88] Alexander contends the emphasis in the Qumran documents (e.g. 1QS 3.20–24; 4Q174 1–3 i 7–9; 4Q510 1 6; 11Q11 5.5–8; 11QPs[a] 19.15) is on the psychological effects

The incantation psalms of the *DSS* reflect an apocalyptic worldview that recognized the presence of evil spirits at work in the world within the divine order. Some of the Scroll texts disclose vulnerability in the human spirit that left a person open to attack by the subordinates of Beliar due to the inclination of the heart.[89] These evil spirits afflicted humanity with physical ailments, spiritual oppression, and possession (cf. 4Q560). In order to counteract the activity of these spirits, Judaism incorporated the practice of magical protection through prayer and the use of incantations. These prayers were used as weapons of spiritual warfare in order to protect the children of light from being persuaded by a host of evil spirits to follow the evil inclination. It can also be understood from the documents that these prayers were only a temporary restraint against the activity of the spirits, but it is also clear that the authors expected a complete destruction of the spirits in the eschaton as described in *BW* (16.1).

6.5 Conclusion

The growing prominence of the belief in demons played a key role in the struggle of good versus evil in the 2TP. As a result, anthropology found in certain documents that recorded how evil spirits influenced a person in an effort to draw him or her away from God and, at the same time, permitted evil spirits to afflict or perhaps take possession of a human body (cf. 11Q5 19 15–16). Within this anthropology and demonology, we have identified three primary motifs at work in the Scrolls that helped to formulate how the problem of evil was being addressed in 2TP Judaism. First, it was understood that humanity had a good and evil inclination. Second, the evil side of this innate characteristic allowed the evil spirits who emerged from the Watcher tradition (i.e. Belial and his lot) to cause people to digress

---

of the evil spirits upon the individual and community rather than the physical harm. Therefore, the primary weapon against the spirits is prayer that glorifies God, see Alexander, "Demonology in DSS," 345–46.

[89] There are several protective prayers or recitations in the Qumran literature, which are used against Belial, or those in his camp. See e.g. 1QS 2.4–10 – "against human followers of Belial"; 1QM 13 – "against Belial and his lot of spirits who plot against the lot of God"; 4Q280 – "against *Melki-resha*, the one who plots against the covenant of God"; 4Q286 frag 7 – "against Belial and the spirits that plot with him." 4Q560 suggests a physical possession or affliction of an individual by an evil spirit (during sleep?) that causes an undefined illness (cf. 4Q266 6.1.5f). 4Q560 frag 1.2 offers an amulet that presumably will protect the individual from these attacks. These types of prayers may be reflected in the instruction given to Noah by the archangel in *Jubilees* 10.12–14 which would protect his children from the attacks of *Mastema* and the evil spirits of the giants. Similar practices can be found in *Tobit* 6.8.

from following God. Third, it is because of these attacks that we see the prominence of the prayers that were used as a defence against the spirits. Within these prayers, we find allusions to the Watcher tradition, which was advanced in the second and first centuries B.C.E. by the Scrolls and other Jewish literature. We also find a reflection of the interaction of demons and humans in the Gospels.

The combination of the themes found in *BW*, *DSS*, and other texts, allowed for the emergence of a theology, demonology, and anthropology within Early Judaism that dissociated God from the origin of evil. These developing motifs in 2TP Judaism would eventually evolve to the point at which we see the emergence of the "kingdom of Satan" in the Gospels (Matt 12.26; Lk 11.18), bringing about a recognized dualism in the spirit world of the first century. The resulting anthropology assumed that human nature is weak, corruptible, and subject to the manipulation of evil spirits. These are the same evil spirits, although reconceived, that the author of *BW* had affirmed exist in his day.

The foregoing exposé of the origin of human suffering through the activity of evil spirits is only attested thus far in sources originating from Judea-Palestine. However, in his treatise *De Gigantibus*, Philo of Alexandria offers a different model in which the cause of human suffering and evil is not personified in the form of evil spirits. Philo's argument centres more on human nature; the responsibility for suffering ultimately rests on the shoulders of humanity. In what follows, I will present a detailed examination of Philo's interpretation of Genesis 6.1–4 in relation to his view of the human soul.

Chapter 7

Philo of Alexandria:
Interpreting Genesis 6.1–4

7.1 Introduction[1]

The previous chapters have argued that the interpretation of Genesis 6.1–4
played an important role in the development of a Jewish demonology in
the centuries leading up to the Common Era. The giantology (i.e. the theme
of evil spirits) and anthropology in the *Book of Watchers* were adopted and
elaborated by the authors of several early Jewish texts during the second
and first centuries B.C.E. These texts, in turn, advanced the giant tradition
of the emergence of evil spirits to the point we find it taken up by the
authors of the Gospels. The Gospel texts reflect a belief in the existence of
evil spirits in certain branches of the Palestinian Jewish worldview. These
evil spirits appear to have the ability to afflict and, at times, invade the
human body for reasons left unspoken. However, it appears that not all
Jews were willing to accept this explanation for elements of human
suffering in the first century C.E. Philo of Alexandria in *De Gigantibus*
offered a very different view, which may be derived in large part from his
own interpretation of Genesis 6.1–4.

This chapter will present an alternative approach to the responsibility
for human suffering articulated by a lone voice in the Alexandrian
Diaspora during the 2TP, one that differs considerably from the tradition
set forth in *BW* and other related texts. As will be seen below, it is difficult
to determine whether Philo knew of the Watcher tradition; it does appear,
however, that he was at least aware of some form of the Rebellious Angel
tradition prevalent in Palestinian Judaism.

In order to understand Philo's approach, we must first try to determine
his place in Early Judaism. I shall do so by presenting the relevant
questions in the debate concerning his method of interpreting scripture.
Several scholars have argued that he is presenting a very Platonic view of
humanity and the cosmos. However, as will be shown below, he is a gifted

---

[1] All Greek texts and translations of Philo are from *Philo in Ten Volumes* (*and Two
Supplementary Volumes*) (trans. F. H. Colson, G. H. Whitaker, and Ralph Marcus; LCL;
Cambridge: Harvard University, 1929–62).

exegete of scripture who uses Greek philosophical language in order to explain effectively the journey of the human soul. I shall discuss the role of Philo's audience(s), which, along with his philosophical language, presents several difficulties for the reader who is attempting to interpret his exegesis of the biblical tradition.

Following the discussion of Philo's role as an exegete, I shall outline his view of the soul in relation to anthropology in the wider cosmos. While developing his anthropology, Philo argues for the existence of two types of souls, a divine soul that remains outside of the physical realm of humanity and the human soul that takes on flesh. Within this anthropology, two interrelated points will be raised that are central to his interpretation of Genesis 6.1–4: the origin of the human soul and its immortality. These two elements, discussed in this broader perspective, will provide a backdrop against which a clearer picture of his anthropology and giantology emerges in the primary text of this chapter, *De Gigantibus*. This discussion will reveal a diversity of Jewish thought in relation to demonology in the first century C.E.

7.2 Philo of Alexandria: Exegete or Philosopher?

Philo of Alexandria has been characterized as both a Jewish exegete and a Greek philosopher. His life and, in part, his writings remain enigmatic to the twenty first century scholar. There are very few references found in Graeco–Roman literature that describe his life in the Jewish community in Alexandria in the first century C.E.[2] Josephus described him as a leading citizen during the late first century B.C.E. and early first century C.E. He writes that Philo's opinions in the community were held in high regard: "Philo, who stood at the head of the delegation of the Jews, a man held in the highest honour, brother of Alexander the Alabarch, and no novice in philosophy, was prepared to proceed with a defence against the accusations."[3] Despite Josephus' exalted praise of Philo, there is little evidence outside of his writings to support this claim. David Runia maintains that there was little regard for Philo's work during his lifetime, and contends that the majority of Jews "either ignored him or condemned him to silence."[4] Runia argues that because of the lack of direct evidence

---

[2] For a brief introduction to the life of Philo in Alexandria, see Erwin R. Goodenough, *An Introduction to Philo Judeaus* (second ed.; Oxford: Basil Blackwell, 1962).

[3] See Josephus, *Ant.*18.259, and Philo's account in *Legat.* of his journey to Rome as a member of the Jewish delegation that went before the emperor.

[4] See David T. Runia, *Philo in Early Christian Literature: A Survey* (*Jewish Traditions in Early Christian Literature* 44; Minneapolis: Fortress Press, 1993), 17.

of rabbinic use of Philo, we should consider a rejection of his work by the rabbinic community due to its exploitation by Christian authors such as Clement, Origen, and Eusebius. He contends that the rejection of Philo was paralleled by the rejection by the rabbinic community of the LXX as a translation of the Hebrew Bible. This rejection is reflected in the revision undertaken in the second century C.E. by Aquila to oppose its Christian exploitation.[5] Despite Runia's explanation of the objection to Philo's writings within first century C.E. Judaism, Philo's interpretation of Jewish scriptures holds an important place in our understanding of early Jewish thought and should be considered in the exegesis of Jewish scriptures.

Peder Borgen concludes that Philo was an important individual from this period in that he was a devoted Jew and at the same time a philosopher in the midst of the Hellenistic world.[6] Consequently, his views of theological issues contribute to an understanding of demonology, as well as other biblical themes, during 2TP Judaism. Borgen argues that the writings of Philo are distinctly Jewish but are presented most often in a philosophical manner. To this end, Borgen states that Philo has interpreted the Laws of Moses for the Jews of Alexandria in a manner acceptable to Hellenistic thinking and exegesis. He has used the language of reason to examine the Scriptures in order to bring a deeper understanding of them to the Hellenistic Jewish community.[7] Consequently, no matter how "Greek" Philo may appear, he was in his own right a faithful Jew. Thus, his philosophy corresponded to his Judaism, or perhaps was formulated from Jewish thought.

Samuel Sandmel suggests that Philo had a close conceptual affiliation to early rabbinic Judaism.[8] In an effort to stress the Jewishness of Philo, Sandmel evaluates three possible ways in which Philo and the rabbis might

---

Although there is little evidence in rabbinic writings of an interaction with Philo, we do have references by later rabbis to a group of interpreters called the *dorshe reshumot* and *dorshe hamurot*. This group is known for their allegorical interpretation of scripture and was opposed by later rabbis. It is possible that Philo was identified as part of this group causing his work to be ignored by the rabbis.

[5] Ibid., 15.

[6] See Peder Borgen, *Philo of Alexandria, An Exegete For His Time* (NovTSup 86; Leiden: E.J. Brill, 1997). Borgen states that Philo has brought together scripture and philosophical works, thus making his work pivotal in the history of thought.

[7] Ibid., 9.

[8] See Samuel Sandmel, *Philo's Place in Judaism: A Study of Conceptions of Abraham in Jewish Literature* (Cincinnati: Hebrew Union College Press, 1956), 5. See also Collins, *Between Athens and Jerusalem*, 16–25. Collins contends for the Jewishness of the writings of Philo and others in the Diaspora. Philo would have been more or less contemporary with four major figures in first–century C.E. Judaism: Hillel, Shammai, Jesus, and Paul. However, it seems highly unlikely that he had contact with any of these individuals.

be compared. First, rabbinic Judaism was an authority in Alexandria in the period 20 B.C.E. – 40 C.E. from which Philo borrowed rabbinic theology and then drafted his thoughts into philosophical form for his audience.[9] However, Sandmel can produce no evidence that this was the case in Alexandria. By offering this theory, Sandmel implies the continuous use of Hebrew in Alexandria and in particular by Philo. This is a major assumption on his part, considering the majority opinion that Philo's Bible was the LXX rather than the Hebrew Bible.[10]

Second, Sandmel suggests that Alexandrian Judaism was independent of Palestine and that corresponding doctrines were due to a similar interpretation of Scripture along with a somewhat limited communication between the two regions. Although some scholars have argued for a "large dependency of Palestine on Alexandria," there is little evidence for this assumption.[11]

Third, Sandmel considers the possibility that Palestinian and Alexandrian Judaism "each developed along its own lines of creativity but without the complete loss of communication." This pattern offers room for the idiosyncrasies of each division of Judaism to develop within its own camp while at the same time allowing for minimum influence on each other. The argument concerning these three choices, as Sandmel states, is entwined with the question of whether or not Philo knew Hebrew, and if so, to what extent. This issue, however, may be entirely irrelevant for two reasons. First, we know that Philo had the LXX and had no real need for the Hebrew Bible.[12] Second, it is conceivable that if it is determined that Philo reflects Palestinian *Halakah*, why is it not possible that these principles were related to him in Greek? After all, if we were going to argue for a tri–lingual Palestine in the first century C.E., why would this be such a difficulty?[13] Philo's Judaism, which is based on his interpretation of

---

[9] The difficulty with this theory is that there is no need to identify a "rabbinic Judaism" during Philo's life. It is likely that concepts that we find in later rabbinic writings were developing in the early first c. C.E. and previoiusly; however, similarities between Philo and the rabbis may be simply that they are interpreting a common scripture.

[10] It should be noted that Greek Bible translations have been found at Qumran, which indicates that Alexandria was not isolated in its "Hellenised" Judaism.

[11] Sandmel, *Philo's Place*, 10.

[12] If Philo were aware of the Watcher tradition in a written form, would this indicate that there was a Greek translation already available in the first century C.E.?

[13] For discussion of the issue of language in the first century C.E., see e.g. Joseph A Fitzmyer, *A Wandering Aramean: Collected Aramaic Essays*. (Atlanta: Scholars, 1979); Maurice Casey, "An Aramaic Approach to the Synoptic Gospels," *Exp Tim* 110 (1999): 275–78; and Loren T. Stuckenbruck, "An Approach to the New Testament through Aramaic Sources: The Recent Methodological Debate," *JSP* 8 (1991): 3–29.

the LXX, presents an Alexandrian post–biblical *Halakah* that was likely based on Palestinian Oral Law.[14]

Many scholars have argued that Philo is a Greek philosopher. A number of philosophical trends have been distinguished in Philo's writings, which can be traced back to the works of Plato, Stoicism, Epicureanism, Pythagoreanism, Scepticism, and Peripateticism.[15] However, philosophy was not Philo's religion; it only served as a medium by which he explicated the biblical text. Philo's favourite linguistic tool for exegesis was allegory. This tool may seem at first to be one of Philo's Greek characteristics, but Philo felt justified in using it because of its use in the Bible (*Plant.* 36). His allegorical interpretation, however, must always be understood in the context of the biblical verse. Therefore, while interpreting Philo's treatises, we should keep in mind: (1) the exegetical function of his philosophical language, and (2) Philo's primary theme is the journey of the soul.[16] R. Melnick argues that Philo understood allegory as the true mystery by which one extracts the letter of the Torah.[17] In doing so, Philo has made Judaism more acceptable to his Greek world. This of course raises the question: who was Philo's audience?

7.2.1 Philo's Audience

There has been relatively little attention devoted to the addressees of Philo's writings. Given that Philo does not overtly identify his readers, they have to be inferred from the texts. Thus, Alan Mendelson offers several alternatives about the nature of Philo's audience.[18] He suggests that in Philo's writings we have a distinct view from outside of Palestine, one that contrasts Jews of two distinct affiliations. Philo's group, thus his audience, is one that appreciates wisdom, while the second group is one that Philo identifies as those who need the literal meaning of the biblical text.[19] Mendelson argues that Philo's group was aware of two complementary beliefs: (1) the Bible was written on a level for the philosophically poor, and (2) scripture could be approached allegorically.[20] According to Mendelson, Philo was writing to the Jewish population in

---

[14] For discussion of Philo and *Halakah*, see Samuel Belkin, *Philo and the Oral Law: The Philonic Interpretation of Biblical Law in Relation to the Palestinian Halakah* (Cambridge, MA.: Harvard University, 1940).

[15] See Ellen Birnbaum, *The Place of Judaism in Philo's Thought, Israel, Jews, and Proselytes* (BJS 290; Atlanta: Scholars, 1996), 21.

[16] See Birnbaum, *Place of Judaism*, 16.

[17] R. Melnick, "On the Philonic Conception of the Whole Man," *JSJ* 11 (1980): 1–32.

[18] See Alan Mendelson, *Philo's Jewish Identity* (BJS 161; Atlanta: Scholars, 1988).

[19] See *Deus.* 61–64.

[20] Philo had carefully thought-out rules of applying allegory to the interpretation of scripture: these are described in *Somn.* 1.102

Alexandria; indeed, he was responding to the "daily needs of the Jewish community in Alexandria."[21]

Ellen Birnbaum presents a more detailed description of Philo's various audiences. She suggests that Philo's works are directed to different or overlapping audiences with different aims for each treatise.[22] Though we can only make intelligent guesses about their respective identities, we do know the audience must have been familiar with Jewish beliefs, practices, and the Jewish people.[23] Birnbaum proposes three particular audiences based upon three genres identified in Philo's works.[24] Accordingly, the audience of his allegorical treatises had a sophisticated knowledge of scripture and philosophy. These Jews were likely looking for a revelation of secrets about the journey of the human soul during life and after death. These allegories, in which Philo most often quoted from the Pentateuch, detailed the soul's struggle with passions and its quest for God.[25]

The second genre of writings is the exegetical commentaries.[26] The audience addressed by these, according to Birnbaum, encompasses a wider Jewish population, who would also have had a sophisticated knowledge of scripture and philosophy. She suggests that the two main texts in this genre, *Quaestiones et Solutiones in Genesin* and *Quaestiones et Solutiones in Exodum*, represented a sourcebook or textbook for the Alexandrian Jews. These two texts answered questions of scripture with literal and symbolic interpretation.

Birnbaum identifies the third genre as Philo's expository treatises.[27] The audience of such compositions would have been rather different from the previous two groups. Birnbaum argues that we cannot assume this group was familiar with scripture; instead, they would have possessed different

---

[21] See Mendelson, *Philo's Identity*, 16.

[22] See Birnbaum, 18, n. 34 for other secondary sources dealing with the purposes of Philo's writings.

[23] See *Mos.* 1.1 which may identify at least part of his audience, "to those who are worthy not to be ignorant of it."

[24] For a discussion of the classification of Philo's writings see Peder Borgen, *Philo of Alexandria: A critical and Synthetical Survey of Research Since World War II* (ANRW II 21 1; Berlin: Haase, 1984), 117–18.

[25] Philo identifies this audience in *Deus.* 10 in which he calls it the "Beloved of God," a clear reference to Israel. However, the question is raised of what Philo meant as Israel. For a thorough discussion on this question, see Birnbaum, *Place of Judaism*, 17–19.

[26] See *QG, QE, Leg., Cher., Sacr., Det., Post., Gig., Deus., Agr., Plant., Ebr., Sobr., Conf., Migr., Her., Congr., Fug., Mut.,* and *Somn.*

[27] *Opif., Abr., Ios., Decal., Spec., Virt., Praem., Contempl., Hypoth.,* and *Mos.* Goodenough argues (on the basis of the content of *Spec.*) that the audience for the expository works was likely Gentiles who had an interest in Jewish religion. The difficulty with Goodenough's view is the final sections of *Praem* 79f. in which the recipients are most likely Jews.

levels of knowledge of the biblical tradition and Greek philosophy. This audience likely included non-Jews who had little knowledge of Jewish practices, and for this reason Philo presented a rewritten bible.[28]

A summary of Mendelson and Birnbaum shows how difficult it is to determine Philo's audiences with any accuracy. Little more can be said than they were Jews and Gentiles who lived in, or at least had contact with, Alexandria. It is at least probable, as David Runia has suggested, that Philo was recording his own search for a deeper meaning of the scriptures in which he allowed others to partake.[29]

7.2.2 Problems of Interpretation

In any of the three genres identified in his writings, it is clear that Philo relies on Jewish methods of exegesis of the scriptures to relate the message to each audience. However, he does leave several points of interpretation ambiguous by using words that have several meanings that cannot be clearly distinguished from one another. In doing so, he offers a symbolic meaning of the text without offering the literal sense of the passage. David Winston argues that Philo uses this method to sidestep clashes between Jewish and Greek thought: "Although [Philo] allows the Jewish side of his thought the dominant place in his presentation, he invariably tones it down by introducing some philosophical twist and allowing the perceptive reader a glimpse of his true position."[30] The different audiences, along with Philo's deliberate mix of Jewish exegesis and philosophical thought, often result in the reader finding it difficult to understand what it is Philo is actually trying to articulate. This problem becomes apparent in the discussion immediately below.

It is not my intent to correct misunderstandings of Philo's work; nevertheless, a reader of Philo ought to realise that his methodology is itself capable of being misunderstood.[31] His unsystematic presentation was a result of the order of the material as it occurs in the Old Greek version of the Torah, rather than an unsystematic theological approach. Borgen is convinced that Philo is engaging in an exegetical "question and answer"

---

[28] Two works that fall into this category are *Hypoth.*, which discusses Jewish Law and the Essenes as a defence of the Jews, and *Contempl.*, which discusses the lives of the *Therapeutae* in an attempt to impress the Jews by the work of the sect.

[29] David T. Runia, "How to Read Philo," *NTT* 40 (1986), 192.

[30] David Winston, "Judaism and Hellenism: Hidden Tension in Philo," *SphA* 2 (1990), 18.

[31] See Harry A. Wolfson, *Philo: Foundations of Religious Philosophy in Judaism, Christianity, and Islam* (second ed.; 1947; repr., Cambridge: Harvard University Press, 1968). Wolfson writes an elaborate presentation of Philo's style of philosophical exegesis.

approach that may be observed in other writings from the period.[32] In support of his thesis of "Philo the Exegete," Borgen states:

[Philo] interprets the laws of Moses and Jewish existence in general by means of Greek ideas and religious traditions. According to Philo, Moses formulated the authentic philosophy, and Greek philosophy contains elements of this true philosophy and is at some points derived from the teachings of Moses.[33]

Philo's discussion of biblical themes prevalent in 2TP Judaism contributes a noteworthy approach with the inclusion of a Jewish perspective of the Scriptures and the philosophical views of the Greeks.[34] His use of philosophical language, however, often leaves the reader with the impression that suggests he is contradicting himself and did not have a coherent understanding of the subject. Borgen explains this potential for confusion by drawing attention to the Jewishness of Philo's argument, that is, he is not afraid to give two answers to the same question.[35] Similarly, Oliver Leaman argues that Philo contradicts himself when he states a point in one of his writings and then states the opposite elsewhere.[36] However, *contra* Leaman, it appears that Philo's sometimes incoherent interpretation does not derive from his misunderstanding of the concepts presented, but from his attempt to intertwine his philosophical reasoning with biblical revelation over what would have been an extended period of writing activity. Philo is attempting to take his Alexandrian audience into a world of Jewish texts that they can only understand against the backdrop of Greek concepts of virtue, wisdom, and the corporeal and incorporeal universe. If modern readers are to avoid confusion in understanding Philo's writings, they must recognize that Platonic thought is the basis of Philo's method of teaching. However, while the influence of Platonic thought on Philo is readily apparent in his writings, his views are not limited to Greek influences as will be seen below.

The primary text upon which this chapter will focus, *De Gigantibus*, demonstrates Philo operating as a Jewish exegete and a philosopher. We

---

[32] Borgen suggests it is possible that these two treatises (*QE* and *QG*) are using a typical rabbinic question and answer format, which was wide spread in 2TP Judaism (and the Greek world), in which the author freely expands on the biblical text, see Borgen, *Philo, An Exegete*, 90.

[33] See Peder Borgen, "Judaism in Egypt," *ABD* 3: 1061–72.

[34] See Borgen, *Philo, An Exegete*. Borgen gives an excellent presentation of the language difficulties and their understanding in light of Philo's Greek/Jewish philosophy.

[35] Ibid., 93.

[36] See Oliver Leaman, *Evil and Suffering in Jewish Philosophy* (Cambridge: Harvard University, 1995), 35.

can perhaps attribute this in part to his implied audience. This audience should be considered a "learned" group of Jews who were perhaps aware of traditions behind his interpretation. In this case, I argue, these traditions may have included themes found in *1 Enoch* and other Qumran material, which, as a result of their familiarity, needed little explanation.

7.3 Philo's View of the Soul

Since in *De Gigantibus* the ψυχή plays such an important role, it is necessary to articulate first how Philo viewed the soul in general and its place in the incorporeal and corporeal worlds. Philo's view of the term ψυχή is by no means easily understood in his writings. He believed that all ψυχαί originated from God prior to the creation of humankind, and argued for the existence of two categories of soul: one that remains in the divine realm, his "true" man,[37] and another that inhabits the human body.

The first type of soul is immortal, but includes some incorporeal (of a spiritual and divine nature) and some corporeal souls (e.g. stars). These ψυχαί, made in the image of the Divine, were of a single nature; they are neither male nor female, of the mind only, and incorruptible.[38] The air is the abode of these beings, for, according to Philo, God filled all parts of the universe with living beings.[39] These creatures exist in the universe and the senses cannot apprehend them, for they abide in the divine realm. Philo describes these beings as "not a living creature only, but mind in the purest kind through and through."[40]

Philo justifies the existence of the first group of souls in *De Opificio Mundi* 143. He describes the universe at the time prior to the creation of humanity as a "well-ordered state" with a constitution. The constitution is composed of the divine laws set up to control the universe.[41] The

---

[37] See *Det.* 84.

[38] See *Opif.* 134–135.

[39] See *Gig.* 7 and *Somn.* I.134–36.

[40] See *Somn.* I.135.

[41] For a text comparison supporting this idea, see James L. Kugel, *Traditions of the Bible: A Guide to the Bible As it Was At the Start of the Common Era* (Cambridge: Harvard University, 1998), 54. This concept can be found in the motif of Prov 8.22: "The Lord possessed me [Wisdom] at the beginning of His way, before His works of old." *4 Ezra* (although there is dispute over the dating, possibly late first century C.E.) speaks of the establishment of the Garden of Eden prior to the earth appearing. See also McNamara, *Targum Neofiti 1: Genesis* on Gen 3.24 and Maher, *Targum Pseudo-Jonathan: Genesis* on Genesis 2.8. Also *2 Baruch* (probably late first century C.E.) speaks of the pre-existence of the Temple in Jerusalem prior to the making of Paradise. In *b. Pesahim* 54a, we find that the Torah was created before the world; the Torah would have been Philo's idea of what the constitution or laws governing the

progression of his theory follows: if a state and laws exist, then there must be citizens who are present in that state. The citizens, described in *De Opificio Mundi* 144, are of a spiritual and divine nature: some are without a body (ἀσώματος), others with bodies, "and who should these be but spiritual and divine natures, some incorporeal and visible to the mind only, some not without bodies, such as are the stars."

It may be suggested that Philo understood these beings as the "us" in Genesis 1.26; an angelic host that assisted God in the creation process ("Let us make *adam*[42] in our image, in our likeness"). Targum *Pseudo-Jonathan* also contains this theme. The author of the Targum elaborates on Genesis 1.26 by clearly identifying the "us" as the angels who minister before God, those who were created on the second day. In addition, other rabbinic sources support this theme (e.g. *Gen Rab.* 8.4; *b. Sanh.* 38b). *Pseudo-Jonathan* also explains the plurality of God's statements in Genesis 3.22; 11.7; and 18.20 as words spoken to the angelic host. It has been suggested that the angels are identified as the "us" in the rabbinic material in order to exclude the possibility of the Christian claim that the "us" indicates the Trinity.[43] *Jubilees* 10.22–23, however, may suggest this interpretation was known and understood as early as the second century B.C.E. The archangels of *Jubilees*, who narrate the story of the Tower of Babel, identify themselves as the "us" in Genesis 11.6. Another possible early source of this interpretation is 4Q417 (4QInstruction).[44] Although this Qumran text does not imply angelic participation in the creation of humanity, it does follow a similar dualistic interpretation of the creation of humanity found in Philo's writings. 4QInstruction suggests the creation of a people in the image of the Holy Ones (= Philo's heavenly ψυχαί) and another that is the "spirit of the flesh" (= Philo's earthly ψυχαί).

Philo presents the ψυχή of a human as vastly different from the ψυχαί that already existed in the image of God (i.e. angelic beings who assisted in creation). Both these beings have as their life source the same divine

---

universe would have been. Although some of these writings are later than Philo's time, the traditions that inform them stand as part of late 2TP thought.

[42] I use *adam* (אדם) to identify humanity in general.

[43] See J. Bowker, *The Targums and Rabbinic Literature* (Cambridge: Cambridge University, 1969) and Maher, *Targum Pseudo-Jonathan*, 19–20, n. 42.

[44] For discussion of the various interpretations of Gen 1.26, see John Collins, "In the Likeness of the Holy Ones: The Creation of Humankind in a Wisdom Text from Qumran," in *The Provo International Conference on the Dead Sea Scrolls: Technological Innovations, New Texts, and Reformulated Issues* (ed. Donald W. Parry and Eugene Ulrich; Leiden: Brill, 1999), 609–18. See also Ben Wold, *Women, Men, and Angels: The Qumran Wisdom Text Musar le Mevin and its Allusions to Genesis 1–3*. (WUNT 2; Tübingen: Mohr Siebeck, forthcoming).

breath.[45] However, he argues in *De Opificio Mundi* 72f. that God had help in the creation of humanity because of its endowment with virtue and vice due to its mind and reason. The human is a mixed nature, an object of sense perception that makes it prone to dualistic contraries: wisdom/folly, courage/cowardice, justice/injustice, good/evil, and virtue/vice.[46] He reiterates the idea of the "image of God" in his description of humankind. It is not that humans are, strictly speaking, in bodily form in the image of God, but rather in the image of God with respect to the mind: "Let no one represent the likeness as one to a bodily form; for neither is God in human form, nor is the human body Godlike. No, it is in respect of the Mind, the sovereign element of the soul, that the word 'image' is used."[47] The beings in this form (ἀσώματος) are able to apprehend divine truth. They are, according to Philo, "wisdom with no material body," and are therefore divine.[48] He seems to be implying that the human ψυχή is constituted in a similar fashion to those ψυχαί created in Genesis 1.26. Therefore, it seems likely that Philo understood that the human soul was capable of transforming itself into a "divine" being.[49]

Philo's assumed exposure to Plato's "World of Forms" may play a part in the creation of humanity and his introduction of the two types of ψυχή. Borgen claims that Philo in his view of creation of humanity is giving a thoroughly Platonic interpretation. Philo may have understood the first type of soul as part of the invisible world that he describes in *De Opificio Mundi* 19. Philo contends, "He [God] constituted and brought to completion a world discernible only by the mind, and then, with that for a pattern, the world which our senses can perceive." He argues that this pattern of creation is not another place, but is the realm of creation in the mind of God. God in his wisdom created the pattern for all existence prior to beginning the creation of the universe.[50] While at first it may appear that

---

[45] See *Opif.* 135 (ὃ γὰρ ἐνεφύσησεν οὐδὲν ἦν ἕτερον ἢ πνεῦμα θεῖον), 139, and *Plant.* 19f.

[46] Cf. similar language in the "Doctrine of Two Spirits" in 1QS 3–4.

[47] See *Opif.* 69.

[48] See *Conf.* 81. See also *Det.* 99.

[49] See *Opif.* 77. Philo argues that the human soul is a life form open to the invisible entrance of God's spirit and that it is the dwelling place of God. This may indicate the possibility that some other type of spirit was able to take up residence in the human soul; see *Cher.* 98–100.

[50] See in particular *Opif.* 25, εἰ δὲ τὸ μέρος εἰκὼν εἰκόνος, δῆλον ὅτι καὶ το ὅλου ("Now if the part is an image of an image, it is manifest that the whole is so also"). Here Philo states that if man is an image then creation itself must be an image. See also *Jubilees* 2.2, here the author is speaking of God (my brackets): "which He hath prepared in the knowledge (of creation) of His heart." This may be interpreted as a pre-existent

is the case, it seems upon scrutiny, as Borgen himself suggests, that Philo is trying to be an exegete of Scripture.[51]

Although creation, exclusive of humans, could be understood to be Plato's World of Forms, it should also be considered that Philo might have been drawing on Exodus 25.9–27.9 in which the pattern of the greater Tabernacle in the heavens is used to build the Tabernacle for God to dwell on the earth. Kugel argues that Philo's alleged use of the Platonic World of Forms is best interpreted in terms of a very Jewish concept of the pre-existence of the world prior to the establishing of the earth.[52] A possible explanation for Philo's interpretation is that he has discovered what appears to be a problem in the biblical text concerning the story of the creation of humanity, since it occurs in the back-to-back text of Genesis 1.27 and 2.7. As any Jewish sage would do, he has chosen to expand the meaning of the text in traditional Jewish fashion. We have now set out in Philo's work, therefore, the origin of the heavenly ψυχή (Gen 1.26) and the creation of humanity (Gen 2.7).[53]

7.3.1 The Immortality of the Soul

The immortality of the ψυχή is a significant concept for Philo in several places in his writing.[54] Despite some points of apparent contradiction, Philo sees the origin of the soul in God as a key to its indestructibility.[55] In *Quaestiones et Solutiones in Genesin* 3.11, he argues that Genesis 15.15 is describing the immortality of the ψυχή. Abraham is told by God, "you shall go to your fathers with peace, nourished in good old age," indicating that at the point of death the soul leaves the mortal body and returns to its place of origin.[56] Philo interprets "go to your fathers" as referring to

---

universe in the heart (mind) of God. Cf. 1QS III.15 – "From the God of knowledge stems all there is and all there shall be. Before they existed he established their entire design."

[51] See Borgen, *Philo, An Exegete*, 11.

[52] See Kugel, *Traditions of the Bible*, 58. Cf. *Sir* 24.9–10, *Wis* 9.8, *1 Enoch* 14.16–20, *T. of Levi* 3.4–6, *11QPs-Hymn to the Creator*. See also Runia, "Philo in Early Christian Literature," 75–7. Runia describes Philo's "patterns" as the same typology used in Hebrews and the Gospel of John. He also points out the striking similarity of Philo's pre-creation world with that written in *Gen Rab.* 1:1. See also Romans 1:20 and Hebrews 8:5 and 9:23f.

[53] See *Opif.* 134f, Philo is drawing a clear distinction between the creation accounts in Genesis 1 and 2.

[54] See for example *Opif.* 154f; *Conf.* 176f; *Somn.* I.181; *Cher.* 114. The concept of an indestructible soul plays a key role in Philo's view of the death of humans and the possibility of "possession."

[55] See Marcus' comments of Philo's methodology in his introduction to *QG* ix–x.

[56] See Leaman, *Evil and Suffering*, 36. In his discussion, Leaman argues that Philo is following what appears to be a common belief at the time concerning the immortality of the soul that at death, it ascends to a place of origin, although, somewhere imprecise.

another life without a body, and to the place of origin of the soul as being with God in the heavenly realm.[57] Philo may have been influenced on this point by Plato's view in *Phaedo* 64C in which Socrates and Simmias are discussing death:

"We believe, do we not, that death is the separation of the soul from the body, and that the state of being dead is the state in which the body is separated from the soul and exists alone by itself and the soul is separated from the body and exists alone by itself? Is death anything other than this?" "No, it is this," said he.

Plato argues that upon the death of the person, the soul will separate from the body and continue its existence.[58] The *Poem of Empedocles* frag 115 offers a similar interpretation of the existence of the soul. The text describes the journey of the soul while in the body. The soul is in exile from its proper place and, wandering about the earth, it feels like a foreigner, an alien from God:[59]

There is an oracle of necessity, an ancient decree of the gods, eternal, sealed with broad oaths: whenever one, in his sins, stains his dear limbs with blood . . . by misdeed, swears falsely, the daemons (that is) who have won long-lasting life, he wanders for thrice ten thousand seasons away from the blessed ones, growing to be all sorts of forms of mortal things through time, interchanging the hard paths of life. I too am now one of these, an exile from the gods and a wanderer, trusting in mad strife.

From these two examples, we can suggest that there was a singular concept of what happens to the soul upon the death of an individual beginning as early as the fifth century B.C.E. in some Greek philosophical circles. If the person had remained virtuous, he or she had the opportunity to return to the place of the gods. Nevertheless, as we see in the *Poem of Empedocles*,

---

[57] Philo appears to change his position on this concept of life after death on several occasions. See *QG* 3.2. Nevertheless, it is clear from a synopsis of his ideas that life after death is attributed to the individual's choices during life in the mortal body.

[58] See Plato, LCL, vol. 1. In *Phaedo*, Socrates raises an argument for the immortality of the soul because of an apparent view that upon death of the person the soul was destroyed and vanished into nothingness. Cf. the *Poem of Empedocles*, which claims the soul, after passing from creature to creature, will eventually wear out and pass away. See Brad Inwood, *The Poem of Empedocles: A Text and Translation with an Introduction* (Toronto: University of Toronto, 1992), 53.

[59] Ibid., 208. This sounds similar to the pericope in Lk 11:24–26 in reference to the unclean spirit, which, when it goes out of a body, searches for a place of rest. The reference is also similar to Paul speaking in Ephesians 2:19, referring to those who have found the truth of God and are now capable of moving on to the realm where God is upon the death of the mortal body.

those individuals who stain themselves with sin return to another life in the body. However, it was generally thought that the ψυχή was capable of existing on its own in a realm apart from the material world.[60]

The issue of purity plays a key role in Philo's concept of the immortality of the soul. In *De Somniis* I.135f., Philo thinks the human ψυχή and the beings of heavenly realm are the same category of being (i.e. souls that do not enter the human realm); both are invisible, not to be apprehended by the senses. In *De Plantatione* 14, Philo states that because of their proximity to the earth some of the ψυχαί are drawn to the corporeal realm and descend into human bodies of the earth-born for a fixed period. Philo refers to this in *De Somniis* I.138: "Of these souls some, such as have earthward tendencies and material tastes, descend to be fast bound in mortal bodies, while others ascend, being selected for return according to the numbers and periods determined by nature." Added to the equation of the incorporeal and incorruptible nature of the human soul is its second nature. This second nature is one made of clay, corruptible and susceptible to the desires of the flesh. However, Philo argued that there is hope for these souls who have lost their way. He is perhaps following Plato's thought in *Phaedrus* 248–250. Plato argues that all souls are in the presence of God prior to becoming human and have beheld the nature of the true being. The ψυχή does this in order to be prepared with knowledge of the Divine in the event that it should pass into a human body. Thus, Plato believed that all humans have a soul that has spent time in the presence of the Divine prior to entering the material realm and taking on a corporeal body.[61] The acquisition of this knowledge allows the soul to escape the "torrents" of the flesh. Nevertheless, in Philo's opinion there is a fixed time that the soul must spend in the body. Philo may have been drawing his concept of fixed time from the Jewish idea of structure and order of the universe.[62] However, there are parallels in Philo's thought to Plato's concept of fixed time in *Phaedrus* 248–49.[63] Here, Plato's notion of the return of the soul to the heavens is quite complex, a cyclical period that can span up to ten thousand years.

---

[60] Cf. Louis Gernet, *The Anthropology of Ancient Greece* (trans. John Hamilton, S. J. and Blaise Nagy; Baltimore: Johns Hopkins, 1981). Gernet argues: "There is no expression of a firm belief in the soul's immortality" in any of the pre-Hellenistic literature.

[61] Cf. *Gig.* 20.

[62] See Borgen, Philo, *An Exegete*, 68.

[63] Colson claims, in his appendix in vol. 5 (p.600 §138), that Philo is perhaps alluding to Plato's idea that the just shall be a part of the corporeal world for three thousand years and the unjust up to ten thousand years.

Now in all these states, whoever lives justly obtains a better lot, and whoever lives unjustly, a worse lot. For each soul returns to the place whence it came in ten thousand years; for it does not regain its wings before that time has elapsed, except the soul of him who has been a guileless philosopher or a philosophical lover; these, when for three successive periods of a thousand years they have chosen such a life, after the third period of a thousand years become winged in the three thousandth year and go their way. (*Phaedrus* 248–49)

This text contains strong allusions to reincarnation, which would likely have created difficulties for Philo. He, of course, would have followed a theological/anthropological line in Judaism that will not allow for reincarnation (in the Platonic sense), and believed that humanity must learn to overcome the passions of the flesh with reason.[64] Otherwise, the ψυχή is a slave to the world and an alien, not a citizen of the heavenly realm, but a mortal that is subject to death.[65]

Philo argues that the "angelic type" ψυχή chooses not to take part in earthly dwellings (i.e. the human body) preferring to dwell in the αἰθήρ region of the heavens as the heaven-born. These beings of Philo's world spend their time going back and forth seeking divine truth. These are what Philo calls the "purest of spirits" (καθαρότης), which are given charge over humanity as agents of God. One might then ask, "Why do all ψυχαί not become human?" Plato's response is that only those having lost their way to the divine truth fall to the earth and take on human form. Philo's response, however, may be that they have kept themselves pure from the passions of the flesh.

Philo's anthropology incorporates a theory of two souls, one that remains pure in its relationship to the Divine realm; and the other that has relinquished the heavenly quest to pursue the passions of the flesh. Thus, the second type of soul is ineligible to remain in the heavenly realm until it has been purified of the carnal passions. Philo discusses his anthropology in detail in his interpretation of Genesis 6.1–4 in *De Gigantibus*.

---

[64] Philo adapts a form of Plato's idea of reincarnation into his anthropology. Philo categorizes living humans as those who are caught in the stream of the passions of the flesh and those who have sought after the genuine philosophy and avoided contact with the vices. It is possible, however, for those who have managed to come out of the stream to again turn from the ways of God and fall back into the fleshly desires. These human souls could be understood as having been "reincarnated" into a fleshly body if this notion can be compared to Plato's cyclical period.

[65] See *Opif.*, 154f.

7.4 *De Gigantibus*: Philo's Giantology and Anthropology

There are three main works in the corpus of Philo's writings that include material on Genesis 6.1–4. These are *De Gigantibus, Quod Deus immutabilis sit,* and *Quaestiones et Solutiones in Genesin.* These three treatises present a detailed, although at times confusing, discussion of anthropology through the story of the angels of God who mate with human women to produce giant offspring. Philo's interpretation of the Genesis passage seems to contain allusions to the Watcher tradition in *1 Enoch* and other 2TP Jewish writings. Although it is difficult to determine if he had direct knowledge of the Watcher tradition of *1 Enoch*, Philo perhaps knew of at least part of the Fallen Angel tradition. It does not appear, however, that he intended to move along the "giant tradition" (as we know it from *BW*) in a similar fashion to what we find in other early Jewish literature.[66] On the contrary, he contends in *De Gigantibus* 58 that the story in Genesis 6.1–4 is not connected to the "myth of the poets about the giants" (e.g. the giants of the Hesiod myth or possibly the Watcher tradition), but rather a description of the struggles of the journey of the human soul.

The title *De Gigantibus* gives the reader the impression that the focus of the text is the giant offspring. Nevertheless, it is perhaps better identified as a discussion of the nature of opposites, a dualistic approach to anthropology in first-century C.E. Judaism. In his opening comment in §1, which compares Noah the righteous to the ἄνθρωποι in Genesis 6.1, Philo implies there is an ethical dualism present within humanity.[67] He picks up this theme in *Quaestiones et Solutiones in Genesin* 89 (on Gen 6.1) in which he argues that the multiplication of humanity is an evil act (i.e. there is an evil element of humanity) based on God's action in Genesis 5.32, the introduction of the righteous (element) Noah and his sons. It is through humanity's "immeasurable wrongdoing that evil comes," which allows Philo to separate God from the responsibility of evil. Philo's *De Gigantibus* describes the journey of the human ψυχή as one of personal responsibility for the decisions and actions by the individual. These personal choices govern the purity of the soul and the person's ability to return to the heavenly realm after his or her death at which time the ψυχή leaves the body.

Philo begins to detail his anthropology in §6 in his comments on Genesis 6.2. He contends that Moses gave the name of angels (ἄγγελοι) to

---

[66] For a similar interpretation of the source of evil, see *4 Ezra* and *2 Bar* 56.10–15. These two documents indicate the source of sin and evil is in the Adamic myth.

[67] See discussion of ethical dualism in chapter 6, *Excursus: Dualism in Relevant Qumran Fragments.*

what Greek philosophers called *daemons* (δαιμόνια).[68] These beings are the souls (ψυχαί) "which fly and hover in the air." Ψυχαί are just one type of being that Philo suggests fill every division of the universe; the earth contains the living beasts, the fire contains the fire-born,[69] and heaven contains the stars. The angels, or *daemons*, are the living beings that fill the air. Although they are invisible to our senses, these souls can be perceived by the mind only, so "that like may be discerned by like."

Philo contends that the air plays a key role in the existence of the soul. He argues in *De Gigantibus* 11 that the air (ἀήρ) is able, through Divine direction, to "bring forth living beings, since to it the seeds of vitality have been committed through the special bounty of the creator." The air contains a host of bodiless souls, mighty beings (δυνάμεις), which are made up of at least two groups of ψυχαί.[70] The first group seems to be disposed to seek after a human body in which to occupy. The second group has a "diviner constitution" with no desire to enter the physical realm. These are what philosophers call heroes, those same beings whom Moses refers to as ἄγγελοι.[71] The ἄγγελοι are described as messengers who carry words back and forth between humanity and the divine.[72] It is clear that Philo is very much aware of the spiritual beings (forces) that are constantly at work in the heavenly realm.

It is from the first group described above (see previous section) that we find a comparison with the Watcher tradition in Philo. He interprets the *bene haelohim* in a fashion similar to the LXX as the angels of God (οἱ ἄγγελοι τοῦ θεοῦ).[73] However, the comparison is in name only, not in

---

[68] Interestingly, in Philo's discussion of the angels and *daemons*, he ignores the negative LXX references to *daemons*. Why has he chosen to compare the angels to the *daemons* of the Greek philosophers and not the demons of the Jewish bible? Does this show his ignorance of the presence of these beings in the Old Testament, or perhaps does it reveal the inaccurate adoption of the term *demon* by Christianity? It has been argued (see Alexander, "Demonology in the DSS," 350–51) that there was no demonology in the exilic/pre-exilic periods of Israelite history, however, how then do we address the spirits sent by God to punish or afflict humans. Furthermore, must we understand demons (i.e. spirits) as evil in this period or can demons be understood in the Greek sense of the *daemon* as a "watcher"?

[69] Cf. *Plant.* 12, Aristotle, *Hist. An.* V. 552b, and Euripides *fragmenta* 943, Strabo *Geographica* 13.4 11.

[70] *Plant.* 14.

[71] Ibid. If we compare this section with §6, it seems to indicate that Philo understood the Greek heroes to be the same as the *daemons*.

[72] Cf. *Gig.* 12, "They are consecrated and devoted to the service of the Father and Creator whose wont it is to employ them as ministers and helpers, to have charge and care of mortal man."

[73] Cf. ἄγγελοι for υἱοι τοῦ θεοῦ in Aldina and Sixtina editions. See also A–72, 56, 75–458, 71, 121–392, 55, and 509.

respect of their actions. The Watcher tradition has described the "angels of God" as a group of rebellious angels who have entered the human realm to fornicate with women. Philo interprets the ἄγγελοι of Genesis 6.2 as ψυχαί that descend to the earth to take on a human body.[74] If we attempt to compare Philo's interpretation with the Watcher tradition, then his understanding would indicate a physical possession of a human body by an angelic spirit. However, it appears that is not his intention. The souls that descend to take on human flesh are merely that, human.[75]

Within Philo's description of the human ψυχή, we find two categories of humans which are based upon his ethical dualism (*Gig.* 13–14). The first ψυχή descends to the earth to take on human flesh,[76] but it is caught up in the "rushing torrent"[77] of the human passions, which in turn results in the corruption of the ψυχή and it is no longer able to return to the heavenly realm (§13).[78] Such a soul seeks no wisdom with which it can overcome the passions of the flesh: "they have abandoned themselves to the unstable things of chance, none of which has aught to do with our noblest part, the soul or mind." The second category of ψυχή is the one who descends to the earth to take on human flesh but is able to rise above the current of the passions. This soul seeks the wisdom of "genuine philosophy" (Judaism) in order to regain the immortal and incorporeal existence in the presence of the Divine, keeping him or herself apart from the passions and remaining pure (§14).[79]

---

[74] See the discussion above of the possibility of the angel's involvement in the creation of humanity, p. 210.

[75] There are hints of possession by an "evil spirit" in *Somn.* I.139. This passage describes souls that have previously been bound in the human body but have since ascended back to the heavenly realm. They then long "for familiar and accustomed ways of mortal life, and again retrace their steps" back to the tomb of a body. This text presents two possible lines of interpretation to the reader: (1) Philo believes in reincarnation, or (2) what we have in this passage is a case of possession by an "evil one." In terms of Philo's allegorical method, this passage could simply be describing someone who had the opportunity to be purified and return to the community, but chose to continue in pursuit of the pleasures of the flesh.

[76] Cf. *Somn.* I.138; *Plant.* 14.

[77] Cf. the torrents of 1QH^a XI 29, 32.

[78] *Opif.* 152 describes bodily pleasure as the "beginning of wrongs and violation of the law," thus bringing impurity upon the individual. The fulfilment of these pleasures results in a life of mortality and corruption. See also *QG* 51f in which Philo argues that the person who follows after the pleasures makes light of the commands of God.

[79] It is possible that this description of the two categories of souls is part of Philo's apology for Judaism. This portion of text seems to allude to ideas familiar to us from Qumran material and the ability of an individual to be transformed out the natural realm into the supernatural realm in angelic fashion.

In *Legum Allegoria* II.6, Philo describes what may be understood as good and evil inclinations within the individual human soul. He identifies them as the irrational and rational portions of the soul. The irrational portion is the senses and passions, which as stated above, if abused can result in the breaking of the Law and the corruption of the individual. The rational portion of the soul is reason. It is by reason that the soul controls the passions and permits the individual to seek the wisdom of genuine philosophy (*Leg.* 70).[80]

In *De Opificio Mundi* 79f., Philo argues that the purpose of humankind, once created, was "to spend his or her days without toil or trouble surrounded by an abundance of all that was needed." He goes on to state that if the irrational pleasures are able to control the ψυχή of a person, then punishment will occur in the present life and it will affect the immortality of the person. He lists those things that will bring destruction if they are sought after or are allowed to take hold of the soul: desire for glory, wealth, power to control life, fear, folly, cowardice, and the worst – injustice. The rational ψυχή seeks to be the dwelling place for God. For this to be accomplished, the human must seek the virtues of the divine that Philo identifies in *Quaestiones et Solutiones in Genesin* 99 as continence, frugality, prudence, courage, and most important – justice.

Philo's description of vices (*Opif.* 79) and virtues (*QG* 99) and the list thereof found in 1QS 3 and 4 are remarkably alike in three particular respects.[81] First, the concept of two spirits within humanity in 1QS 3 is noticeably similar to Philo's concept of a rational and irrational entity within the human soul.[82] Second, we note the inclusion of similar lists of vices and virtues found in 1QS 4 3–6 (virtues) and 9–11 (vices). These traits, depending on the path the spirit chooses to follow, can lead the human into the divine realm or to destruction and recall Philo's opinions

---

[80] Philo describes the human soul as threefold: the seat of reason (the head–reason), the seat of high spirit (the heart–passion), and the seat of desire (the abdomen–lust). Each of these regions has an attached virtue, which helps it over come evil desires. Reason has prudence, which helps the soul know what and what not to do. The passion of the heart has courage and the lust of desire is given self-mastery, which is to heal the desires (*Leg.* 70).

[81] See James H. Charlesworth et al., eds., *The Dead Sea Scrolls Hebrew, Aramaic, and Greek Texts with English Translations, Rule of the Community and Related Documents* (vol. 1 of *Princeton Theological Seminary Dead Sea Scrolls Project*; Tübingen/ Louisville: J. C. B. Mohr (Paul Siebeck)/Westminster John Knox, 1994), 12–18.

[82] See *Opif.* 73–74; *Deus.* 4, and *Gig.* 34–38. Cf. 1QS 4 2–8 which describes the characteristics of what could be understood as the "good inclination" (spirit of truth – Philo's rational mind?), spirit of meekness, patience, compassion, goodness, etc. 1QS 4 9–14 describe characteristics that could be understood as the "evil inclination" (spirit of deceit – Philo's irrational mind?), greed, injustice, wickedness, falsehood, pride, etc.

expressed in *De Gigantibus* 12–17. Third, the notion that the sins and unrighteousness of a person can be atoned for by heeding the counsel of the community, which will guide that person back to the spirit of truth, is present in Philo's writings and in the *DSS*. Here we may note particularly Philo's discussion of the Θεραπευταί in *De Vita Contemplativa*. These people are members of an isolated community who are described as "healers" of the soul. According to Philo, the task of the Θεραπευταί is to bring healing to the soul that is oppressed by the vices of the flesh.[83] The Θεραπευταί do this by giving wisdom to the person that will guide him or her back to the divine truth.[84]

Philo's concept of the human soul envisions two interrelated sets of dualism. There are two categories of spirit that originate in the heavenly realm. The soul that has nothing to do with the earthly realm remains as a messenger of God. The other cannot resist the draw of the human flesh and descends to take on a human body. Within this category of soul, there are again two types. The first is swallowed up by the pleasures of the flesh and succumbs to the vices that come with them. The second type finds the strength to continue to seek the divine through genuine philosophy and will some day return to the heavenly realm to be once again in the service of God.

7.4.1 Angels and Daemons

In *De Gigantibus* 16, Philo continues to press the theme of ethical dualism. He argues that ἄγγελοι, δαίμονια, and ψυχαί are "different names for the same one underlying object," which we must assume is ψυχή.[85] Each of the three categories of beings has dualistic characteristics; there are good and bad angels, demons, and souls. It is within this section that we have the most likely allusion to the Watcher tradition. Philo appears to argue against the existence of evil spirits by ordering his readers "You will cast from you that most grievous burden, the fear of demons or superstition." While at first sight it may be difficult to identify the Jewish Watcher tradition as the source for the fear of demons, there does not appear to be anything within the Greek tradition that would have given rise to such a

---

[83] There is very little textual evidence in the *DSS* that refers to the actual healing of an individual. See e.g. 4Q266 frag 6.1.5f.; 4Q196 and 197 (*Tobit*); 1Q20 20 16–22 (*Genesis Apocryphon*); 4Q242; and possibly 4Q511 frag 8.

[84] See also *Opif.* 155f. Philo refers to the soul that continues to succumb to the pleasures of the flesh and does not seek help from the Θεραπευταί. These souls are subject to banishment from the heavenly realm and possible death of the soul. Cf. 4Q417 frag 2.1.16f (4Q418 43, 44, 45.1.13). In this document, the one who leads the person back into the "divine" is the Angel of Light. See also 1QS 3 20f.

[85] Cf. *Somn.* 140–141; *QE* 13.

notion.[86] This fact may suggest that Philo had some knowledge of the Watcher tradition, with its story of the origin of evil spirits.[87] However, it is likely that he disagreed with this interpretation of Genesis 6, a matter reflected in his neglect or dismissal of *daemons* as evil spirits in *De Gigantibus*.[88]

A second point of comparison with the Watcher tradition is found at the end of *De Gigantibus* 16 in which Philo identifies "those [angels] who are unholy and unworthy of the title." John Dillon suggests that Philo may be concerned with the Fallen Angels (of Genesis 6.2) who are no longer "ambassadors backwards and forwards between men and God . . . but are those who are unholy and unworthy of the title."[89] Philo contends these are the angels in Psalm 77.49 (LXX), the ἀγγέλων πονηρῶν, evil angels (מלאכי רעים). He argues these "evil ones" are pretending to be angels, angels who do not pursue, with reason, the virtues of the divine. Instead, they "court the pleasures which are born of men, pleasures mortal as their parents, pleasures endowed not with the true beauty, which the mind alone can discern, but with the false comeliness, by which the senses are deceived."[90]

De Gigantibus 16 is perhaps one of the most significant passages in this treatise and at the same time one of the most confusing. If we are to understand that Philo is talking about the "evil angels" of Psalm 77, while at the same time identifying them as human souls, he has taken the verse completely out of context (this is not to say he has misunderstood the passage, but rather he has read the passage in a very distinctive way). The angels of Psalm 77.49 are the angels of God's wrath who function as

---

[86] If we accept the idea that *daemons* and heroes are one and the same in Philo's thought, there is nothing within the history of their existence that indicates fear or superstition would be associated with them. Following their death, they are understood as semi–divine beings that are guardians of the living. *Daemon* is identified as a *genie* or as a divine being, but, generally, it does not carry negative connotations.

[87] See John Dillon, "Philo's Doctrine of Angels," in *Two Treatises of Philo of Alexandria* (BJS 25; ed. David Winston and John Dillon; Chico, CA.: Scholars, 1983), 204. Dillon argues that Philo may be acquainted with something of the tradition on which *1 Enoch* depends.

[88] He may argue for the existence of the evil influence of demons in *Gig.* 3 where he claims that creation follows the theory of the existence of opposites; because there are good angels, there must exist evil angels.

[89] Ibid., 200. We should keep in mind that the angels in the Watcher tradition are known to have transformed into humans on occasion. It is possible that this transformation had some influence upon Philo's interpretation of the angelic ψυχαί transforming into human form to pursue the human passions.

[90] Cf. *1 Enoch* 8.1.

agents of divine punishment sent against evil humanity.[91] If he is identifying these angels as evil human souls, which in keeping with his view in §12 must be the case,[92] then it is possible to conclude that he believes that God will use wicked humanity in his divine economy.

There appear to be other possible parallels between his interpretation of Genesis 6.2 and the Watcher tradition. He identifies the daughters of humanity (בנות האדם) as the pleasures of the mortal flesh.[93] These pleasures have seduced the "evil ones" with every possible human pleasure imaginable (*Gig.* 18).[94] At first glance, these evil ones appear to be those which are described in *1 Enoch* 6. However, §19, "Among *such as these* [beings in §17–18] then it is impossible that the spirit of God should dwell and make forever its habitation," clearly identifies them as human (Gen 6.3): "My spirit shall not abide forever among men, because they are flesh," (see discussion of the interpretation of ידון, ch. 3, 3.2.3).[95] In §29, Philo suggests the spirit of God cannot abide permanently in the soul of a human because it is flesh which results in ignorance. He argues that the ignorance caused by the flesh prevents the wisdom of the divine from coming to its fullness in the human soul. He suggests that things of everyday life (marriage, rearing of children, poverty, and the business of private and public life) prevent the "flower of wisdom" from coming to full bloom in the soul, and maintains that souls that are free from the flesh (ἄσαρκοι) and body (ἀσώματοι) spend their time without hindrance seeing and hearing things divine (*Gig.* 31).

---

[91] Philo is very much aware of the existence of such beings. He identifies them as κολαστήριος in *Sacr.* 132 and *Spec.* I.307.

[92] Valentin Nikiprowetsky, "Sur Une Lecture Démonologique De Philo D'Alexandria, *De Gigantibus* 6–11," in *Hommage à Georges Vajda: Etudes D'histoire et de Pensée Juives* (ed. G. Nahon and C. Touati; Leuven-Paris: Peeters, 1980).

[93] Cf. *Deus.* 3. Philo seems to imply the presence of actual angels in the Genesis 6.4 passage. He describes them as "messengers of falsehood" (ψευδαγγελουΰτων – false angels of *Gig.*17), which could be understood as the Watchers of *1 Enoch* 16.3. He again uses dualistic language of light and darkness (οἱ τοῦ σκότους) to distinguish between the soul that uses reason to seek wisdom and the soul that seeks the "nerveless and emasculated passions." Philo argues that the "and after that" of Genesis 6.4 is referring back to the departure of the Divine spirit from humans, and that when the Divine spirit departs the human, the ψυχή joins up with the "daughters of humanity" to produce vices which are not godly.

[94] This may be an allusion to the Watcher tradition in *Jubilees*, where the women are assigned blame for seducing the angels with their comeliness.

[95] Philo omits τούτοις from his version of the LXX text of Gen 6.3, which indicates he is not looking at a specific group of men. He reinforces this thought in §20, "the spirit sometimes stays awhile, but it does not abide forever among us, the mass of men (τοῖς πολλοῖς ἡμῖν)."

The *daemon*, also considered a ψυχή, appears to be in a class by itself, although Philo leaves its role somewhat ambiguous. The role of the *daemon* in Greek writings is usually classified as a divine being, an impersonal power, agent of fate, or a god. *Daemons* operated in the human sphere on behalf of the Olympian gods.[96] Philo equated the *daemon* with the Jewish idea of angel, a mediator of knowledge between God and humanity. Soteriologically speaking, the *daemon* represented a mediator between the state of unrighteousness and impurity in the cycle of reincarnation and at the same time mediated a state of purity and justification, which brought about a return of the individual to the region of the Divine. This second function was probably Philo's understanding of the *daemon*, since this being had the ability to lead the human back from a fleshly existence to his or her intended angelic state in the realm of the Divine.

7.4.2 Philo's "Giantology"

As we have seen, the giants of the Watcher tradition are described as spiritual beings that were born with a human type of body. They belong to one of three categories of spirit (angel, human, and giant) within *BW* that can be identified as distinct from the Spirit of God. The giants are seen as categorically evil because they are an illegitimate mix of human and angel. Their function in the physical world of *1 Enoch* was to destroy humanity. Following their death, their purpose as evil spirits was to tempt humans and to draw them away from God.

Philo has clearly offered a major reinterpretation of the Genesis 6.1–4 passage in comparison with the tradition found in *1 Enoch*. It is therefore possible to say that the relationship between *BW* and *De Gigantibus* should not be conceived as one of "positive influence." Although it is possible that Philo was familiar with the Watcher tradition, or some form of it, it

---

[96] It is possible that this was the role of the Watcher angels in *1 Enoch* and *Jubilees* prior to their fall. For discussion of the δαίμων in Greek literature, see Lars Albinus, "The Greek δαίμων Between Mythos and Logos" in *Demons, The Demonology of Israelite-Jewish and Early Christian Literature in Context of their Environment* (eds. Armin Lange, Hermann Lichtenberger and K. F. Diethard Römheld; Tübingen: Mohr Siebeck, 2002), 425–446; Bernard Dietrich, *Death, Fate, and the Gods: The Development of a Religious Idea in Greek Popular Belief and in Homer* (University of London Classical Studies 3; London: Athlone, 1967); and Søren Skovgaard Jensen, *Dualism and Demonology: The Function of Demonology in Pythagorean and Platonic Thought* (Copenhagen: Munksgaard, 1966). See e.g. use of δαίμων as a synonym for θεός Homer's *Iliad* 1.222, 3.420; "departed heroes" in Hesiod *Opera et Dies* 121–28; a being somewhere between the departed heroes and the gods ("watchers over humanity") in Plutarch *De E apud Delphos* 390E; "guardian angel" in Plato's *Timaeus* 90a and ἀγαθοὺς δαίμονας in *Gig.* 16. See also Sorensen, *Possession and Exorcism*, 80–84.

seems that any possible influence it had in reality encouraged him to write a corrective to *1 Enoch*. If Philo is being corrective, he is not necessarily opposed to the entire Watcher tradition, but specifically against the first century idea that evil spirits are the cause of human suffering. Philo therefore has set out his interpretation of what the giants are in reference to corruption of humanity.

The giants of Philo should not be understood as either physical or spiritual entity. Rather, the offspring of the angels of God and the daughters of humanity, "nerveless and emasculated passions," are the irrational vices (*Deus.* 4). The task of these giants is to create discord within the individual and the community. These vices result in an internal conflict within the human soul that holds him or her beneath the water in the torrent of the stream. The human must avoid the "pleasures which are akin to the body" (*Gig.* 34) and live as the "true man," the one who lives the life of virtue not "compounded of soul and body."[97] Humans must avoid anything that will ignite the lusts of the flesh and "embrace that spirit of frugal contentment which is the friend of virtue rather than things that belong to the body" (*Gig.* 35). Philo indicates that the vices are numerous and represent a deadly threat to humans; as he contends in §35, "let us subdue the vast and countless host of her deadly foes."[98]

Though Philo does not regard his giants as evil spirits, we can perhaps draw a possible comparison between the giants of the Watcher tradition and the giants of *De Gigantibus*, since both threaten the survival of humanity. The giant of *1 Enoch* is considered a physical threat while it occupies a body (*1 En* 7.3–5) and later becomes a spiritual threat to the soul of an individual by physical affliction or drawing him or her away from God (*1 En* 15.11–12; 19.1). Philo's giants represent a similar threat to the spiritual survival of humanity in that they bring out or contribute to the impurity of an individual, which results in his or her inability to enter into the region of the Divine. Both traditions imply human duty and responsibility to reject the advances of the giants (although *Jub* 10 puts the case more strongly than either *1 En* or Philo). The spirits of giants in the Watcher tradition represent an external threat, which operates against the internal good inclination of the individual. Philo's giants correspond to the internal pleasures of the flesh that are allowed to operate, or not operate, by the irrational and rational sides of the soul. These pleasures drive the

---

[97] This statement seems to imply that Philo is talking about the ψυχή who has not joined with human flesh, but remains in the region of the air.

[98] Philo argues in *Opif.* 81 that there is a war going on in the human soul between the vices and virtues.

individual to seek external vices.[99] *De Gigantibus* 37–38 indicates there are
external vices that easily draw the soul away from its goal of purity and
holiness in the presence of the Divine. These vices include money, glory,
or bodily strength. Philo argues that these things are not in and of
themselves evil, but will become a vice to the individual if they are
pursued (*Gig.* 35).[100] He implies in §31 that those who pursue pleasures are
not being obedient to the Law, thus they cannot be endowed with the
Divine spirit.[101]

Philo encourages his readers to avoid the pitfall that the angels of God
fell into by pursuing the daughters of humanity, the irrational pleasures
(*Gig.* 40). He instructs them not to be moved from the "rank in God's array
where they that are so posted must all seek to be the bravest, nor desert to
pleasure, the cowardly and invertebrate, pleasure who harms her friends
and helps her enemies" (*Gig.* 43). For the individual to accomplish this he
or she must seek out the true beauty of virtue, which will "bind you fast to
the object of your desire." By doing this, the individual will remain with
the fullness of God near him or her (*Gig.* 47).

7.5 Conclusion

In *De Gigantibus* 58, Philo attempts to reveal the true meaning of the
Genesis 6.1–4 passage. He declares it is not a myth about the giants
(although he is likely referring to the giants [or Titans] of Homer and
Hesiod), but rather Moses' account of three levels of humanity, the
earth-born, the heaven-born, and the God-born. The earth-born are those
ψυχαί who take part in the pleasures of the body, not concerning
themselves with the virtues of the holy life.[102] The heaven-born are lovers
of learning, those who remain in the heavenly realm pursuing the things of
the mind. The God-born are priests and prophets who refuse to enter into

---

[99] *Opif.* 160 may imply that there are forces at work alongside the "pleasures" that
may be understood as demonic forces: "pleasure employs ten thousand champions and
defenders, who have undertaken to look after her and to defend her."

[100] Cf. 1QS 4. 9–11. This text lists the characteristics of a person who walks in the
paths of darkness.

[101] Cf. *Opif.* 152; Philo argues that bodily pleasure is the beginning of the violation of
the Law – for the sake of pleasure men bring upon themselves the life of mortality and
wretchedness in lieu of immortality. This may have affinities with *1 Enoch* 15.3–4 in
which the angels give up their immortality for pleasure with human women.

[102] It is possible that §60–61 serve as part of Philo's apology of Judaism. The three
types of ψυχαί may represent three people groups in Philo's day. The earth-born appear
to represent the pagans of society (Egyptians?); the heaven-born may represent the Greek
philosophers; and the God-born may represent Israel, priests and prophets.

the worldly sector of humanity, but chose to remain as "freemen of the commonwealth of Ideas" (§61). Philo offers Abraham as an example of the men of God who through his study of the upper world of heaven was transformed in what can be described as "angelmorphic" language.[103] This is Philo's encouragement to all his readers: they should follow the example of Moses and Abraham and seek the transformation into the divine realm, forever in the fullness of God.[104]

The following chart reveals how Philo and the *Book of Watchers* differ in their presentation of the key figures in the Genesis 6.1–4 passage.

Philo	1 Enoch Watcher Tradition
Equates human soul and spirit	Unclear if soul and spirit are the same
Soul is identified as human, angel, *daemon*	Soul is part of human (only?)[105]
Body – human only	Body – human and giant[106]
Spirit – human, angel, and *daemon*	Spirit – human, giant, and angel[107]
Giants – not seen as physical nor spirit	Giants – physical and spiritual being[108]
Giants – internal vices that tempt humanity	Giants – spirits that tempt humanity[109]
Humans – can be angelic	Humans – physical and spiritual being
One type of soul/spirit outside of God	Three types spirits outside of God
Spirit – Good or bad on 3 levels	
Angelic type beings that are celestial bodies	Angels described as stars in the *Animal Apocalypse*
Good/bad angels – can transform to human	Good/bad angels – can take on human form[110]

---

[103] Cf. *Opif.* 77; see also *Somn.* I.140 which describes the transformation of humanity to the realm of "perfect purity and excellence" with the angels of the ruler of the universe.

[104] See *Somn.* I.143: Philo describes Moses in angelic language.

[105] See *1 Enoch* 9.3, 10; 22.3; 4Q530 2 1

[106] See *1 Enoch* 15.8

[107] See (for human) *1 Enoch* 20.3; 22.3, 9, 11, 13; (for giants) 15.9; *Jubilees* 10.7, 11; (for angels) *1 Enoch* 13.6; 15.7

[108] See *Jubilees* 15.8, 9 and possibly *Sibylline Oracles* 1.105.

[109] See *1 Enoch* 15.12; *Jubilees* 7.27; 10.7, 11.

[110] See *1 Enoch* 19.1 and 86.3.

Philo	1 Enoch Watcher Tradition
Good/bad humans – can become angelic	Good/possibly bad humans – cannot be angelic[111]
No giant spirits	Evil spirit of giants – unclean mix of human/angel[112]

In this summary of Philo's giantology and anthropology, we can see clear distinctions between his ideas and those of *BW*, while at the same time some overlapping themes are visible. The contrasts begin with Philo's equating of the human soul and spirit, while *BW* is unclear about the identity of the two entities; although it is possible, they are one and the same. Philo identifies the soul as the key element in the make up of humans, angels, and *daemons*. *BW* apparently assigns the soul only to humans. The physical body is singled out for humans in Philo, while it is given to humans and, for a short period, also to the giants. As noted above, the spirit and soul are equated and thus can be understood as an element of the human, angel, and *daemon*. *BW* identifies a spirit in humans, angels, and giants.

A major contrast between the two traditions appears in their different interpretation of the giants. Philo avoids assigning any spiritual element to the giants in *De Gigantibus*. He identifies them symbolically with the pleasures of the human body, which bring corruption through vices. *BW* identifies the giant offspring of the angels and women following their demise as evil spirits. The work of the giants in both writings is to afflict and tempt humanity in order to draw away from God and his Law. As a result, in both cases humanity is corrupted and, consequentially, they are incapable of entering into the divine region.

Some possible overlap exists between Philo's interpretation of Genesis 6.1–4 and the interpretation found in *BW* in relation to the concept of angel. Philo argues that there is only one form of soul/spirit apart from God. However, within this single form he identifies three categories of soul (human, angel, and *daemon*); each of these three categories has good and bad elements. *BW* identifies three distinct spirits apart from God (angel, human, and giant). There are good and bad angels, good and bad humans, but there are only bad giants. In addition, Philo only understands the giants as a bad element. Philo identifies both good and bad angels. Those who remain in the heavenly region in the service of God are good, while those who descend to take on human flesh are bad. We can perhaps

---

[111] See *1 Enoch* 19.2; *Jubilees* 4.15—implied evil humanity in the seduction of the angels.
[112] See *1 Enoch* 15 and 86.6.

consider this descent as a transformation to human form in order to take part in human pleasures. Similarly in *BW*, we find the Watchers transforming into human form in order to take part in the human pleasure of fornication with human women.

Philo's explanation of physical humanity can be troublesome. Human beings apparently begin their existence in the presence of the Divine, but for quite ambiguous reasons, they chose to take on physical form. They were once angels, but they surrendered their place of communication with the Divine, in order to create their own "giants" much the same as the Watchers did when they entered into the human realm. Once these ψυχαί take on human form, we are not told the odds that they will return to the heavenly region.[113] We are informed only that those who do return do so by dedicating themselves to the study of genuine philosophy (i.e. Jewish Law). It is through this study that they are purified and able to return to the divine realm. Humanity plays a much more passive role in the story in *BW*. Men and women are victimized to a degree by the Watchers, the giants, and eventually by the evil spirits. Their only hope appears to be deliverance by God Himself on the Day of Judgment when he will destroy evil completely in the cosmos. It is at this point that there may be some kind of transformation for humans into an angelic state.

The interpretation of Genesis 6.1–4 by Philo of Alexandria offers a very different representation of the problem of human suffering in the first-century C.E. Jewish Diaspora when compared with other (early) Jewish writers. The interpretation of the Genesis passage by the author of the *BW* presented an aetiology of evil spirits (among other possibilities) that was espoused by other Jewish authors and further developed as an answer to the problem of evil. However, it appears that Philo was not willing to accept this rationale and chose to explain the struggles of humanity in light of individual responsibility to overcome temptations of evil.

Although Philo's writings can appear at times confusing, this can be explained in part by the genre and presumed audience of each particular treatise.[114] While embracing this knowledge, modern readers must recognize that Platonic thought was a basis of Philo's method of teaching along with his presentation of an exegetical tradition that was consistent with that of the Jewish Torah centred worldview in Palestine. Philo has

---

[113] It is unclear if the Watchers remain in human form until their judgment and destruction, as is the case with what appears to be a majority of the angels who descend in *Gig.* to take on human form.

[114] See Ellen Birnbaum, *The Place of Judaism in Philo's Thought Israel, Jews, and Proselytes* (BJS 290; Atlanta: Scholars, 1996), 18f, for discussion of Philo's audience.

implemented both these methods in his interpretation of the biblical text in order to present his views concerning the journey of the soul.

It is evident that Philo's angelology is much more integral to his anthropology than in the Watcher tradition, which assumes a more stratified universe. As a result, Philo's concept of the human soul identifies two parallel dualisms at work (cosmic and ethical dualism). He recognizes two spirits in the heavenly realm; one spirit that remains angelic and a second spirit that takes on human flesh. The second category of spirit contains two types of souls, one that succumbs to the temptation of the flesh and another that seeks to find a return to the heavenly realm. This dualism carries with it the sense that the responsibility for evil rests with humanity rather than with an external force, an opinion common in other writing of the period.[115] It is within this understanding of the soul that Philo gives an interpretation of the Genesis 6.1–4 passage. Our review and comparison thereof with the Watcher tradition suggests that he was at least aware of some form of the Watcher tradition of *1 Enoch* and other 2TP writings; and it would seem that he was attempting to "correct" such an understanding of the problem of evil and its origins.

---

[115] See *Leg.* 2.107. Philo argues that it is for the sake of pleasure that humans do evil acts thus reinforcing his idea that evil in the world is ultimately the responsibility of the individual.

Chapter 8

Results and Conclusions

Although a great deal of research has been undertaken concerning Genesis 6.1–4 and the *Book of Watchers*, the distinctive approach of this thesis lies in a detailed and exhaustive examination of the reception of the giant tradition of Genesis 6 in *BW* and its place in the development of Jewish demonology in the 2TP. Our preceding discussion has asked how the author of *BW* interpreted the story of the *bene haelohim* in Genesis 6.1–4 in order to explain the presence of evil spirits and human suffering. Answers to this question have been identified in an examination of the biblical and post-biblical traditions within Judaism and other non-biblical traditions (i.e. Greek and Near Eastern myths). Within this examination, I have endeavoured to present a systematic presentation of the evidence that establishes *BW*, because of its interpretation of Genesis 6.1–4, as the basis from which a demonology, alongside an anthropology, began to develop in the 2TP literature.

Chapter 2 offers a thorough review of the recent research of *BW*, which, to date, had not been undertaken. As a result, I have presented the various conclusions concerning the date, possible sources, and function of *BW*. This examination demonstrates the great scholarly contribution that has been made thus far, while at the same time pointing out its shortcomings in relation to the interpretation of *BW*.

Chapter 3 presents a thorough examination of the difficult terms and expressions that are found in Genesis 6.1–4. Each of the four verses contains terminology that could result in the passage being construed within the wider context of Genesis 6–9. As a result, I have interacted with several works that have offered theories concerning the function of the passage in the larger Flood narrative. The results suggest there are several options from which the author of *BW* could have understood the characters as villainous. Within the biblical and post-biblical traditions of early Judaism, various interpretations of *bene haelohim* have been identified (e.g. angels of heaven, Watchers [LXX Dan 4.10, 14, 20], archangels [4Q534 ii.18], "angels of the nations" [Deut 32.8], and the "host of heaven" [Ps 148.2]). Within the examination of these traditions, I offer an extensive presentation of the various interpretations of the Genesis passage in the Aramaic *targumim* that to date have been used little in research on *BW*. Although it is the consensus of scholars that the dating of the *targumim* is late, I suggest that the ambiguity of the *targumim* offer viable options of possible iniquitous interpretations of the characters of Genesis 6.1–4 during the 2TP. The knowledge of these various traditions allowed the author of *BW* to elaborate the story of the *bene haelohim* to strengthen any negative nuances that the traditions themselves may have implied. Within each of these possible identities of the *bene haelohim*, there is a strong theme of rebellion by the characters involved.

Chapters 4 and 5 examine how *BW* adopted and expanded the motif of the *bene haelohim*, which included the introduction (or the taking up) of the Shemihazah and Asa'el/Instruction traditions. I have offered a detailed examination of the linguistic evidence concerning the names of the two main Watcher characters in *BW*, Shemihazah and Asa'el. As a result, I argue that Hanson's suggestion that the Leviticus "Day of Atonement" motif lies behind the author's use of the name Asa'el (Azazel) should not be considered original to the Aramaic version of *BW*. I have also argued that the idea that marriage has taken place in Genesis 6.2, and subsequently *1 Enoch* 6.2, should be reconsidered. I contend that, linguistically, it is not apparent or necessary that this is the case. If so, then Suter's proposal that *BW* is a polemic against the Jerusalem priesthood for marrying foreign women must be questioned, if not rejected.

Within the Shemihazah and Asa'el/Instruction traditions, we can observe clearly the negative effect the action of the angels brought upon themselves, humanity, and creation. The action of the Watchers resulted in their punishment and removal from any further participation in the cosmos. Their removal perhaps suggests that the early Christian tradition that identifies the Fallen Angels as demons needs to be reconsidered. The rebellion of the Watchers and their sexual contact with humans resulted in the defilement of all of creation, which; thereafter, required a ritual cleansing of the earth. However, all this is secondary to the introduction of evil spirits into the worldview of 2TP Judaism.

The sexual relations between the angels and the women produced giant offspring, which *BW* describes as hybrid beings that embodied both the physical attributes of humans, and the spiritual nature of the angels. Consequently, at the time of their physical death, their spirits, which were created in rebellion, continued to roam the earth as evil spirits. However, this can only be understood alongside the developing anthropology affirmed in *BW*, owing to its teaching that humans are subject to the actions of these apparently stronger "angelic" spirits (see Mk 5.3–4). These evil spirits, like their angelic fathers, have the ability to roam the earth unseen, and, because of their corrupt nature, continually seek to destroy humanity. Their former physical nature is most likely responsible for the implied desire to reoccupy a human body, as indicated in *BW*, although this aspect of possession is identified more clearly in the Gospels (see Mk 5.12). Nevertheless, there are indications in the *DSS* that this issue had been addressed earlier and was a concern in the second and first centuries B.C.E.

Chapter 6 argues the Watcher tradition was taken up by authors of the Qumran material and was further developed in the cosmic and ethical dualisms of the Scrolls. The evil spirits develop as a group that operate under the leadership of a chief spirit who is known by the names of Belial, Beliar, and Mastema, and who probably evolves into the "Satan" figure in later Christianity. The evil spirits in the Scrolls seem to be an adaptation of the *Jubilees* Watcher tradition, which places them within the divine economy as instruments of God to punish and test humanity (*Jub* 10). Within the demonology of the Scrolls, I have shown the apparent human susceptibility to attack from evil spirits is due to the innate evil inclination within humanity that allows the evil spirits to lead the person astray from the path of God. It is because of these developments that we see, within the anthropology and demonology of the Scrolls, a need for prayers of protection from the affliction and possible possession of humans by such spirits. Several of these prayers have revealed a formulaic process of incantation that invokes the divine name or other methods of protection against the spirits. At the same time, it is understood that humans also have a good inclination, which directs them (assisted by spiritual, likely angelic, forces) to keep God's commandments.

Chapter 7 identifies a distinctive stream of thought concerning the affliction of "evil spirits" in the works of Philo of Alexandria. The journey of the human soul is the central theme of Philo's writings. In *De Gigantibus*, he describes the journey of the ψυχή in the world of temptation and sin in relation to the problem of human suffering. Philo's interpretation of Genesis 6.1–4, in contrast to the Watcher tradition, offers a distinctly different account of the "giants." Nevertheless, it is unclear why Philo's interpretation is significantly different to the degree that it is from the older material. It is possible that the geographical location of the author of *BW* influenced his interpretation of the Genesis passage, in that the oppression of the nation within the land of Israel required such a presentation. Although we know that the Jews of Alexandria were, at times, under the oppression of the Egyptians during Philo's lifetime, Philo's "giants" do not play the role of oppressor as they are understood to do in *BW*. Philo's interpretation of the passage is derived from his method of exegesis and in relation to his anthropology. It is difficult to find a solution to Philo's diverse interpretation, except by noting that Philo and the author of *BW* reveal diversity within 2TP Judaism, which may be consistent with the variety of Jewish groups known to exist.

The author's purpose in *BW* in expanding the story of the *bene haelohim* of Genesis 6 was probably to produce a multifaceted explanation of the problem of evil. It is clear, however, that the evil spirits of the giants did become the central characters of the story. As a result, Jews may have understood them as the force behind the gentile nations that oppressed Israel, as supernatural powers driving a corrupt leadership, or as spirits that afflicted individuals. Based on the adaptation of the Watcher tradition in subsequent Jewish writings (i.e. Pseudepigrapha, *DSS*, and N.T.), it is clear the spirits of the giants assumed an important place in the understanding of human suffering and the problem of evil within the developing 2TP demonology and anthropology. Consequently, the results of this study may serve as a foundation for further investigation of the demonology and anthropology in other early Jewish and Christian writings.

Bibliography

Biblical Material

Masoretic Text. 1990 Edition of *Biblia Hebraica Stuttgartensia*. All translations from this edition are mine unless otherwise noted.

Septuagint. Two editions were used: 1) A. Rahlfs' 1979 edition; and 2) the Göttingen edition. All translations from these editions are mine unless otherwise noted.

New Testament. 1998 twenty-seventh edition of *Novum Testamentum Graece*. All translations are mine unless other wise noted.

Apocrypha. Translations from The Apocrypha or Deuterocanonical Books NRSV. Cambridge: Cambridge University Press, 1989.

Mishnah. All translations of Mishnaic sources are taken from the 1933 edition translated by H. H. Danby.

Texts and Translations of Primary Texts

Allegro, John M. *Qumrân Cave 4 I (4Q158–4Q186)*. Vol. 5 of *Discoveries in the Judean Desert*. Edited by Emanuel Tov. Oxford: Clarendon, 1968.

Attridge, Harold W. and Robert A. Oden, Jr. *Philo of Byblos the Phoenician History: Introduction, Critical Text, Translation, Notes*. Catholic Biblical Quarterly Monograph Series 9. Washington, DC: Catholic Biblical Association of America, 1981.

Baillet, Maurice. *Qumrân Grotte 4 III (4Q482–4Q520)*. Vol. 7 of *Discoveries in the Judean Desert*. Edited by Emanuel Tov. Oxford: Clarendon, 1982.

Baumgarten, Joseph M. and Daniel R. Schwartz. *The Dead Sea Scrolls Hebrew, Aramaic, and Greek Texts with English Translations: Damascus Document, War Scroll, and Related Documents*. Vol. 2 of *The Princeton Theological Seminary Dead Sea Scrolls Project*. Edited by James H. Charlesworth, et al. Tübingen/Louisville: Mohr Siebeck/Westminster John Knox, 1995.

Black, Matthew. *Apocalypsis Henochi Graece*. Pseudepigrapha Veteris Testamenti Graece 3. Leiden: Brill, 1970.

Boyce, Mary, ed. and trans. Textual Sources for the Study of Zoroastrianism. Manchester: Manchester University, 1984.

Charles, R.H. The Apocrypha and Pseudepigrapha o f the Old Testament in English *with Introduction and Critical and Explanatory Notes to Several Books*. 2 vols. Edited by R. H. Charles, et al. Oxford: Clarendon, 1913.

–. The Book of Enoch, or 1 Enoch: Translated from the Editor's Ethiopic Text, and edited with the introduction notes and indexes of the first edition wholly recast, enlarged and rewritten; together with a reprint from the editor's text of the Greek fragments. Oxford: Clarendon, 1912.

–. *The Book of Enoch*. London: SPCK, 1917. Repr., edited by Paul Tice. Escondido, CA: The Book Tree, 2000.

–. *The Book of Jubilees or Little Genesis*. London: SPCK, 1917. Repr., Eugene, OR.: Wipf and Stock, 2001.

Charlesworth, James H. ed. et al. *The Dead Sea Scrolls Hebrew, Aramaic, and Greek Texts with English Translations Rule of the Community and Related Documents*. Vol. 1 of *Princeton Theological Seminary Dead Sea Scrolls Project*. Tübingen/Louisville: Mohr Siebeck/Westminster John Knox, 1994.

–., ed. et al. *The Dead Sea Scrolls Hebrew, Aramaic, and Greek Texts with English Translations Damascus Document, War Scroll, and Related Documents*. Vol. 2 of *Princeton Theological Seminary Dead Sea Scrolls Project*. Tübingen/Louisville: Mohr Siebeck/Westminster John Knox, 1995.

–., ed. *The Old Testament Pseudepigrapha*. 2 Vols. New York: Doubleday, 1983–85.

Clarke, E. J., ed. *Targum Pseudo-Jonathan of the Pentateuch: Text and Concordance*. Hoboken, NJ: KTAV, 1984.

De Lagarde, Paul. *Hagiographa Chaldaice*. Lipsiae: In Aedibus B. G. Teubneri, 1873.

Díez Macho, Alejandro. *Neophyti 1 Targum Palestinense MS De La Biblioteca Vaticana Genesis*. Madrid: Consejo Superior De Investigaciones Científicas, 1968.

Dillmann, August. *Das Buch Henoch uebersetzt und erklärt*. Leipzig: Vogel, 1853.

Fitzmyer, Joseph A. *The Genesis Apocryphon of Qumran Cave 1*. Biblica Et Orientalia 18A. Rome: Biblical Institute, 1971.

Freedman, H. and Maurice Simon, eds. *Midrash Rabbah*. Vol. 1 of *Midrash Rabbah in Ten Volumes*. Translated by H. Freedman and Maurice Simon. London: Soncino, 1961.

García Martínez, Florentino and Eibert J. C. Tigchelaar, eds. *The Dead Sea Scrolls Study Edition*. 2 vols. Leiden/Grand Rapids: Brill/Eerdmans, 1997–98.

García Martínez, Florentino, Eibert J. C. Tigchelaar and Adam S. Van der Woude, eds. *Qumran Cave 11 II 11Q2–18, 11Q20–31*. Vol. 23 of *Discoveries in the Judean Desert*. Edited by Emanuel Tov. Oxford: Clarendon, 1998.

Grossfeld, Bernard. *The Targum Onqelos to Deuteronomy*. Vol. 9 of *The Aramaic Bible*. Edited by Michael Maher, Martin McNamara and Kevin Cathcart. Edinburgh: T & T Clark, 1988.

–. *The Targum Onqelos to Genesis*. Vol. 6 of *The Aramaic Bible*. Edited by Michael Maher, Martin McNamara and Kevin Cathcart. Edinburgh: T & T Clark, 1988.

–. *The Targum Onqelos to Leviticus and the Targum Onqelos to Numbers*. Vol. 8 of *The Aramaic Bible*. Edited by Michael Maher, Martin McNamara and Kevin Cathcart. Edinburgh: T & T Clark, 1988.

Hesiod. *The Homeric Hymns and Homerica*. Translated by Hugh G. Evelyn-White. Loeb Classical Library. Cambridge: Harvard University, 1936.

Holladay, Carl R. *Fragments From Hellenistic Jewish Authors*. Chico, CA.: Scholars, 1983.

Homer. *The Iliad*. Translated by A. T. Murray. Loeb Classical Library. Rev. 2nd ed. 2 vols. Cambridge, MA.: Harvard, 1999.

–. *The Odyssey*. Translated by A. T. Murray. Loeb Classical Library. Rev. 2nd ed. 2 vols. Cambridge, MA.: Harvard, 1995.

Inwood, Brad. *The Poem of Empedocles: A Text and Translation with an Introduction*. Toronto: University of Toronto, 1992.

Josephus. Translated by H. St. J. Thackeray et al. 10 vols. LCL. Cambridge: Harvard University, 1926–1965.

Knibb, Michael A. *Ethiopic Book of Enoch*. 2 Vols. Oxford: Clarendon, 1978.

Maher, Michael. *Targum Pseudo-Jonathan: Genesis, Translated with Introduction and Notes.* Vol. 1B of *The Aramaic Bible.* Edited by Michael Maher, Martin McNamara and Kevin Cathcart. Edinburgh: T & T Clark, 1992.

McNamara, Martin. *Targum Neofiti 1: Deuteronomy.* Vol. 5A of *The Aramaic Bible.* Edited by Michael Maher, Martin McNamara and Kevin Cathcart. Edinburgh: T&T Clark, 1997.

–. *Targum Neofiti 1: Genesis.* Vol. 1A of *The Aramaic Bible.* Edited by Michael Maher, Martin McNamara and Kevin Cathcart. Edinburgh: T & T Clark, 1991.

–. *Targum Neofiti 1: Numbers and Targum Pseudo-Jonathan: Numbers.* Vol. 4 of *The Aramaic Bible.* Translated by Ernest G. Clarke and Shirley Magder. Edited by Michael Maher, Martin McNamara and Kevin Cathcart. Edinburgh: T&T Clark, 1995.

Milik, J. T. *The Books of Enoch: Aramaic Fragments of Qumrân Cave 4.* Oxford: Clarendon, 1976.

Puech, Émile. *Qumrân grotte 4 XXII Textes Araméens.* Vol. 31 of *Discoveries in the Judean Desert.* Edited by Emanuel Tov. Oxford: Clarendon, 2001.

Pfann, Stephen and Philip S. Alexander, et al. *Qumran Cave 4 XXVI Cryptic Texts and Miscellanea Part 1.* Vol. 36 of *Discoveries in the Judean Desert.* Edited by Emanuel Tov. Oxford: Clarendon, 2000.

Philo. Translated by F. H. Colson, G. H. Whitaker, and Ralph Marcus. 10 vols. and 2 supp. vols. Loeb Classical Library. Cambridge: Harvard University, 1929–62.

Plato. *Euthyphro, Apology, Crito, Phaedo, Phaedrus.* Translated by Harold N. Fowler. Loeb Classical Library. Cambridge/London: Harvard University, 1917. Repr. 1999.

Sanders, James A. *The Psalms Scroll of Qumran Cave 11 (11QPs^a).* Discoveries in the Judean Desert, 4. Oxford: Clarendon, 1965.

Sperber, Alexander, ed. *The Bible in Aramaic: Volume 1 The Pentateuch According to Targum Onkelos.* Leiden: Brill, 1959.

Strugnell, John and Daniel J. Harrington, S.J. *Qumran Cave 4 XXIV Sapiential Texts, Part 2 4Qinstruction (Mûsār L^e Mēvîn): 4Q415 ff.* Vol. 34 of *Discoveries in the Judaean Desert.* Edited by Emanuel Tov. Oxford: Clarendon, 1999.

Stuckenbruck, Loren T. *The Book of Giants from Qumran, Texts, Translation, and Commentary.* Texte und Studien zum Antiken Judentum 63. Tübingen: Mohr Siebeck, 1997.

Ulrich, Eugene, et al, eds. *Qumran Cave 4 VII Genesis to Numbers.* Vol. 12 of *Discoveries in the Judean Desert.* Edited by Emanuel Tov. Oxford: Clarendon, 1994.

VanderKam, James C. *The Book of Jubilees.* Corpus Scriptorum Christianorum Orientalium 511. Lovanii: Aedibus E. Peeters, 1989.

Vergil. *Aeneid.* Translated by H. Rushton Fairclough. Rev. ed. Cambridge: Harvard University, 1965.

Wevers, John W., ed. *Genesis.* Septuaginta Vetus Testamenta Graecum 1. Göttingen: Vandenhoeck und Ruprecht, 1974.

–, ed. *Numeri.* Septuaginta Vetus Testamentum Graecum 3. Göttingen: Vandenhoeck und Ruprecht, 1982.

Ziegler, Joseph, ed. *Iob* [Job]. Septuaginta Vetus Testamentum Graecum 11. Göttingen: Vandenhoeck und Ruprecht, 1982.

Other Reference Material Consulted

Alexander, Patrick H., John F. Kutsko, James D. Ernest, Shirley A. Decker-Lucke, and David L. Petersen, eds. *The SBL Handbook of Style for Ancient Near Eastern, Biblical, and Early Christian Studies* (Peabody, MA.: Hendrickson, 1999).

Borgen, Peder, Kare Fuglseth and Roald Skarsten. *The Philo Index, A Complete Greek Word Index to the Writings of Philo of Alexandria.* Grand Rapids: Eerdmans, 2000.

Brown, Francis, S.R. Driver, and Charles A. Briggs. *The New Brown – Driver – Briggs – Gesenius Hebrew and English Lexicon with an Appendix Containing the Biblical Aramaic.* Peabody, MA.: Hendrickson, 1979.

Clines, David J., et al. *The Dictionary of Classical Hebrew, vol. IV.* Sheffield: Sheffield Academic, 1998.

Hatch, Edwin and Henry A. Redpath, eds. *A Concordance to the Septuagint and Other Greek Versions of the Old Testament.* Oxford: Clarendon, 1897. Repr., Graz, Austria: Akademische Druck-und-Verlagsanstalt, 1975.

Jastrow, Marcus. *A Dictionary of the Targumim, the Talmud Babli and Yerushalmi, and the Midrashic Literature.* 2 vols. New York: The Judaica Press, 1971. Repr., from 1903.

Koehler, L. W. Baumgartner, and J. J. Stamm. *The Hebrew and Aramaic Lexicon of the Old Testament.* Translated and edited by M. E. J. Richardson. 4 vols. Leiden: Brill, 1994–2000.

Liddell, H. G., R. Scott, and H. S. Jones. *A Greek-English Lexicon* 9th ed. with revised supplement. Oxford: Clarendon, 1996.

Van der Toorn, Karel, Bob Becking, and Pieter W. van der Horst, eds. *Dictionary of Deities and Demons in the Bible: DDD.* 2nd ed. Leiden/Grand Rapids: Brill/Eerdmans, 1999.

Secondary Sources

Adler, William. "Berossus, Manetho, and 1 Enoch in the World Chronicle of Panodorus." *Harvard Theological Review* 76 (1983): 419–42.

–. *Introduction to Jewish Apocalypses in Christian Settings.* Compendia Rerum Iudaicarum Ad Novum Testamentum 4. Edited by James C. VanderKam and William Adler. Assen, The Netherlands: Van Gorcum, 1996.

Albinus, Lars "The Greek δαίμων Between Mythos and Logos" Pages 425–446 in *Demons: The Demonology of Israelite-Jewish and Early Christian Literature in Context of their Environment.* Edited by Armin Lange, Hermann Lichtenberger and K. F. Diethard Römheld. Tübingen: Mohr Siebeck, 2003.

Alexander, Philip S. "The Targumim and Early Exegesis of 'Sons of God' in Genesis 6." *Journal of Jewish Studies* 23 (1972): 60–71.

–. "The Demonology of the Dead Sea Scrolls." Pages 331–53 vol. 2 of *The Dead Sea Scrolls After Fifty Years A Comprehensive Assessment.* Edited by Peter W. Flint and James C. VanderKam. Leiden: Brill, 1999.

–. "Wrestling Against Wickedness in High Places: Magic in the Worldview of the Qumran Community." Pages 318–37 in *The Scrolls and Scriptures Qumran Fifty Years After.* Edited by Stanley E. Porter and Craig A. Evans. Sheffield: Sheffield Academic, 1997.

Alon, Gedalia. *Jews, Judaism, and the Classical World: Studies in Jewish History in the Times of the Second Temple and Talmud.* Translated by Israel Abrahams. Jerusalem: Magnes Press, 1977.

Andersen, F. I. "2 (Slavonic Apocalypse of) Enoch." Pages 91–213 vol. 1 in *The Old Testament Pseudepigrapha.* 2 vols. Edited by James H. Charlesworth. New York: Doubleday, 1983–85.

Anderson, Gary. "The Status of Torah Before Sinai." *Dead Sea Discoveries* 1 (1994): 1–29.

Assmann, J. "Nephilim." Pages 618–20 in *Dictionary of Deities and Demons in the Bible: DDD.* Edited by Karel van der Toorn, Bob Becking and Pieter W. van der Horst. 2d ed. Leiden/Grand Rapids: Brill/Eerdmans, 1999.

Attridge, Harold W. and Robert A. Oden, Jr. *Philo of Byblos the Phoenician History: Introduction, Critical Text, Translation, Notes.* Catholic Biblical Quarterly Monograph Series 9. Washington, DC: Catholic Biblical Association of America, 1981.

Bamberger, B. J. "Philo and the Aggadah." *Hebrew Union College Annual* 48 (1977): 153–85.

Bapp, K. "Prometheus," in *Ausführliches Lexicon der griechischen und römischen Mythologie.* Edited by W.H. Roscher. Leipzig: Teubner, 1902–09.

Barker, Margaret. *The Old Testament: The Survival of Themes from the Ancient Royal Cult in Sectarian Judaism and Early Christianity.* London: SPCK, 1987.

Barr, James. "Aramaic-Greek Notes on the Book of Enoch I, II." *Journal of Jewish Studies* 23 (1978): 187–98.

–. "The Question of Religious Influence: The Case of Zoroastrianism, Judaism and Christianity," *Journal of the American Academy of Religion* 53 (1985): 201-235.

–. Review of J. T. Milik, *The Books of Enoch: Aramaic Fragments of Qumran Cave 4. Journal of Theological Studies* 29 (1978): 517–30.

Bartelmus, Rüdiger. *Heroentum in Israel und seiner Umwelt.* Zürich: Theologischer Verlag, 1979.

Batto, Bernard F. *Slaying the Dragon Mythmaking in the Biblical Tradition.* Louisville: Westminster John Knox, 1992.

Bauckham, Richard. *The Fate of the Dead, Studies on the Jewish and Christian Apocalypses.* Supplements to Novum Testamentum 93. Leiden: Brill, 1998.

Baumgarten, Joseph M. "On the Nature of the Seductress in 4Q184." *Revue de Qumran* 15 (1991): 133–43.

–. "The 'Sons of Dawn' in *CDC* 13:14–15 and the Ban on Commerce among the Essenes." *Israel Exploration Journal* 33 (1983): 81–5.

Beckwith, Roger T. "The Earliest Enoch Literature and Its Calendar: Marks of Their Origin, Date, and Motivation." *Revue de Qumran* 10 (1981): 365–403.

Belkin, Samuel. *Philo's Midrash.* New York: Yeshiva, 1989.

–. *Philo and Oral Law.* Harvard Semitic Series 11. Cambridge, MA.: Harvard University, 1940.

Betz, Hans Dieter. "On the Problem of the Religio-Historical Understanding of Apocalypticism." *Journal for Theology and the Church* 6 (1969): 134–56.

Beyer, Klaus. *Die Aramäischen Texte vom Toten Meer.* Göttingen: Vandenhoeck und Ruprecht, 1984.

Bickerman, Elias J. *The Jews in the Greek Age.* Cambridge: Harvard University, 1988.

Birnbaum, Ellen. *The Place of Judaism in Philo's Thought: Israel, Jews and Proselytes.* Studia Philonica Monographs 290. Atlanta: Scholars Press, 1996.

Black, Matthew. *The Book of Enoch or 1 Enoch.* Studia in Veteris Testamenti Pseudepigrapha 7. Leiden: Brill, 1985.

–. "The Twenty Angel Dekadarchs at 1 Enoch 6.7 and 69.2." *Journal of Jewish Studies* 32 (1981): 227–35.

Boccaccini, Gabriele. *Beyond the Essene Hypothesis: The Parting of the Ways Between Qumran and Enochic Judaism.* Grand Rapids/Cambridge: Eerdmans, 1998.

Borgen, Peder. *Early Christianity and Hellenistic Judaism.* Edinburgh: T & T Clark, 1996.

–. "Judaism in Egypt." Pages 1061–72 in vol. 3 of *The Anchor Bible Dictionary.* Edited by David N. Freeman. New York: Doubleday, 1992.

–. *Philo of Alexandria: A Critical and Synthetical Survey of Research Since World War II.* Aufstieg und Niedergang der römischen Welt II 21 1. Berlin: Haase, 1984.

–. *Philo of Alexandria, An Exegete for His Time.* Supplements to Novum Testamentum 86. Leiden: Brill, 1997.

Bowker, J. *The Targums and Rabbinic Literature.* Cambridge: Cambridge University, 1969.

Boyce, Mary. *A History of Zoroastrianism.* 3 vols. Leiden: Brill, 1975–1991.

–. "On the Antiquity of Zoroastrian Apocalyptic," *Bulletin of the School of Oriental and African Studies* 47 (1984): 57–75.

Brekelmans, C. "The Saints of the Most High and Their Kingdom," *Old Testament Studies* 14 (1965): 305–29.

Bremmer, Jan. *The Early Greek Concept of Soul.* Princeton: Princeton University, 1983.

Brentlinger, John A. *The Symposium of Plato.* Translated by Suzy Q. Groden. Amherst, MA.: University of Massachusetts, 1970.

Breytenbach, Cilliers and Peggy L. Day. "Satan." Pages 726–32 in *Dictionary of Deities and Demons in the Bible: DDD.* Edited by Karel van der Toorn, Pieter van der Horst and Bob Becking. Leiden/Grand Rapids: Brill/Eerdmans, 1999.

Bright, John. *A History of Israel.* 3d ed. Philadelphia: Westminster, 1981.

Brock, Sebastian. Review of J. T. Milik, *The Books of Enoch: Aramaic Fragments of Qumran Cave 4. Journal of Jewish Studies* 29 (1978): 98–9.

Burrelli, Robert J. "A Study of Psalm 91 with Special Reference to the Theory That it Was Intended as a Protection Against Demons and Magic." Ph.D. diss., University of Cambridge, 1993.

Carr, Wesley. *Angels and Principalities.* Cambridge: Cambridge University, 1981.

Cassuto, U. *A Commentary on the Book of Genesis.* Translated by Israel Abrahams. Jerusalem: Magnes, 1961.

Casey, Maurice. "An Aramaic Approach to the Synoptic Gospels." *Expository Times* 110 (1999): 275–78.

Chazon, Esther. "Hymns and Prayers in the Dead Sea Scrolls" Pages 244–70 vol. 1 of *The Dead Sea Scrolls After Fifty Years A Comprehensive Assessment.* Edited by Peter W. Flint and James C. VanderKam. 2 vols. Leiden: Brill, 1998.

Childs, B.S. *Myth and Reality in the Old Testament.* London: SCM, 1960.

Clines, David J. "The Significance of the 'Sons of God' Episode (Genesis 6:1–4) in the Context of the 'Primeval History' (Genesis 6–11)." *Journal for the Study of the Old Testament Supplemental Series* 13 (1979): 33–46.

Cohen Naomi G. "The Jewish Dimension of Philo's Judaism." *Journal of Jewish Studies* 38 (1987): 165–86.

Collins, John J. *Apocalyptic Imagination: An Introduction to Jewish Apocalyptic Literature.* 2d ed. Grand Rapids: Eerdmans, 1998

–. *Apocalypticism in the Dead Sea Scrolls.* London: Routledge, 1997.

–. "The Apocalyptic Technique: Setting and Function in the Book of Watchers." *The Catholic Bible Quarterly* 44 (1982): 91–111.

–. *Between Athens and Jerusalem: Jewish Identity in the HellenisticDiaspora.* Grand Rapids: Eerdmans, 2000.

–. "In the Likeness of the Holy Ones: The Creation of Humankind in a Wisdom Text from Qumran," Pages 609–18 in *The Provo International Conference on the Dead Sea Scrolls: Technological Innovations, New Texts, and Reformulated Issues.* Edited by Donald W. Parry and Eugene Ulrich. Leiden: Brill, 1999.

–. "Methodological Issues in the Study of 1 Enoch: Reflections on the Articles of P. D. Hanson and G. W. Nickelsburg." Pages 315–22 in the *SBL Seminar Papers, 1978.* Missoula: Scholars, 1978.

–. "The Origin of Evil in Apocalyptic Literature and the Dead Sea Scrolls," Pages 25–38 in *Supplements to Vetus Testamentum Congress Volume Paris 1992.* Edited by J.A. Emerton et al.; Leiden: E.J. Brill, 1995.

–. "Sibylline Oracles." Pages 317–472 vol. 1 of *The Old Testament Pseudepigrapha.* 2 Vols. Edited by James H. Charlesworth. New York: Doubleday, 1983–85.

–. "Watchers." Pages 893–95 in *Dictionary of Deities and Demons in the Bible: DDD.* Edited by Karel van der Toorn, Bob Becking and Pieter van der Horst. Leiden/Grand Rapids: Brill/Eerdmans, 1999.

Conybeare, F. C. "The Demonology of the NT." *Jewish Quarterly Review* 8 (1896): 576–608.

Coxon, P. W. "Gibborim." Pages 345–46 in *Dictionary of Deities and Demons in the Bible: DDD.* Edited by Karel van der Toorn, Bob Becking and Pieter W. van der Horst. Leiden/Grand Rapids: Brill/Eerdmans, 1999.

Crombie, I. M. *An Examination of Plato's Doctrines.* London: Routledge and Kegan Paul, 1962.

Culianu, I. P. *Psychanodia I: A Survey of the Evidence Concerning the Ascension of the Soul and Its Relevance.* Leiden: Brill, 1983.

Darnell, D. R. "Hellenistic Synagogal Prayers." Pages 671–97 vol. 2 of *The Old Testament Pseudepigrapha.* 2 Vols. Edited by James H. Charlesworth. New York: Doubleday, 1983–85.

Davidson, Maxwell J. *Angels at Qumran: A Comparative Study of 1 Enoch 1–36, 72 108, and Sectarian Writings from Qumran.* Journal for the Study of Pseudepigrapha Supplemental Series 11. Sheffield: JSOT, 1992.

Day, P.L. *An Adversary in Heaven: Śāt̞ān in the Hebrew Bible.* Harvard Semitic Monographs 43. Atlanta: Scholars, 1988.

Delcor, Mathias. "Le Mythe de La Chute des Angles et de L'origine des Geants Come Exlication du Mal Dans Le Monde Dans L'apocalyptique Juive: Histoire Des Traditions." *Revue de l'histoire des religions* 190 (1976): 3–53.

Delitzsch, Franz. *A New Commentary on Genesis 2 Vols.* Clark's Foreign Theological Library 36. Translated by Sophia Taylor. Edinburgh: T & T Clark, 1888–89.

Delling, Gerhard. "The 'One Who Sees God' in Philo." Pages 27–41 in *Nourished in Peace: Studies in Hellenistic Judaism in Memory of Samuel Sandmel.* Edited by F. Greenspan. Chico, CA.: Scholars, 1984.

Dequeker, L. "The 'Saints of the Most High' in Qumran and Daniel." *Old Testament Studies* 18 (1973): 108–87.

Dietrich, Bernard. *Death, Fate, and the Gods: The Development of a Religious Idea in Greek Popular Belief and in Homer.* University of London Classical Studies 3. London: Athlone, 1967.

Dillon, John. *Middle Platonists: A Study of Platonism 80 BC to AD 220*. London: Duckworth, 1977.

–. "Philo's Doctrine of Angels." Pages 197–205 in *Two Treatises of Philo of Alexandria: A Commentary on De Gigantibus and Quod Deus Sit Immutabilis*. Edited by David Winston and John Dillon. Atlanta: Scholars, 1983.

Dimant, Devorah. "1 Enoch 6–11: A Fragment of a Parabiblical Work." *Journal of Jewish Studies* 53, (Autumn 2002): 223–37.

–. "1 Enoch 6–11: A Methodological Perspective." Pages 323–39 in *SBL Seminar Papers 1978*. Missoula: Scholars, 1978.

–. "The Biography of Enoch and the Books of Enoch." *Vetus Testamentum* 33 (1983): 14–29.

–. "The Fallen Angels in the Dead Sea Scrolls and in the Apocryphal and Pseudepigraphic Books Related to Them." Ph.D. diss., Hebrew University, 1974 [Hebrew].

–. "The 'Pesher of the Periods' 4Q180 and 4Q181." *Israel Oriental Studies* 9 (1979): 77–102.

–. "Qumran Sectarian Literature" Pages 483-550 in *Jewish Writings of the Second Temple Period*. Compendia Rerum Iudaicarum ad Novum Testamentum 2/2; ed. Michael Stone; Assen: van Gorcum, 1984.

Doran, R. "Pseudo-Eupolemus." Pages 873–82 vol. 2 of *The Old Testament Pseudepigrapha*. 2 Vols. Edited by James H. Charlesworth. New York: Doubleday, 1983–85.

Duhaime, J. "Dualistic Reworking in the Scrolls from Qumran," *Catholic Biblical Quarterly* 49 (1987): 32–56.

Duling, D. C. "Testament of Solomon." Pages 935–87 vol. 1 of *The Old Testament Pseudepigrapha*. 2 Vols. Edited by James H. Charlesworth. New York: Doubleday, 1983–85.

Dunn, J. D. G. and Graham H. Twelftree. "Demon-Possession and Exorcism in the NT." *Churchman* 94 (1980): 210–25.

Eslinger, Lyle. "A Contextual Identification of the *Bene Ha'elohim* and *Benoth Ha'adam* in Genesis 6:1–4." *Journal for the Study of the Old Testament* 13 (1979): 65–73.

Feldman, Louis H. "Hengel's *Judaism and Hellenism* in Retrospect." *Journal of Biblical Literature* 96 (1977): 371–82.

–. "The Portrayal of Sihon and Og in Philo, Pseudo-Philo and Josephus." *Journal of Jewish Studies* 53 (Autumn 2002): 264–72.

Ferguson, Everett. *Demonology of the Early Christian World*. New York: E. Mellen, 1984.

Fernández Marcos, Natalio. *The Septuagint in Context: Introduction to the Greek Version of the Bible*. Translated by Wilfred G. E. Watson. Leiden/Boston/Köln: Brill, 2000.

Fishbane, Michael. *Biblical Interpretation in Ancient Israel*. Oxford: Clarendon, 1985.

Fitzmyer, Joseph A. "Implications of the New Enochic Literature from Qumran." *Theological Studies* 38 (1977): 332–45.

–. "Now This Melchizedek." *Catholic Bible Quarterly* 5 (1963): 305–21.

–. *A Wandering Aramean: Collected Aramaic Essays*. Atlanta: Scholars, 1979.

Flusser, David. "Qumran and Jewish 'Apotropaic' Prayers." *Israel Exploration Journal* 16 (1966): 194–205.

Fossum, Jarl. "Gen. 1:26 in Judaism, Samaritanism, and Gnosticism." *Journal of Jewish Studies* 16 (1985): 202–39.

Freiden, Ken. "Language of Demonic Possession: Keyword Analysis." Pages 41–52 in *Daemonic Imagination, Biblical Text and Secular Story*. Edited by Robert Detweiler and William G. Doty. Atlanta: Scholars, 1990.

Frey, Jörg. "Different Patterns of Dualistic thought in the Qumran Library. Reflections of their Background and History," Pages 275-336 in *Legal Texts and Legal Issues: Proceedings of the Second Meeting of the International Organization for Qumran Studies, Cambridge 1995, Published in Honour of Joseph M. Baumgarten*. Studies on the Texts of the Desert of Judah 23. Edited by Moshe Bernstein, Florentino García Martínez and John Kampen; Leiden: Brill, 1997.

Fuhs, H. F. "Die äthiopische Übersetzung des Henoch: Ein Beitrag zur Apokalyptikforschung der Gegenwart." *Biblische Notizen* 8 (1979): 36–56.

Gammie, John G. "The Angelology and Demonology in the Septuagint of the Book of Job." *Hebrew Union College Annual* 56 (1985): 1–19.

García Martínez, Florentino. *Qumran and Apocalyptic, Studies on the Aramaic Texts From Qumran*. Studies in the Texts of the Desert of Judah 9. Leiden: Brill, 1992.

Gaylord, Harry E. "How Satanel Lost His-El." *Journal of Jewish Studies* 33 (1982): 303–09.

Gernet, Louis. *The Anthropology of Ancient Greece*. Translated by John Hamilton, S. J. and Blaise Nagy. Baltimore: Johns Hopkins, 1981.

Gese, H. "Der bewachte Lebensbaum und die Heroen, zwei mythologische Erwägungen zur Urgeschichte der Quelle J." Pages 77–85 in *Wort und Geschichte. Festschrift zum 70 Geburrstag von Karl Elliger*. Edited by H. Gese and H. P. Rüger. Kevelaer: Butzon and Bercker, 1973.

Gignoux, P. "L'apocalyptique iranienne est-elle vraiment la source d'autres apocalypses?" *Acta Antiqua Academiae Acientiarum Hungaricae* 31 (1988): 67–78.

Gilbert, M. "Wisdom Literature." Pages 283–324 in *Jewish Writings of the Second Temple Period*. Vol. 2 of *The Literature of the Jewish People in the Period of the Second Temple and the Talmud*. Edited by Michael Stone. Translated by K. Smyth. Assen/Philadelphia: Van Gorcum/Fortress, 1984.

Ginzberg, Louis . *The Legends of the Jews*. 10 vols. Translated by Henrietta Szold. Repr., Philadelphia: Jewish Publication Society of America, 1954.

Glasson, T. F. *Greek Influence in Jewish Eschatology*. London: SPCK, 1961.

Goodenough, Edwin R. *By Light, Light: The Mystic Gospel of Hellenistic Judaism*. New Haven: Yale University, 1935.

–. *An Introduction to Philo Judeaus*. 2d ed. Oxford: Basil Blackwell, 1962.

Grabbe, Lester L. "Philo and Aggada." *Studia Philonica Annual* 3 (1991): 153–66.

–. "The Scapegoat Tradition: A Study of Early Jewish Interpretation." *Journal of the Study of Judaism* 18 (1987): 152–67.

Greenfield, Jonas C. and Michael E. Stone. Review of J.T. Milik, *Books of Enoch: Aramaic Fragments of Qumran Cave 4*. *Numen* 26 (1979): 89–103.

–. "The Enochic Pentateuch and the Date of the Similitudes." *Harvard Theological Review* 70 (1977): 51–65.

Grelot, Pierre. "La géographic mythique d'Henoch et ses sources orientales." *Review Biblique* 65 (1958): 33–68.

–. "La legende d'Henoch dans les apocryphes et dans la Bible: Origine et signification." *Recherches de Science Religieuse* 46 (1958): 5–26, 181–210.

Grossfeld, Bernard. *An Analytic Commentary of the Targum Neofiti to Genesis: Including Full Rabbinic Parallels*. New York: KTAV, 1992.

Gruppe, Otto F. "Aithiopenmythen." *Philologus* 47 (1889): 328–343.

–. "War Genesis 6:1–4 Urspruenglich Mit der Sintflut Verbunden?" *Zeitschrift für die alttestamentliche Wissenschaft* 9 (1889): 135–155.

Gunkel, Hermann. *Genesis*. Mercer Library of Biblical Studies. Translated by Mark E. Biddle. Macon, GA.: Mercer University, 1997.

Hanhart, Robert. *The Translation of the Septuagint in the Light of Earlier Traditions and Subsequent Influences*. Atlanta: Scholars, 1992.

Hanson, Paul. "Rebellion in Heaven, Azazel and Euhemeristic Heroes in 1 Enoch 6–11." *Journal of Biblical Literature* 96 (1977): 195–223.

Harl, Marguerite, ed, *La Bible D'Alexandrie La Genese*. 2d ed. Vol. 1 of *La Bible D'Alexandrie*. Paris: Editions Du Cerf, 1986.

Harrington, D. J. "Pseudo-Philo." Pages 297–377 vol. 2 of *The Old Testament Pseudepigrapha*. 2 Vols. Edited by James H. Charlesworth. New York: Doubleday, 1983–85.

Hartman, Lars. *Asking for a Meaning: A Study of 1 Enoch 1–5*. Coniectanea Biblica New Testament Series 12. Lund, Sweden: CWK Gleerup, 1979.

Hastings, J. "Bastard." Page 91 in *Dictionary of the Bible*. 2d ed. Edited by James Hastings. Rev. by Fredrick C. Grant and H. H. Rowley. Edinburgh: Clark, 1963.

Hendel, Ronald. "The Nephilim Were on the Earth: Genesis 6.1–4 and Its Ancient Near Eastern Context." Pages 11–34 in *Fall of the Angels*. Themes in the Biblical Narrative 6. Edited by Christopher Auffarth and Loren T. Stuckenbruck. Leiden: Brill, 2003.

–. "Of Demigods and the Deluge: Toward an Interpretation of Genesis 6.1–4." *Journal of Biblical Literature* 106 (1987): 13–26.

Hengel, Martin. *Judaism and Hellenism*. 2 vols. Edinburgh: T & T Clark, 1974.

Henten, J. W. van. "Mastemah." Pages 553–54 in *Dictionary of Deities and Demons in the Bible: DDD*. Edited by Karel van der Toorn, Bob Becking and Pieter W. van der Horst. Leiden/Grand Rapids: Brill/Eerdmans, 1999.

Hertz, J. H. *The Pentateuch and Haftorahs*. London: Oxford University, 1929.

Himmelfarb, Martha. *Ascent to Heaven in Jewish and Christian Apocalypses*. Oxford: Oxford University, 1993.

Horst, Pieter W. van der. "Evil Inclination." Pages 317–19 in *Dictionary of Deities and Demons in the Bible: DDD*. Edited by Karel van der Toorn, Bob Becking and Pieter W. van der Horst. Leiden/Grand Rapids: Brill/Eerdmans, 1999.

Howard, J. Keir. "New Testament Exorcism and its Significance Today." *Expository Times* 96 (1985): 105–09.

Huggins, Ronald V. "A Canonical 'Book of the Periods' at Qumran?" *Revue de Qumran* 15 (1992): 421–36.

–. "Noah and the Giants: A Response to John C. Reeves." *Journal of Biblical Literature* 114 (1995): 103–10.

Hull, John. *Hellenistic Magic and Synoptic Tradition*. London: SCM, 1974.

Isaac, Ephraim. "1 Enoch." Pages 5–89 vol. 1 in *The Old Testament Pseudepigrapha*. 2 vols. Edited by James H. Charlesworth. New York: Doubleday, 1983–85.

Isaacs, Marie. *The Concept of Spirit: A Study of Pneuma in Hellenistic Judaism and its Bearing on the New Testament*. London: Heythrop College, 1976.

Jacobs, Louis. "Jewish Cosmology." Pages 66–86 in *Ancient Cosmologies*. Edited by Carmen Blacker and Michael Loewe. London: George Allen and Unwin, 1975.

Jacoby, Felix. *Die Fragmente der griechischen Historiker*, III C 1. Leiden: Brill, 1958.

Janowski, B. "Azazel." Pages 128–31 in *Dictionary of Deities and Demons in the Bible: DDD*. Edited by Karel van der Toorn, Bob Becking and Pieter W. van der Horst. Leiden/Grand Rapids: Brill/Eerdmans, 1999.

Jensen, Søren Skovgaard *Dualism and Demonology: The Function of Demonology in Pythagorean and Platonic Thought.* Copenhagen: Munksgaard, 1966.

Jeremias, Joachim. *Jerusalem in the Time of Jesus: An Investigation Into Economic and Social Conditions During the New Testament Period.* Translated by F. H. and C. H. Cave. Philadelphia: Fortress, 1969.

Kee, Howard C. "Testaments of the Twelve Patriarchs." Pages 775–828 vol. 1 of *The Old Testament Pseudepigrapha.* 2 Vols. Edited by James H. Charlesworth. New York: Doubleday, 1983–85.

–. *Miracle in the Early Christian World.* New Haven: Yale University, 1983.

Kilmer, A. D. "The Mesopotamian Concept of Overpopulation and its Solution Reflected in Mythology." *Orientalia* 41 (1972): 160–77.

Kittel, Bonnie P. *The Hymns of Qumran, A Translation and Commentary.* Society of Biblical Literature Dissertation Series 50. Missoula: Scholars, 1981.

Klein, J. "The Bane of Humanity: A Lifespan of 120 Years." *Acta Sumerologica* 12. (1990).

Knibb, Michael A. "Martyrdom and Ascension of Isaiah." Pages 141–76 vol. 2 of *The Old Testament Pseudepigrapha.* 2 Vols. Edited by James H. Charlesworth. New York: Doubleday, 1983–85.

Kobelski, Paul J. *Melchizedek and Melchireša.* Catholic Bible Quarterly Monograph Series 10. Washington, DC: Catholic Bible Quarterly Monograph, 1981.

Kotansky, R. "Demonology." Pages 269–73 in *Dictionary of New Testament Background: A Compendium of Contemporary Biblical Scholarship.* Edited by Craig A. Evans and Stanley E. Porter. Downers Grove, IL.: InterVarsity, 2000.

Kraeling, Emil G. "The Significance and Origin of Gen. 6:1–4." *Journal of Near Eastern Studies* VI (Oct. 1947): 193–208.

Kugel, James L. *Traditions of the Bible: A Guide to the Bible As It Was At the Start of the Common Era.* Cambridge: Harvard University, 1998.

Kuhn, Harold B. "The Angelology of the Non-Canonical Jewish Apocalypses." *Journal of Biblical Literature* 67 (1948): 217–32.

Kvanvig, Helge S. *Roots of Apocalyptic: The Mesopotamian Background of the Enoch Figure and the Son of Man.* Wissenschaftliche Monographien zum Alten und Neuen Testament 61. Neukirchen-Vluyn: Neukirchener Verlag, 1988.

Lange, Armin. *The Essene Position on Magic and Divination.* Pages 377–436 in *Legal Texts and Legal Issues: Proceedings of the Second Meeting of the International Organization for Qumran Studies, Cambridge 1995, Published in Honour of Joseph M. Baumgarten.* Studies on the Texts of the Desert of Judah 23. Edited by Moshe Bernstein, Florentino García Martínez and John Kampen; Leiden: Brill, 1997.

–. "Spirit of Impurity." Pages 254–68 in *Demons, The Demonology of Israelite-Jewish and Early Christian Literature in Context of their Environment.* Edited by Armin Lange, Herman Lichtenberger and K.F. Diethard Römheld. Tübingen: Mohr Siebeck, 2003.

–. *Weisheit und Prädestination. Weisheitliche Urordnung und Prädestination in den Textfunden von Qumran.* Studies in the Texts of the Desert of Judah 18. Leiden E.J. Brill, 1995: 6-20.

Langton, Edward. *Essentials of Demonology: A Study of Jewish and Christian Doctrine, Its Origins and Development.* London: Epworth, 1949.

Laporte, Jean. "Philo in the Tradition of Biblical Wisdom Literature." Pages 103–41 in *Aspects of Wisdom in Judaism and Early Christianity.* Edited by R. Wilken. Notre Dame, IN.: University of Notre Dame, 1975.

Larson, Erik W. *The Translation of Enoch: From Aramaic into Greek.* New York: New York University, 1995.

Leaman, Oliver. *Evil and Suffering in Jewish Philosophy.* Cambridge: Harvard University, 1995.

Leaney, A.R.G. *The Rule of Qumran and its Meaning.* London: SCM, 1996.

Levenson, Jon D. *Creation and the Presence of Evil: The Jewish Drama of Divine Omnipotence.* San Francisco: Harper Row, 1988.

Levine, Etan. *The Aramaic Version of the Bible Contents and Context.* Berlin/New York: Walter de Gruyter, 1988.

Levison, John R. *The Spirit in First century Judaism.* Leiden: Brill, 1997.

Mach, Michael. *Entwicklungsstadien des Jüdischen Engelglaubens in Vorrabbinischer Zeit.* Tübingen: Mohr Siebeck, 1992.

Mack, Burton L. "Wisdom and Apocalyptic in Philo." *The Studia Philonica Annual Studies in Hellenistic Judaism* 3 (1991): 21–39.

McVann, Mark. *Dwelling Among the Tombs: Discourse, Discipleship, and the Gospel of Mark 4:35–5:43.* Atlanta: Emory University, 1984.

Melnick, R. "On the Philonic Conception of the Whole Man," *Journal of the Study of Judaism* 11 (1980): 1–32.

Mendelson, Alan. *Philo's Jewish Identity.* Brown Judaic Studies 161. Atlanta: Scholars, 1988.

Merrill, Eugene H. *Qumran and Predestination: A Theological Study of the Thanksgiving Hymns,* Studies on the Texts of the Desert of Judah, 8 Leiden: Brill, 1975.

Metso, Sarianna. *The Textual Development of the Qumran Community Rule* in Studies on the Texts of the Desert of Judah, 21. Leiden: Brill, 1997.

Milgrom, Jacob. "Israel's Sanctuary: The Priestly Picture of Dorian Gray." *Revue Biblique* 83 (1976): 390–99.

–. *Leviticus 1–16: A New Translation with Introduction and Commentary.* The Anchor Bible. New York: Doubleday, 1991.

Milik, J. T. "Problemes de la Litterature Henochique a la Lumiere des Fragments Arameens de Qumran." *Harvard Theological Review* 64 (1971): 333–78.

Molenberg, Corrie. "A Study of the Roles of Shemihaza and Asael in 1 Enoch 6–11." *Journal of Jewish Studies* 35 (1984): 136–46.

Montefiore, C. G. and H. Loewe. *A Rabbinic Anthology.* New York: Schocken Books, 1974.

Moran, W. L. "Atrahasis: The Babylonian Story of the Flood." *Biblica Commentarii Trimestres* 52 (1971): 51–61.

Morgenstern, Julian. "The Mythological Background of Psalm 82." Pages 29–126 in *Hebrew Union College Annual.* Edited by Zevi Diesendruck, David Philipson and Julian Morgenstern. Cincinnati: Hebrew Union College, 1939.

Murray, Robert. "The Origin of Aramaic *'Ir,* Angel." *Orientalia* 53 (1984): 303–17.

Mussies, G. "Giants." Pages 343–45 in *Dictionary of Deities and Demons in the Bible DDD.* Edited by Karel van der Toorn, Bob Becking and Pieter van der Horst. Leiden/Grand Rapids: Brill/Eerdmans, 1999.

Newsom, Carol. "The Development of 1 Enoch 6–19: Cosmology and Judgment." *Catholic Biblical Quarterly* 42 (1980): 310–29.

–. "An Apocryphon on the Flood Narrative." *Revue de Qumran* 13 (1988): 23–1.

Nickelsburg, George W. E. *1 Enoch 1 A Commentary on the Book of 1 Enoch, Chapters 1–36; 81–108.* Hermeneia–A Critical and Historical Commentary on the Bible. Minneapolis: Augsburg Fortress, 2001.

–. "Apocalyptic and Myth in 1 Enoch 6–11." *Journal of Biblical Literature* 96 (1977): 383–405.

–. "The Books of Enoch in Recent Research." *Religious Studies Review* 7 (1918): 210–17.

–. "Enoch, Levi, and Peter: Recipients of Revelation in Upper Galilee." *Society of Biblical Literature* 100 (1981): 575–600.

–. *Resurrection, Immortality, and Eternal Life in Intertestamental Judaism*. Harvard Theological Studies 26. Cambridge: Harvard University, 1972.

Niehoff, Maren R. "Philo's Mystical Philosophy of Language." *Jewish Studies Quarterly* 2 (1995): 220–52.

Nikiprowetsky, Valentin. "Sur une Lecture demonologique de Philo D'Alexandria, *De Gigantibus* 6–11." Pages 55–99 in *Hommage a Georges Vajda: Etudes D'histoire et de Pensee Juives*. Edited by G. Nahon and C. Touati. Leuven/Paris: Peeters, 1980.

Nitzan, Bilhah. *Qumran Prayer and Religious Poetry*. Studies in the Texts of the Desert of Judah 12. Translated by Jonathan Chipman. Leiden: Brill, 1994.

Nock, A. D. *Essays on Religion and the Ancient World*. Cambridge: Harvard University, 1972.

Noth, Martin. *Die israelitischen Personennamen im Rahmen der gemeinsemitischen Namensgebung*. Stuttgart: Kohlhammer, 1928.

Oden, R. A. "Divine Aspirations in Atrahasis and in Genesis 1–11." *Zeitschrift für die alttestamentliche Wissenschaft* 93 (1981): 197–216.

Oesterley, W. O. E. *The Jews and Judaism During the Greek Period: The Background of Christianity*. New York: Macmillan, 1941.

Oesterreich, T. K. *Possession: Demonological and Other*. London: Kegan Paul, Trench, Trubner, 1930.

Olofsson, Staffan. *God is my Rock: Study of Translation Techniques and Theological Exegesis in the Septuagint*. Coniectanea Biblica Old Testament Series 31. Stockholm: Almqvist and Wiksell, 1990.

–. *The LXX Version: A Guide to the Translation Technique of the Septuagint*. Coniectanea Biblica Old Testament Series, 30. Stockholm: Almqvist &Wiksell, 1990.

Pagels, Elaine. *The Origin of Satan*. New York: Vintage Books, 1995.

Paramelle, Joseph. *Philon D'Alexandrie: Questions Sur La Genese*. Geneva: P. Cramer, 1984.

Pearson, Birger. *Gnosticism, Judaism, and Egyptian Christianity*. Minneapolis: Fortress, 1990.

Pearson, Brooke A. "A Reminiscence of Classical Myth at II Peter 2,4." *Greek, Roman, and Byzantine Studies* 10 (1969): 72–5.

Pearson, Brook W. R. "Resurrection and the Judgment of the Titans: In LXX Isaiah 26:19." *Journal for the Study of the New Testament: Supplement Series* 186 (1999): 33–51.

Penney, Douglas L. and Michael O. Wise. "By the Power of Beelzebub: An Aramaic Incantation from Qumran." *Journal of Biblical Literature* 113 (1994): 627–50.

Petersen, David L. "Genesis 6.1–4, Yahweh and the Organization of the Cosmos." *Journal for the Study of the Old Testament Supplement Series* 13 (1979): 47–64.

Philonenko, Marc. "Philon D'Alexandrie et L'Instruction Sur Les Deux Espirits." Pages 61–68 in *Hellenica et Judaica*. Edited by A. Caquot et al. Leuven/Paris: Peeters, 1986.

Ploeg, J. P. M. van der. "Le psaume XCI dans une recension de Qumran." *Revue Biblique* 72 (1965): 210–17.

Puech, Émil. "11QPsApᵃ: Un ritual d'exorcismes. Essai de reconstruction." *Revue de Qumran* 14 (1990): 377–408.

–. "Les fragments 1à 3 du *Livre des Géants* de la grotte 6 (pap 6Q8)." *Revue de Qumran* 19 (1999): 227–38.

Rabin, Chaim. *The Zadokite Documents.* 2d ed. Oxford: Clarendon, 1958.

Rad, Gerhard von. *Deuteronomy A Commentary.* The Old Testament Library. Translated by Dorothea Barton. London: SCM, 1966.

–. *Genesis A Commentary.* The Old Testament Library. Translated by John H. Marks. London: SCM, 1961.

Rahlfs, A., ed. *Psalmi Cum Odis.* Septuaginta Societatis Scientiarum Gottingensis 10. Göttingen: Vandenhoeck und Ruprecht, 1931.

Reeves, John C. *Jewish Lore in Manichaean Cosmogony, Studies in the Book of Giants Traditions.* Cincinnati: Hebrew Union College, 1992.

–. "Utnapishtim in the Book of Giants." *Journal of Biblical Literature* 112 (1993): 110–15.

Reimer, Andy M. "Rescuing the Fallen Angels: The Case of the Disappearing Angels at Qumran." *Dead Sea Discoveries* 7 (2000): 334–53.

Rohde, Erwin. *Pysche and the Cult of Souls and Belief in Immortality Among the Greeks.* Translated by W. B. Willis. London: Kegan, Paul, Trench and Truener, 1925.

Rokeah, David. "Philo of Alexandria, Midrash, and Ancient Halakhah." *Tarbiz* 55 (1986): 433–39.

Rubinkiewicz, R. "Apocalypse of Abraham." Pages 686–705 vol. 1 of *The Old Testament Pseudepigrapha.* 2 Vols. Edited by James H. Charlesworth. New York: Doubleday, 1983–85.

Runia, David T. "How to Read Philo." *Norsk Teologisk Tidsskrift* 40 (1986): 192.

–. *Philo in Early Christian Literature: A Survey.* Jewish Traditions in Early Christian Literature 44. Minneapolis: Fortress, 1993.

–. *Philo of Alexandria and Timaeus of Plato.* Philosophia Antiqua 44. Leiden: Brill, 1986.

Sacchi, Paolo. *Jewish Apocalyptic and Its History.* Translated by William J Short. Journal for the Study of the Pseudepigrapha Supplemental Series 20. Sheffield: Sheffield Academic, 1990.

Samuelson, Norbert M. *Judaism and the Doctrine of Creation.* Cambridge: Cambridge University, 1994.

Sanders, James A. Review of J. T. Milik *The Books of Enoch: Aramaic Fragments of Qumran Cave 4.* *Journal of Biblical Literature* 97 (1978): 446–47.

Sandmel, Samuel. "Parallelomania." *Journal of Biblical Literature* 81 (1962): 1–13.

–. *Philo's Place in Judaism: A Study of Conceptions of Abraham in Jewish Literature.* Cincinnati: Hebrew Union College, 1956.

Sarna, Nahum M. *Genesis.* JPS Torah Commentary 1. Philadelphia/New York/Jerusalem: Jewish Publication Society, 1989.

Schereschewsk, Ben Zion. "Mamzer." Pages 840–42 in vol. 11 of *Encyclopaedia Jududaica.* Edited by C. Roth and G. Wigoder. 16 vols. New York/Jerusalem: Macmillian/Keter, 1971

Schüer, Emil. *The History of the Jewish People in the Age of Jesus Christ.* Rev. ed. by Geza Vermes and F. Millar. Edinburgh: T & T Clark, 1986.

Schwarzbaum, Haim. "The Overcrowded Earth." *Numen International Review for the History of Religions* (1957): 59–74.

Scodel, R. "The Achaean Wall and the Myth of Destruction." *Harvard Studies in Classical Philology* 86 (1982): 37–42.

Scott, James H. *Adoption As Sons of God.* Tübingen: J. C. B. Mohr, 1992.

Segal, Alan F. *The Other Judaisms of Late Antiquity.* Brown Judaic Series 127. Atlanta: Scholars, 1987.

Smith, J. Z. "Towards Interpreting Demonic Powers in Hellenistic and Roman Antiquity." *Aufstieg und Niedergang der Römischen Welt* 2, 16.1 (1978): 425– 39.

Soggin, J. Alberto. *Das Buch Genesis: Kommentar.* Darmstadt: Wissenschaftliche Buchgesellschaft, 1997.

Sokoloff, Michael. "Notes on the Aramaic Fragments of Enoch From Qumran Cave 4." *Maarav* 1 (1978–79): 197–224.

Sorensen, Eric. *Possession and Exorcism in the New Testament and Early Christianity.* Wissenschaftliche Untersuchungen zum Neuen Testament, 2. Reihe 157. Tübingen: Mohr Siebeck, 2002.

Sperling, S. David. "Belial." Pages 169–71 in *Dictionary of Deities and Demons in the Bible: DDD.* Edited by Karel van der Toorn, Bob Becking and Peiter W. van der Horst. 2d ed. Leiden/Grand Rapids: Brill/Eerdmans, 1999.

Stone, Michael E. "The Book of Enoch and Judaism in the Third Century B.C.E." *The Catholic Biblical Quarterly* 40 (1978): 479–92.

Stuckenbruck, Loren T. "4Qinstruction and the Possible Influence of Early Enochic Traditions: An Evaluation." Pages 245-61 in *The Wisdom Texts From Qumran and the Development of Sapiential Thought.* Bibliotheca Ephemeridum Theologicarum Lovaniensium 159. Edited by C. Hempel, A. Lange and H. Lichtenberger; Leuven: Peeters, 2002.

–. "An Approach to the New Testament through Aramaic Sources: The Recent Methodological Debate." *Journal for the Study of Pseudepigrapha* 8 (1991): 3–29.

–. "The 'Angels' and 'Giants' of Genesis 6:1–4 in Second and Third Century B.C.E. Jewish Interpretation: Reflections on the Posture of Early Apocalyptic Traditions." *Dead Sea Discoveries* 7 (2000): 354–77.

–. "Angels of the Nations." Pages 29–31 in *Dictionary of New Testament Background: A Compendium of Contemporary Biblical Scholarship.* Edited by Craig A. Evans and Stanley Porter. Downers Grove, IL: InterVarsity, 2000.

–. *Angel Veneration and Christology.* Wissenschaftliche Untersuchungen zum Neuen Testament 70. Tübingen: Mohr Siebeck, 1995.

–. "Giant Mythology and Demonology: From the Ancient Near East to the Dead Sea Scrolls." Pages 31–38 in *Demons: The Demonology of Israelite-Jewish and Early Christian Literature in Context of their Environment.* Edited by Armin Lange, Hermann Lichtenberger and K. F. Diethard Römheld. Tübingen: Mohr Siebeck, 2003.

–. "The Origins of Evil in Jewish Apocalyptic Tradition: Interpretation of Genesis 6:1–4 in the Second and Third Centuries BCE." Pages 86–118 in *Fall of the Angels.* Themes in the Biblical Narrative 6. Edited by Christopher Auffarth and Loren T. Stuckenbruck. Leiden: Brill, 2003.

–. "Revision of Aramaic—Greek and Greek—Aramaic Glossaries in *The Books of Enoch: Aramaic Fragments of Qumran Cave 4* by J. T. Milik." *Journal of Jewish Studies* 41 (1990): 13–48.

Suter, David. "Fallen Angel, Fallen Priest: The Problem of Family Purity in 1 Enoch." *Hebrew Union College Annual* 50 (1979): 115–35.

–. *Tradition and Composition in the Parables of Enoch.* Society of Biblical Literature Dissertation Series 47. Missoula, MT.: Scholars, 1979.

Tawil, Hayim. "Azazel The Prince of the Steepe: A Comparative Study." *Zeitschrift für die alttestamentliche Wissenschaft* 92 (1980): 43–59.

Tcherikover, Victor. *Hellenistic Civilization and the Jews* [Ha-Yehudim Ve'haYevanim Batekufah Ha-Kelenistit]. Translated by S. Applebaum. Jerusalem: Magnes, 1959.

Tiller, Patrick A. *A Commentary on the Animal Apocalypse.* Atlanta: Scholars, 1993.

Tobin, Thomas H. *The Creation of Man, Philo and the History of Interpretation.* Catholic Biblical Quarterly Monograph Series 14. Washington, DC: Catholic Biblical Association, 1983.

Torczyner, H. "A Hebrew Incantation Against Night Demons From Biblical Times." *Journal of Near Eastern Studies* 6 (1947): 18–29.

Tov, Emanuel. *The Greek and Hebrew Bible: Collected Essays on the Septuagint.* Supplements to Vetus Testamentum, 72. Edited by H. M. Barstad, et al. Leiden: Brill, 1999.

–. *Text-Critical Use of the Septuagint in Biblical Research.* Jerusalem Biblical Series 3. Jerusalem: Simor, 1981.

Tur-Sinai, N. H. "The Riddle of Genesis VI. 1–4." Pages 348–50 in *Expository Times.* Edited by A. W. Hastings and E. Hastings. Edinburgh: T & T Clark, 1960.

Twelftree, Graham H. *Jesus the Exorcist: A Contribution to the Study of the Historical Jesus.* Peabody: Hendrickson, 1993.

Uhlig, Siegbert. *Das äthiopische Henochbuch* Jüdische Schriften aus hellenistisch-römischer Zeit 5, fascile 6. Gütersloh: Mohn, 1984.

Ullendorf, Edward. "An Aramaic 'Vorlage' of the Ethiopic Text of Enoch?" *Problemi attuali di scienza e di cultura, quaderni* 48. (1960): 259–67.

VanderKam James C. "1 Enoch, Enochic Motifs, and Enoch in Early Christian Literature." Pages 33–101 in *The Jewish Apocalyptic Heritage in Early Christianity.* Edited by James C. VanderKam and William Adler. Vol. 4 of *Jewish Traditions in Early Christian Literature.* Edited by P.J. Tomson, et al. Compendia Rerum Iudaicarum ad Novum Testamentum, Section 3. Assen, The Netherlands: Van Gorcum, 1996.

–. "The Angel of the Presence in the Book of Jubilees." *Dead Sea Discoveries* (2000): 378–93.

–. *The Angel Story in the Book of Jubilees.* Studies on the Texts of the Desert of Judah 31. Leiden: Brill, 1999.

–. *Biblical Interpretation in 1Enoch and Jubilees.* Journal for the Study of Pseudepigrapha Supplement Series 14. Sheffield: JSOT, 1993.

–. *Enoch: A Man for All Generations.* Columbia, SC.: University of South Carolina, 1995.

–. *Enoch and the Growth of an Apocalyptic Tradition.* Catholic Biblical Quarterly Monograph Series 16. Washington DC.: Catholic Biblical Association of America, 1984.

–. "Enoch Tradition in Jubilees and Other Second-Century Sources." Pages 229–51 in *SBL Seminar Papers* J. Missoula: Scholars, 1978.

–. "The Interpretation of Genesis in 1 Enoch." Pages 129–48 in *The Bible at Qumran: Text, Shape, and Interpretation.* Edited by Peter Flint and Tae Hun Kim. Grand Rapids: Eerdmans, 2001.

–. "Some Major Issues in the Contemporary Study of 1 Enoch: Reflections on J. T. Milik's *The Books of Enoch: Aramaic Fragments of Qumran Cave 4.*" *Maarav* 3 (1982): 85–97.

–. "The Textual Base for the Ethiopic Translation of 1 Enoch." Pages 247–62 in *Working with No Data: Studies in Semitic and Egyptian Presented to Thomas O. Lambdin.* Edited by D. M. Golomb. Winona Lake, IN.: Eisenbrauns, 1987.

Vermes, Geza. *Post-Biblical Jewish Studies*. Studies in Judaism in Late Antiquity 8. Leiden: Brill, 1975.

Wacholder, Ben-Zion. *Eupolemus, A Study of Judaeo-Greek Literature*. Cincinnati: Hebrew Union College, 1974.

Wahlen, Clinton. *Jesus and the Impurity of Spirits in the Synoptic Gospels*. Wissenschaftliche Untersuchungen zum Neuen Testament, 2. Reihe 185. Tübingen: Mohr Siebeck, 2004.

Walcot, P. *Hesiod and the Near East*. Cardiff: University of Wales, 1966.

Weingreen, J. "Construct Genitive." *Vetus Testamentum* 4 (1954): 50–59.

Wernberg-Møller, Preben. "A Reconsideration of the Two Spirits in 1QS 3: 13 4:26." *Römische Quartalschrift für christliche Altertumskunde und Kirchengeschichte* 3 (1961–62): 413–41.

–. "A Reconstruction of the Two Spirits in the Rule of Community." *Revue de Qumran* 3 (1961): 413–41.

West, M. L. *Early Greek Philosophy and the Orient*. Oxford: Clarendon, 1971.

–. *The East Face of Helicon*. Oxford: Clarendon, 1997.

–. *The Orphic Poems*. Oxford: Clarendon, 1983.

Westermann, Claus. *Genesis 1–11: A Commentary*. Translated by John J. Scullion. London: SPCK, 1984.

Wevers, John W., ed. *Deuteronomium*. Translated by U. Quast. Septuaginta Vetus Testamenta Graecum 3. Göttingen: Vandenhoeck and Ruprecht, 1977.

–. *Notes on the Greek Text of Genesis*. Society of Biblical Literature Septuagint and Cognate Studies Series 35. Atlanta: Scholars, 1993.

Wickham, L. R. *The Sons of God and the Daughters of Men: Genesis VI 2 in Early Christian Exegesis*. Oudtestamentische Studieen 19. Leiden: Brill, 1974.

Winston, David. "The Iranian Component of the Bible, Apocrypha and Qumran." *Harvard Review* 5 (1966): 188–89.

–. "Judaism and Hellenism: Hidden Tension in Philo." *SphA* 2 (1990): 18.

–. *Philo of Alexandria: The Contemplative Life, the Giants, and Selections*. New York: Paulist, 1981.

–. *The Wisdom of Solomon*. The Anchor Bible 43. New York: Doubleday, 1979.

Winston David and John Dillon, eds. *The Two Treatises of Philo of Alexandria: A Commentary on De Gigantibus and Quod Deus Sit Immutabilis*. Brown Judaic Series 25. Atlanta: Scholars, 1983.

Wold, Ben. *Women, Men, and Angels: The Qumran Wisdom Text Musar le Mevin and its Allusions to Genesis 1–3*. Wissenschaftliche Untersuchungen zum Neuen Testament 2. Tübingen: Mohr Siebeck, forthcoming.

Wolfson, Harry A. *Philo: Foundations of Religious Philosophy in Judaism, Christianity, and Islam*. 2d ed. Cambridge: Harvard University, 1947. Repr., 1968.

Yamauchi, Edwin. "Magic or Miracle? Diseases, Demons and Exorcisms." Pages 89–183 in *Gospel Review: The Miracles of Jesus*. Edited by David Wenham and Craig Blomberg. Sheffield: JSOT, 1986.

Zaehner, R. C. *The Dawn and Twilight of Zoroastrianism*. London: Weidenfeld and Nicolson, 1961.

Ziegler, Joseph, ed. *Susanna, Daniel, Bel Et Draco*. Goettingen: Vandenhoeck and Ruprecht, 1954.

Zlotowitz, Meir and Nosson Scherman. *Bereishis: Genesis A New Translation with a Commentary Anthologised From Talmudic, Midrashic and Rabbinic Sources*. 2d ed. Bereishis 1. New York: Mesorah, 1980.

Index of References

1. Hebrew Bible and LXX

2. New Testament

3. Apocrypha and Pseudepigrapha

4. Dead Sea Scrolls

5. Ancient Authors

6. Rabbinic and Other Jewish Literature